Promissory Notes

D1557527

PROMISSORY NOTES
Women in the Transition
to Socialism

edited by
Sonia Kruks, Rayna Rapp,
and Marilyn B. Young

MONTHLY REVIEW PRESS
NEW YORK

Library of Congress Cataloging-in-Publication Data
Promissory notes : women in the transition to socialism / edited by
   Sonia Kruks, Rayna Rapp, and Marilyn B. Young.
      p.   cm.—(New feminist library)
   Bibliography: p.
   Includes index.
   ISBN 0-85345-770-0 : $36.00.—ISBN 0-85345-771-9 (pbk.) : $18.00
   1. Women and socialism.   I. Kruks, Sonia.   II. Rapp, Rayna.
III. Young, Marilyn Blatt.   IV. Series.
HX546.P76   1989
335'.0088042—dc19   89-2987
                                                                       CIP

Monthly Review Press
122 West 27th Street
New York, NY 10001

Manufactured in the United States of America

10 9 8 7 6 5 4 3 2 1

Contents

6 Contents

Introduction

Sonia Kruks, Rayna Rapp, and Marilyn B. Young

Everything about the subject of this book is contentious, including its title. *Promissory Notes* implies a transaction that might be considered illegitimate. It can be read as implying a contract, in which socialism promised to bring forth women's liberation in exchange for women's support in revolutionary struggle. At least some of our contributors dispute that there ever was such a contract. Yet it seems to us there was, if not a contract, certainly a very strong belief, present in both the original theory and later practice, that the participation of women in revolutionary socialist movements was the only way in which their liberation could and would be realized.

Since at least the mid-nineteenth century, socialist political movements have held out explicit promises of women's liberation, conceiving of it as an *integral* part of the revolutionary project. The situation of women did not play the same role in contemporary liberal politics. Popular movements for the abolition of slavery, for the extension of the franchise to all men (and later to women), and for the right to free speech and association considered such universalization of legal rights enough. The liberation of women was not an integral aspect of their vision and could not be, given the limits of liberal theory. The subject of liberal theory was the individual: inequities of race, class, and gender would be dissolved in the acid bath of individual legal rights.

It was strikingly otherwise with socialist movements. Whether one looks at the Utopian Socialists in France and England, the works of Marx, or the tremendous influence of Bebel and Engels in Western Europe or, somewhat later, the early USSR and the formal platforms of Socialist and Communist parties throughout the contemporary world, the necessary connection between social transformation and social justice for women is everywhere articulated. Yet veterans of recent political movements also know how unfinished the task of women's liberation has proven to be.

In those states in which a government informed by Marxism, or Marxism-Leninism, came to power—or seized it—both the promise and the frustration are of particular interest. Some of the reasons for the frustration (as for other limitations in socialist transformation) are fairly obvious. These include the material constraints imposed by the consequences of a colonial and neocolonial history—lack of an industrial base, costly wars of national liberation, the persistence of unequal terms of international trade, and enforced underdevelopment. Political-military destabilization, as in Mozambique and Nicaragua, is another obvious reason. It can be equally devastating whether it takes the form of economic warfare—trade embargoes, manipulation of aid and the "food weapon" for political ends—or of outright invasion. In fact, no revolution in the twentieth century has enjoyed an unhindered free space in which to develop, and this means that neither economic stability nor widespread civic democracy has been part of the legacy of socialist states. In the light of this history, sympathetic supporters have tended to interpret ongoing contradictions (with respect to women as well as other social issues) as the product of circumstances rather than structure.

There are also less obvious and more structural reasons for the failure to resolve the "Woman Question" in socialist states and movements. The very language of the problematic, the "Woman Question," recalls the nineteenth-century discourse in which it was first framed. The analysis of women as separate from the rest of the society socialists wished to transform inevitably had consequences for the total vision socialists embraced. The Woman Question would be *answered* by socialism along with all other social problems. Women as a category had nothing to contribute to the *theory* of socialism.

Contemporary socialist feminists have creatively confronted some of the limitations of classic Marxist theory. In particular they have pointed to its inability to sufficiently analyze and incorporate the centrality of the gender division of labor in all spheres. They have also explored its lack of concern with sexuality and reproduction and its failure to recognize the material force of gender ideology. Classic Marxist theory, Western socialist feminists have argued, does not admit the possibility that women's *specific* experiences can contribute in a positive way to revolutionary transformations. Indeed, the contrary. Women are portrayed in classic Marxist theory as backward because of their exclusion from social production and their entanglement in domestic responsibilities. Thus, by incorporating women in social production, revolution will automatically liberate them. So far, however, the efforts to wed socialist-feminist critiques of classic theory to the history of the movements and states which have in fact tried to live it out remain inadequate.

Promissory Notes grows out of our mutual conviction that the diverse and scattered materials on women in socialist states should be brought together in a way that can be useful to activists, students, and scholars. Included on our agenda is a careful analysis of both the insights and limitations of the Marxist heritage and its Leninist practice. Our approach begins with an examination of the early theoretical bases in European

Marxism for a position on the Woman Question. Within socialist movements there emerged both a utopian and a "scientific" theory of women's subordination. Both pictured the bourgeois patriarchal nuclear family, with its origins in the development of private property, as the locus of women's ongoing subordination. Women's status came to be considered a barometer of social justice. Utopian socialist movements often encouraged experimentation in changing the forms of child care, marriage, community planning, and the like in an effort to end women's subordination. Within "scientific socialism" the majority view held to a more comfortable assumption: both the evolution of women's consciousness and the material bases for its transformation would be the direct result of the massive entry of women into the world of waged work and workers' struggles. In their proletarianization and in their anticipated subsequent participation in the revolutionary movement lay women's liberation. Experiments that preceded these most basic of all possible changes were either irrelevant or dangerous distractions.

The enduring power of these early debates should be underlined. They have resonated through every socialist movement in the twentieth century without exception. On the whole, the "scientific socialist" position triumphed. From China to Nicaragua, this nineteenth-century model has been consciously adopted, even when its appropriateness was, at the least, open to question. While other aspects of the Marxist-Leninist program (such as analyses of the peasantry, or where the commanding heights of the economy were located) have been adapted to national conditions, this element has remained remarkably unchanged, whether the country deploying the theory was Asian, Southeast Asian, African, European, or Latin American. The model has been applied whether a given country's social relations were taken to be feudal, tribal, or protocapitalist, whether the country had been fully colonized or not, whether the state in question had been unified or had remained fragmented. Nor did differences in the form of kinship and marriage impede application of the nineteenth-century view that located women's subordination in private property relations, whether family forms were monogamous or polygynous, involved dowry or brideprice (or in China, for example, both).

Despite these shortcomings, Western socialist feminists continue to look to the socialist countries in order to examine how a theoretical commitment to female liberation might work in the context of the effort to achieve total social transformation. Some of us share the theory's root belief that private property and the family are indeed the major source of women's oppression. Others of us argue that the control of women's sexual and reproductive capacities runs deeper than bourgeois family and property forms. But all of us remain attracted to a theory that would simultaneously eliminate all class, race, and gender oppression. Yet, when we turn to the history of socialist countries, the extent to which the bourgeois family form, however disguised in socialist rhetoric, seems to endure as the general norm to which socialist leaderships aspire is striking. If there is one theme which pervades all the essays in this book, it is the complex interplay of continuity and contradiction among an older European theory, contemporary socialist regimes, and current Western socialist-feminist concerns.

Taken together, the essays in *Promissory Notes* reveal tensions in the theory and practice of socialist states. One significant difficulty is the failure of most socialist regimes to directly address the full implications of the division of labor by gender. Good faith policies directed at incorporating women into full social production and lightening their domestic responsibilities inevitably run into contradictions between what the leadership considers to be general economic necessities and the concrete situation of many women. The contradictions are acknowledged to different degrees in different societies. They may include problems of population policies, as in the one-child family policy in China or the pronatalist programs of the Eastern bloc; conflicts over the mobilization of women for production despite inadequate commitments to public child-care and household services; or in rare instances struggles over changing the division of labor within the family. Even when problems such as these are acknowledged, political and economic constraints often make them hard to address. For example: scarce resources make adequate day care genuinely difficult to provide; the necessity to defend a new revolution often leads to a militarization of society, with attendant conservative implications for women in the family.

Another set of difficulties highlighted in the essays arises from the productionist bias in Marxism-Leninism. This orientation often influences the establishment of policy priorities. While policies related, for example, to military expenditure or the production of machine tools directly impinge on the lives of women, their specific interests are rarely taken into account. It is simply assumed that they will share in the general benefits of the building of socialism. This is often true. But it is also the case that women do not usually participate, as women, in the setting of transformational agendas. Women's organizations focus solely on what are regarded as women's issues, such as eliminating "feudal" family practices or winning maternity benefits. Yet macro planning issues (such as production goals for light over heavy industry) and even micro issues (such as providing running water or designing public housing) which have a differential impact on women and men, are regarded as national and therefore genderless.

A further "given" in Marxism-Leninism is a political theory whose organizational imperative—the vanguard party—can be inimical to the interests of women. Women's interests are assumed to be a subset of class interests. Such views make autonomous bases of women's self-organization at least problematic. In an unconscious echo of General Motors, what is good for the working classes is thought to be good for women. As a result, conceptions of women's interests that are not directly subsumed to class frequently remain only indirectly articulated. In this, women are hardly alone. With rare exceptions (Nicaragua comes to mind) present socialist states allow little space for autonomous self-organization by any social group. Mass organizations which in the revolutionary period expressed group interests (youth, women, peasants, etc.) in the postrevolutionary state become simply (or complexly) organs through which the vanguard party mobilizes sections of the population to fulfill national goals set by the leadership.

Socialist transformation of course involves tensions and difficulties beyond those discussed in *Promissory Notes*. There is a notable silence on the part of most of our contributors on the subject of sex and sexuality. This reflects, at least in part, the way in which our authors—some would say correctly—discuss the issues in terms of the agenda set by their subject. In part it reflects the state of current research and the difficulty of exploring what remains a largely taboo subject in socialist societies—for reasons this volume *does* address.

Promissory Notes is essentially a collection of case studies, rather than a contribution to the explicitly theoretical debate about the marital status of feminism and socialism. Indeed, even in the first section of the book, which deals directly with theory, what is offered is in fact a contextualized history of that theory. Our hope is that attention to the intersection of theory and specific histories will renew the debate by grounding it more concretely.

We have organized the book in five parts. Part 1, "The European Heritage," describes the way in which the theoretical agenda was set in Europe, primarily in the work of Marx and his followers. Its later elaboration and codification in the Second and Third Internationals is traced: this codification reflected in particular the form that the socialist struggle took first in late nineteenth- and early twentieth-century Germany and then, from 1917 to the mid-1920s, in Russia. By the 1920s, to all intents and purposes, a canonical analysis of the Women Question was elaborated. Our intention here is not to provide the usual historical "background" but to demonstrate the remarkable continuity which exists between mid-nineteenth and late twentieth-century theoretical formulations and concomitant practices.

In Part 2, "The First Experiments," two articles offer original research on the experiences of women in the early years of the USSR and the founding moments of the Chinese Communist Party. Both essays capture a sense of the open possibilities and the immense constraints of these early revolutionary struggles in a period before the socialist canon had been fully established.

Part 3, "The 'Woman Question' in Third World Revolutions," draws on

the history of Cuba, Nicaragua, Mozambique, Yemen, Vietnam, West
Bengal (India), and post-Maoist China to examine regimes in which the
codified statement of the Woman Question established by the Third
International is a principal point of reference. What is striking, across this
vast geographic, social, and historical landscape, is the extent to which the
analysis used and the policies developed are similar. Thus in each place,
the very same problems remain unresolved and the very same questions
are left unaddressed.

Part 4, "Women in Industrialized Socialist Regimes," explores the
current situation in three Eastern European socialist countries: Hungary,
the German Democratic Republic, and the Soviet Union. Because the
standard of living and industrial development in these countries is more
comparable to the West than any of the countries examined in Part 3, they
allow us to make a variety of interesting and important comparisons. On
the one hand, they provide an exemplar to the capitalist West in terms of
such readily quantifiable social goods as child care, maternity benefits,
access to middle-level political power, and more equal earning power—
real benefits seldom addressed even in socialist-feminist debates. On the
other hand, the very extent of these successes highlights the limits to
women's liberation possible within presently existing socialism. The problems in the formulation of the Woman Question, discussed in Part 1, here
become starkly apparent in practice.

Rather than pretend to give a theoretical resolution that we think
remains unattainable, given the state of current research and thinking, we
have chosen to end the volume on an open and interrogative note. Part 5
presents a roundtable to which we have invited scholars and activists to
contribute. These short pieces engage all the central issues of the current
theoretical debate—from questioning the possibility of the development of
an autonomous feminist position within existing socialisms which would
influence the definition of socialism itself, to illuminating the way in
which colonialism has hopelessly distorted the potential dialogue between
socialism and feminism in much of the third world. Underlying the efforts
of editors and authors alike is the conviction that, without underestimating
the difficulties, more feminist roads to socialism, and more socialist roads
to feminism, remain open, deeply desirable possibilities.

We would like to thank those students at the New School who participated in our seminar on Women and Socialism: without their enthusiasm
and curiosity this project would not have been conceived. Thanks go also
to Karen Judd at Monthly Review Press, for without her patience and per-
severance, as well her editorial skills, this book would not have been born.

Part 1
The European Heritage

Marxism and the "Woman Question"

Joan B. Landes

For the past century, Marxists have credited Friedrich Engels with placing the "Woman Question" on a firm scientific basis, that is, with elaborating the most adequate theoretical position on the topic of woman's emancipation for our age.[1] This is a curious but revealing claim. While Marxism signals its commitment to women, it regards feminism as by itself inadequate, standing in need of a reformulation that Marxism can best provide. What does Marxism offer women? Not only a theorization of women from the standpoint of the family, "the social relations of reproduction," but a historical and materialist approach to the family. Marxism rescues women and their cause from the defeatist ring of naturalizing, patriarchalist discourse. It opens women's oppression to human, political intervention. In the most optimistic Marxist vision, then, women may become subjects as well as objects of emancipation. Their cause is no longer partial, but joined to that of the proletariat. The feminist project becomes a dimension of the liberation of society in its entirety. But if this is so, it is also because feminism is subsumed (necessarily) within a more universal perspective.

The long-standing relationship between the two movements is marked from the outset by Marxist ambivalence toward feminism. An appreciation of the full scope of this ambivalence requires the sort of detailed investigation provided by subsequent chapters of this book. Here, I will chart the implications of the ways in which the founders of scientific socialism understood women's emancipation, and indicate the extent to which they attempted to appropriate feminism to Marxism. In posing the problem this way, I have already hinted at a fact that is usually neglected in orthodox Marxist treatments of the subject. By the 1840s, when Marx and Engels first turned their attention to the Woman Question, there existed a legacy of women's protest and feminist demands dating at least to the revolution of 1789, surfacing again in the revolutions of 1830 and 1848 in France. Utopian socialists invited women's full participation in the coming world order, which they hoped to bring about through a peaceful social transfor-

mation. The French feminists of the 1830s—Flora Tristan, Suzanne Voil-
quin, Reine Guindorf, Claire Démar, Pauline Roland, Prosper Enfantin,
and Charles Fourier—were utopian socialists. In the 1840s feminists were
attached to republican socialist movements; later in the century they
flocked either to liberal republicanism or to mutualist socialism. In England, male and female followers of the utopian Robert Owen enthusiastically advanced feminist demands, and large numbers of often militant
women inhabited the Chartist movement.[2] By 1884 (the publication date
of Engels' *The Origin of the Family, Private Property and the State*),
women's organizations were well established throughout North America
and Europe. Consequently, the affirmative but conflicted relationship
between feminism and socialism involved a practical as well as a discursive
dimension. My task in this essay will be to examine Marxist discourse on
the Woman Question, but I do so in light of these historical circumstances.

The Origin of the Family, Private Property and the State was an immediate success. August Bebel, a leading German social democrat and author
of *Women Under Socialism*, quickly revised his own popular book to
incorporate Engels' discoveries—an amalgam of nineteenth-century ethnography and German philosophy.[3] In the title and structure of this work,
Engels drew into socialist discourse the major categories of "objective
spirit." Following Marx, he reversed Hegel's priorities.[4] He grounded his
account of class history and the "world historic defeat of the female sex" in
Hegel's middle term, *civil society*, and he located the real basis of civil
society in private property. Engels presents a dialectical account of the
manner in which alienated property relations are mediated through the
antagonistic structure of the family and the state. In the preface the family
is accorded equal status with the labor process. Engels asserted that "according to the materialistic conception the determining factor in history is,
in the final instance, the production and reproduction of immediate life."
This is said to be of a twofold character: social production and the
propagation of the species, the labor process and the family. The argument
of *Origin* can be summarized as follows: whereas a kinship-based family
order is the basis of social structure *prior to* the development of class
divisions and a state-oriented political order, all class history proper is
characterized by "a society in which the system of the family is completely
dominated by the system of property."[5] In the course of social evolution
reproduction is eclipsed by production, the family by the labor process.
Engels advances a theoretical and historical claim as to the manner in
which social production comes to exert an ever more determining influence on social life, especially after the transition from a primitive society
organized around kinship to class-based civilizations with differentiated
political systems.

In his study of prehistory, Engels allowed for the possibility that social reproduction, on the side of family life, has a partially independent influence. This pertains to a kinship society in which all production relations are subsumed within kin terms. On the other hand, the transparency of production relations in capitalism is highlighted by the actual separation between family life and the sphere of production, as well as by the breakdown of kinship-based social relations and the rise of market relations. But even in capitalism the picture is clouded. Throughout his lifetime, Marx referred to uncompleted projects to supplement his analysis of production relations. Similarly, we overburden any discussion of the family by addressing it solely in the context of stages in the social division of labor, or by viewing women only from the perspective of different forms of ownership. Even *Origin* is strikingly partial: it is a study of the family and only incidentally of women's oppression; a study primarily of prehistory and only superficially one of the family in capitalist society.

Thus, a problem arises insofar as the social division of labor and social relations of production fail to explain aspects of sexual and family life. What cannot be accounted for on this basis is abandoned by Marx and Engels to the residual category of a natural division of labor. Moreover, many of the difficulties posed by Engels' work derives from his failure to address the Woman Question directly. Nor do Marx's writings redress the balance. Indeed, both men consistently treated the Woman Question under the topic of the family. While in principle this may not be so troublesome, the status of the family within Marxist writings fluctuates between two views of ethical and natural existence: first, the Hegelian ethical position that treats the family as a central moral structure in modern society; second, the Utopian Socialist attack on the patriarchal, sexually oppressive form of the family, which is linked in turn to social and political domination. The fate of women and personal life in Marxist argument is refracted through these two competing views.

In an 1842 editorial in the *Rheinische Zeitung*, Marx defended divorce while upholding the ethical content of the family in the manner of Hegel. He emphasized the moral responsibilities of parents toward their children, and admonished those who would reduce marriage to a capricious sexual union.[6] Hegel had insisted that the modern family is (or should be) an "ethical root of the state," conforming to the logic of neither political nor economic relationships.[7] He denied the patriarchal claim that the father's relationship to his wife and children is analogous to the king's relationship to his subjects, the liberal contention that all relationships (even those between parent and child) are conventional, and the Utopian Socialist denunciation of the link between male power in the family and bourgeois class power in civil society and the state. As is evident by its imitative format, this editorial on divorce was written prior to Marx's sustained efforts to come to terms with Hegelian philosophy, beginning in 1843 in the *Critique of the Philosophy of Right*. In contrast, the *Communist Manifesto*, coauthored by Marx and Engels in 1848, reads as a forceful utopian repudiation of a mystified Hegelian view of the family. Capitalism is charged with reducing bourgeois women to instruments of production for the male bourgeoisie, transforming proletarian children into "simple articles of commerce and instruments of labor," destroying proletarian family life with women driven into prostitution and exploitative working conditions. Sexual oppression is conceived as a derivative of the social division of labor and its products, private property and the capitalist cash nexus. [8]

Likewise the major writings of both writers in the 1840s are shot through with caricatures, borrowed from the Utopian Socialists, of the manner in which private property erodes all ethical content, exposing the family's true political and economic determinations. Prostitution is a favorite theme, both as a description of (working) women's fate and as a metaphor for the worker's degradation by capital. The utopian rhetoric underscores the socialist advocacy of women's cause. In *The Holy Family*, Marx asserted that "the general position of women in modern society is inhuman."[9] He quoted approvingly from Fourier's list of crimes against women, including the hypocritical, unequal punishment of adultery and seduction, the choice between forced infanticide and illegitimate birth for a woman whose child is born out of wedlock, the virtual "sale" of daughters to marital bidders, the prostitution underpinning the "marital trade," the manner in which civilized societies raise to a higher and more hypocritical level the debasement of women under barbarism.

Nevertheless, throughout the corpus of Marx's and Engels' writings, one hears strong echoes of Hegel's ethical approach. Even though Hegel's arguments are radically transformed, exploded through an immanent critique, they are never entirely set aside. Indeed, ambiguities arise within the classical Marxist canon as a result of a shifting interpretation of family life, a fact that has burdened later Marxists in their effort to develop a strategy for women's liberation. Played in a major key—and here is where Marx and Engels appear in their most utopian, anti-Hegelian posture—the destruction of the family is regarded as a favorable development. Although they never believed that capitalism emancipates women, Marx and Engels argued that the sexual division of labor in agricultural, preindustrial societies gives way to a capitalist form of the social division of labor. In other words, patriarchy, like "all fixed, fast frozen relations, with the[ir] train of ancient prejudices and opinions [is] swept away" to be supplanted in the socialist future by new forms of human association.[10] Modern industry overturns the economic foundation of the traditional family and its corresponding form of female labor, thereby "unloosen[ing] all traditional ties."[11] Family life will be supplanted by new forms of human association in the socialist future. For the present, women's entry into the public workforce was deemed to be a necessary condition for the emancipation of the class as a whole, by way of a "radical revolution, universal human emancipation."[12]

Played in a minor key, the social dissolution of the working-class family and the corresponding abuse of female and child laborers provide powerful images of the scourge of capitalism—a profile of what Albrecht Wellmer once referred to as the "moral physiognomy of capitalist society" in Marxist criticism.[13] Engels' *The Condition of the Working Class in England* reads like a passionate outcry against the industrial conditions that produced the "universal decadence of family life among the workers."[14] Similarly, the substitution of female for male labor is treated as emblematic of the absolute degradation of human labor by capital. In a typical vein, Marx observed: "as labour becomes more and more unsatisfying, more repulsive, competition increases and wages decrease. . . . Machinery brings about the same results on a much greater scale, by replacing skilled workers with unskilled, men by women, adults by children."[15] Likewise, in *Capital*, Marx commented upon capital's ability to depress wages by employing women and children. In fact, in its secret drive to reduce the worker to a mere object, capital discovers an ideal, because pliant and docile, subject/object in married women and children. The decline of working-class resistance to capitalist work conditions is as much a consequence of the new composition of the labor force as of changes in the technical division of labor.[16]

There is a subtle shift of emphasis, then, between the two versions of the relationship between capitalism and family life. On the one hand, the family (without qualification, e.g., all family life) is depicted as a negative *institution*, a product of class society that will disappear in the socialist future. As Marx proclaimed in the *Theses on Feuerbach*, "after the earthly family is discovered to be the secret of the holy family, the former must then itself be destroyed in theory and practice."[17] On the other hand, the family, working class or bourgeois, exists as a negative *effect* of the operation of the laws of capital. It is not family life as such, but its particular capitalist form that is condemnable. By recognizing the most dehumanizing effects of the capitalist organization of society, we are directed toward the discovery of new forms of human association wherein social relationships are not dominated by property forms, sexual life is not reduced to animal-like drives, and the emancipation of all the senses is possible.[18] It is not hard to see, therefore, why later Marxists have held fast to at least two differing interpretations of the original texts in order to support their own contention that socialists ought to promote free love and communal living arrangements, or more likely, that socialists should condemn "bourgeois" marriage and its flip side, libertinage, in order to defend the working-class family, the model of uncorrupted family life in a property-based society.

Underlying these competing versions of a Marxist theory of the family there exists an uncertainty about the nature of human freedom and sexual emancipation, which itself bespeaks a conflict between a model of identity and unity, on the one hand, and one of difference and diversity, on the other. In a central passage of the *1844 Manuscripts*, Marx addressed the sexual relationship as a measure (or metaphor) of the level of humanization of the species as a whole in the manner of Fourier and eighteenth-century Enlightenment authors. The central polarities of the age, naturalism and humanism, individuality and community, are represented as core expressions of a fundamental antagonism between man and woman. In contrast, Marx appealed to an undivided sexual ideal. For, he wrote, "in the relationship . . . is *sensuously manifested*, reduced to an observable *fact*, the extent to which, therefore, the *other* person has become for him a need—the extent to which he in his individual existence is at the same time a social being."[19] Although the relationship between man and woman has an objective, material basis in the natural world and in our own physical nature (in desire), Marx emphasized what is peculiarly human in our approach to another human being. Only through a process of humanization, socialization, and individuation predicated on a mutual relationship between independent selves-in-community, capable of transcending the moment of immediate animal desire, can the relationship between two persons cease to operate in a determined fashion.

I will draw two inferences from this discussion. First, sexual antagonism derives from a wholly external source. According to Marx, it is capitalism—and by extension, any property-based social order—that destroys the senses and impoverishes the intersubjective realm. There is no acknowledgment of other possible sources of sexual antagonism. As elsewhere in the classical account, Marx posits a model of perfect, undivided family life to supersede the conflicts of class society and to reproduce, on a higher level, the outline of early human society (primitive communism), which grounds later formulations of a theory of social evolution by Marx and Engels.

Second, humanization or socialization requires sublimation or delayed gratification, to employ a psychological vocabulary. In another statement from this same period, Marx insisted pessimistically that the metabolic interaction with nature always involves a necessary measure of self-denial.[20] Paralleling his reflections in the *Manuscripts*, he wrote elsewhere: "In order that man may become as man his real object, he must conquer his relative existence, the power of desire and of mere nature in himself."[21] In other words, Marx adopted a Hegelian attitude toward labor as the deferral of immediate gratification. This much is familiar. But how did his view of the transposition of human need for animal desire as a basic constituent of freedom relate to the principle of women's emancipation?

Marx hinted that this too might require a certain level of sublimation. He did not believe that woman's emancipation would be achieved through a romantic appeal to a cult of womanhood and nature. In this respect, Marx endorsed a rupture with the Hegelian ethical ideal of family life. In an 1850 review article, Marx emphatically repudiated the reactionary patriarchal content of the particular work under scrutiny.[22] There, in an extremely rare remark, he scorned the ideology of motherhood. Despite this prescient insight, however, Marx never adequately resisted the unreflected category of the natural. Throughout the classical texts, the other side of the dialectic of labor makes its appearance in the concept of a natural division of labor. And one witnesses a repetition of the movement between the release of difference, on the one hand, and the impulse toward unity, on the other.

In the familiar account of *Origin*, slavery, private property, and the subordination of women are said to arise simultaneously and to culminate in the formation of state structures. But Engels' theoretical reconstruction of prehistory implies that the contradictions of tribal society are based on the sexual division of labor: that is, they precede the formation of class society. For one thing, the differential access to instruments of production that men and women possess within tribal society has enormous consequences for the "world historical defeat of the female sex." Earlier, in *The German Ideology*, Marx and Engels pointed directly to the social significance of the sexual division of labor, which they somewhat paradoxically regarded as a "natural" division of labor based on sexual difference, the ability of women to bear children, and the differential physical strength of men and women, which accounts for the "latent slavery" of women and children in the family.[23]

I will reserve several important qualifications that could be introduced in order to advance my assertion in the strongest possible manner. I view the society depicted in *The German Ideology* as not differing markedly from that portrayed in much patriarchal literature.[24] Moreover, despite its occlusion behind the matriarchy thesis, the natural division of labor is present and indeed undermines the presumed equality of tribal society as portrayed in *Origin*. Apart from the important fact that women do not occupy equal positions in the political arena of tribal social life, there are socially significant demarcations within the sexual division of labor itself. The splits between private and public, inside and outside, domestic work and wage labor, are, in a surprisingly ahistorical fashion, transposed back onto early human social organization by Engels. The man and wife of his matriarchal household might comfortably occupy gender roles in Victorian society. "The man fights in the wars," he writes, "going hunting and fishing, procures the raw materials and the tools necessary for doing so. The woman looks after the house and the preparation of food and clothing, cooks, weaves, and sews. They are each master in their own sphere: The man in the forest, the woman in the house."[25]

Marx and Engels each deployed the concept of a natural division of labor. On the one hand, insofar as the sexual division of labor does not entail exchange of surplus it is regarded as a simple division of subsistence labor within the household. On the other hand, for example in *Origin*, women are excluded from the ownership or control of surplus-producing cattle because of their differential access to certain means of production and to the products of labor within communistic tribal society. The contradiction between these two positions can be resolved once we see that there is no sharp cleavage between a natural and a social division of labor. The natural division of labor itself harbors the private property that is supposed to be exclusive to the social division.[26] The simple domestic mode of production is a variation on the patriarchal household community, which Engels posited as the transitional form between mother right and institutionalized monogamy. Sexual equality during the stage of primitive matriarchy turns out to be strictly a surface phenomenon, concealing a sexual division of labor wherein *natural difference* and inequality between men and women are already well established.

Neither Marx nor Engels fully escaped the patriarchal assumptions of their age, even as they sought to escape them. Equally disturbing is the way in which the metaphors of matriarchy and maternity reify the existing social differences among men and women. In the *Manuscripts* Marx had deplored the narrowing of sexual drives to procreative behavior. Yet in *Origin*, Engels treated sexuality mainly from the standpoint of procreation, and there is little evidence in his published writings that Marx thought otherwise. Both men conceived of communism as a dialectical regression to the original stage of primitive matriarchy, at which time patriarchal domination, class society, and the alienation of labor were not yet institutionalized. Properly understood, the Marxist theory of primitive matriarchy or primitive communism is a consciously constructed (though not entirely original) alternative to the patriarchalist version of human origins wherein a natural family structure of male preeminence and female subordination explains (naturalizes) all future forms of social and political domination. It is the theoretical point of reference for classical Marxism's effort to join women's emancipation to the socialist project. But this theory conforms to the priorities of a class theory rooted in the possession and nonpossession of property in the means of production, thereby obscuring other sources of social divisiveness, including sexual antagonism.

The analysis does affirm the commitment of socialism to the emancipation of women. However, such a maternal image of women was used frequently to repress women's sexuality in the name of economic goals and to restrict their political involvement for the sake of family interests. In effect, the domestic imagery of primitive matriarchy and the natural division of labor obscured fears of women and free sexuality among Second and Third International Marxists suspicious about the autonomous goals of feminists—especially their demands for birth control and sexual freedom. To summarize, an unexamined privileging of social unity and identity (an unexpurgated Hegelian theme) in the Marxist theory of human origins moderated considerably the accompanying theory of sexual emancipation. Coexisting, discordant elements were suppressed by the founders of historical materialism, relegated to the level of natural life, the prehistorical world, the world without social implications. Woman is different, but allowed no voice in this theory for her difference, for difference is an essential feature of woman's embodiment.

It may be that Marxism is not unlike all other theories that accept the role of sexual dimorphism in an uncritical manner. Yet Marxism promised to undermine the Western philosophical enterprise and its essentialist and naturalistic appeals. Nevertheless, its central texts on the Woman Question, most especially *Origin*, narrate a story in which sexual equality both precedes and comes after the enormous parenthesis in which human history and class struggle are said to occur. In this narrative, women have no independent or autonomous role to perform; they are passive recipients of either good or mis-fortune. But even during the most auspicious moments, as in primitive matriarchy, inequalities exist. No adequate acknowledgment is made that the sexual division of labor might generate social antagonisms of equal consequence to those occuring in the property order and even foster class divisions between men and women.

There is no definitive public record of Marx's or Engels' attitude toward feminism. The best indications are that they never achieved a thoroughly consistent position on the subject. In principle, to be sure, they endorsed the Utopian Socialist goal of building a movement of equality and cooperation between men and women. As late as 1868, Marx wrote in a private correspondence that "major social transformations were impossible without ferment from women."[27] Moreover, he set a precedent for the participation of women in socialist politics by naming a woman, Harriet Law, to the General Council of the First International, and by promoting the organization and admission of groups of women workers. On the other hand, when a dispute arose over the American sections' membership in the First International, Marx eventually recommended their expulsion on the grounds that they gave "precedence to the women's question over the question of labor." In response, the American delegate retorted: "The labor question is also a women's question and the emancipation of woman must precede that of the workers."[28]

In subsequent years further tensions between men and women beset the working-class movement. Female suffrage and protective legislation became two of the most heatedly debated topics within reform circles: the former largely a feminist demand that received strong socialist endorsement; the latter a socialist position that stirred considerable controversy among feminists. When Marx penned his important *Critique of the Gotha Programme* he made no mention of the internal German socialist debate over female suffrage, ignoring the draft article that called for "universal, equal and direct suffrage by secret ballot for all males who have reached the age of 21."[29] The resolution finally adopted at Gotha involved a shrewd compromise: while avoiding any explicit mention of women, it permitted their inclusion under the concept of citizen. Judging from these remarks, Marx also seemed to accept the restriction of female labor. He made no argument against either claim, requesting only that the party clarify whether it intended that such prohibitions and restrictions were to be interpreted as a byproduct of the health needs of the female body or as a moral protest on behalf of the female sex. In striking contrast, Marx firmly objected to the clause professing the prohibition of child labor. He pronounced this goal either impossible to achieve under large-scale industry or reactionary since "an early combination of productive labour with education is one of the most potent means for the transformation of present-day society."[30]

What are we to think of the inconsistencies between Marx's views on female and child labor? After all, when he penned his response, the abuses of child labor were an open scandal, yet Marx persisted in seeing something beneficial, or at least necessary, in it. On the other hand, was Marx simply reiterating an unexamined bourgeois sentimentality when he endorsed the demand for protective legislation? The latter is still a vexed issue among feminists. There is no doubt that the demand possessed a double character. On the one hand, the resulting legislation did sometimes protect women from the most excessive abuses of an industrial work environment. On the other hand, it often served to secure male privileges in the labor market, to deny women access to jobs by very spurious criteria, and to encourage a female self-image tied to domesticity, subordination, and nonparticipation in the public sphere.

Marx and Engels, like other socialists of their age, failed to recognize the limitations of this demand. Their shortened vision was only accentuated by the growing hostility of socialists toward middle-class women's movements. Socialists began to defend protective legislation as a class issue. Organizationally, it offered a convenient compromise between those who upheld women's right to work and those who wished to restrict female labor in the name of a conventionally conceived family life. Engels resorted to this class-bound perspective in a letter to the German feminist Gertrud Guillaume-Schack. He deemed it necessary to qualify the feminist demand for equal pay in order to protect the "health of future generations," in his estimation a more important concern than the "absolute formal equality of the sexes during the last years of the capitalist mode of production." Although Engels reaffirmed the socialist dedication to "equal wages for equal work to either sex," he distinguished socialist from feminist strategies. "The English women who championed the formal right of members of their sex to permit themselves to be as thoroughly exploited by the capitalists as the men, are mostly, directly or indirectly, interested in the capitalist exploitation of both sexes," he declared. [31]

What is at stake here is the relationship of women to the nondomestic sphere of labor. Strangely, Engels branded these English feminists with a position that approximates the general logic of capitalism as set forth in the *Communist Manifesto*: to abolish all differences among persons and to eradicate all privileges among groups in time. This involved the supercession of male by female labor, and the eventual dissolution of all differences of age and sex within the working class as all workers are reduced to "instruments of labor," so that the various interests and conditions of life within the ranks of the proletariat will be more or less equalized. [32]

In effect, Engels condemned feminists for advancing the very process he and Marx had once regarded as an inevitable and beneficial feature of capitalist change; that is, for undercutting all existing artificial and archaic divisions between men and women. Protectionism purported to "save" women from their fate. But such motivations call into question the very definition of the proletarian struggle as the "self-conscious, independent movement of the immense majority." [33] In his letter to Guillaume-Schack, Engels also referred to women's "special physiological functions" as a possible explanation for restricting their participation in the labor force, thereby suggesting a serious lacuna in the Marxist theory of the revolutionary subject. In the case of women, we are led to assume that the normal operation of the laws of capitalist production will result in the dissolution of the preindustrial, patriarchal sexual division of labor and the subsumption of women under class relations. Yet Engels and Marx maintained strong reservations about this trajectory. They resolved to resituate ethical and naturalistic arguments about family life within a historical materialist framework, especially by examining how class and property relations transform the structure of personal life. Yet, an overly comfortable identity of women and family, hence of women with larger socialist goals, tended to suppress the search for a framework within which the social construction of female identity and the social sources of women's oppression might be independently scrutinized. [34] Moreover, because women are theorized almost exclusively through their location in the family, there is little impetus provided for an understanding of women's relationship to the political domain. For example, in *Origin*, women's absence from the state is not accounted for except by way of a discussion of the mechanisms through which the state supports the monogamous family of bourgeois property.

I conclude, therefore, by returning to my initial observations. I have charted the way in which the Woman Question in Marxism has been reduced to an ambivalent approach to the family that vacillates between different poles: a Hegelian approach in which women are tied to the ethical whole (now proletarian instead of bourgeois family existence), and the Utopian attack on the property basis of family life and the resulting prostitution of women and labor within capitalist society. Finally, subsuming both these positions, the position of women and the family are conceived as features of a natural, sexual division of labor. What is missing in these competing accounts, however, is a treatment of the explicitly political fate of women in the world of liberal (and revolutionary) democracy. The absence of a full treatment of the public sphere, and especially the suppression of public speech and action by women, within the classical texts of Marxism has proved to be especially unfortunate in light of the future history of women within socialist movements. As at the outset, the Woman Question remains subordinate to the fate of the working-class movement, and political, social, and gender questions are all too easily dismissed by way of a naturalizing discourse on matters of sexuality and family life. Following Engels, social democrats and communists have recommended public housekeeping—the socialization of domestic work—as the solution to women's domestic oppression. In this prescription, there is no recognition of the need for women and men to wage a conscious struggle to transform interpersonal relations, nor of the political requirements of such a task.

Notes

1. I recognize that Engels is a controversial figure, even among Marxists. Many wish to sever the two founders of Marxism, labeling Engels a vulgar materialist. I do not want to enter this debate, only to acknowledge at the outset that no consideration of the Marxist contribution to feminism can ignore Engels' role. He, more than any other figure, with the possible exception of August Bebel, is responsible for setting feminism on the Marxist agenda.

2. See Claire Goldberg Moses, *French Feminism in the Nineteenth Century* (Albany: State University of New York Press, 1984); Barbara Taylor, *Eve and the New Jerusalem: Socialism and Feminism in the Nineteenth Century* (New York: Pantheon, 1983).

3. August Bebel, *Women Under Socialism*, trans. Daniel De Leon, intro. Lewis Coser (New York: Schocken Books, 1971). Bebel's work was probably the most widely read socialist classic of the late nineteenth century and the book credited most often by its readers with introducing them to the socialist movement. Likewise, other popular treatments and public addresses delivered by Eleanor Marx, Edward Aveling, Clara Zetkin, Alexandra Kollontai, to name just the most prominent, all followed Engels' broad outline. Even Wilhelm Reich's later attempt to update Engels' ethnography by reference to the twentieth-century results of Malinowski and others was conducted in the spirit of a defense of Engels' work. See Wilhelm Reich, "The Imposition of Sexual Morality," in Lee Baxandall, ed., *Sex-Pol Essays* (New York: Vintage, 1972), pp. 89–249.

4. Marx attacked Hegel for mystifying the actual relationships between family, civil society, and the state. By undertaking a transformative criticism of Hegel's political philosophy, he demonstrated that the real starting point is not Hegel's Idea, but the family and civil society. Marx also charged that Hegel reverted to a "body politics," a patriarchal principle, in that he based his state on a hereditary constitutional monarchy. See Karl

Marx, *Critique of Hegel's Philosophy of Right*, ed. Joseph O'Malley (Cambridge: University Press, 1970), pp. 8–9, 94–95.

5. Friedrich Engels, *The Origin of the Family, Private Property and the State: In Light of the Researches of Lewis H. Morgan*, intro. and notes Eleanor Burke Leacock (New York: International, 1972), pp. 71, 72.
6. Karl Marx, "On a Proposed Divorce Law," in Lloyd D. Easton and Kurt H. Guddat, eds., *Writings of the Young Marx on Philosophy and Society* (Garden City, N.Y.: Doubleday, 1967), pp. 136–142.
7. G. W. F. Hegel, *Philosophy of Right*, trans. T. M. Knox (New York: Oxford University Press, 1952), paragraph 255. For a critique of Hegel's theory see my article, "Hegel's Conception of the Family," *Polity* 14, no. 1 (Fall 1981): 5–28.
8. "The Communist Manifesto," in Karl Marx and Friedrich Engels, *Selected Works in One Volume* (New York: International, 1968), pp. 31–63; pp. 49–51.
9. In Karl Marx and Friedrich Engels, *Collected Works*, Vol. 4 (New York: International, 1975) p. 195.
10. "The Communist Manifesto," p. 38.
11. Marx continues: "However terrible and disgusting the dissolution, under the capitalist system, of the old family ties may appear, nevertheless, modern industry, by assigning as it does an important part in the process of production, outside the domestic sphere, to women, to young persons, and to children of both sexes, creates a new economic foundation for a higher form of the relations between the sexes" (Karl Marx, *Capital: A Critique of Political Economy*, Vol. 1 [New York: International, 1967], pp. 489–90).
12. Marx, "A Contribution to the Critique of Hegel's 'Philosophy of Right,'" in *Critique of Hegel's 'Philosophy of Right'*, p. 139.
13. Albrecht Wellmer, *Critical Theory of Society*, trans. John Cumming (New York: Herder and Herder, 1971), p. 61.
14. Friedrich Engels, *The Condition of the Working Class in England*, trans. and ed. W. O. Henderson and W. H. Chaloner (Stanford: Stanford University Press, 1958), p. 161.
15. Karl Marx, "Wage Labour and Capital," in *Selected Works*, p. 92.
16. Marx, *Capital*, pp. 402–3. A plausible implication of this line of argument (endorsed by many in the labor and socialist movements) involved the defense of the family wage and the "traditional" working-class family with a male breadwinner and nonlaboring wife and children. For two contrasting perspectives on this strategy, see Heidi Hartmann, "Capitalism, Patriarchy, and Job Segregation by Sex," *Signs* 1, no. 3, pt. 2 (Spring 1976 Supplement): 137–70; and Jane Humphries, "Class Struggle and the Persistence of the Working-Class Family," *Cambridge Journal of Economics* 1 (1977): 241–58.
17. In *The German Ideology, Part One*, ed. C. J. Arthur (New York: International, 1970), p. 122. Translators of the *Theses* have rendered this important passage with interesting variations demonstrating that quotation and translation are also interpretation. It is as if the translators have allowed their own moral dispositions toward family life to guide their English phrasing. If so, this would only support further my argument that Marx's and Engels' views on the relation of family to capitalism are intrinsically antinomical. Consider the following examples, in addition to the version already cited in the text: (1) "Hence, for example, once the earthly family is disclosed as the secret of the holy family, the former must now be annihilated both theoretically and practically"; (2) "Thus, for example, once the earthly family is discovered to be the secret of the holy family, the former must itself be destroyed in theory and in practice"; (3) "For instance, after the earthly family is found to be the secret of the holy family, the former must then be theoretically and practically nullified"; (4) "Thus, for instance, once the earthly family is discovered to be the secret of the holy family, the former must then itself be criticized in theory and revolutionised in practice"; (5) "Thus, for instance, once the earthly family is discovered to be the secret of the holy family, the former must then itself be theoretically criticized and radically changed in practice" (the last two versions are attributed to

Friedrich Engels). Sources, in order of presentation: Nathan Rotenstreich, *Basic Problems of Marx's Philosophy* (Indianapolis: Bobbs-Merrill, 1965), p. 24; Ernst Bloch, *On Karl Marx*, trans. John Maxwell (New York: Herder and Herder, 1971), p. 55; *Writings of the Young Marx*, p. 401; *Selected Works*, p. 29; Friedrich Engels, *Ludwig Feuerbach and the Outcome of Classical German Philosophy* (New York: International, 1941), p. 83.

18. See especially, Karl Marx, *Economic and Philosophic Manuscripts of 1844*, trans. Martin Milligan, ed. Dirk J. Struik (New York: International, 1964), p. 63.
19. Ibid., p. 134.
20. Alfred Schmidt, *The Concept of Nature in Marx* (London: NLB, 1971), p. 139.
21. Karl Marx, "Doctoral Dissertation," cited in ibid., p. 137.
22. Karl Marx and Friedrich Engels, "Review of G. Fr. Daumer's *The Religion of the New Age*," in Karl Marx and Friedrich Engels, *On Religion*, intro. Reinhold Niebuhr (New York: Schocken, 1964), p. 96.
23. See Marx and Engels, *The German Ideology*, pp. 52–53.
24. I am not alone in this view. See the excellent discussion by Beverly Brown, "Natural and Social Division of Labour—Engels and the Domestic Labour Debate," *m/f* 1 (1978): 24–48.
25. Engels, *Origins*, p. 218.
26. Brown, "Natural and Social Division of Labour," pp. 38, 39.
27. Karl Marx, Letter to Kugelman, December 12, 1868, cited in Richard Stites, *The Women's Liberation Movement in Russia: Feminism, Nihilism, and Bolshevism 1860–1930* (Princeton: Princeton University Press, 1978), p. 235.
28. Cited in Mari Jo Buhle, *Women and American Socialism, 1840–1920* (Urbana, Chicago, and London: University of Illinois Press, 1981), p. xiv. The American sections attracted an unusually large percentage of women, including Victoria Woodhull, who published her own newspaper urging the International to support the advancement of women.
29. Editor's note 261 to Karl Marx, "Critique of the Gotha Programme," in *Selected Works*, pp. 315–35, p. 737.
30. Marx, "Critique of the Gotha Programme," p. 334.
31. Letter to Gertrud Guillaume-Schack in Beuthen (London, July 5, 1855) in Karl Marx and Friedrich Engels, *Selected Correspondence* (Moscow: Progress Publishers, 1975). Despite Engels' private reservations, socialist parties generally supported the demand for equal pay.
32. "The Communist Manifesto," p. 42.
33. Ibid, p. 45.
34. Cf. Rosalind Coward, *Patriarchal Precedents: Sexuality and Social Relations* (London: Routledge & Kegan Paul, 1983).

In the Shadow of the Comintern: The Communist Women's Movement, 1920–43

Elizabeth Waters

In June 1920, twenty-one women representing nineteen countries met in Moscow for the First Communist Women's Conference. A celebratory meeting in the Bolshoi theater with an orchestra and an audience of local factory women was followed by two days of discussions in the Kremlin. Delegates proclaimed their commitment to women's emancipation and socialist revolution and pledged their allegiance to the Third International, an organization established the previous year with the declared aim of coordinating the global struggle of the proletariat and its allies to abolish class society and build communism.

As its name implied, it was the third in a series. The First International, founded in 1864, lasted for little over a decade. The Second International, set up in 1889 in response to the rise of social-democratic parties in several European countries, grew spectacularly. At regular congresses, members passed resolutions on matters of mutual concern, including militarism, which they deplored, and proletarian internationalism, which they invoked as their defense against capitalist warmongering. When war broke out in 1914, however, the vast majority of socialists found the pull of nationalism to be irresistible and rallied in support of their governments against the "foreign enemy." This had led the Russian socialist Lenin, leader of the Bolshevik Party, to announce the death of the Second International and urge the creation of a "Third International" to take its place. At the time few can have taken him seriously, for he and his party were relatively unknown and socialist opposition to the war was negligible. By 1920, when the delegates assembled for the First Communist Women's Conference, the world had changed beyond recognition: Lenin was the head of a Bolshevik government in Russia; across Europe workers were demonstrating, occupying factories, and calling for radical social transformation; and the Third International (also known as the Communist International or Comintern to emphasize the ideological divide between it and its predecessor) was preparing for its Second Congress, its membership on the increase, its adherents confident that world revolution was only a matter of time.

The victory of communism was expected to bring with it the liberation of women. A connection between the emancipation of the female sex and the emancipation of labor had long been acknowledged by socialist theorists and both the First and the Second Internationals had argued the case for women's equality. By the beginning of the twentieth century, social-democratic women were organizing for greater recognition within the socialist movement and for their rights in the wider society. Under the auspices of the Second International, two socialist women's conferences had taken place, in Stuttgart (1907) and Copenhagen (1910).[1] Delegates to the First Communist Women's Conference meeting in 1920 paid tribute to those socialists who had struggled before the war for women's emancipation. At the same time they claimed that their movement represented a new departure: while the Second International, initially committed to achieving full equality for women, had eventually abandoned its aim, the Third International, in contrast, would liberate women "not only on paper, but in reality, in actual fact."[2] This was the promise made in the *Theses on the Communist Women's Movement*, a lengthy document discussed by the delegates at the Moscow conference and ratified in 1921 by the Third Congress of the Communist International.[3]

The communist movement set great store by theory, believing that policies could successfully mobilize the masses only if they were based on a correct appraisal of the mechanisms of history and of current economic, social, and political developments; organization was also considered a matter of central importance, if revolutionary situations were to be exploited to the full. The *Theses* accordingly examined the origins of female oppression, assessed the implications for women of recent events, and listed the different measures the communist parties should endeavor to implement, depending on whether they were operating in postrevolutionary, capitalist, or precapitalist societies; they also included an analysis of the organizational weaknesses of the prewar socialist movement and a detailed outline of the organizational structure to be adopted by communist women. The *Theses* linked the struggle for the emancipation of .women with the emancipation of the working class more firmly than any of the documents of the Second International. At the same time, the connection between class and sexual divisions within society was left vague and the primacy of the former over the latter taken for granted: in the final analysis, the inequality of women remained a secondary consideration, and the women's movement was expected to occupy a subordinate role, organizationally as well as ideologically.

The *Theses* were intended as a definitive statement on the "Woman Question," a guide for the movement in the years to come. As is often the case with manifestos of this kind, events soon left the *Theses* behind. By the

mid-1920s the politics and organizational practices of the women's movement already differed considerably from the model envisaged by the First
Communist Conference. By the end of the decade, the only aspect of the
Woman Question to receive the regular attention of the communist movement was the industrial exploitation of working women, and even this was
allotted an increasingly minor place. The organizational prescriptions of
the *Theses* relating to the structure of the women's movement at the
national level were implemented according to the letter rather than the
spirit, while at the international level they were largely ignored.

The redirection of the movement, of both policies and organizational
forms, was more than a necessary accommodation to the political realities
of the interwar period, a time of inflation and unemployment, not of
revolutionary upheaval and socialist revolution—it was a rejection of the
underlying principles of the *Theses*. This gap between intention and
performance was not the inevitable result of any essential incompatibility
between socialism and feminism in general, nor of fatal theoretical flaws in
the *Theses* in particular. It was the product of events both ideological and
organizational, both within and outside the women's movement, which
served over a number of years to silence and exclude a feminist voice.

Perspectives and Policies

The *Theses of the Communist Women's Movement* presented to the first
conference in 1920 began by proclaiming the International's commitment
to the political equality of women and the guarantee of their social rights.
A second paragraph traced the origin of the privileged social position of
men to the institution of private property and to women's isolation within
the domestic economy and the family, drawing from this the conclusion
that female emancipation could be won only when private property was
collectivized and women worked in social production. A lengthy assessment of the Second International was followed by an evaluation of the
postwar political and economic situation: capitalism was found wanting,
and only communism was recognized as capable of righting the wrongs of
women. Thus, the destinies of women and of the proletariat were linked
historically, in the origins of oppression and exploitation, and also strategically, in the struggle to overthrow capitalism and create a better world.
Women's struggles were ineffective, it was argued, unless conducted in
connection with the communist movement, but proletarian victory would
not be assured unless women took their place in the political process.
"Without the conscious and active participation of the mass of women who
sympathize with communism . . . a fundamental and far-reaching transformation of the economic basis of society and all its institutions and all its
cultural life is impossible."[4]

Confidence in the inevitability of revolution influenced the manner in which the *Theses* presented their demands. Basic civil and political rights such as had featured in the program of prewar social democracy were to be fought for in capitalist and precapitalist countries, but were given a new twist.[5] Suffrage, for example, was described as a "fig leaf" covering dependence and exploitation. Communists were advised to encourage women to use their vote in the interests of the proletariat and revolutionary change, at the same time making clear to them the limitations of parliamentarianism and bourgeois democracy.[6]

The women's movement in postrevolutionary societies was instructed to work for "the inclusion in the public economy of the traditional and now outmoded domestic economy of the individual family, run as it is along the lines of the artisanal production of the medieval guilds, and [for] the transformation of the housewife, the serf of the domestic hearth, into a free participant in the mighty public economy."[7] As a first step in this direction, a number of model public amenities offering services usually provided by the household were to be established. Such demands had never featured in the programs of the Second International. Socialist women in the prewar period might read Engels' *Origin of the Family* and quote approvingly his prediction that "private housekeeping" would be "transformed into a social industry," but for them it remained a prediction, a forecast of events that were to take place after the revolution; in the meantime they confined themselves to the struggle for improved welfare provisions from the bourgeois state.[8] When Lily Braun, a member of the German Socialist Party, published in 1901 a plan for cooperative housing with provisions for community catering and child care, Clara Zetkin, the recognized authority in the party on the Woman Question and the leader of its women's movement, damned it as the "latest blossoming of Utopianism in its most dangerous, opportunistic form."[9] The orthodox view was, in other words, that what might be desirable in a socialist society could be counterproductive at an earlier stage of social development. It was consistent with this view of history unfolding in a series of stages that the *Theses* should suggest measures to eliminate the domestic economy in countries that had already experienced a successful revolution. The *Theses* went further and demanded of communists in capitalist countries that they explain to women the outmoded character of the domestic economy and its waste of time and energy and resources, and that they establish "institutions designed to lighten the position of the working woman, as mistress of the home and as mother, to transfer women's usual household obligations to society, and to complement the domestic upbringing of the child with a system of public upbringing that has been fundamentally overhauled to make it capable of providing an education in that which counts most, in social solidarity."[10] In precapitalist countries, communists were to take measures and to set up institutions "that will convince women by example and experience, that the individual domestic economy leads to their subjugation."[11] The inclusion of these demands in the *Theses* represented a break with the social democratic approach; it suggested that the Woman Question was central to the socialist project, that the liberation of women was cause as well as effect of socialist change.

There was in the period of the Russian revolution a growing recognition of the place of housework in the making of women's subordination. The household, its economic function, social effects, and possible substitutes were all subjects for discussion. Henriette Roland Holst, an influential member of the Dutch Communist Party, described the never-ending routine of household chores:

> Alone in her kitchen or in her small apartment, [the woman] performs the work that is essential for the upkeep of the household. She stands in front of her stove or she sits and mends clothes; whatever she does, the work demands all her concentration. She is never free; there are always other jobs she could be doing. Even if she is lucky enough to have a husband who is good to her, she is still a slave to the polishing and cleaning and cooking and darning and can never say that her work is done.[12]

In a short essay on communism and the family that went through several editions in the first few years after the Russian revolution, Alexandra Kollontai, a prominent Bolshevik, traced the history of the domestic economy to show how the transition from feudal to capitalist relations had affected housework. Whereas peasant women in the old days produced items for sale at the market, she wrote, in modern society the only responsibility of the housewife was to service her family, a job less onerous than it had once been; if previously the housewife knitted her own stockings and made her own jam, nowadays clothes and preserves were bought ready-made, and the spread of public amenities such as shops and restaurants reduced further the variety and importance of domestic tasks, leaving the housewife only the monotonous and repetitive duties of dusting and cleaning day after day.[13] Like Henriette Roland Holst she believed that the work performed free of charge by the housewife for her family should become the responsibility of the community and that the "socialization" of domestic life was an integral part of the creation of a communist society. Inessa Armand, another Bolshevik, the first head of the party's women's department (Zhenotdel), told delegates to the All-Union Congress of Working and Peasant Women in November 1918 that domestic servitude had to be abolished immediately and "not in some distant future."

> The bourgeois system is being done away with. We have entered the period of socialist construction. Private, separate domestic economies have become harmful anachronisms which only hold up and make more difficult the carrying out of new forms of distribution. They must be abolished. The tasks carried out earlier by the housewife for her family within her tiny domestic

economy must become independent branches of social labour. We must replace the thousands and millions of tiny, individual economies with their primitive, unhealthy and badly-equipped kitchens and primitive wash tubs by clean and shining communal kitchens, communal canteens, communal laundries, run not by working women/housewives but by people paid specially to do the job. [14]

Though these theorists identified housework as a source of female oppression and one of the causes of women's political backwardness, they nonetheless insisted that it be accorded the same status as other forms of labor and that its contribution to the economic well-being of communities receive recognition. Sylvia Pankhurst, the militant English suffragist and (by 1917) ardent revolutionary, was quick to correct the British government's Industrial Unrest Commissioners when they spoke in a wartime report of the economic dependence of women. "The men of the mining community are dependent upon the women who cook their meals, wash their clothes and clean their homes," she wrote. "Not merely their comfort, but their earning capacity is increased by the labour of these women."[15] Housewives, in her view, had their part to play in ending the rule of the rich and eliminating the wage slavery of the poor, and she urged women to set up their own committees—Soviets of the Streets—that could tackle local problems and elect delegates to represent them in the wider community.

> The Soviet Revolution is coming, but the working women ought not to wait until it is here to set up their street committees. These are the workshop committees of the mothers, for the streets and the houses they live and work in are *their* workshop. They should start the Soviets of the streets as soon as possible. [16]

The implication here was that household responsibilities were not necessarily a drag on the development of political consciousness and could even serve as the focus for revolutionary activity.

The *Theses* too took it for granted that housewives would take part in the struggles to create the new society, without, though, allocating them a central role. Women were referred to several times as *trudyashchiesya*, a word that caused trouble to Comintern translators who could find nothing better in English than "toiling women." The Russian phrase had none of this awkwardness and encompassed all who worked, whether in the factory or the field or the home. In other words, recognition of the economic contribution of the housewife was built into the vocabulary employed in the *Theses*. There were direct references to housewives as well: in capitalist societies, housewives of the proletariat and unpropertied layers of the population were to be encouraged to participate in election campaigns and if elected their collaboration in the Soviets was to be sought; wives of the laboring masses who wanted to be free of "class and sexual slavery" were enjoined to throw in their lot with the International.[17]

By identifying the reform of the household as a part of the struggle against capitalism instead of a byproduct of socialist revolution the *Theses* were breaking new ground. In other respects they kept within the same theoretical framework as social democracy; like the programmatic documents of the Second International, they made no mention of Marx's prediction that the family would "wither away," nor did they discuss measures that could in the short term create more egalitarian families. In the section on methods of work in capitalist countries, the *Theses* made a passing reference to "egotistical morality," condemned prostitution, and demanded an end to the double morality; communists in precapitalist countries were instructed to eliminate "superstitions, customs, moral values, religious and legal norms which reduce the woman to the role of domestic slave, working for her husband and serving his pleasure."[18] Apart from this there was no hint that the construction of communism might include struggles to change attitudes and patterns of behavior. The *Theses* had nothing to say about the regulation of reproduction and in this too they mirrored the resolutions and other official declarations of the Second International.

The silences of the *Theses* on family and fertility did not indicate lack of concern for these matters among the women who supported the Third International. Alexandra Kollontai, for example, identified the family as an institution of bourgeois oppression and argued that the transition to socialism would necessarily require a restructuring of the family and a reshaping of relationships between men and women and between parents and children. Her short story *Soon*, published in 1922, described the world as she imagined it would be in 1970, a world in which individuals lived in groups based on age and personal preference instead of blood relationship and conventional marriage.[19] She wrote elsewhere of the pernicious effect of the capitalist system on the moral values of society and on the emotional life of individuals, advocating a new code of behavior based on equality and sensitivity to the dynamics of power in human relationships.[20] Other women with connections to the communist movement—Nelly Roussel and Madeleine Pelletier in France, Stella Browne in Britain, and Crystal Eastman and Rose Pastor Stokes in the United States—argued for the legalization of abortion and the accessibility of contraception. The left-wing Ohio paper *The Toiler*, sympathetic to the communist cause, declared: "If the workers are going to build together a firmer and happier world one of the first steps is to get that knowledge of their own bodies which is an essential part of freedom, and the foundation of an intelligent control of our own lives."[21]

Among the women who gave their support to the new International were erstwhile members of social-democratic parties, including Henriette Roland Holst, Alexandra Kollontai, and Inessa Armand, adherents in the main of the left wing, and active in the socialist women's movement. Others were feminists who had steered clear of the Second International, critical of what they saw as its neglect of women, but who thought that the Comintern would honor its promises of equality and liberation. In France an independent feminist newspaper, Voix des femmes, wrote enthusiastically about the aims and activities of the Bolsheviks and several of its contributors joined the fledgling French Communist Party.[22] Another feminist paper, La Lutte féministe (The Feminist Struggle), changed its name to La Lutte féministe pour le communisme (The Feminist Struggle for Communism); its editor, Hélène Brion, visited Moscow to see for herself the new life that was in the making and subsequently traveled around France speaking for the Soviet cause.[23] Madeleine Pelletier, the anarchist and advocate of women's rights, also journeyed to Russia and came away favorably impressed.[24] Sylvia Pankhurst helped found the British Communist Party. These women believed that the socialist and feminist revolutions for which they had struggled so long were imminent and that a society free from oppression and exploitation was in their grasp. They examined the institutions and ideologies responsible in their view for sexual inequalities and searched for ways to bring justice and freedom for women.

The full range of ideas debated during the revolutionary period did not, then, find expression in the Theses. In 1920, the Bolsheviks were the only communist party to have staged successfully a revolution and it was they who had taken the initiative in calling the First Communist Women's Conference and in preparing the position paper for the occasion. The Theses reflected above all the ideas and preoccupations of the Soviet women delegated to draft them—their certainty that an attack on the "domestic hearth" was of central concern in the struggle for women's emancipation, their low ranking of demands for fertility control, and their view that family and sexuality could be discussed in the press, but should not be mentioned in anything as official as a program.[25] The foreign delegates who debated the draft Theses at the Moscow conference did not raise any serious objections to their content, or suggest any amendments of substance. Most of them, it seems likely, did not share the Bolsheviks' high regard for programmatic statements; none of the feminists recently won to the communist cause, who might well have found the analysis incomplete and the demands imprecise, were among the delegates. Clara Zetkin, unable to attend the conference but in charge of the final editing of the Theses, was in broad agreement with the Bolshevik approach and made few alterations to the text.[26]

More fully than anything produced by the socialist movement previously, the Theses translated into a political program the idea expressed by

Engels in *Origin of the Family* that female emancipation must be a twofold process, incorporating both the entry of women into the national labor force and the socialization of domestic labor. The revolutionary optimism of the Comintern served to place the Woman Question on the immediate agenda, at the same time, discouraging a careful analysis of women's social subordination or its integration into socialist theory: incentive for the communist movement to theorize sexual oppression and its relationship to class exploitation was lacking, because the revolution that would sweep away every vestige of oppression and exploitation was supposed to be at hand. The solution offered in the *Theses* to the problem of women's isolation within the home—the replacement of domestic responsibilities by public amenities—suggested a radical reappraisal of the social order, but the force of this critique was blunted by its narrowly economic emphasis. The domestic household was objected to on grounds of inefficiency and productive irrationality; its contribution to the creation and perpetuation of gender differences was overlooked. The assumption appeared to be that provided women worked for the national economy, the type of work they did was unimportant. References in the *Theses* to women as wives and mothers in the future society reinforced the impression that despite the profound social and economic transformations that revolution would allegedly bring, considerable distinction between the social roles of men and women would remain.

Organizational Prescriptions

The *Theses* presented to the First Women's Conference in 1920 diagnosed organizational shortcomings as partly to blame for the poor showing of the socialist women's movement in the prewar period. The Second International was accused of failing to establish a medium for monitoring the implementation of congress resolutions ("no body was set up to carry out the basic principles and demands of women's equality") or to grant the women's movement representation at congresses and a vote in the International Bureau.[27] Further, it was criticized for leaving the individual parties to decide whether or not to carry out central directives, a delegation of responsibility that was said to have created a "precipice between theory and practice." The organizational structure of the communist women's movement set down in the *Theses* was designed to ensure that this "precipice" would disappear from the political landscape and that henceforth demands for women's emancipation would be implemented without delay or modification. Communist parties were to establish women's agitational commissions at every level, from the local to the national, with permanent representation on the relevant party committee, a full vote on matters relating to women, and a consultative vote on other issues. This organizational pyramid was to be topped by an International Women's Secretariat (IWS) consisting of three to six members elected by the International Communist Women's Conference and with representation on the Executive Committee of the Communist International (ECCI).

The activities of the different levels of the hierarchy were specified in detail. In the localities, agitational committees were to encourage women to support party campaigns, supervise theoretical and practical training, and appoint an editor to the women's page of the local party paper; district committees were to organize conferences, distribute literature, and initiate campaigns; the national committee, over and above these same duties, had responsibility for gathering and circulating information and publishing a journal. The duties of the International Women's Secretariat were listed as follows: maintenance of contacts with and between national committees; collection of informational and agitational material; publication of a journal; and organization of international conferences.[28]

While six pages were devoted to the organizational structure of the women's movement, the relationship between the movement and other women's organizations outside the party was, in contrast, touched upon only in passing. In the section dealing with the history of the prewar period, the Second International was commended for having made "a clear demarcation between the socialist and the bourgeois women's movement."[29] One of the opening paragraphs of the *Theses* indicated why such demarcation was essential:

> Communism, the great emancipator of the female sex, can never be the result of the united struggle of women of all classes for the transformation of bourgeois society. . . . It can be achieved only and exclusively by the united class struggle of women and men of the exploited against the privileges and power of men and women of the exploited classes.[30]

There was no further discussion of the matter anywhere in the text, presumably because the death of the bourgeoisie and all its political organizations was held to be imminent and the hegemony of the proletariat assured. These assumptions proved to be mistaken and the position taken in 1920 was to become, in subsequent years, the subject of controversy.

The relationship between the women's movement and the party was also dealt with in the *Theses* in a couple of sentences: the communist parties were obliged to organize a women's movement, the local and national commissions were instructed to keep in close contact with the national party, and to refer all decisions to the relevant party committees for ratification. Such was the faith of communist women in the revolutionary virtue of the Third International and in its commitment to the emancipation of women that they viewed this subordination with equanimity. The Comintern, however, did not live up to their expectations and in the years to come complaints of the parties' neglect of the women's movement were as frequent as they were bitter; the subordinate role accepted with such casual alacrity in the *Theses* was never shaken off.

The Politics of the Communist Women's Movement, 1920–43

In the years after the First Women's Conference, the feminist influences on the movement rapidly diminished. Feminists did not secure places on committees or on delegations and their ideas lost ground. Hélène Brion, Madeleine Pelletier, Crystal Eastman, Sylvia Pankhurst, and others like them soon ended their association with the communist movement, disillusioned with its politics, which they found authoritarian and insufficiently responsive to the needs of women. Several of those who had come to the Comintern from the left wing of West European social democracy also broke with the communist movement. Stella Browne left to campaign in the British Labour Party; Henrietta Roland Holst, tired of what she called the intellectual suffocation and the dogma of the Comintern, handed in her resignation in 1927; a number of women were expelled for belonging to Trotskyist or other oppositional factions.[31]

The vacancies created by these resignations and expulsions were filled by women of very different political outlook and party status, whose beliefs had not been shaped in an era of suffrage campaigning and feminist debate and for whom the subordination of women in society was not a burning issue. These new leaders rarely carried much weight in the communist hierarchy and were more accustomed to obeying orders than to formulating policies. The loss of Clara Zetkin, who withdrew from active involvement in the International Women's Secretariat (IWS) in the mid-1920s, was a particular blow to the movement because of her high standing within the Comintern and her commitment to maintaining links between the women's sections of the national parties. Thereafter, the international women's movement was organized solely from Moscow. Here too the women's movement had lost its keenest champions (Inessa Armand died in 1920 and Alexandra Kollontai was demoted to diplomatic duties some two years later).[32] They were replaced by women who were neither as dedicated to the cause of emancipation nor as well-placed in the party.

Changes in leadership were paralleled over the years by changes in perspectives and policies. It is not easy to sum up the ideology and campaigning practice of a movement which spanned five continents, whose national sections operated in countries at such various stages of economic and cultural development and with such different political traditions. No generalizations can be entirely satisfactory; nevertheless, despite considerable diversity, certain common patterns are visible: the dual aim, advocated in the *Theses*, of full incorporation of women in public life, at work and in politics, and the reorganization of the private sphere through the socialization of household tasks, was gradually abandoned in favor of a single focus on industrial struggles. Within this productionist perspective the specific interests of women were subordinated to the perceived interests of the working class.

Talk of the elimination of domestic labor was abandoned soon after the First Communist Women's Conference, as hopes for world revolution in the West were dashed. The socialization of the household was judged by the new generation of leaders to be utopian and irrelevant. Neither national party newspapers nor Comintern publications gave the matter coverage, except for the occasional article on the Soviet catering system.[33] During the civil war which followed the Russian revolution hundreds of thousands of Soviet townspeople were fed in state-run dining halls and the Zhenotdel included the extension of this system as one of its campaigning slogans. However, once the war was over canteens came to be seen as a complement to, rather than a replacement for, the private kitchen. The government decision to legalize private trading in 1921 gave the food stores and the markets a new lease on life just as budget reorganization cut the number of canteens and other public amenities. With the years of war and revolution finally over, the majority of the population—the communists as well as the masses, women as well as men—desired a return to familiar patterns of everyday living. Sole responsibility for cooking, cleaning and child care passed once again to the family and the inevitability of this state of affairs was no longer seriously challenged.

Housewives in Soviet Russia were encouraged to join cooperatives, educate themselves and participate in the construction of the new society. In the West they were also called upon to join cooperatives, fight inflation, and support the industrial struggles of their husbands. In the first half of the 1920s, housewives were for many communist women's sections a chief target of ideological and organizational work. They were nevertheless viewed with a certain ambivalence, as possibly a "valuable ally," but more probably, unless properly supervised, a liability, capable of infecting the movement with their petty-bourgeois mentality and of sapping the militancy of their husbands. *International Press Correspondence* observed: "If workers' wives keep back their husbands on the eve of a strike, if the workers' wives persuade their husbands and brothers at a time when armed struggles for power are being prepared, we cannot properly prepare for these struggles."[34]

A housewife in the Soviet Union who wanted to join the party had to produce more references and undergo a longer period of probation than almost any other category of candidate. In many Western countries housewives constituted a large proportion of the membership of the communist women's sections, yet they were still spoken of as "backward" and of less "decisive significance" than proletarian women in the factories.[35] Kate

Gitlow, Secretary of the U.S. United Council of Working-Class House-wives, wrote with satisfaction of how the American worker's wife was learning "that the most important struggle goes on in the industrial field."[36] By 1930 the "excessive proportion of housewives" in the move-ment was a matter for open dissatisfaction.[37] "Work among housewives" was largely dropped, except for propaganda to neutralize their allegedly harmful influence.

While the housewife was looked at with increasing suspicion, hopes were pinned on the "working woman," the paid industrial laborer. By the late 1920s, industrial exploitation was the staple ingredient of communist coverage of the women's movement. The poor conditions, the long hours, and the low wages of working women were regularly documented. A typical article in *International Press Correspondence* reported that ra-tionalization had been introduced at the ribbon mills in the French town of Comines, as a result of which the wages of the textile workers, many of whom were women, dropped by 15 percent.[38] Another described a linen mill in Sofia, operated by girls aged between ten and fifteen, who were more or less confined to the premises, worked in shifts of twelve hours, and in their free time did washing for the manager and cleaned the work-shops.[39] By the end of the decade women's equality was understood primarily in terms of their access to paid employment and participation in factory struggles.

As industrial exploitation became the central concern of the movement, less attention was paid to struggles for abortion and contraception rights, which, while not mentioned in the *Theses*, had been a focus for campaign-ing in some countries during the twenties. A number of postwar Western governments, concerned with the falling birth rate and confident of their right to intervene in the private affairs of individuals, began to enforce more rigorously the anti-abortion legislation already on their books, and even banned the sale of contraceptive devices. Women who needed jobs and wanted to limit the size of their families did not share this anxiety about low population growth nor appreciate state intrusion in their lives; repressive legislation became a source of public resentment, a circum-stance to which communist women in several countries had responded. In Canada they demanded the establishment of Mothers Clinics which would, among other things, provide contraceptives free of charge.[40] In Denmark, they set up the Working Women's Information Bureau (*Arbe-jderkvindernes Oplysningsforbund*), one of whose objects was to make knowledge of birth control available to proletarian women. In Germany, they launched a campaign against Paragraph 218 of the legal code, which banned abortion.

The departure from the communist movement in the early 1920s of several well-known campaigners for abortion and contraception rights had not put an end to debate within the movement, but did alter its parameters.

Communists tended to conflate support for fertility control with neo-Malthusianism, a doctrine of which they were highly critical because it allegedly offered birth control as an alternative to class struggle. They dismissed as reformist the argument that limiting family size would enable working class families to improve their living standards, and considered equally unacceptable the feminist view that every woman had the right to decide if and when she had children. Choice in matters of reproduction was not recognized as women's right. Access to contraception and abortion was viewed rather as a necessary evil that would continue only so long as society was unable to guarantee the material means for a properly prosperous and happy childhood for all. The decree passed in Soviet Russia in 1920, permitting abortions that were performed in state hospitals by trained doctors, gave the present poverty of the country as justification.[41] The communist campaign in Germany against Paragraph 218 constantly tied its attack on the repressive abortion law to the demand for better maternity provisions, rarely mentioning birth control; it was woman's right to motherhood and not to choice that was emphasized. Hertha Sturm's confused and defensive speech at the Third Communist Women's Conference in 1924 exemplified the unease that many communist women felt when forced to confront the question of fertility regulation:

> We all know very well that in a bourgeois state a worker-mother has every right to avoid having children that she cannot feed and bring up. In bourgeois society, the party has conducted and is conducting a fight for the rights of working women to free themselves from hunger and exhausting pregnancy. But this is miles away from some special theory that preaches refusal of maternity as some kind of communist slogan. We must declare merciless war on this petty-bourgeois distortion.[42]

The IWS made no attempt to coordinate local or national campaigns for abortion and contraception rights or to criticize or discipline sections that failed to organize them. In Britain it was left to the socialists to take the initiative. The first national conference of communist women, held in 1924, discussed the international situation, factory conditions, education, and nursing, but made no mention of reproduction; in contrast, the Labour Women's Conference, meeting the same month, passed a resolution in favor of birth control by an overwhelming majority. Three years later a similar resolution was passed by the conference, again with a big majority, earning this rebuke from one of the most senior women members of the communist party: "As a matter of fact the most burning questions concerning women in industry were pushed into the background by the Standing Orders Committee while a long discussion on Birth Control was allowed to take up the time of the conference.[43] Such criticism was to become commonplace over the next few years as the communist women's movement concentrated single-mindedly on industrial struggles. At the beginning of the 1930s, Canadian communists ceased their agitation for contraception, and even in in Germany, where at the end of the 1920s a major attack against Paragraph 218 had been launched, campaigning was scaled down and subjected to strict party control.[44]

The vision of a new world free of exploitation and oppression had encouraged the communists to challenge sexual inequalities and promise an end to women's social subordination; as the vision faded so too did hopes for the radical restructuring of women's lives. By the beginning of the 1930s, the campaigning of the communist women's movement was limited in most countries to defending the working and living conditions of the proletariat and supporting the various political offensives of the communist parties, which had little relevance to the specific interests of women. When in 1935, the Seventh World Congress of the Communist International belatedly recognized the menace of fascism and authorized political alliances with other parties and groups outside the communist movement, women were urged to participate in campaigns for democracy and peace. This change of tactic was successful in attracting women to the communist movement, and in some countries the women's sections took a new lease on life. There was no return, however, to the radical and feminist concerns of the *Theses*; instead, the Comintern promoted a traditional view of women as wives and mothers who instinctively abhorred tyranny and war.

Organizational Practice 1920–43

While the perspectives and policies of the *Theses* were abandoned, the organizational prescriptions laid down for national communist parties, disregarded or followed selectively and sporadically at first, were gradually imposed, though for reasons and with consequences other than those envisaged by the First Communist Women's Conference.

In the years immediately following the 1920 conference, the IWS frequently circulated reminders to the communist parties of their obligation to undertake "work among women." If communist parties were sluggish in their response, the IWS put pressure on them to change; if work was carried out in an unorthodox fashion, the Secretariat showed more tolerance than a reading of the *Theses* might have led one to expect. When communist women in Holland chose to join an already existing independent revolutionary socialist women's union, instead of setting up a women's section of the party, *Die Kommunistishche Fraueninternationale*, the official journal of the IWS, to whom the Dutch women had sent a letter explaining their decision, expressed disapproval; the editors characterized the communist women's movement in Holland as "organisationally and ideologically still in its infancy," its members as "comrades who 'seek communism with their souls' but have not as yet conquered the world of communist theory."[45] Nevertheless, they published the Dutch women's report and made no suggestion that disciplinary proceedings be started against them. It was assumed that the getting of wisdom took time and that the Dutch women would eventually themselves recognize the error of their ways.

In the mid and late 1920s a very different attitude was adopted toward those who strayed from the path of orthodoxy. Learning from experience was a luxury that the IWS was no longer prepared to afford, and any failure to comply with organizational norms was construed as evidence of unsound political tendencies. The most common unorthodoxy at this stage was not the failure of parties to establish a women's movement (sections were in existence almost everywhere) but the isolation of these sections from their national parties, a circumstance said to foster feminist and reformist deviationism. The offenders were ordered to conform, and eventually they did; by the early 1930s close relations between the sections and the parties had finally been established.

Views on the proper relationship between the communist women's movement and noncommunist organizations underwent a similar evolution. In the early 1920s, the appropriateness of the organizational exclusiveness advocated by the *Theses* was called into question; the assumption that communist women would work always within party confines and never seek outside alliances was felt by many to be too restrictive. Feminist organizations remained small and weak during this period, but the Second International, far from disappearing from the historical scene as the Comintern had once predicted, made a remarkable comeback. In the competition between reformist and revolutionary politics, the communists were the losers right across the board, not excepting the struggle for the hearts and votes of women. Furthermore, apart from the thousands of proletarian women who joined social democratic parties, there were the millions who remained outside the orbit of any political party. If the communist women's sections worked only within their national parties they would doom themselves, it was feared, to irrelevance.

In the discussion about ways of broadening the appeal of the communist women's movement, Clara Zetkin took a prominent part; supported by fellow German communist Hertha Sturm, she argued in the IWS for flexibility and urged the creation of women's organizations that were outside the party and formally separate from it, able to spread the communist message beyond the small band of the faithful and bring together women from diverse social backgrounds and with a range of political allegiances. A number of sections, in fact, created so-called non-party organizations quite independently of the debate within the International Women's Secretariat: the Working Women's Information Bureau was one case in point; the Canadian Federation of Women's Labor Leagues, set up by communist women in Toronto in 1924, was another.[46] Doubts about the ideological soundness of such organizational forms were soon raised and toward the end of the 1920s doubt became certainty. The Secretariat condemned nonparty organizations and cautioned the women's movement against such initiatives. Initially these instructions were not always heeded, but by the time the Canadian Federation of Women's Labor Leagues was disbanded in 1931, a very large degree of organizational uniformity had already been achieved.[47] From then on, until the introduction of popular frontism at the Seventh World Congress, the communist women's movement kept itself to itself. The letter if not the spirit of the *Theses* had triumphed.

The implementation of the *Theses* at the international level was far less successful. Whereas the Comintern, up until its sudden dissolution in 1943, held frequent congresses or plenums, published journals, and maintained a large organization, the international apparatus of the communist women's movement had all but disappeared by the mid-1920s. A sub-bureau set up in Berlin in 1921 to coordinate activities in Western Europe was closed in 1924 and the following year the movement's official journal, *Die Kommunistische Fraueninternationale*, stopped publication.[48] The last international conference of the women's movement was held in 1926.[49] The IWS itself, entrusted by the *Theses* with the task of coordinating the international movement, remained throughout the 1920s a small and shadowy body and by the early 1930s had effectively ceased to function. All institutional means for the sharing of experience and the exchange of opinion had been dismantled, leaving in place only a channel for the dispatch of directives from the center.

Unfavorable Climates

The history of the interwar period confounded communist expectations. Instead of communist revolution, the world experienced the Depression and the rise of fascism; instead of gaining in size and influence, the international women's movement remained small and powerless.

On the face of it the prospects for the communist women's movement in the years after the Russian revolution had seemed good. A Swiss communist woman, Minna Tobler-Christingen, remembered:

> In the historical years 1918 and 1919 there were optimists who believed that the working woman was about to emerge from her passivity and become an active and historically decisive factor in the labour movement. Even greater optimists believed that in the coming struggles the working women would not only take an active part but a leading one.[50]

In the immediate postwar period European women had been advised to return to the home and many were given no choice but to hand over their jobs to the soldiers back from the fronts. Employers were quick to relearn the advantages of a female workforce and the number of gainfully employed women was before long on the increase. The number of single women and of women-headed families had risen sharply as a consequence of the war, and more and more women were forced to seek employment. The female membership of trade unions continued to rise and this was interpreted by the communist movement as a sign of militancy to come. Housewives and mothers were also expected to turn in ever larger numbers to the International as they experienced "the endlessly increasing cares, deprivations, sufferings and hardships" of capitalist society and struggled to cope with rising prices and the housing crisis. [51]

In the event, few women displayed industrial or political militancy or flocked to join the International. Paid employment and trade union membership failed to serve as an apprenticeship to communist politics in the way the Comintern had hoped. The introduction of technology and the de-skilling that went with it gave management a greater measure of control over the workforce. More women were chasing a limited number of jobs, and those who succeeded in finding work were not disposed to quibble about rates of pay or conditions of work. At home, women were too preoccupied with the task of making ends meet to have energy and enthusiasm for politics. The networks of friendship and neighborhood support that in times past had formed the basis for protest movements against prices and other local grievances were less visible in this period, perhaps because migration, the growth of cities, and the changes in domestic and family life had undermined the previous pattern of urban communities. As Minna Tobler-Christingen sadly observed, optimism had been misplaced and women "scarcely came to the fore, either as mass or as an active element."[52] Faced with such unfavorable climates, there could be no question of following blindly the policies listed in the *Theses*; campaigns had to be trimmed to the times.

In the Shadow of the Comintern

The women's movement operated under considerable constraints, yet its reorientation should not be interpreted merely as an inevitable adaptation to the narrower political interests of its constituency in the interwar period. Demands for the transformation of the domestic household and an end to bourgeois morality may well have evoked little support among the majority of women in this period. The female masses, though, were less homogeneous than communist rhetoric tended to assume, and the young, the unmarried, the urban, and the educated were not interested only in the politics of the workplace, as the success of local campaigns for birth control and against repressive abortion legislation indicated. At the end of the 1920s the communist women's movement in fact argued its more or less exclusive focus on industrial struggles not on the grounds that these were the ones that mattered to proletarian women at that particular time, but that these were the only ones that were ideologically correct. Concern for motherhood benefits or an interest in matters of sexual hygiene were condemned as symptoms of petty-bourgeois and feminist deviationism.

This change of direction cannot be explained solely by the unfavorable conditions for communist campaigning; neither can it be explained solely by the movement's flawed theoretical premises. The *Theses* of 1920 were imprecise in their definition of sexual inequality, left unresolved the problematic relation between the struggle for female emancipation and the struggle for socialism, and by ascribing primacy to class divisions undoubtedly opened the way for a future revision of theory that would relegate still further the Woman Question within the catalog of communist concerns. However, direction was changed gradually, over a number of years, more rapidly in some countries than in others, more thoroughly over some issues than over others, and not without fierce internal conflict. Unraveling the pace and pattern of these developments and the significance of ideological debates and political battles is crucial for understanding the history of the communist women's movement.

Changes in the leadership of the women's movement reflected, albeit sometimes with considerable time lag, developments within the Comintern: when the Comintern discovered a "left deviation" in its ranks, "leftists" were sooner or later expelled from the women's movement; when "rightwingers" were declared the enemy, the women's sections eventually took up the hunt. Any study of the history of the communist women's movement must address the question of the relationship between the women's sections and their national parties, between the women's sections and the Comintern. The metamorphosis of the women's movement remains incomprehensible unless it is seen in the context of the history of the Comintern itself.

The women's sections were locked into the hierarchical structure of the communist movement, subordinate to the national parties and ultimately to the central apparatus of the Comintern. Even when, by default, they enjoyed a degree of autonomy, they could never entirely escape their dependent status. The Congress of the International was the supreme policymaking body of the communist movement and its resolutions were binding on all sections of the movement. The slogans communist women adopted and the campaigns they waged were formulated in response to Comintern decisions, passed down to them via the national parties. When at its Third Congress in 1921, the International announced a temporary "stabilization of the capitalist system," the women's movement had to adjust its policies accordingly; when in 1928 the Sixth World Congress predicted the imminence of wars and revolutions, further revisions were required. As well as being dependent upon the national parties and the Comintern for their political line, women's sections relied on them for the funds with which to print their newspapers and pamphlets, to hire halls, and to run campaigns.

This ideological and organizational dependence served from 'the very beginning as a brake upon the movement, instituting inequalities of power and inhibiting debate and initiative. Undoubtedly, though, the burden was carried far more lightly in the early years than it was from the mid-1920s onward, when the Stalinist system in the Soviet Union began to take shape and the centralizing tendencies of the Comintern became firmly entrenched. After world revolution failed to materialize, the Bolsheviks faced the task of governing a country that was still overwhelmingly rural and unindustrialized, without outside assistance. Under the pressures of economic underdevelopment and international isolation, the state, instead of withering away, grew inordinately. The party changed in style and direction as its ranks were swelled by new members, for whom socialist ideals and democratic practices were less important than economic progress and personal advancement. The party elite became all-powerful, crushing, first, all political groups outside the party (including the other socialists) and, then, all internal oppositions. As it became clear that for the immediate future the Bolsheviks would remain the only communists in government, their authority within the Comintern grew, until to challenge it was interpreted as nothing less than an act of treachery. The Bolsheviks' brand of Marxism, deterministic and productionist, became compulsory for all, and their every twist and turn of policy was to be slavishly followed. At the Fifth Comintern Congress held in 1924, a program of "Bolshevization" was launched; foreign parties were instructed to model themselves on the Russians, firstly by recognizing the proletariat as the chief target of campaigns ("Face to the Factories" was the watchword) and secondly by reorganizing party cells on an industrial instead of a residential basis.

"Bolshevization" marked an important stage in the political marginalization of the Woman Question and the women's movement. Nonindustrial struggles were downgraded and eventually pronounced ideologically unsound. Thus a speaker at the 10th plenum of the Executive Committee of the Communist International (ECCI) leveled the following accusation against rightwingers:

> In times of big economic conflict they took them to botanical gardens, spoke to them of the electrification of the home, but did not tell them about the wage problem. I could give you dozens of examples showing that the work amongst women was done in such a way as to keep them away from the struggles of the working class. [53]

Women and the working class came to be regarded as mutually exclusive categories, and for communists it became increasingly hard to understand how "work among women" contributed to the class struggle. Better conditions of work and pay for the woman worker were the only legitimate demands, and even these were in danger of being lost as the emphasis on proletarian unity obscured the special interests of women within the working class. By the mid-1920s the number of women writing for the communist press and the number of articles on women's issues had fallen sharply.[54] And while the Third and Fourth World Congresses devoted a whole session to the discussion of the Woman Question, the Fifth Congress in 1924 confined itself to a brief resolution, and plenums later in the decade gave the matter an even more cursory treatment.

The organizational marginalization of the women's movement followed a similar course. The status of the international women's movement within the Comintern, already low, fell even further.[55] This was partly as a result of changes within the women's movement itself, such as the emergence of a new and less influential leadership and the closing of *Die Kommunistische Fraueninternationale* after Clara Zetkin stood down as editor. These were not entirely internal matters, though, since it was the Comintern that set the official pecking order and took decisions about journal publications; it could, if it so chose, have conceded greater importance within the movement to representatives of the IWS and allocated funds for a new women's journal. Comintern indifference to the fate of the women's movement was a major reason for the gradual decline of its international apparatus. Far from making an effort to reverse this process, the Comintern acted to hasten it. The new statute of the ECCI passed at the "Bolshevization" Congress in 1924 ruled that members of the Secretariat were to be appointed by the Executive Committee instead of elected by the international women's conference. As Soviet control of the International increased, as administration was centralized and initiative crushed, the existence of auxiliary bodies such as the IWS became inconvenient and superfluous. In April 1926, the Secretariat lost its independent status, becoming the women's department of the ECCI.[56]

At the national level the story was very much the same. As early as 1921, when the women's sections were still in the process of formation, the first complaints against the communist parties for their cavalier attitude toward the women's movement were heard. At the Third Comintern Congress, all three representatives of the IWS spoke of the lack of support from the communist parties for their work; one of them, the French delegate Lucie Colliard, began her speech with the following words: "Comrades, I am speaking on behalf of the women communists, but first of all I must make it clear that I have been sent here by a communist party which has never done anything to attract women to its ranks."[57]

Over the next few years the French Communist Party did nothing to improve its record. In October 1922 the women's paper *L'Ouvrière* ceased publication for several months, the party pleading lack of funds, and five years later it was closed down again, this time for good; in 1925 the party arranged a meeting to commemorate the Paris Commune for March 8, obliging the women to move their celebration of International Women's Day to another date.[58] During 1927, the party journal *Cahiers du Bolchevisme* published only one article on women.[59] The French party may have been particularly recalcitrant but it was by no means exceptional. As national parties implemented Bolshevization they took their cue from the Comintern and crossed the Woman Question off their agendas, relegating their women's sections to the sidelines.

Organizational orthodoxy was a stick that the Comintern and the national parties could use to impose their political will. Though many of the new generation of leaders of the women's movement were, as we have seen, willing to accept orders from above and zealously call for orthodoxy and conformity, there was also considerable resistance to Bolshevization, as the debate about the so-called delegates meetings indicated. The delegates meeting, a type of organization employed for many years and with considerable success in Soviet Russia, was first championed by the central apparatus of the Comintern in 1923, and was promoted persistently over the next couple of years as a replacement for nonparty organizations, of which the Comintern disapproved.[60] In the USSR, the elections of delegates and their activities when in office had always been firmly supervised and controlled by the women's department and ultimately by the party, and it was this aspect of their operation that the Comintern officials found to their liking, just as the difficulty of policing activities outside the communist movement was the chief reason for their negative attitude toward nonparty organizations. Despite a string of resolutions passed by the Comintern in 1925 and 1926 declaring the superiority of delegates meetings, some women's sections were slow to try them or to give up nonparty organizations.[61] The marginalization of the IWS and of the national women's sections in the mid-1920s was thus not simply the desire of a central bureaucracy to streamline its organizational structure; the women's movement contained stubborn and disobedient elements whose power to influence events, however small, was not to be countenanced. While the interventions of the Comintern to this end did not everywhere achieve immediate success, time was on its side. As Moscow extended its hold over the national parties, the reflex of discipline was learned, and if women's sections were unwilling to reform themselves, the Comintern was only too willing to do it for them.

Conclusions

The communist women's movement was launched in the wake of the Russian revolutions, which had toppled the 300-year-old Romanov dynasty, proclaimed "proletarian dictatorship," and promised a new world. For socialists of the Left this was a period of unprecedented optimism and all manner of utopian ideas flourished. Not surprisingly in such a climate there was an attempt to rethink the relationship between the Woman Question and the socialist revolution. Women's right to equality in the public sphere was reaffirmed and plans for the socialization of the household and of domestic labor were made. But hopes were disappointed. The IWS remained weak and ineffectual. It abandoned the principles on which it had originally based itself. The struggle for emancipation came to be understood in terms of the workplace, and other inequalities in women's lives were ignored. By the end of the 1920s, any special emphasis on women's social subordination in communist propaganda or campaigning came to be regarded as a capitulation to bourgeois feminism; the movement's aim was no longer the advancement of women but their mobilization for the advancement of the Comintern.

The reorientation of the communist women's movement was more than a question of adapting strategy and tactics in the face of economic depression and an absence of working-class militancy; it reflected a fundamental shift in political outlook. Since the women's sections were tied ideologically and organizationally to their national parties, explanations for the change of direction must ultimately be sought in the history of the Comintern: the rise of the Stalinist system in the USSR, the dominance of the Soviet party within the communist movement, and the increasing centralization of the Comintern apparatus accentuated and institutionalized the already existing tendency to overlook gender as a source of conflict and a site of struggle.

The Comintern proved as incapable as its predecessor of integrating the ideas and practices of socialism and feminism. Indeed, the Comintern would seem to have provided a less favorable environment for the pursuit of feminist aims, its hierarchical structure and its overwhelming focus on production and the public sphere allowing little space for the development of politics that were responsive to gender as well as class relations. If the history of the IWS underlines the importance of political autonomy for women, it also suggests that unless the central theoretical principles and organizational practices of socialist movements are rethought and reconstructed, women's movements will continue to live in their shadow.

Notes

The major general histories of the Comintern, such as J. Braunthal, *History of the International* (London: Nelson, 1967) and F. Claudin, *The Communist Movement* (New York: Monthly Review Press, 1975), make no mention of the communist women's movement. A number of recent books and articles specifically address aspects of the national and international history of the women's movement: Aurelia Camparini, *Questione femminile e terza internazionale* (Bari: De Donato, 1978); Silvia Kontos, *Die Partei kampft wie ein Mann* (Frankfurt: Roter Stern, 1979); Robert F. Wheeler, "German Women and the Communist International: The Case of the Independent Social Democrats," *Central European History*, June 1975, pp. 113–39; D. Tartakowsky, "Le PCF et les femmes (1926)," *Cahiers d'histoire de l'institut Maurice Thorez*, no. 14 (1975): 194–99; J. Heinen, "De la l-ere e le ll-e Internationale, la question des femmes," *Critique Communiste*, no. 20–21 (1977–78): 109–79; Atina Grossmann, "Abortion and Economic Crisis: The 1931 Campaign Against Paragraph 218 in Germany," *New German Critique*, no. 14, (1978): 119–37 (reprinted in Renate Bridenthal, et al., eds., *When Biology Became Destiny* (New York: Monthly Review Press, 1984); A. Buttafuoco, "The Feminist Challenge," in C. Boggs and D. Plotke, eds., *The Politics of Eurocommunism* (Boston: South End Press, 1980), pp. 197–219.

In the writing of this chapter I have also drawn on the documents and contemporary press reports of the international women's movement.

I am grateful to the many people who have shared with me their knowledge of communist movements and communist women's movements, in particular to Juliet Ash, Martin Durham, Holly Kirkconnell, and Eva Schmidt.

1. No one has yet written a comprehensive history of the socialist women's movements associated with the Second International. See Jean Quataert, *Reluctant Feminists in German Social Democracy* 1885–1917 (Princeton: Princeton University Press, 1979), pp. 228–40, for a discussion of European socialist women's movements, and Charles Sowerwine, *Sisters or Citizens?: Women and Socialism in France Since* 1876, (Cambridge: Cambridge University Press, 1982), pp. 117–23 for information on the Stuttgart and Copenhagen conferences.
2. "Tezisy po kommunisticheskomu dvizheniyu sredi zhenshchin, vyrabotannye komissiei vo glave s tov. Klaroi Tsetkin i utverzhedennye kommunisticheskim Internatsionalom," in P. Vinogradskaya, ed., *Pervaya mezhdunarodnaya konferentsiya kommunistok* (Moscow, 1920), p. 100.
3. The *Theses* were edited by a commission elected at the First Conference of Communist Women and submitted for ratification to the Third Comintern Congress in 1921. The edited version was published in *Kommunisticheskii Internatsional* ("Proekt tezisov dlya kommunisticheskogo zhenskogo dvizheniya,") no. 15 (1920): 3452–72, and, with slight stylistic variation, as an appendix to the report of the proceedings of the First Communist Women's Conference, "Tezisy po kommunisticheskomu dvizheniyu sredi zhenshchin, vyrabotannye komissiei vo glave s. tov. Klaroi Tsetkin i utverzhdennye kommunisticheskom Internationalom," pp. 99–123). All references below are to this latter text.
4. "Tezisy," pp. 104–5.
5. The Erfurt program adopted by the German Socialist Party in 1891 had sought "the abolition of all laws which discriminate against women as compared with men in the public or private legal sphere." See W. Thonnessen, *The Emancipation of Women: The Rise and Decline of the Women's Movement in German Social Democracy* 1863–1933 (London: Pluto, 1976), p. 47. By the early twentieth century almost all socialist parties were committed to the fight for women's civil rights, in particular the franchise.
6. "Tezisy," p. 115.
7. Ibid., pp. 102 and 113–4.
8. Friedrich Engels, "Origin of the Family, Private Property and the State," in *Karl Marx and Friedrich Engels, Selected Works* (Moscow: Progress Publishers, 1970), p. 503.
9. Letter from Clara Zetkin to Karl Kautsky, quoted by Quataert, *Reluctant Feminists*, p. 122.
10. "Tezisy," p. 116.
11. Ibid., p. 117.

12. H. Roland Holst, "L'Homme et la femme dans la classe ouvrière," L'Ouvriere, April 7, 1923.
13. A. Kollontai, *Sem'ya i kommunisticheskoe gosudarstvo* (Moscow, 1919), included as "Communism and the Family" in *Selected Writings*, trans. Alix Holt (London: Allison and Busby, 1977), pp. 53–56.
14. I. Armand, "Osvobozhdenie ot domashnego rabstva," *Kommunisticheskaya partiya i organizatsiya rabotnits. Sbornik statei, rezolyutsii i instruktsii* (Moscow, 1919), pp. 31–34. An abridged version of this article is included in a selection of Inessa Armand's writings published in the Soviet Union in 1975 (I. F. Armand, *Stat'i rechi pis'ma* [Moscow, 1975], pp. 65–67). Of the passage quoted above the second and third sentences have been omitted. Evidently these days the tiny domestic economy is not regarded as an anachronism.
15. E. Sylvia Pankhurst, "The Home and the Housewife," *Workers Dreadnought*, October 13, 1917.
16. "The Soviets of the Streets: An Appeal to Working Women," *Workers Dreadnought*, March 27, 1920.
17. "Tezisy," p. 115 and p. 112. In postrevolutionary society, it was expected that everyone would have employment in the "national economy" and no one would be engaged exclusively in housework, hence in this instance the *Theses* called on all women (rather than specifically housewives) to fight for the "creation, formation and administration of those institutions which aim to lighten the position of the woman-housewife and woman-mother."
18. "Tezisy," p. 117.
19. Kollontai, *Skoro, ili cherez 48 let* (Omsk, 1922).
20. Kollontai, *Novaya moral' i rabochii klass* (Moscow, 1918); "Tezisy o kommunisticheskoi morali v oblasti brachnykh otnoshenii," *Kommunistka*, nos. 12–13 (1921): 28–34; "Pis'ma k trudyashcheisya molodezhi," *Molodaya gvardiya*, no. 1–2 (1922): 137–44; "Pis'mo vtoroe. Moral' orudie klassovogo gospodstva i klassovoi bor'by," *Molodaya gvardiya*, no. 6–7 (1922):128–36.
21. G. Nafe, "The Strike and the Wife," *The Toiler*, December 4, 1920.
22. In September 1921, *Voix des Femmes* included a front-page article by Charles Rappoport entitled "Pourquoi les femmes doivent être communistes?" ("Why should women be communists?").
23. In an article published early in 1921 in *The Communist International* ("One of the Aims of French Communism," nos. 16–17, p. 101) Hélène Brion wrote: "For us women . . . the Russian revolution is doubly interesting because it is practically realising the principles of emancipation in both respects: as workers and as women."
24. For an account of her journey and her impressions of Soviet Russia, see M. Pelletier, *Mon voyage aventureaux en Russie communiste* (Paris: Marcel Giard, 1922).
25. The legalization of abortion in Soviet Russia in November 1920, a few months after the First Communist Women's Conference, was in the main the work of lobbying by doctors and lawyers. Delegates at the Second Communist Women's Conference in 1921 attended a meeting on the "New Morality" but omitted any reference to the topic in the documents passed at its sessions.
26. The original Soviet draft has not been available. Clara Zetkin wrote an introduction to the edited version of the *Theses* defending sections of the document that, she said, might seem "superfluous to the Russian women." Presumably the issues she picked out as requiring comment—the attitude to be taken by the communist movement in the capitalist countries to the suffrage movement, and the demands, again in the capitalist countries, for full political and legal rights for women, for equal education and access to professional employment, and for maternity protection—can be taken as the ones she had inserted into the original draft. See K. Tsetkin, "Vvedenie k russkomu izdaniyu

tezisov po internatsional'nomu kommunisticheskomu zhenskomu dvizheniyu," *Kommunisticheskii Internatsional*, no. 16 (1920): pp. 3945–50.

27. "Tezisy," p. 111.

28. Ibid., pp. 118–23.

29. Ibid., p. 109. The conference of socialist women held in 1907 in Stuttgart had resolved that "socialist women must not ally themselves with the feminists of the bourgeoisie, but lead the battle side by side with the socialist parties." See Sowerwine, *Sisters or Citizens*, p. 118. Many parties, it should be noted, resisted all attempts at demarcation and continued in spite of this resolution to form alliances with feminists.

30. "Tezisy," p. 103–4.

31. For biographical information on Henriette Roland Holst, see B. Lazitch and M. M. Drachkovich, *Biographical Dictionary of the Comintern* (Stanford: Hoover Institution, 1973), pp. 344–45. Stella Browne is the subject of Sheila Rowbotham's *A New World for Women: Stella Browne—Socialist Feminist* (London: Pluto, 1977).

32. Alexandra Kollontai was one of the leaders of the Workers Opposition, a group that at the Tenth Congress of the Russian Communist Party in 1921 opposed official policy on the trade unions and challenged party perspectives on the economic and political development of the country.

33. A. Chalatov, "The Participation of Women Workers in the Activities of Public Feeding," *International Press Correspondence*, no. 87 (1925): 1322–23.

34. Vassiliev, "Work Among Working Women," *International Press Correspondence*, no. 10 (1931): 188.

35. E. Baum, "The Women's Question at the IV World Congress," *International Press Correspondence*, no. 2 (1923): 29.

36. K. Gitlow, "Women's Work in the United States," *International Press Correspondence*, no. 31 (1927): 642.

37. See "The Work Among Women and the Task of the Communist Parties. Resolution Adopted by the Conference of the Chiefs of Women's Departments of European Communist Parties', *International Press Correspondence*, no. 49 (1930): 1023–28.

38. Y. Robert, "The Life of the Working Women in the Textile Industry in France," *International Press Correspondence*, no. 73 (1928): 1341–42.

39. S. Blagojeva, "The Working Conditions of Women in Bulgaria," *International Press Correspondence*, no. 75 (1928): 1459.

40. The first birth control bureau in Canada was reportedly opened in the small town of Kitchener, Ontario, by a footwear manufacturer, Mr. Kaufmann, the second by a philanthropic widow, Mary Hawkins. See T. M. Bailey, *For the Public Good: A History of the Birth Control Clinic and the Planned Parenthood Society of Hamilton, Ontario, Canada* (Hamilton: Planned Parenthood Society, n.d.). The sale or display of birth control devices was illegal in Canada at this time (the ban was not lifted until 1969) and communist women, who lacked the social status and the respectability enjoyed by shoe manufacturers and philanthropists, were no doubt anxious to keep on the right side of the law. It is more than likely, though, that they provided information and assistance in an informal way. *The Working Woman*, the paper of the Women's Labor Leagues, whose editor Flora Custance was a Communist Party member, noted that after Mr. Winthrow had delivered a lecture on birth control to the Toronto Women's Labor League, several women asked him for his card. See "Notes and Happenings," *The Working Woman*, no. 1 (1926): 2–3.

41. "Decree on the Legalisation of Abortions of November 18, 1920," in R. Schlesinger, *The Family in the USSR: Documents and Readings* (London: Routledge & Kegan Paul, 1949), p. 44.

42. L. Reisner, "Na mezhdunarodnoi konferentsii kommunistok," *Pravda*, July 15, 1924. Reisner does not provide a verbatim report; this passage from Hertha Sturm's speech is

her paraphrase. The proceedings of the Third Communist Women's Conference were never published and the fullest record available is the press coverage.

43. C. Cant, "The British Labour Women's Conference," *International Press Correspondence*, no. 37 (1927): 790.

44. Atina Grossman, "Abortion and Economic Crisis: The 1931 Campaign Against Paragraph 218 in Germany," *New German Critique*, no. 14 (1978): 136 (reprinted in Bridenthal et al., eds., *When Biology Became Destiny.*).

45. "Nachschrift der Redaktion," *Die Kommunistische Fraueninternatsionale*, no. 1 (1921): 23–25.

46. The origins of the Women's Labor Leagues are obscure. Holly Kirkconnell dates the first one to Fort William in 1919 (see "The Women's Labor Leagues of Canada," unpublished paper, University of Toronto, 1978, p. 1, but according to *Canada's Party of Socialism: History of the Communist Party of Canada* 1921–1976 (Toronto: Progress Books, 1982, p. 32), the leagues were already in existence in the prewar period. At the Fourth Communist Women's Conference in Moscow in 1926, Hertha Sturm remarked on the enormous number of proletarian women's organizations that existed despite the fact that the women's movement had earlier "categorically rejected any form of special women's organization" (see "On the International May Conference Among Women," *International Press Correspondence*, no. 44 [1926]: 723).

47. In 1931 the Women's Labor Leagues were ordered to disband and affiliate to the communist-controlled Workers' Unity League. "After this point," writes Holly Kirkconnell (p. 22) "the information about the Women's Labor Leagues ends."

48. *Die Kommunistische Fraueninternationale* was published only in German, but the subbureau had translated the most important material into other languages. See H. Sturm, "Past and Future of the International Communist Women's Movement," *International Press Correspondence*, no. 17 (1922): 125.

49. It is symptomatic of the low ranking of the women's movement within the Comintern that historians have been uncertain of the conference dates. W. S. Sworakovski, in *The Communist International and Its Front Organizations* (Stanford: Hoover Institution, 1968, p. 461), writes of the international women's movement as follows: "Comintern records reveal that an international women's consultation took place during the founding Congress in 1919 and three international conferences of communist women took place in 1921, 1924 and 1926." According to *The Red Notebook: The Communist International at Work* (London, 1939, p. 17), the "Women's Communist International" was founded in 1925.

50. M. Tobler-Christingen, "The Swiss Working Women's Movement," *International Press Correspondence*, no. 11 (1929): 189.

51. "Tezisy," p. 105.

52. Tobler-Christingen, "Swiss Working Women's Movement," p. 189.

53. Comrade Moirova, "10th plenum of ECCI," *International Press Correspondence*, no. 48 (1929): 1025. In 1929, the Bolshevik party launched a campaign against Bukharin and his followers, accusing them of "right deviationism." Over the next few years all opponents—and imaginary opponents—of the Comintern line were labeled "right-wingers."

54. Articles on strikes published in the communist press during the late 1920s and 1930s rarely provide information on the sex breakdown of the workforce or on any special demands made by the women. Examples of this blind spot are E. Gere, "Nekotorye uroki stachki tekstil'shchikov v Frantsii," *Kommunisticheskii internatsional*, no. 7 (1938): 54–63, and G. Reiman, "Sotsial'nyi upadok germanskogo rabochego klassa i razyitie sotsial'noi differentsiatsii," *Kommunisticheskii internatsional*, no. 31 (1931): 36–43.

A lengthy article in the same journal in 1938, on the twenty-fifth anniversary of the death of August Bebel, omitted any mention of his advocacy of women's rights or of his famous book *Woman and Socialism*. See V. Pik, "Avgust Bebel (k 25-i godovshchine so dnya smerti 1840–1913)," *Kommunisticheskii Internatsional*, no. 7 (1938): 22–31.

55. Even in the early 1920s the international women's movement ranked lower than the youth movement. According to Tivel, the compiler of a book of documents and statistical information on the first five years of the Comintern (5 *let Kominterna v resheniyakh i tsifrakh*, M., 1924, p. 18), six youth organizations at the Second Congress had full voting rights and no fewer than twenty-eight at the Third, while national women's organizations had no representatives at the Second Congress and only one with a consultative vote at the Third. The same author reports that between the Third and Fourth congresses the Presidium of the Executive Committee of the Comunist International discussed youth twenty-one times, Profintern ten times, Sportintern four times, and the IWS six times (p. 45).

56. *Tatigkeitsbericht der Exekutive der Kommunistischen Internationale*, February-November 1926 (Hamburg, 1926), p. 32.

57. *Protokoll des 111 Kongress der Kommunistischen Internationale, Moskau, 22. Juni bis 12. Juli 1921* (Hamburg, 1921), pp. 923–24.

58. S. Blagojeva, *Istoriya 8 marta* (Moscow, 1928), p. 10.

59. Jean-Louis Robert, "Die Kommunistische Partei Frankreichs und Die Frauenfrage 1920–1939," unpub. paper, p. 3.

60. In Soviet Russia, delegates were elected at meetings of working women in the factories and of housewives in residential districts. They attended literacy and political classes and worked for Soviet departments, usually those of health and education, visiting day-care centers, assisting with homeless children, and the like.

61. E. H. Carr provides a brief discussion of the debates on delegates meetings in *Socialism in One Country 1924–1926* (Harmondsworth: Penguin, 1972), pp. 1018–24. See also "Organisation Conference on the Work Among Women Arranged by the Organisation and Women's Departments of the Comintern during the Session of the Enlarged Executive on 5 and 6 April 1925," *International Press Conference*, no. 56 (1925): 765–73, and H. Sturm, "On the International May Conference on Work Among Women," *International Press Conference*, no. 44 (1926): 723–24.

Part 2
The First Experiments

Women, the Family, and the New Revolutionary Order in the Soviet Union

Wendy Zeva Goldman

In 1927, precisely ten years after the October revolution, working-class and peasant women from every corner of the USSR bundled up clothing and provisions and began the long journey to Moscow. Leaving remote peasant huts, crowded working-class dormitories, communal apartments, and eastern tents, they traveled by train, in carts, and on foot, to gather, more than one thousand strong, at the All-Union Congress of Working and Peasant Women to discuss women's liberation.

Many delegates, never before having ventured beyond their local areas, trembled as they approached the podium of the great hall to speak on behalf of the women at home. They spoke passionately of the problems of child care, poverty, family disintegration, and male chauvinism. One woman from Kostroma province succinctly summarized the comments of many speakers. "What hinders us?" she asked. "Women are hindered by difficult material conditions." Other women angrily denounced the men in their villages and factories for their lack of cooperation and their hostility toward women's equality. One woman declared that peasant men were "unconscious, uncultured, and nasty to look at, undermining the work [of women] at every step." Working-class men did not fare much better in the delegates' estimation.[1]

The women's comments combined a powerful understanding of the material obstacles to women's liberation and a wholly new awareness of the role played by patriarchy in their oppression. Although they lacked a theoretical understanding of women's position in society, they tentatively articulated a perspective that combined class and gender in new and unprecedented ways. The congress revealed that despite the enormous poverty and material backwardness of the country, the potential existed for a women's movement composed of working-class and peasant women actively engaged in the struggle for women's equality in the home, the factory, and the village. Empowered and given voice by the first socialist revolution, these women—uneducated, even illiterate—discussed their practical work in terms that could not help but expand the categories of Marxist analysis.

Many contemporary feminists and historians have assessed women's relationship to socialism not in terms of material possibilities or the concrete actions of working women, but rather in terms of ideology and politics. Feminists have penned numerous ideological critiques of Marxism, stressing the need to expand its narrow analytical categories to include the study of gender roles, sexuality, housework, and the power relations between men and women.[2] While many confined their critique to the theoretical realm, others extended this analysis to history, arguing that socialism's failure to liberate women stemmed from an ideological incapacity to conceptualize fully—and therefore to remedy—women's oppression. In the words of the historian Alfred Meyer, "the relative neglect of the 'women question' was built into Marxist theory."[3] Other historians argue that the Bolsheviks never had an independent commitment to women's liberation, but used women to organize support for other ends.[4] Ideology, according to these interpretations, is the ultimate arbiter of the historical process.

Yet the fate of women's liberation in Russia was determined not only by ideology, but by a number of historical factors: the extent of women's participation in the revolution, the presence of self-consciously feminist demands, the degree to which women were organized and capable of representing their interests, the ability of the postrevolutionary state to realize its vision of liberation, and the prevailing material conditions of social life. All of these factors were of course closely interrelated. Women's participation in the revolution influenced their ability to keep their needs before the state, and the material conditions profoundly affected the state's ability to implement its programs.

Although women played a role in the Russian revolution, there was no significant independent feminist group actively committed to socialism. Further, working-class women were slow to participate in strikes and union activity or to voice self-consciously feminist demands. Before 1905, women workers never raised the issue of wage equality with men, nor did they question the segregation of women in low-paying, unskilled jobs. Yet despite their previous passivity, after 1905 women became increasingly involved in strike activity and the workers' movement.[5] With the onset of World War I, they entered production in greater numbers, and by 1917 one-third of Petrograd's factory workers were women. The Bolsheviks, influenced by this growing militance, published a paper for women workers, *Rabotnitsa*, and encouraged women to join factory committees and unions. Split over the question of organizing women, the party moved steadily in 1917 toward a policy of separate organizations for women. Support for the Bolsheviks, in turn, grew among laundresses, domestic servants, restaurant and textile workers, and soldiers' wives. Although the party was theoretically opposed to separate organizations for women, in practice, the success of *Rabotnitsa's* staff resulted in the organization of the Petrograd Conference of Working Women in November 1917 and the formation of the Zhenotdel, or women's department, within the party in 1919.[6]

Throughout the 1920s, the Zhenotdel tried to create a foundation for women's liberation through the establishment of child-care centers, communal dining halls, and other services, but its attempts were limited by a ruined economy and the persistent lack of state resources. Local officials were often hostile to its activities, and the vast majority of its constituency was illiterate, unorganized, and unconscious of their interests as women.[7]

Despite the Zhenotdel's best efforts, material scarcity crippled the Bolshevik vision of liberation, although jurists and party officials maintained their commitment to the "withering-away" of the family, and convocations such as the Women's Congress in 1927 showed the potential of an active socialist women's organization. This potential was cut short in the 1930s with the decision to disband the Zhenotdel, to end open discussions of women's liberation, and to resurrect the family.

This essay seeks to show that the retreat of the 1930s was not motivated by Bolshevik opportunism or the ideological inadequacy of Marxism. It argues that Soviet policymakers, jurists in particular, manifested a powerful and sincere interest in women's liberation throughout the 1920s. The main obstacle to women's liberation in this period was not a poverty of philosophy, but rather a crushing material poverty. In fact, the Bolshevik vision of social liberation far surpassed the ability of both state and society to sustain it. Bolshevik policy toward women was not static, but developed in dynamic relation to material conditions, local interests, and the activities and opinions of working-class and peasant women. The essay examines the early Bolshevik ideals in light of the specific material conditions of the time, assessing Soviet family policy in the 1920s against the social experiences of three broad sections of the Soviet population: the homeless children (*besprizorniki*), the peasantry, and urban working-class women.

The First Family Code

The Bolsheviks came to power with an ideological approach to the family based on the ideas of Karl Marx, Friedrich Engels, and August Bebel. According to the Marxist tradition, capitalism itself gradually undermined the family by involving women in production outside the home. Under socialism, the state would assume the basic functions of the family. Communal laundries, day-care centers, and dining halls staffed by paid workers would eliminate domestic labor. Women would enter the world of waged work on an equal footing with men. The state would cease to interfere in the union of the sexes, marriage would become superfluous, and the family itself would eventually "wither away."[8] The Marxist approach did not promote gender conflict: the redivision of domestic tasks between men and women, although endorsed by Lenin, was not seen as the primary solution to the problem of women's unpaid domestic labor.[9] The collective, not individual men, would assume responsibility for women's work in the home.

The first Family Code of the new socialist state, ratified in 1918, constituted the most progressive family and gender legislation the world had ever seen.[10] The Family Code abolished the inferior legal status of women and created equality under the law. It set up local bureaus of statistics (known as ZAGS) for the registration of marriage, divorce, birth, and death; and it gave legal status to civil marriage only. Divorce was permitted at the request of either spouse (no grounds were necessary) and an unlimited term of alimony in cases of need and disability entitled men and women to the same guarantees of support. Although some women criticized the alimony provision for fostering women's dependence on men, most jurists considered alimony necessary in the transitional period, recognizing that the state was still too poor to create a comprehensive social welfare system that would free women from their dependence on men.[11]

Centuries of property law and male privilege were swept away with the Family Code provisions abolishing illegitimacy and entitling all children to parental support. All children had equal rights regardless of whether they were born within or outside a registered marriage. The establishment of familial obligations independent of the marriage contract thus severed the concept of family from marriage.[12]

In the belief that the state would be a better guardian than the individual family, the Family Code forbade adoption. In a primarily agrarian society, jurists feared that adoption would allow peasants to exploit children as unpaid labor. Educators and jurists eagerly awaited a time when all children would enjoy the benefits of collective upbringing. The abolition of adoption, in their view, was the first step in transferring child care from the family to the state.[13]

The duties and responsibilities of the marriage contract were sharply restricted in accordance with the prevailing idea of marriage as a union between equals. Marriage did not create community of property between spouses: a woman retained full control of her property and earnings after marriage and neither spouse had any claim on the property of the other. This provision was later modified to permit the housewife a share in the property acquired in the course of marriage with her husband's earnings. In a remarkable ruling, the Supreme Court acknowledged that housework, as well as waged work, constituted a form of socially necessary labor.[14]

From a comparative perspective the 1918 Family Code was remarkably ahead of its time. Similar legislation concerning divorce, legitimacy, and property has yet to be passed in any of the major European countries.[15] The emphasis on equality, independence, and free union drew on a long tradition in the Russian and European radical movements.[16] Yet the free and egalitarian relations of the revolutionary movement were not easily transposed to a larger population where different cultural and social forms prevailed. The application of Bolshevik ideals to a largely rural, poverty-stricken country created unforeseen consequences, which, ironically and tragically, had the greatest impact on women and children.

Family Law and the Peasantry

In the early 1920s the overwhelming majority (84 percent) of the Russian population lived within a centuries' old agricultural system in which marriage and the family were central.[17] The application of family law to the countryside posed unique problems for peasants and jurists alike. Family law granted peasants the right to live apart from one's spouse, to divorce, and to receive alimony and child support, but all of these rights conflicted squarely with the system of family-based agricultural production. Soviet family law, emphasizing the values of personal freedom and independence, was strikingly at odds with the economy and social customs of the village.

The age-old institutions of the household (*dvor*) and the commune (*mir, obshchina*) still governed agricultural production and village life in the 1920s. The family/household, a kin-based, patrilocal unit often spanning several generations, was the basic unit of production. Women who married went to live in their husbands' households; young men remained in the *dvor* of their fathers. In peasant parlance, "Every daughter is someone else's booty."[18] The family held in common the land, livestock, implements, buildings, and other property. Apart from the wife's dowry, small personal items, and some money wages, all crops and income belonged to "the common pot." The household collectively consumed what it produced; the property or profits were not divided into "definable shares."[19]

Although the members of the household owned the property in common, the household was not managed democratically.[20] The head of the household (*domokhoziain*) exercised strong patriarchal control over the entire family. A woman became the head of a household only under rare circumstances, and even then she was limited in her rights and powers.[21] Customary law granted men and women different property rights. If a household split (*razdel*), the land and property were divided equally among the men; women were not entitled to a share. Divorce was virtually unknown among the peasantry in prerevolutionary society and peasant justice had little sympathy for a woman who left her husband's household.[22] Women had little say in the household, and no say in the commune or the *skhod* (the governing body of the commune), despite their crucial contributions to the productive and reproductive life of the household.

The Soviet Land Code, ratified in 1922, combined peasant customary law with a new, revolutionary insistence on gender equality. It abolished private ownership and granted all citizens, "regardless of sex, religion, or nationality," rights to the land. Women had the right to full participation in the commune and the *skhod*, and a *dvor* could "be composed of a single person (regardless of sex)." A newly married woman acquired rights in her husband's *dvor* and lost her rights in her father's *dvor*. Unlike customary law, in which a woman's rights depended on the presence of her husband or sons, the Land Code ensured that a woman entering a *dvor* by marriage had the right to an equal share. If the household split, land and property were divided among all household members, not only the adult males.[23]

The Land Code represented a compromise between the Bolsheviks and the peasantry. Despite its emphasis on gender equality, it legitimized the traditional relations of production in the countryside and affirmed the centrality of the household. While it granted women new rights within the household, it did little to alter the patriarchal institutions so central to peasant life. A woman still left her father's *dvor* to enter the *dvor* of her husband; production was still centered around the family; and peasant society remained patrilocal.

The Family Code, however, offered a more radical vision of change by extending rights to individuals that undermined the unity and economic interests of the household. Women not only had the right to a share of the household property, but now had the right to leave the household as well. While the Land Code guarded the interests of the household unit, the Family Code emphasized the rights of the individual. Not surprisingly, the conflicts between the household and the individual, between the Land Code and the Family Code, emerged most clearly in questions concerning property. The extension of gender equality and "modern" notions of individuality to a patriarchal social order raised a host of questions concerning women's and children's property rights that neither the Land Code, the Family Code, nor subsequent juridical decisions could resolve.

One of the most pressing questions centered on the property rights of the peasant woman after divorce. Did she have the right to take her share of the land, draft animals, tools, and buildings if she left the household? The Commissariat of Land never provided a clear answer. On the one hand, a divorced woman could not be left destitute, but on the other hand, a woman leaving an extended household of ten could hardly remove one-tenth of the hut, the cow, and the plow. Moreover, the division of land into ever smaller plots would only lead to greater inefficiency and a reduction in output, an outcome that the leaders of a grain-starved nation could scarcely endorse. Although the Commissariat of Land issued a series of directives on women's rights, officials never worked out a clear policy. Practice varied widely from region to region depending on the availability of land, the economic assets of the individual household, the length of the marriage, and the practice of the local land commission.[24]

Yet even if a woman received a share of the land after divorce, she still faced great difficulties. Frequently she was forced to rent her plot out because she had no livestock and no way to plow it, or hire herself out for wages so she could pay a man to do the physical jobs she could not handle.[25] The Family Code granted a woman rights to alimony and child support, but even these rights conflicted with the organization of peasant agriculture. According to the Land Code, a member of the *dvor* could not use the common property to meet personal debts or obligations. If a peasant divorced his wife or had a child outside of marriage, he could not use the money, produce, livestock, or land of the *dvor* to pay alimony or child support.[26] Yet most peasants had few personal possessions and no independent source of income. The combination of poverty and joint property deprived women and children of their rights granted by the Family Code.

In 1923, the Commissariats of Land and Justice ruled that if the personal means of the father were insufficient to provide support, the woman and the child had the right to draw upon the common property of the *dvor*.[27] This ruling created enormous resistance among the peasantry. If the entire household was held responsible for the obligations of one member, the economic well-being of all was threatened. One peasant insisted, "Rarely do a man and wife live alone. They live with a whole family, and thus all suffer in the case of divorce. Why should my brother suffer if I divorce my wife and the court orders me to pay?"[28]

For the peasants, marriage was an economic institution in which property considerations took precedence over sentimental attachments. They believed that the marital bond should be "*pripechaten*" or "sealed" as tightly as possible.[29] Yet the divorce rate in the countryside was surprisingly high: in 1927, almost 11 percent of all men and 9 percent of women entering marriage in the countryside had been previously married and divorced. The average length of marriage ending in divorce in the countryside was only 2.4 years.[30] The brief duration of these unions created complications for women's property claims. A woman could return to her parents' household, but often she was not welcomed there, especially if she had children. From the peasants' point of view, a divorced woman was like a stray slice of a loaf, an "*otrezannyi lomot'*." She was "*ni baba, ni devka*," neither married women nor maid, and there was little place for her in village life.[31]

Peasant women complained angrily about their problems after divorce.

Belitskaia, a peasant delegate to the Women's Congress, rhetorically asked her fellow delegates, "What rights does a woman have in the countryside?" She posed the hypothetical case of a divorced woman with two children: "What part of the property does she get?" Belitskaia asked. "Only one-third and only from the moveable property. The land is not divided because we have too little suitable land to divide." Belitskaia explained that although a peasant woman might receive a small alimony award, she still had nowhere to live and no way to support herself.[32]

Men often refused to pay the awards, small though they were. About half of the peasant women who were awarded alimony were unable to collect anything.[33] Many peasants swore that alimony could only lead to the ruin of the *dvor* and developed numerous ruses for avoiding payment.[34] Although the courts, especially at the higher levels, tended to side with the woman and the child against the household, the main problem was that the majority of peasants were terribly poor, living barely above a subsistence level. As late as 1929, 35 percent of peasants cultivated less than 5.4 acres, did not own a horse or a cow, and were forced to rent tools and draft animals to cultivate their land. Fifty percent of peasants had only one draft animal.[35] According to one study, more than 80 percent of rural alimony cases involved middle or poor peasant households. The courts usually levied sums of three to ten rubles a month, but many households simply could not afford to pay these amounts.[36] Even if the household owned a horse or a cow, the animal could not be cut in half. Some of the cases that came to court were simply unresolvable. One local people's court judge wrote, "Neither of the sides had anything. It is a good thing they were reconciled in court. But how do we handle similiar cases in the future?" The judge noted grimly that collecting alimony in the countryside was "hellish work."[37]

The Family Code, with its emphasis on individual rights and freedoms, created great conflict in the countryside. Not only did it challenge centuries of patriarchal values, it undermined the collective principle of the household, the very basis of agricultural production. Moreover, the challenge to patriarchy it contained provoked a conflict of economic interests among women. Pitting the divorced woman against the household, the provisions on alimony and child support granted the woman some measure of independence at the expense not only of her ex-husband, but the women and children remaining in the household as well. Jurists, committed to extending gender equality to the countryside, encountered deep structural obstacles: extreme poverty, the relative absence of an independently waged population, the economic indivisibility of the household, the importance of physical strength in the division of labor, the powerful dependence of women on men, and the patrilocal focus of social relations. The liberation of peasant women required no less than a complete transformation of the mode of production—the introduction of machinery, development beyond the primitive level of production, the penetration of waged relations, and the destruction of the collective principle of the household—as well as a revolution in traditional social values and practices.

Yet despite the enormous structural obstacles to women's liberation in the countryside, a small minority of peasant women were profoundly affected by the party's educational efforts and the activities of the Zhenotdel. Delegates to the Women's Congress spoke proudly of their struggle as single women to retain their share of the land in the village, to attend meetings of the *skhod,* and to organize agricultural cooperatives for women. Mothers of illegitimate children and divorced peasant women defied centuries of patriarchal tradition and fought the household in court for the right to child support and alimony. One peasant woman, hardly representative of the majority but noteworthy nonetheless, wrote, "In the countryside they look at a woman like a work horse. You work all your life for your husband and his entire family, endure beatings and every kind of humiliation, it doesn't matter, you have nowhere to go—you are bound in marriage. So it has always been under very strong marriage. I myself am a peasant and I was in this bind. We don't need such strong marriage now."[38] The Land Code and the Family Code offered a measure of protection to the single, the outcast, and the landless, as well as a new sense of entitlement for all. Although the codes prompted great gender conflict in the countryside, they also offered a new vision of gender relations, which a small but significant number of peasant women eagerly embraced.

The Besprizorniki

The second major obstacle to women's liberation that bedeviled the Soviet regime almost from its inception was the presence of hundreds of thousands of homeless children known as the *besprizorniki,* literally "shelterless ones."[39] Although the 1918 Family Code had optimistically prohibited adoption in the belief that the state would care for orphaned and needy children, by 1922 it was estimated that there were 7.5 million "starving and dying" children in Russia.[40] Many, having lost one or both parents, fled broken families that could no longer feed them. They traveled alone and in bands, illegally riding the rails from one end of the country to the other. Gathering in shifting crowds in the railroad stations and marketplaces, they stole, begged, picked pockets, and prostituted themselves to survive. Their numbers stood as a direct index of the disruption of social life; their treatment, a direct barometer of the state's attitude toward the family.

The origins of *besprizornost'* lie in what one historian called the "demographic earthquake" that tore Russia apart in the years 1914–21. As a result of World War I, the Civil War, epidemics, and famine, Russia lost 16 million people.[41] In the 1920s, new sources of *besprizornost'* appeared in the large numbers of widowed mothers, the high levels of female unemployment, the inability of single peasant women to eke out a living in the countryside, the high divorce rate, and the continuing poverty and difficulty of life.[42]

The early efforts to deal with *besprizornost'* were imbued with an idealistic commitment to socialized childrearing. In the first All-Russian Congress for the Protection of Childhood, three hundred delegates met in Moscow in 1919 to formulate state policy. One delegate declared, "There can be no wretched children belonging to no one. All children are the children of the state." The state, she suggested, should create "family" type institutions on the estates of the former nobility. With the assistance of a few hired personnel, the children themselves would "establish and maintain order." Women delegates spoke enthusiastically of the liberation that would attend the socialization of childrearing.[43]

Yet reality quickly belied the promise of utopia. While Soviet theorists dreamed of a new children's democracy, thousands of children were starving in institutions that lacked even the most basic provisions. Il'ina, a delegate to the Congress for the Protection of Childhood, argued that all talk of abolishing the family was irrelevant as long as the state could not assume the upbringing of children. It would be pointless, she insisted, to replace the family with children's homes as long as the homes did not take on the other "basic features of the family, namely its economic independence and its productivity."[44]

Yet as conditions worsened, the state had little choice but to assume responsibility for thousands of children whose families could no longer feed them. In 1918, the government began evacuating famine-stricken children from the cities to the abandoned estates of the nobility in the grain-producing regions. A year later it passed decrees authorizing free food for children under sixteen. The Central Executive Committee (CEC) created the Commission for the Betterment of the Lives of Children (Detkomissia) in 1921 with representatives from the Commissariats of Provisioning, Enlightenment and Health, the Cheka (secret police), and other organizations to ensure provisioning for the children's institutions, coordinate relief activities, and to care for the *besprizorniki*.[45]

The number of children in state facilities steadily increased from 30,000 in 1917 to 75,000 in 1918; 125,000 in 1919; 400,000 in 1920, and 540,000 in 1921.[46] One observer described the miserable state of the children's homes in 1920. The children were going about in rags, and there was no cloth, thread, stockings, or blankets. In the winter, the rooms were dark and freezing, for there was no electricity and no oil. "It was useless to think of any educational scheme in this nightmare," she wrote. "The children did absolutely nothing. The older ones played cards, smoked and drank, and girls of sixteen and seventeen abandoned themselves to prostitution."[47]

In the spring of 1921, severe drought hit the southeast. Homeless, abandoned, starving children fled the rural areas and poured into the towns. A frantic telegram from a relief worker told of "corpses freezing in the streets." In Ufa there were 68,000 homeless children; in Orenburg, 55,000; Simbirsk, 36,000; and Cheliabinsk, 48,000. Between 200 and 500 children showed up every day, begging admittance to children's homes illequipped to feed, house, or clothe them.[48] In a forced retreat from the provision of the 1918 Family Code prohibiting adoption, the government began placing children with better-off peasant families. Although officials knew that the peasants regarded such children as little more than unpaid labor, there were few alternatives under the desperate pressure of mass starvation.

With the adoption of the New Economic Policy (NEP) in 1921 and the strict curtailment of state spending, the government reduced funding to the children's institutions and transferred responsibility for their upkeep to local governments.[49] In practice, there were few local funds available and thousands of children's institutions folded, leaving their largely female staffs without work. The decrease in the number of facilities coupled with great need led to severe overcrowding in the remaining homes. Throughout 1921–22 the party and the state issued a series of decrees aimed at reducing the number of children in the homes. New rules stipulated that only orphans and children who had lost a parent in the Red Army were eligible for care.[50] Local officials began emptying the homes, sending children to relatives, private guardians, production cooperatives, workshops, and peasant families. More than one thousand children's institutions closed between 1923 and 1925.[51] The remaining homes were to be reorganized into self-sufficient working colonies; land plots were allotted so they could feed the children themselves.[52] Children were to pay their own way as much as possible: either through their labor in an individual peasant family, in a workshop apprenticeship, or in a self-sufficient colony.

Day-care centers or preschool institutions also suffered cutbacks during the transition to NEP, creating new hardships for single working mothers. Children from impoverished single-parent homes, left alone without supervision, often joined the ranks of the *besprizorniki*. A circular to all the local departments for social upbringing frankly admitted, "The existing grid of pre-school institutions does not serve even the neediest part of the working population."[53]

The needs of women and the needs of children formed the tight, alternating links on a chain that became a vicious circle. Single mothers who lost jobs and access to day care as a result of cutbacks in state enterprises were unable to support or supervise their children, who consequently ended up on the streets. The large number of *besprizorniki* forced the state in turn to divert scarce resources from day-care centers to children's homes, decreasing the funds available for day care, adding to the burden of single mothers, and ultimately increasing the number of *besprizorniki.*

Educators, jurists, and social workers were disturbed not only by the children, who were hungry, sick, and ragged, but by the social problems they created. The children, who often survived by petty crime, were responsible for at least half of all juvenile crimes nationwide and an even greater percentage in the large cities. According to law, children who were sixteen and under could not be tried in adult court or sentenced to adult penalties. Local commissions, staffed by pedagogues, jurists, and doctors, were established to hear juvenile cases. Between 1922 and 1924, the commissions' caseload increased by 19,885 cases.[54] Although the commissions were becoming more effective, they could not keep pace with the influx of new cases.

Unlike the courts, the commissions did not possess punitive powers. Depending on the severity and the circumstances of the case, they could remand the child either to a children's institution, to a guardian, or to the parents.[55] The shortage of funds and overcrowding in the children's homes sharply reduced the number of available places, and most adults, especially urban workers, were reluctant to assume the burden and expense of a strange child. With so few alternatives, the commissions generally opted to send the children back to their parents, most often a single mother who could not provide the needed care. Many children, despite terrible deprivations, became accustomed to life on the streets. They had difficulty adjusting to authority, work, and an organized institutional environment. Educators and social workers began to speak of the problem of "chronic *besprizornost.*" They feared that years of war and disruption had produced a generation of vagabonds who would never be capable of work or a steady life.[56]

The problems of chronic *besprizornost'* and crime put sharp pressure on jurists and state officials to clear the children from the streets. The Detkomissiia issued a series of decrees in 1924 encouraging local administrators to create new places in the children's homes by sending the older inmates out to work.[57] Many local officials, resenting the financial drain imposed by the homes, eagerly took advantage of the new decrees to expel the teenagers and close the homes. They arranged mass transfers of children, without permission from the central authorities, and with no assurance that the children would be accepted at their assigned destinations.[58] Thousands of children, victims of the covert war over funding between the central authorities and local administrators, eventually returned to the streets.

The problems of crime, overcrowding in the homes, crippling costs, and local resentment gradually convinced policymakers that a new approach was needed to solve the problem of chronic *besprizornost'* and train children for work at the least possible expense to the state. In April 1926, the CEC issued a decree reversing the prohibition against adoption in the 1918 Family Code and encouraging peasant families to adopt the children in state institutions.[59] The decree had two aims, both freely admitted: to cut state expenditures on orphans and to prepare the children for future employment.[60] Here was tacit recognition that the family performed an essential function—bringing up children—at a minimum social cost. Each peasant household that accepted a child received an extra plot of land—free of agricultural taxes for three years—and a lump-sum payment of thirty to fifty rubles. The terms of the decree were clearly designed to make adoption economically attractive. The households most likely to adopt were those in need of an additional worker. The children would be used as hired labor, although they had no rights to wages or a share in the household's property. The peasant family received tax privileges, a lump sum, an extra plot, and a free laborer. The child received "job training."[61]

The Commissariat of Enlightenment recognized that the decree was a far cry from the early plans to ensure state support for all needy children; its letter to the Department of Peoples' Education spoke of a forced retreat.[62] Although educators dreamed of children's towns where every child could be "an artist and a composer," as early as 1921 children were placed in peasant families where they faced lives of endless work, poverty, and exploitation. The 1926 decree simply codified the final outcome of a decade of struggle between vision and reality.

The problem of *besprizornost'* defied an easy solution. The sheer numbers of needy, homeless children would have taxed the resources of a far richer, more developed country. Urban workers showed little desire to take the children into their cramped quarters; peasants had to be offered compelling economic inducements. Local governments balked at assuming the expenses of caring for a mobile population of orphans. All these responses demonstrated the programmatic limits of voluntarism and decentralization in coping with a problem of such huge social dimensions.

Moreover, *besprizornost'* proved a major obstacle to the realization of the early Bolshevik vision of women's emancipation. The orphaned children constituted a tremendous drain on state and local resources, diverting funds from preschool institutions and other support systems. The starving, filthy children of the streets graphically demonstrated the social costs of the withering away of the family.[63] The state, barely able to feed its orphans, could do little to free mothers from their traditional family responsibilities. The early dream of socialized upbringing was swiftly overtaken by the nightmare of chronic *besprizornost'* and crime. The family was resurrected as a solution to *besprizornost'* because it was the one institution that could feed, clothe, and socialize a child at almost no cost to the state.

Urban Women and "Free Union"

The Bolsheviks believed strongly in "free union," the idea that men and women should come together and separate freely, unfettered by the contractual bonds of marriage. The commitment to free union naturally made itself felt in family law that permitted divorce simply on request of either spouse. Divorce, virtually unknown in tsarist Russia, quickly skyrocketed after the revolution. By the mid-1920s, the Soviet Union had the highest divorce rate of any European country: almost three times as high as Germany's, 3.5 times as high as France's, and 26 times that of England and Wales.[64] In the European SSSR in 1926, there were 145.4 divorces for every 1,000 marriages or approximately one divorce for every thirteen marriages.[65] In the large cities there was one divorce for every 3.5 marriages in 1926. Moscow's divorce rate in 1926 was the highest of all: 477.1 divorces for every 1,000 marriages (practically one out of every two!) followed by Tver—359, Yaroslavl—279, and Leningrad—265.[66]

Some women undoubtedly used the new law to escape oppressive and abusive husbands, but even so, divorce often had extremely painful consequences. One of the implicit assumptions of the divorce law was that both spouses were independent individuals, free to make personal decisions on the basis of choice rather than economic necessity. Yet unemployment, especially for women, proved a serious problem during NEP. Large numbers of women lost their jobs to demobilized soldiers after the Civil War and peasant newcomers to the cities had difficulty finding work. Korotkova, a delegate to the Women's Congress from Krym, exclaimed, "If you look in the labor registry offices you will find only women. No one wants to hire them because they have no skills."[67] Moreover, the progressive features of Soviet labor legislation, such as paid maternity leave and work restrictions for pregnant and nursing women, often prompted managers to fire women first.[68]

Under such conditions, the high divorce rate had a special significance for the urban woman. If her husband divorced or abandoned her, she was often unable to support herself or her children. Dziuba, a delegate from the Ukraine, emphasized the special plight of the housewife after divorce. "Comrades, workers and peasants," she proclaimed, "I ask you to consider that the wife of the worker, your sister, has been overlooked. If a woman worker leaves her husband, she only loses a husband, she works independently. But when the wife of a worker leaves her husband, she is considered a non-laboring (*netrudnyi*) element, left in the street as *besprizornoi*. There is nowhere for her to turn, all is closed and everyone turns away from her."[69] Without an independent wage, women were in no position to exercise their right to free union. Vera Lebedeva, the head of the Department for the Protection of Maternity and Infancy, grimly summed up the future of many divorced women: "The weakness of the marital tie and divorce create masses of single women who carry the burden of child care alone. Imagine yourself such a woman, without support from your husband, with a child on your hands, laid-off due to a reduction in staff, and thrown out of the dormitory . . . with no possibility to continue supporting yourself. Where do these thousands go?" Lebedeva asked. "There is one exit—the street."[70] Like the female *besprizorniki*, many women who were unable to find work sold themselves on the streets. Prostitution represented the most painful, but not the most improbable, fate of the husbandless woman under NEP.

While unemployment stood as an unmistakable barrier to women's independence, the concentration of women in poorly paid, unskilled jobs also reinforced their dependence on men. Women earned only 65 percent of what men earned in the mid-1920s.[71] However meager the pooled salaries of the working-class family, the man's higher wages ensured a better standard of living for his wife and children. Even if a woman worked, divorce signified a substantial drop in her standard of living.

The delegates to the Women's Congress were quick to connect the problems of *besprizornost*,' divorce, and single motherhood to women's lack of skills and lower salaries. Women were the most vulnerable to dismissal, and low salaries reinforced their dependence on the family. One delegate argued that a woman's inability to support a family without a man was an important cause of *besprizornost*.' "Imagine the position of a woman, receiving a low salary," she said, "who has four children on her hands, and does not even have the hope that she will be able to provide for them in the future." Lebedeva noted that single peasant women, driven out of the countryside, were often forced to abandon their children when they failed to find work in the towns. The problem of *besprizornost*' had to be solved at the root: by giving women skills.[72]

Yet if women's economic independence was the solution to *besprizornost*,' the lack of available child care proved an enormous obstacle to economic independence. The imprisoning circle of poverty and scarcity seemed to have no exit, as the problems of *besprizornost*,' child care, lack of skills, and unemployment interlocked, each reinforcing the other. Given the obstacles to women's independence, thousands of divorced and abandoned women turned to the courts to sue for alimony and child support. The courts were generally lenient in their awards to women: they used flexible criteria in their determination of paternity and attempted to provide a fair sum after divorce. Yet judges were severely restricted in determining the size of the award because men's salaries were frequently too small to provide adequate support for a woman with children. If a man remarried, or his ex-wife was unemployed, or if they had children, both parties suffered. Women could not live on the court-ordered awards, and men could not afford to pay them.[73] Men were victims as well as women. A surprising number of men requested custody of their children because they were unable to pay the child support ordered by the courts. Although such requests were common among peasant men, they were made by wage-earners as well. Once a man remarried and had a second family, he often could not afford to send the court-ordered "third" of his wages to his first wife and child. Thousands of men left town or changed jobs to avoid paying alimony, and only about half of the men on the bailiffs lists were ever apprehended.[74]

Working-class and peasant women spoke out angrily against frequent divorce and male promiscuity. Women criticized men for taking advantage of the easy divorce law to abandon their wives and children. One woman from a rural area wrote, "In the towns and in the country it is possible to find no small number of families abandoned by husbands. Although they sometimes pay alimony, it is not enough to live on, and often they simply stop paying. This affects children most painfully of all. . . . In some cases women are responsible for these tragedies, but mainly it is men."[75] Women explained that divorce has radically different consequences for men and for women. One working-class housewife noted with grim honesty, "Women in the majority of cases are more backward, less skilled, and therefore less independent than men. . . . To marry, to bear children, to be enslaved by the kitchen, and then to be thrown aside by your husband— this is very painful for women. This is why I am against easy divorce."[76]

Many women spoke directly against free union, insisting that a limit be placed on the number of divorces possible under the law. One textile worker said, "My request from the other women workers is to pass a decree ending serial marriages."[77] Other women went ever further, demanding that people who had extramarital affairs be punished. A group of ten housewives argued that the government should "strengthen the punishment for husbands who get involved with other women, and also establish punishment for these women."[78] Other women sought to revoke the provision of the 1918 Family Code entitling all children to parental support. They argued that an illegitimate child did not deserve support if the father was already married and supporting a family.[79]

In 1926, after a year of intense nationwide debate, the Central Executive Committee ratified a new Family Code that sought to address many of the social problems of NEP. The 1926 Family Code legalized adoption, gave the housewife a right to property acquired with her husband's wages, extended alimony rights to the unemployed, and offered protection to women in *de facto* marriages by extending the same legal rights to unmarried partners as to those in registered marriages. At the same time, it undermined the significance of marriage registration and simplified the divorce procedure even further.[80] Although it sought to address the problems of social breakdown and family dissolution, the new policy also showed the influence of those who sought to hasten the "withering away" of the family and the advent of free union. In the debate over the new legislation, many peasants and women registered their opposition to the more libertarian proposals, such as the recognition of *de facto* marriage and the simplification of divorce.

In contrast to the jurists who promoted free union, many working-class and peasant women mistrusted the freedom embodied in Soviet family law. Bitter experience taught them that without adequate child-care services, full employment, and equal wages, free union benefited only men. If the family withered away before the state could assume its functions, women were left in a desperate position. Substantial structural changes were necessary before a new ideology of family and social relations could play a constructive role.

Conclusion

The Bolshevik commitment to women's liberation throughout the 1920s was not only genuine, it was doggedly persistent in the face of huge obstacles. Educators and state officials, overwhelmed by thousands of homeless children, overcrowded institutions, crime, and the specter of "chronic *besprizornost*'," frankly acknowledged adoption as a necessary but unfortunate measure, but maintained a commitment to collective upbringing. Officials in the commissariats of land and justice repeatedly refused to accede to peasant demands to abolish divorce and alimony, and continued to support the rights of the vulnerable, the weak, and the landless peasant woman. Although increased grain production was clearly a major state priority, the land and family codes established rights for women that could only engender a decrease in plot size and production, as well as powerful opposition from the household. Jurists in 1926 opted to solve the problems of abandoned women and families by recognizing *de facto* marriage rather than by restricting divorce. The problems of poverty, backwardness, and scarcity severely undermined the Bolshevik vision, yet jurists maintained a flexible commitment to women's liberation and the "withering away" of the family.

At the same time, the libertarian premises of family law sparked resistance from many sectors of the population. Local officials resented the burden of the *besprizorniki* and eagerly grasped any opportunity to close the homes and rid themselves of the children. Peasant men and women frequently resented the imposition of a "foreign" morality, and opposed the laws on divorce and alimony for clear economic reasons. Women, both urban and rural, spoke out vehemently against promiscuity and laws that threatened their shaky family economies. All these popular attitudes emerged from the collision of a policy of social liberation and a society that could not materially sustain it.

In 1928, under Stalin's leadership, the party launched a massive drive to collectivize agriculture and industrialize the economy. Collectivization eliminated the patriarchal household as the basic unit of production, and in principle might have offered a new basis for gender relations in the countryside. Industrialization involved millions of women in production, thereby promising new possibilities for women's economic independence and the socialization of domestic labor. Yet collectivization was carried out in a brutal and often senseless manner that provoked the fierce hostility of peasant women.[81] The spiraling chaos of industrialization created severe shortages of housing, child care, and other social services.[82] The earlier problems of *besprizornost'*, divorce, and family breakdown—still unre-solved—were exacerbated by new social stresses.

In 1930, the party abolished the Zhenotdel and began to retreat from its earlier vision. New repressive laws stressing family responsibility were passed in an effort to halt the massive social dislocation. Parents who abandoned their children were subject to criminal prosecution.[83] Chil-dren over the age of twelve who committed theft, rape, or murder were liable to trial in adult court and subject to adult sentences. The more lenient local commissions on juvenile crime were disbanded. Parents were subject to large fines for damages incurred by their children's mischief or hooliganism.[84] In 1936, a new law made divorce much more difficult to obtain, increased the punishment for nonpayment of alimony to two years in prison, prohibited abortion, provided aid to women with many chil-dren, and extended the funding for day care.[85] The early belief in the "withering away" of the family was branded as "petty-bourgeois," and the "strong, socialist family" was widely extolled as a proper model for social relations. Men were informed in no uncertain terms that the revolution had not exempted them from family responsibilities.[86] The sharp debates over family law came to an end as the free-thinking jurists of the 1920s were compelled to parrot set phrases in support of the new law.

The roots of this reversal go back to the terrible scarcity and under-development of the 1920s. Many working-class and peasant women had experienced the "freedom" of this period simply as social chaos. Among the groups that had suffered most from libertarian family policy, there was a measure of support for the resurrection of the family and the new emphasis on responsibility.[87] The irony and, ultimately, the tragedy of the Soviet attempt to liberate women is that conditions had changed suffi-ciently by the 1930s to permit the realization of the vision that jurists and activists defended so stubbornly in the 1920s. Yet by this time the orientation of the party had also changed, and a new mixture of political repression, criminal sanctions, and traditional values took the place of democratic debate, humanist concerns, and social experimentation. The great potential of the socialist experiment, as evoked by the Women's Congress in 1927, was never realized.

Notes

1. *Vsesoiuznyi s'ezd rabotnits i krest'ianok. Stenograficheskii otchet. 10–16 Oktiabria 1927 goda* (Moscow, 1927), pp. 240, 258. Hereafter cited as Women's Congress.

2. See, for example, Zillah R. Eisenstein, "Developing a Theory of Capitalist Patriarchy and Socialist Feminism," in *Capitalist Patriarchy and the Case for Socialist Feminism* (New York, London: Monthly Review Press, 1979); Heidi Hartmann, "The Unhappy Marriage of Marxism and Feminism: Towards a More Progressive Union," and Carol Erhlich, "The Unhappy Marriage of Marxism and Feminism: Can it Be Saved?" in Lydia Sargent, ed., *Women and Revolution* (Boston: South End Press, 1981); Alison M. Jaggar, *Feminist Politics and Human Nature* (Totowa, NJ: Rowman & Allanheld, 1983), pp. 207–47; Alena Heitlinger, "Marxism, Feminism and Sexual Equality," in Tova Yedlin, ed., *Women in Eastern Europe and the Soviet Union* (New York: Praeger, 1980); Joyce Outshoorn, "The Dual Heritage," in Anja Meulenbelt et al., eds., *A Creative Tension: Key Issues of Socialist-Feminism* (Boston: South End Press, 1984); Batya Weinbaum, *The Curious Courtship of Women's Liberation and Socialism* (Boston: South End Press, 1978); and Lise Vogel, *Marxism and the Oppression of Women* (New Brunswick, NJ: Rutgers University Press, 1983).

3. See Alfred G. Meyer, "Marxism and the Women's Movement," in Dorothy Atkinson, Alexander Dallin, and Gail Lapidus, eds., *Women in Russia* (Stanford: Stanford University Press, 1977), p. 99. Beatrice Farnsworth criticizes Sophia Smidovich for her "conservatism" in the debate over sexuality in the 1920s, but never explores the ramifications of "free" sexuality for women in this period. See her "Communist Feminism: Its Synthesis and Demise," in Carol R. Berkin and Clara M. Lovett, eds., *Women, War and Revolution* (New York: Holmes & Meier, 1980), pp. 150, 147; see also Harold Benenson, "Victorian Sexual Ideology and Marx's Theory of the Working-Class," *International Labor and Working Class History*, Spring 1984, pp. 1–23.

4. Gail Lapidus, "Sexual Equality in Soviet Policy: A Developmental Perspective," in Atkinson et al., eds., *Women in Russia*; Anne Bobroff, "The Bolsheviks and Working Women, 1905–1920," *Soviet Studies* 26, no. 4 (1974). For work that sees the initial commitment of the Bolsheviks to women's liberation as genuine, see Carol Eubanks Hayden, "The Zhenotdel and the Bolshevik Party," *Russian History* 3, Part II (1976); Alix Holt, "Marxism and Women's Oppression: The Bolshevik Theory and Practice in the 1920s," in Tova Yedlin, ed., *Women in Eastern Europe and the Soviet Union*; Elizabeth Waters, "From the Old Family to the New: Work, Marriage and Motherhood in Urban Soviet Russia, 1917–1931," Ph.D. diss., University of Birmingham, February 1985.

5. Rose L. Glickman, *Russian Factory Women: Workplace and Society, 1880–1914* (Berkeley: University of California Press, 1984), chs. 5 and 6.

6. M. Donald, "Bolshevik Activity Amongst the Working Women of Petrograd in 1917," *International Review of Social History* 27, Part 2 (1982): 131. Donald shows the complex relationship between the Bolsheviks' attitude toward organizing women and the growing militance of women workers.

78   The First Experiments

7. Hayden, "The Zhenotdel and the Bolshevik Party," and Richard Stites, "Zhenotdel: Bolshevism and Russian Women, 1917–1930," in *Russian History* 3, Part II (1976); and Holt, "Marxism and Women's Oppression."

8. See August Bebel, *Women Under Socialism* (New York, 1910); Friedrich Engels, *The Origin of the Family, Private Property and the State* (New York: International, 1972), and *The Condition of the Working Class in England* (New York: International, 1969); Karl Marx, *Capital: A Critique of Political Economy* I, trans. Ben Fowkes (New York: Random House, 1977), pp. 620–21, and "The German Ideology," in Marx and Friedrich Engels, *Selected Works* I (Moscow: Progress Publishers, 1969), pp. 63–64.

9. Hartmann, in "The Unhappy Marriage of Marxism and Feminism," notes that Marxist analysis consistently focuses on women in relation to an economic system, not to men (p. 3).

10. *The Marriage Laws of Soviet Russia: The Complete Text of the First Code of the RSFSR* (New York; Russian Soviet Government Bureau, 1921).

11. For criticism see the comments of the delegate Roslavets in *Piatyi sozyv vserossiiskogo tsentral'nogo ispolnitel'nogo komiteta: Stenograficheskii otchet* (Moscow, 1919), p. 151; and A. M. Kollontai, "Brak i Byt," *Rabochii sud* 5 (1926): 363–78.

12. The legal expert Zinaida Tettenborn notes that marriage was the primary legal basis for constructing the family under Western European law. See her "Vnebrachnye Deti," *Proletarskaia revoliutsiia i pravo* 8–10 (1918): 9.

13. A. G. Goikhbarg, "Pervyi Kodeks Zakonov RFSFR," *Proletarskaia revoliutsiia i pravo* 7 (1918): 6; and Zinaida Tettenborn, "Roditel'skie Prava v Pervom Kodekse Zakonov RSFSR," *Proletarskaia revoliutsiia i pravo* 1 (1919): 20–28.

14. "Iz Deiatel'nosti Narodnogo Komissariata Iustitsii," *Ezhenedelnik sovetskoi iustitsii* 11–12 (1922): 12. Hereafter cited as *ESIu*.

15. On the history of European family law, see Mary Ann Glendon, *State, Law and Family* (New York, Amsterdam: Elsevier, 1977).

16. Three excellent works on women in the revolutionary movement include Richard Stites, *The Women's Liberation Movement in Russia: Feminism, Nihilism, and Bolshevism, 1860–1930* (Princeton: Princeton University Press, 1978); Barbara Alpern Engel, *Mothers and Daughters: Women of the Intelligentsia in Nineteenth Century Russia* (Cambridge: The University Press, 1983); and Barbara Evans Clements, "Bolshevik Women: The First Generation," in Yedlin, ed., *Women in Eastern Europe and the Soviet Union.*

17. Teodor Shanin, *The Awkward Class: Political Sociology of Peasants in a Developing Society, 1910–1925* (Oxford: Oxford University Press, 1972), p. 19.

18. A. Petrov, "V Narodnom Sude," *Sud idet!* 12 (1925): 729.

19. Shanin, *Awkward Class*, p. 31; N. Semenov, "Krest'ianskii Dvor," *Revoliutsiia prava* 1 (1927): 192–194.

20. Shanin, *Awkward Class*, p. 221.

21. Semenov, "Krest'ianskii Dvor," pp. 187–88.

22. Beatrice Farnsworth, "The Litigious Daughter-in-Law: Family Relations in Rural Russia in the Second Half of the Nineteenth Century," *Slavic Review* 1 (Spring 1986): 57.

23. *Zemel'nyi kodeks RSFSR* (Moscow, 1922), pp. 5, 6, 10, 11, 12, 13–16. As in customary law, property division was permitted only if a new household was economically viable on the smaller share.

24. G. Ryndziunskii, "Voprosy Deistvuiushchego Semeinogo Prava," *ESIu* 14–15 (1922): 11–12, and "Voprosy Deistvuiushchego Semeinogo Prava," *ESIu* 18 (1922): 4; N. V. Gendzekhadze and I. B. Novitskii, eds. *Zemel'nyi kodeks s dopolnitel'nymi uzakoneniiami i raz'iasneniiami narkomzema RSFSR na 1 avgusta 1927 goda* (Moscow, 1927), p. 104; and E. Dombrovskii, "O Krest' ianskikh Semeino-Imushchestvennikh Razdelakh," *Proletarskii sud* 8–9 (1925): 8–9.

25. *Women's Congress*, p. 262. See also Barbara Evans Clements, "Working-Class and

Peasant Women in the Russian Revolution, 1917–1923," *Signs* 8, Part 2 (Winter 1982), on the problems of single peasant women.

26. Gendzekhadze and Novitskii, eds.; *Zemel'nyi kodeks RSFSR*, p. 14.
27. Abramov, "Vzyskanie Alimentov s Chlena Krest'ianskogo Dvora po Novomu Kodeksu o Brake, Sem'e i Opeke," *ESIu* 9 (1927): 251.
28. "Stenograficheskii Otchet Zasedaniia 2 Sessii Vserossiiskogo Tsentral'nogo Ispolnitel'nogo Komiteta 12 Sozyva 20 Oktiabria 1925 Goda," in *Sbornik statei i materialov po brachnomu i semeinomu pravu* (Moscow, 1926), p. 167. Hereafter cited as 1925 VTsIK.
29. A. M. Bol'shakov, *Derevnia* (Moscow, 1927), p. 319.
30. M. Kaplun, "Brachnost' Naseleniia RSFSR," *Statisticheskoe obozrenie* 7 (1929): 91, 96.
31. Bol'shakov, *Derevnia*, p. 318; M. Ia. Fenomenov, *Sovremmenaia derevnia*, Vol. II (Leningrad, Moscow, 1925), p. 18.
32. Women's Congress, p. 249.
33. A. Sidorov, "K Voprosu Alimentnogo Prava v Derevne," *Rabochii sud* 1 (1926): 14.
34. Sometimes the household would make a fictitious *razdel* and give very little property to the member responsible for alimony, thus absolving the rest of the household for liability for his debts. Other tricks for avoiding payment included cutting back on production and raising only what the household needed, or not reporting extra income. See Fisunov, "Stranitsa Praktika," *ESIu* 24 (1927): 739; V. Solov'ev, "Stranitsa Praktika," *ESIu* 22 (1927): 673.
35. Moshe Lewin, *Russian Peasants and Soviet Power: A Study of Collectivization* (New York: W. W. Norton, 1975), pp. 36, 30.
36. Sidorov, "K Voprosu Alimentnogo," pp. 13–14.
37. *Ibid.*, p. 14.
38. "Chto Predlagaiut Rabotnitsy," *Rabotnitsa* 14 (1926): 15.
39. There is almost no research on the link between *besprizornost'* and the obstacles to women's liberation in the 1920s. For a brief mention of the connection see Roger Pethybridge, *The Social Prelude to Stalinism* (New York: St. Martin's Press, 1974), p. 55.
40. "O Bor'be s Detskoi Besprizornost'iu: Utverzhdennoe Kollegiei NKP Postanovlenie Vserossiiskogo S'ezd Zav. ONO," in S. S. Tizanov and M. S. Epshtein, eds., *Gosudarstvo i obshchestvennost' v bor'be s detskoi besprizornost'iu* (Moscow, Leningrad, 1927), p. 35.
41. Moshe Lewin, "State, Society, and Ideology During the First Five-Year Plan," in his *The Making of the Soviet System* (New York: Pantheon, 1985), p. 210.
42. I. Daniushevskii, "Kak Preduprezhdat' Detskuiu Besprizornost'," in Tizanov and Epshtein, *Gosudarstvo i obshchestvennost'*, p. 10.
43. TsGAOR, fond 2306, opis' 13, delo 11, pp. 9–14.
44. *Ibid.*, p. 47.
45. Ya. A. Perel' and A. A. Liubimova, *Bor'ba s detskoi besprizornost'iu* (Moscow, Leningrad, 1932), pp. 61–63.
46. Z. Sh. Karamysheva, "Pedagogicheskie Problemy Sotsial'no-Pravovoi Okhrany Nesovershennoletnikh v RSFSR 1917–1932" (Candidate Thesis, Nauchno-Issledovatel'skii Institut Obshei Pedagogiki Akademii Pedagogicheskikh Nauk SSSR, Moscow, 1976), p. 17.
47. A. Kalinina's description is cited by Vladimir Zenzinov, *Deserted: The Story of the Children Abandoned in Soviet Russia* (London: H. Joseph, 1931), pp. 23–25.
48. TsGAOR, fond 5207, op. 1, delo 14, pp. 5–6.
49. The New Economic Policy, adopted by the party in 1921, permitted a limited form of private enterprise in small and medium-sized industry, replaced grain requisitioning with a fixed tax, placed industry on a strict cost-accounting basis, and closed many of the unprofitable sectors of the service industry.

50. Karamysheva, "Pedagogicheskie Problemy," pp. 63, 66.
51. TsGAOR, fond 5207, op. 1, delo 10, p. 6.
52. Karamysheva, p. 72.
53. TsGAOR, fond 2306, op. 1, delo 2744, p. 12.
54. I. I. Sheiman, "Komissii po Delam o Nesovershennoletnikh," in *Detskaia besprizornost' i detskii dom. Sbornik statei i materialov II vserossiiskogo s'ezd SPON* (Moscow, 1926), pp. 142, 139.
55. *Ibid.*, p. 145.
56. See, for example, T. E. Segalov, "Poniatie i Vidy Detskoi Besprizornosti," *Pravo i zhizn'* 4–5 (1925): 95–101.
57. "Vsem Gub-i, Oblzemupravleniiam Narkomzemam Avtonomykh Respublik, Vsem Gub-, Oblotdelam Vserabotzemlesa, Vsem Obl-, Gubispolpomoshennym po Ulushcheniiu Zhizni Detei, Detkomissiiam Avtonomykh Respublik, GubONO, Narkomprosam Avtonomykh Respublik," and "Vsem Krest'ianskim Komitetam Obshchestvennoi Vzaimopomoshchi i Otdelam Narodnogo Obrazovaniia," in Tizanov and Epshtein, eds., *Gosudarstvo i obshchestvennost'*, pp. 41–44.
58. "Vsem Tsentral'nym Ispolnitel'nym Komitetam Avtonomykh Respublik Kraevym, Oblastnym, i Gubernskim Ispolnitel'nym Komitetam," in *Ibid.*, pp. 24–26.
59. "O Poriadke i Usloviiakh Peredachi Vospitannikov Detskikh Domov v Krest'ianskii Sem'i dlia Podgotovki k Sel'skokhoziastvennomu Trudu," in *ibid.*, pp. 47–48.
60. *Instruktivnoe pis'mo ob usynovlenii* (Sverdlovsk, 1926), p. 2.
61. *Kak peredavat' besprizornikh i vospitannikov detdomov v trudovye khoziastva i proizvodit' usynovlenie* (Viatka, 1928), p. 5.
62. *Instruktivnoe pis'mo ob usynovlenii* (Sverdlovsk, 1926), p. 1.
63. Heitlinger, "Marxism, Feminism and Sex Equality," p. 12, notes that Marx and Lenin generally underestimated the costs of the socialization of household labor.
64. L. Lubnyi-Gertsyk, "Estestvennoe Dvizhenie Naseleniia SSSR za 1926," *Statisticheskoe obozrenie* 8 (1928): 89.
65. *Ibid.*, p. 85.
66. *Estestvennoe dvizhenie naseleniia RSFSR za 1926 god* (Moscow, 1928), p. LIV; Lubnyi-Gertsyk, "Estestvennoe Dvizhenie," p. 86.
67. Women's Congress, p. 287.
68. P. M. Chirkov, "Sovetskii Opyt Resheniia Zhenskogo Voprosa v Period Stroitel'stva Sotsializma (1917–1937)" (Diss. for Doctor of Historical Science, Moscow State University, 1979), p. 172.
69. Women's Congress, p. 452.
70. V. L. "Vliianie Novoi Ekonomicheskoi Politiki na Byt Trudiashchikhsia Zhenshchin," *Kommunistka* 3–5 (1922): 15, 16.
71. B. Markus, "Zhenskii Trud v SSSR v 1924 gody," *Kommunistka* 4 (1925): 49.
72. Women's Congress, pp. 240–241.
73. See workers' budgets as constructed by E. O. Kabo, *Ocherki rabochego byta* (Moscow, 1928), p. 19.
74. "Diskussiia po Povodu Proekta Kodeksa Zakonov o Brake, Sem'e i Opeke," *Rabochii sud* 3 (1926): 233.
75. "Mysli Krest'ianka," *Krestianka* 6 (1926): 7.
76. "Chto Predlagaiut Rabotnitsy," *Rabotnitsa* 15 (1926): 16.
77. 1925 VTsIK, p. 143.
78. "Chto Predlagaiut Rabotnitsy," *Rabotnitsa* 15 (1926): 16.
79. "Chto Predlagaiut Rabotnitsy," *Rabotnitsa* 13 (1926): 14.
80. *The Soviet Law on Marriage: Full Text of the Code of Laws on Marriage and Divorce, the Family, and Guardianship* (Moscow, 1932).
81. Lynne Viola, "Bab'i Bunty and Peasant Women: Protest During Collectivization," *Russian Review* 45 (1986).

82. Moshe Lewin coined the term "quicksand society" to characterize the enormous up-heavals of the first Five Year Plan. See his "Society, State, and Ideology During the First Five-Year Plan," in *The Making of the Soviet System.*

83. Ya. A. Perel', ed., *Okhrana zhenshchiny-materi v ugolovnom zakone* (Moscow, Leningrad, 1932), p. 208.

84. *O likvidatsi detskoi besprizornosti i beznadzornosti* (Voronezh, 1935), p. 9.

85. *Proekt postanovleniia TsIK i SNK Soiuza SSR o zapreshchenii abortov, uvelichenii material'noi pomoshchi rozhenitsam, ustanovlenii gosudarstvennoi pomoshchi mnogose-meinym, rashirenii seti rodil'nykh domov, detskikh iaslei i detskikh sadov, usilenii ugolov-nogo nakazaniia za naplatezh alimentov i o nekotorykh izmeneniiakh v zakonodatel'stve o razvodakh* (1936).

86. *Krepkaia sovetskaia sem'ia. Sbornik* (Voronezh, 1936), p. 53.

87. Janet Evans notes in her examination of the 1936 law that although many women opposed the prohibition on abortion, there was support for the other provisions of the law. See her "The Communist Party of the Soviet Union and the Woman's Question: The Case of the 1936 Decree 'In Defense of Mother and Child,'" *Journal of Contemporary History* 16 (1981).

Gender, Politics, and Patriarchy in China: The Experiences of Early Women Communists, 1920–27

Christina Gilmartin

The role of women in the early Chinese communist movement is not easily appreciated. Most Chinese and Western works on the early history of the Chinese Communist Party (CCP) render these women invisible or allude to their presence by mentioning one or two well-known representatives, such as Xiang Jingyu and Deng Yingchao. The general impression conveyed in the scholarly literature is that a few women became token leaders in the CCP during its first phase of existence, but that they were insignificant in the making of party history and in the women's movement of their era. Thus, the CCP of the 1920s has been portrayed as an essentially male-centered organization that gave lip-service to the cause of women's emancipation, but had little real interest in involving women in the revolutionary process as agents of their own emancipation.

This view of the early CCP has gained greater credence with the recent proliferation of scholarship demonstrating the historical incompatibility between Marxism and feminism. Given the experiences of other communist parties, it has seemed reasonable to assume that the Chinese case represented yet one more example of proletarian ideology meeting and overcoming bourgeois feminism. Indeed, it has been argued that high-ranking communist women leaders in the 1920s shunned the independent women's movement and refused to put a high priority on gender issues because of their steadfast belief in the primacy of class-based revolution.[1] This portrayal of the CCP as unwilling to incorporate its ideal of women's emancipation into its women's program has prompted scholars to conclude that the party missed a key opportunity in the mass upsurge of the national revolution (1923–27) to reform the oppressive traditional kinship structure and improve conditions for the bulk of Chinese women.[2]

Because this interpretation seemed to ring so true—it conformed not only with the communist ideological expostulations on the "Woman Question" during the next phase of the Chinese Communist revolution (1928–49), but more importantly with current attitudes of Chinese communist leaders—scholars surmised that little was to be gained by conducting an in-depth study of women in the communist movement during the 1920s.[3] However, by looking at the early years of the CCP through the prism of the present, we have failed to recognize the vast differences between the policies on women in the 1920s and those that came after. In fact, the first Chinese Communists were strongly influenced by the blossoming of feminist ideas during the May Fourth Movement (1915–21), and strove to integrate these ideas into its women's program. With the concluding of an alliance between the Communist and Guomindang parties in 1923 and the rise of social revolutionary ferment in 1925, women were designated as an important group to be mobilized for the cause of the national revolution. They assumed visible political roles as leaders and grass-roots organizers in both parties and were provided with a unique opportunity to oversee what grew into a massive mobilization of women from various classes. The tremendous popular response to this campaign attested to the drawing power of feminist issues, especially among younger women, and raised the expectation that fundamental gender reform of the kinship system would be instituted.

However, as large numbers of women tried to reshape their culture through political participation, other mobilized groups in the revolutionary coalition began to object to female actions that were too explicitly feminist. The conflict over the politicization of gender issues welled up in the Guomindang and Communist parties and was instrumental in the breakdown of their collaboration. In the aftermath of 1927, these tensions were reflected in a shift in the popular imagery of female organizers from ardent, willowy patriots to shrill and sexually promiscuous malcontents. Female activism also came to be viewed as a disturbing indicator of a world turned upside down. Thus, although women's mobilization in the mid-1920s secured important gains for women in the 1930s, such as the vote, legal rights, and greater access to education and employment, women were discouraged from actively pursuing feminist objectives in the realm of mainstream politics in Guomindang China, and even the radical CCP set definite boundaries on women's political roles and the use of gender issues in female mobilization after 1927.

Male Feminists in the Early Communist Movement

Most early male Communists were remarkably sensitive to women's issues. In this respect, they carried on a tradition in Chinese political culture that had existed since the tumultuous 1890s. At that time, strains of indigenous feminist thought that had been present in China for many centuries emerged as a distinct political creed.[4] Its most prominent proponents were men, constitutional reformers and political revolutionaries who advocated women's equality in order to increase the strength of the nation. Liang Qichao, for instance, equated the lives of Chinese women with the miserable lot of slaves or domesticated animals. He argued that China could not become a strong state in the world community until its female "parasites" had been transformed into independent and productive citizens.[5] For Liang and many others of his political persuasion at the turn of the century, the condition of Chinese women came to symbolize the national weakness that had to be transformed if China was to stand up to the Western challenge. Thus from its inception, modern feminism was a handmaiden to nationalism.

During the first two decades of the twentieth century, feminism became more firmly planted in Chinese soil and was fueled by the intellectual vitality and social ferment of the 1910s, which later came to be called the May Fourth Movement. A key target of the new intellectual leaders who aimed to make an irrevocable break with the past was the transformation of the family—necessary, they argued, in order to allow China to become a modern nation-state. Foremost among these May Fourth cultural revolutionaries was Chen Duxiu, who exerted enormous influence over Chinese students through his iconoclastic writing in the widely read *New Youth* magazine and his position as dean of Beijing University. In his articles, Chen lambasted the Confucian familial norms for relegating women to an inferior social position, restricting them to physically and spiritually abnormal lives in their homes, barring them from discussing public issues, and inculcating them with the value of total submission to patriarchal authority. In his view, these traditional principles of proper social conduct for women were incompatible with a modern way of life, which must be based on the concepts of equality and independence.[6] As a result of his championing of women's emancipation, Chen has been credited with rendering this issue into a critical item of discourse among Chinese intellectuals and students in the May Fourth period (1915–21).[7]

When Chen Duxiu embraced Marxism in early 1920 and formed the first communist cell in Shanghai, this May Fourth attack on familial norms prescribing women's conduct was integrated into the fledgling communist movement along with a Marxist materialist analysis of women's oppression drawn from Friedrich Engels' *The Origin of the Family, Private Property and the State*. Thus, the two currents of May Fourth feminism and the Marxist critique of the family mingled in the communist movement as part of a single historical trend and for a few years served to enshrine the ideal of women's emancipation within the movement itself. The impact of this trend was witnessed in the voluminous flood of writings of early male Communists on women's emancipation, which invigorated the feminist press.[8] These men indicted the Confucian morality code, particularly the traditional value of female chastity, provided a materialist interpretation of the development of patriarchy, argued for the importance of women acquiring an education and becoming economically indepen-dent, and echoed Engels' critique of the institution of marriage as analo-gous to prostitution, with the role of the wife differing from that of the hooker only in the duration of her services.[9]

The sheer volume of such writings, to say nothing of the high percent-age of early communists who wrote about women's issues, attests to the strong attraction of the early communist movement to feminist ideas. To be sure, from what little information is available to us about the personal lives of these communist male feminists, some discrepancies certainly existed between what they preached and how they conducted their inti-mate relationships with women.[10] But if the notion of gender equality was not always fully practiced, it was felt strongly enough to compel early communist men to recruit women and develop female organizers who could involve large numbers of women in the revolutionary process as agents of their own emancipation.

Soon after the First Party Congress in July 1921, plans were put in motion to establish a communist women's action program, which included an alliance with an established women's association in Shanghai, the setting up of a women's journal, and the founding of a school for women. Thus the early communist movement readily made the transition from discussion to action. In so doing, it transplanted its feminist ideological orientation into its organization program, thereby providing women with a unique opportunity to build their own institutions within a Chinese political party.

Ideology was not the only factor motivating the communists to take this step. An equally compelling reason was their awareness of the subtle alteration in women's status wrought by deep-seated economic, political, and social changes that had been underway for decades. The unfolding of large-scale historical processes, such as the breakdown of the Chinese imperial state, the beginning of industrialization, the rebuilding of the nation-state, Western cultural imperialism, urbanization, the dissemina-tion of women's education, and the crisis of the elite family, had weakened traditional constraints on female behavior and helped women of various classes step across the boundary between the domestic and the public domains.

Women's entry into the realm of politics symbolized the changes in prescribed gender roles more dramatically than any other single female pursuit, as the wielding of power and authority was central to the cultural construction of male gender roles. In the first decade of the twentieth century, a small number of women involved themselves in revolutionary politics, devoting themselves to the overthrow of the Qing imperial gov-ernment. Soon after the establishment of a republic, women agitated for an equal rights clause to be incorporated into the new constitution. When they learned of the legislature's failure to take decisive action on the issue, women took the unprecedented step of bursting into the halls, breaking windows, and trampling on the guards. This confrontational demonstration of female agency was regarded with widespread popular dismay, as it jarred with conventional norms that women should be passive and accepting of male authority.

The next upswing in female political participation was motivated by the anti-imperialist May Fourth demonstrations in 1919, in which over a thousand women marched in the capital, an unprecedented development. Soon after, women's organizations were established in many Chinese cities to promote nationalistic and women's rights issues, including the right to elect women to office. The Hunan Women's Association stunned the nation when it actually orchestrated the election of one of its members, Wang Changguo, to the Hunan Provincial Assembly.[11] Some of the male assembly members reacted with disdain to her election, arguing that she had disgraced her ancestors by assuming such a public role. An assemblyman by the name of Chen Zhishu was further irked when she sat in one of the most prominent seats, rather than in the rear, at which he uttered the insulting remark: "Are the 190 members of the Hunan Provincial Assembly sons of this Wang Changguo?"[12] His response was indicative of the stiff resistance women entering politics in China still encountered.

Early male CCP members viewed these changes in women's public visibility and instances of female agency as positive indicators that a women's action program could succeed in attracting large numbers of women who were interested in social change. Party newspapers contained articles reporting on examples of militancy among female industrial workers. In addition, the rise of women's groups after the May Fourth Incident caught the attention of communist leaders. When Chen Duxiu was in Canton in late 1920, he delivered a speech to the Guangdong Women's Association in which he identified women's emancipation as one of the most pressing issues of the revolution.[13]

These are but a few of the indications that the CCP in mid-1921 looked to women as a potential group to be mobilized for the revolution. Such a belief was consistent with the general attitudes in the larger nationalistic political culture that had given birth to the fledgling communist movement. However, communist men knew that they could not serve as effective organizers of women, as conventional gender codes proscribed social interaction between the sexes, except within the confines of the family. In order to begin the process of social mobilization, the party had to develop a core of female organizers.

Wang Huiwu and the First Women's Program

Although the delegates at the CCP's First Congress in July 1921 were entirely male, there were women in and around the communist movement from its inception. The first woman member of the Chinese Communist Party was Miao Boying, a Hunanese who was drawn into radical politics while studying at the Beijing Normal College and joined the CCP in November of 1920. She was followed by Liu Qingyang, who became a member in France in January of 1921. In addition, a number of women were involved in Communist activities at that time who did not possess party membership status, the most prominent of whom were Xiang Jingyu in France, Yang Kaihui in Changsha, and Gao Junman and Wang Huiwu in Shanghai. [14]

From what we know of their backgrounds, these women shared several characteristics: they were southerners who came from either merchant or gentry families—though their economic situations varied markedly—and they had been privileged enough to acquire at least a middle-school education. A significant factor in these women's politicization process was their attendance at girls' schools, which served as breeding grounds for nationalist and feminist ideas—even in cases where the principals were very conservative and upheld traditional norms of female conduct and appearance.

For most of these women who entered the communist movement in its first years, breaking with the traditional standards of female conduct was a critical component of their radicalization. The enormity of this struggle should not be underestimated. Women who were raised to be docile and self-effacing confronted tremendous psychological difficulties in their effort to break with prescribed gender roles and participate in public life. As these women gravitated toward the CCP—usually through student networks, the influence of a teacher, or marriage—the issue of women's emancipation remained prominent in their political identities. In the early years of the party, their dual commitments to Marxism and feminism seemed compatible. They found an environment that was very supportive of the cause of women's emancipation and that allowed women to work side by side with men in an equalitarian fashion. In contrast to the fairly segregated lives that most women led in Chinese society, the communist subculture that was emerging offered them a unique opportunity to remove themselves from patriarchal control and conduct their lives in accordance with their ideals of gender equality. Equally significant, it also offered them the possibility of entering into a free-choice marriage or a consensual union with men with values similar to their own. [15]

Of the handful of women in the communist movement in 1921, Wang Huiwu emerged as the first female organizer of a women's program. Her radicalization as a student and the maturation of her political ideas as she gravitated toward the CCP are illustrative of the first generation of Communist women. Atypical for her times, she stood out from the mainstream of Chinese women for her dual commitment to socialism and feminism as well as for her indefatigable energy, her resourcefulness, and her organizational and communication skills.

Like other women in the communist movement, Wang Huiwu com-
menced her career in politics by participating in student protests against
the Paris Peace Conference while she was at the Hunjun Academy for
Girls in Zhejiang. Soon afterward, she published an article in the *Young
China* magazine bitterly assailing the arranged marriage system, which she
felt imprisoned women for their entire lifetimes. She also singled out as
particularly dangerous to women's equality the acceptance of Confucian
ideas of female obedience to the male members of the family, the notion
that women should obey their husbands at all times, and the belief that
women should aspire only to become virtuous wives and excellent mothers, as knowledge in women was deemed a vice. In Wang's view, these
traditional ideals blinded women to the real nature of their subjugation and
allowed them to fall into the trap of arranged marriages.[16] Thus by her
early twenties, Wang Huiwu displayed the major qualities that would later
be manifested in her leadership of the Communist women's program:
iconoclasm, feminism, commitment to journalism, and political activism.

The choice of Wang Huiwu to oversee the women's program in the
summer of 1921 reveals much about the process by which women assumed
power in the CCP. The two criteria that recommended Wang Huiwu for
this role were her strong record of activism and her relationship to an
important male leader in the CCP hierarchy. Ironically, her decision to
marry Li Da, who had been elected to a three-person Central Bureau at
the First Party Congress, gave her access to this important role, but her
position and power within the CCP were never officially sanctioned. In
fact, she lacked formal party membership status. Rather, she wielded
informal power that was seen as a natural extension of her husband's power
and authority in the CCP. She attended most meetings, for instance,
including the First Party Congress.[17] Similarly, Li Da was named the
principal of the Shanghai Common Girls' School, even though Wang
Huiwu did the main planning, curriculum design, teacher selection, and
overseeing of the day-to-day functions. Such contradictions between her
actual roles and her official titles seemed to go unnoticed by Communist
men in Shanghai, who believed themselves to be firm upholders of social
emancipation for Chinese women, and thus saw no need to subject their
assumptions about women's access to formal positions within the party
hierarchy to rigorous scrutiny.

Wang Huiwu began to build a women's program by forming a tactical
alliance with the Shanghai Women's Association, a group founded in the
spring of 1919. Though she was committed to the realization of a proletarian revolution, Wang felt no hostility toward an independent women's
group whose main purpose was to promote a breakdown in gender restrictions and women's entrance into the public realm. Her friendship with
Huang Zonghan, the president of the Shanghai Women's Association, was
instrumental in her ability to form the collaboration, which spawned two

important projects, a journal entitled *The Women's Voice* and the Shanghai Common Girls' School. The sponsorship of these two projects by the Shanghai Women's Association provided legality and legitimacy, for the CCP had to operate as an underground organization in Shanghai.

An important characteristic shared by these two projects under Wang Huiwu was that they were intended to encourage cross-class collaboration among women. To this end, a curriculum was designed to attract "common" women from the lower classes as well as graduates of middle schools who needed further preparation for entrance to university. However, although a number of destitute women came to the school, it proved difficult to recruit workers. One woman student was married to a worker, who demanded she live separately from the rest of the students so as not to pick up their unrestrained and unconventional manners. For this one male worker at least, education was seen as desirable for a wife, while new attitudes and behaviors that might upset family patterns were not. The school's failure to attract women workers was ameliorated partially by the establishment of social investigation classes, which were designed to expose students to conditions in the silk and textile mills of Shanghai.

In a similar vein, while *The Women's Voice* carried articles on many subjects—birth control, women's education, women's literature—an important theme was the plight of women workers; yet the magazine was aimed at women students and intellectuals. Wang sought to convince these women to assume leadership roles in a new women's movement that would involve women from several classes. [18] In essence, Wang Huiwu's women's program was directed at organizing women of the newly emerging middle class.

When the Shanghai Common Girls' School opened its doors to students on February 10, 1922, it was intended to provide women with a basic education that would encourage consciousness of class and gender oppression and foster independence. In contrast to most women's schools, which Wang criticized for training a small group of elite women to become good wives and mothers and for perpetuating traditional rules of propriety, this school offered young women a "modern," scientifically oriented education and at the same time provided work for those women who had no other means of support. To this end, the curriculum included courses in sociology, English language, mathematics, economics, Chinese, physics, and chemistry. In addition, a work program supplied instruction, equipment, and materials for three kinds of jobs: sock-knitting, tailoring, and weaving. Ideologically the program stood as a concrete embodiment of Engels' principle that women ultimately would be liberated by achieving economic independence. Here women had the opportunity to learn a skill that could help remove them from patriarchal control. For Wang Huiwu, these reasons served as a justification for the tremendous outlay of time and energy required to set up and run the program.

Wang also created an environment in the school that encouraged the twenty to thirty women students to become independent of traditional roles and family controls. A number of students shed their surnames as a sign of their complete rejection of the patriarchal kinship system. Later, discovering that the lack of surnames proved too inconvenient, they decided to adopt very common, simple ones instead. At least six students saw the Shanghai Common Girls' School as a refuge from the system of arranged marriage. Schools at this time in fact served as an important institution in facilitating young girls' efforts to gain greater decisionmaking power over their own lives. The poignancy with which the dilemma of arranged marriages was felt by some young girls in the 1920s was aptly revealed in a letter by one student to her parents that was published in a Shanghai newspaper after she had sought asylum at the Shanghai Common Girls' School. She wrote:

> The reason I have left home is because of my arranged marriage with Mr. Wang. This matter was undertaken with my best interests in mind, but marriage ought to be based on love. . . . Although our country is corrupt, our civil law stipulates that marriage is to be decided by the people involved and only then is the permission of the parents gained. In April of 1916 the Supreme Court decided in favor of a daughter who objected to an arranged marriage. Although Mr. Wang and I are relatives, we have no feelings toward one another. Our relationship is like ice. Such a marriage could not produce love. Mr. Wang is the same generation as my grandfather. According to old conventions, this is not a good marriage. I argued against this marriage agreement both before and after the engagement, but my pleas fell on deaf ears. As parents, you were concerned about my honor, but not my feelings. I am a person and have my rights. For my future happiness, I have no choice but to leave home. . . . My suffering is unbearable. I hope you won't do this to my sister. [19]

Wang Huiwu assumed that the quest of fostering women's independence and education would ultimately predispose many women toward becoming revolutionaries. For this reason, the Shanghai Common Girls' School was intended primarily to be an educational institution rather than a cadre training school. She believed that knowledge was a powerful force in turning women into social revolutionaries, that englightenment was the first step toward political activism. In this regard, both the school and the women's journal were concrete expressions of CCP support for the cause of women's emancipation. Moreover, they served to develop a critical mass of females within party circles in Shanghai.

Despite the benefits that accrued from these two projects, the CCP allowed *The Women's Voice* to stop publication in June 1922 and the school to close down in the fall. This withdrawal of party support calls into question the seriousness of the communist commitment to these feminist-oriented programs. It might well be argued that party leaders, in response to ideological tensions between Marxism and feminism, had decided to terminate the women's program because of its feminist objectives. The historical evidence, however, indicates that the reasons for the demise of Wang Huiwu's two projects were due to Communist inexperience in institution-building, lack of financial resources, and most importantly the serious erosion of Wang Huiwu's stature in the party due to the demotion of her husband from the Central Committee at the Second Party Congress in July 1922. Ultimately, the fledgling CCP, despite its radicalism, bowed to patriarchal influences and replaced Wang Huiwu with another capable communist woman, Xiang Jingyu.

Wang Huiwu's year of developing a women's program for the CCP did net some important tangible results. Most importantly, the Second Party Congress decided to formally establish a Women's Bureau. This separate organizational structure provided communist women with their own power base and proved to be critical to the future successes of the women's mobilization campaigns during the national revolution. In addition, Wang Huiwu's school brought several students into the communist movement, all of whom were to play significant roles in the unfolding revolution. Wang Yizhi entered the party in August 1922, as the first woman to be accepted formally by the Shanghai branch.[20] Qian Xijun joined the CCP in 1925, later establishing a place for herself in the annals of the revolution by taking part in the Long March (1934–36) along with twenty-nine other women. Two others from the school made contributions at later dates. Ding Ling joined the CCP in 1931 and Qin Dejun served as a member of the National People's Consultative Congress after 1949.

Xiang Jingyu's Development of the Communist Women's Bureau

Soon after the Second Party Congress Xiang Jingyu, having recently arrived in Shanghai from Montargis, where she had participated in a work-study program for Chinese students in France, was charged with the responsibility of meeting the challenge of developing a coherent and viable Communist Women's Bureau. No doubt, her appointment was influenced by the election of her husband, Cai Hesen, to the Central Committee of the CCP. However, she became the most famous and influential communist woman of this period as a result of her own deeds. A dramatic and intriguing figure, Xiang Jingyu fashioned the strategy that proved so successful in mobilizing women for the national revolution. As the architect of the Women's Bureau, she became involved with many types of women's groups that were concerned with improving women's political, social, and economic status: women's rights, suffrage, and professional organizations; women's schools and universities; student associations; women strikers and unions; and the feminist press.

Xiang Jingyu illustrates the particular fashion in which feminist issues were wedded to revolutionary commitments for Communist women of her time. In some respects, she displayed traditional traits typical of earlier Chinese heroines; in other respects, she was representative of the May Fourth generation of individualistic, liberated women; in still other respects, she manifested the tensions of radical women who had to correlate political responsibilities with personal concerns. Although her achievements were extraordinary, her career as a political and social revolutionary is illustrative of the motivations and dilemmas of her contemporaries in the communist movement. With her execution in 1928 in the White Terror following the bloody breakdown in the alliance between the Guomindang and Communist Party, she became a revolutionary martyr who inspired countless other revolutionary women in the continuing effort to achieve a communist revolution.

In contrast to Xiang Jingyu's stature in the CCP at the height of her career, she began her life as a communist unceremoniously in late 1921. Xiang Jingyu's membership seems to have been considered as a natural, automatic extension of that of her husband, Cai Hesen.[21] Later, this practice changed in the Shanghai branch with the establishment of the Women's Bureau, which prompted the adoption of formal membership procedures for women. However, while the Women's Bureau provided Communist women in Shanghai with a way out of the confines of the informal power structure, it did not eradicate this structure. In the realm of Communist high politics, women had a voice but not a vote. Xiang Jingyu thus participated at higher echelon party meetings on an informal basis only and she was not an elected official of the Central Committee or an official delegate to the party congresses, as has often been claimed in hagiographic biographical sketches.[22]

Contrary to what has generally been asserted in Western scholarship, the main thrust of the Women's Bureau program under Xiang Jingyu was to form tactical alliances with the various groups of the independent women's movement and attract women students in order to develop a core of Communist women organizers to launch a massive social mobilization of women for the national revolution.[23] Thus, Xiang not only did not ignore the struggles of women outside of the working class, but she also attached importance to the cause of women's liberation. To this end, she argued that specific issues regarding women had to be addressed in the course of the revolution—that women had to be incorporated into the revolutionary process as agents of their own emancipation. In this respect, she perpetuated the feminist orientation of the Communist women's program that had existed from its inception.

To be sure, Xiang Jingyu did not completely embrace female intellectuals. In fact, from time to time she expressed her concern for the narrowness of their vision and their lack of interest in the plight of Chinese women workers. In her most harsh indictment of women's rights and suffrage groups during her three-year tenure as head of the Women's Bureau, she described them as made up of the "cream of women intellectuals," who were used to lives of leisure and were totally dependent on the support of men—fathers, husbands, and sons. Moreover, she wondered whether these women's involvement in the women's movement amounted to anything more than a passing fancy.[24] However, to interpret such statements as deep-seated hostility toward female intellectuals or as a strong indication that the Women's Bureau under her direction was not interested in combating gender oppression fails to put them into the context of her political objectives or the full body of her writings.

An important political priority of Xiang Jingyu was to use the Women's Bureau to support the coalition with the Guomindang party that had been discussed at a special planning session in Hangzhou in August 1922 and formally accepted by the CCP at its Third Party Congress in June 1923. Xiang Jingyu wholeheartedly endorsed the United Front, which she argued represented a necessary stage in national unity that would enable China to ward off the danger of imperialist intervention.[25] What was most unusual about her stand was that it was radically opposed to the views of her husband, who objected vociferously to the idea of an alliance and reportedly remained aloof from the Guomindang after the alliance was agreed upon and often criticized its leaders.[26] In this, Xiang Jingyu displayed an unusual degree of independence for a woman of her era.

To cement the United Front in the area of women's work, Xiang Jingyu accepted a post as one of the main editors of *The Women's Weekly*, an eight-page weekly supplement of the Guomindang newspaper in Shanghai, *The Republic Daily*, in order to persuade educated women in Shanghai, including feminists, to support the national revolution. Following the Guomindang's First Party Congress in 1924, she became the head of the Guomindang Shanghai Women's Movement Committee. Not only did she shape the Guomindang women's program, but she also correlated her role in the United Front with the orientation of the Communist Women's Bureau. For instance, she drafted a resolution on women for the Third Party Congress of the CCP in June 1923 that specified that an important function of the Communist Women's Bureau would be to gain influence over the "general women's movement," which she defined as comprising women's rights, suffrage, and social reform groups.[27]

As part of her effort to convince women to participate in the national revolution, Xiang Jingyu went to great lengths to show her support and encouragement for the struggle to alter gender relations. Her articles in *The Women's Weekly* stressed many positive features of the women's rights movement, which she termed "the human rights and civil rights movement of women."[28] On another occasion she wrote:

> The women's rights movement is born out of the need to solve the specific problem of the female sex. . . . Sometimes the problem might appear super-

ficially to be that of a few or a certain group of women, but actually it has
general significance. The significance of the women's rights movement is to
wipe out the oppression of the female sex, develop equality between men and
women, and restore the human rights to which women are entitled.[29]

While writing in support of these women's groups, Xiang Jingyu nevertheless maintained that they could not accomplish their goals unless they
became involved in revolutionary politics. She contended that they could
not ignore the fact that warlord politics and foreign control were "wrecking
China" and "trampling" on civil rights, seriously impairing all efforts to
win equality for women. Without such involvement, she warned, their
achievements would all disappear like "sand castles," as had happened in
Hunan when the "diehards had offhandedly abolished" women's hard-won
right to own property.[30]

What was unusual about Xiang Jingyu's message to these groups is that
she did not merely promise that the revolution would ultimately benefit
women, but she also stressed the importance of women participating in the
revolutionary movement to further their own cause.[31] A distinctive feature
of Xiang Jingyu's leadership was that she was able to integrate such an
orientation into her political program. Thus, when Sun Yatsen omitted
women in his call for a national convention of Chinese leaders from all
professions (politicians, businessmen, educators, etc.) to end militarism
and unify the nation peacefully in 1924, Xiang initiated a mass campaign
to involve women in this convention, arguing that only women could truly
represent women's interests.[32]

This issue struck such a responsive chord in women that Xiang Jingyu
was able to mobilize many women's groups and individuals to agitate for
female participation in the proposed conference to discuss national issues.
Hundreds of people, most of them women, attended meetings in major
metropolitan areas where they established groups to promote women's
participation in the convention. In February 1925 women in this mobilization campaign were further aroused when a National Assembly planning session called by Duan Qirui, the chief executive of the warlord
government in Beijing, adopted draft regulations that specified that only
men would be enfranchised. In essence, women were being defined as
political nonentities in the formation of institutions that might shape a new
nation-state. Led by Xiang Jingyu in her official capacity as head of the
Guomindang Women's Movement Committee in Shanghai, women
around the nation publicly condemned Article 14 and demanded that the
word *nanzi* (men) be replaced with *guomin* (citizen). In so doing, they
were demanding the right to participate as full citizens of the Chinese
state.

The campaign to revise Article 14 failed because of the steadfast refusal
of Duan Qirui's committee to grant women citizen status, but oddly
enough this failure ultimately proved to be a triumph for the revolutionary

forces. For those women who had been mobilized into this campaign and those who watched the course of events in the hope that women might be accommodated into the existing political system, this outcome revealed in stark terms that their interests were best served by the revolutionary camp which was gaining political strength in the south. Moreover, the securing of Guangdong as a base of the Guomindang now made it seem possible that a national revolution could be accomplished. Thus, through this campaign many women's groups became amenable to actively participating in the national revolution.

When Xiang Jingyu assumed the head of the Womens' Bureau, she not only accepted the challenge of convincing women's groups to participate in the national revolution, she also had to convince some of the skeptics in her own party—including perhaps her husband—that these women's groups had revolutionary potential. Tensions about Communist involvement in the women's rights movement first surfaced in the CCP in 1922 with the formation of the Women's Rights League, which advocated sweeping legislative changes for women in the areas of politics, family, education, and labor reform. Miao Boying, a student at Beijing Higher Girls' Normal Institute and the first woman to become a member of the CCP, was one of the founding members of the Women's Rights League. After the league's Beijing membership reached more than three hundred, Miao Boying traveled to Shanghai and Nanjing, where she helped to found new chapters. In Shanghai, Wang Yizhi (recruited into the CCP from the Shanghai Common Girls' School) became a founding member and expounded the reasons for her decision in a prominent women's magazine. She wrote:

> We Shanghai sisters ought to take advantage of this opportunity to strive together with our sisters from Beijing for the rights we ought to have. . . . All rights in the constitution should be held equally by men and women. . . . When we obtain the right to participate in government, we can elect representatives to all levels of the legislative assemblies who will formulate laws beneficial to us and advocate rights that will benefit us. Thus, now in particular, we should struggle for our suffrage rights.[33]

Critical responses to the Women's Rights League were quickly published by several Communist men in Shanghai. Chen Wangdao condemned the league as unrevolutionary because it ultimately bolstered bourgeois oppression.[34] An even more doctrinaire indictment was issued by Gao Junyu, a member of the Central Committee, in *The Weekly Guide* (a CCP organ) in November 1922. Gao assailed the leaders of the Women's Rights League for their lack of socialist and class consciousness. Gao Junyu was particularly critical of the group's first aim: to achieve equality between men and women. It showed, he argued, that the members of the group aspired for equality with capitalists, not with coolies, and thus were not interested in the struggle of the proletariat, despite the obvious fact that most women were "becoming new-style slaves of capitalism."[35]

When Xiang Jingyu drafted her "Resolution on the Women's Movement" for the Third Party Congress in 1923, she strove to combat the deep-seated contempt some members felt toward the women's movement. She argued that this movement was important politically, despite its history of strong divisions and lack of action. She warned her comrades that if the CCP were to succeed in its bid to assume leadership of the women's movement, they should not show disdain toward "ladies," "young misses," and "women politicians" and should not scare them away by stressing the theory of class struggle.[36]

Although Xiang Jingyu could not specifically address the criticism of her male comrades in her published articles for *The Women's Weekly*, her writings contain veiled references to their continuing disapproval of the women's movement. In 1925, for instance, she argued against the view among "certain people" that all women except workers were straggling behind the revolutionary movement, regardless of whether they were traditional or modern-minded. Moreover, Xiang contended that female conservatism could be directly attributed to women's environment—traditional educations, their seclusion from society, and their economic dependency. She also insisted that her experiences and investigations demonstrated that women were by no means impervious to revolutionary influences.[37]

One further indication of Xiang Jingyu's commitment to promoting female agency in the national revolution was her willingness to draw attention within the CCP to instances of gender conflict in the revolutionary working class. In an internal party document, she argued that this conflict stemmed from deep-seated disregard for women by male workers. Although she did not air her concerns about the persistence of patriarchal biases among the male proletariat in the public arena, it is significant that she called on Communist labor leaders to "vigorously educate" male workers and convince them of the importance of discarding such disdainful attitudes. Moreover, Xiang's decision to use the occasion of the Third Party Congress in 1923 to raise such issues concretely demonstrated her continuing commitment to the struggle for women's equality and the eradication of patriarchal oppression.[38]

Xiang's battle with patriarchy was not restricted to the political realm. Although political goals remained her first priority, she was committed to an alternative personal lifestyle as well. Her involvement in an affair with Peng Shuzhi, a high-ranking member of the CCP, showed her to be the epitome of a liberated woman of her time. Like many women Communists in the 1920s, her break with conventional gender roles meant defining marriage as a consensual union that would bring some measure of personal fulfillment and could be terminated if either partner so desired.

Thus, Xiang's experimentation with social relationships was far from an unheard of occurrence in the communist subculture of Shanghai. Although the reasons for the deterioration of her relationship with Cai Hesen are not known, the combination of his almost obsessive passion for politics, which often included all-night work stints, with his long bouts of debilitating asthma attacks may have had a detrimental effect. Xiang's and Cai's differences over the Communist collaboration with the Guomindang no doubt added to the tension in their relationship.

Although the social norms of the communist subculture supported Xiang's right to seek personal happiness in another relationship when her marriage no longer fulfilled her needs, the repercussions of her actions on her political status in the party were quite severe. After Xiang and Cai ended their marriage, she lost her standing on the Central Executive Committee and her command of the Communist Women's Bureau. Nor was she given delegate status or any other official position at the Fifth Party Congress in 1927, a meeting that formally elected some women to high posts in the party hierarchy in recognition of the strong role that women were playing in the mobilization campaigns for the national revolution. Had she continued her relationship with Peng Shuzhi, she might have been able to assume positions commensurate with his high political status. But as an unattached female, she lost her access to the world of high politics in the CCP. Xiang's experiences showed that a woman had to be related to an important male figure in the CCP in order to both gain and retain an influential position in the party hierarchy, and that the quality of her performance in the position had little bearing on the matter.

High Tide of Revolutionary Ferment

Widespread popular outrage at the shooting of Chinese demonstrators in the foreign concession of Shanghai by British and Sikh police on May 30, 1925, ushered in a period of revolutionary ferment that lasted for almost two years. The miscalculation of British authorities about the depth of public sentiment against high-handed foreign treatment of Chinese citizens provided Communist organizers with an issue that transformed thousands of students, including girls, into vocal rebels who shut down their schools and paraded through the streets, spreading the message that this national insult should not be tolerated. By the same token, women workers were drawn into the CCP in Shanghai and began to serve as political organizers. Perhaps the most impressive example of Communist inroads into the female working class was made in the silk industry, where a large-scale strike in 1926 demonstrated the party's new-found strength and its victory over more conservative labor union leaders who had held sway for four years.

Meanwhile, the Shakee massacre, a tragic encounter between Chinese demonstrators and British concession police in the southern city of Guangzhou a few weeks after the May Thirtieth Incident, served to sustain this revolutionary tempo by unleashing a multitude of outraged students and sparking a massive Canton–Hong Kong strike and boycott that lasted for more than a year. The fruits of this popular agitation were more readily reaped in this city because of the recent success of the Guomindang in consolidating its political and military control there. Guangzhou thus became the cradle of the nationalist revolution. Partisans to the cause streamed down to this revolutionary capital to enlist their services in the cause. At the end of 1925 plans were set in motion to launch a large military expedition against the regional warlord governments. When the Northern Expedition, as it came to be called, left Guangzhou in July 1926 to defeat warlord armies in such provinces as Hunan, Hubei, Jiangxi, and Fujian, it left a massive social mobilization of broad sectors of society, including women, in its wake.

The large-scale women's movement that emerged in the course of the national revolution was encouraged and directed by the Guomindang Women's Department and the Communist Women's Bureau. As part of the collaboration agreement between the two parties, Communist women, such as Deng Yingchao and Cai Chang, held prominent positions in the Guomindang Central Women's Department in Guangzhou. They facilitated the development of Guomindang institutions, such as the establishment of a training institute for women grass-roots organizers, and aided the establishment and growth of Communist-sponsored mass women's associations. Initially proposed by Xiang Jingyu, these Communist women's associations first appeared in Beijing and Shanghai at the time of the May Thirtieth Incident. The revolutionary exuberance of the moment facilitated their rapid expansion throughout Guangdong Province in the latter part of 1925 and then into Hunan and Hubei in the wake of the Northern Expedition. By 1927, they drew on the energies and resources of 300,000 members.[39]

The objective of these Communist-sponsored women's associations was to harness the dynamics of both the social revolution and the national revolution against warlord regimes and foreign domination. While the journals of many urban associations stressed nationalist priorities, arguing that women's emancipation could not occur without a national revolution, in the south, at a grass-roots level, the more radical social revolutionary themes received equal if not greater emphasis than nationalist ones.[40] A resolution of the Guomindang Congress in the eastern part of Guangdong stated: "Women are oppressed by old feudal ethics, the old-style family, the old marriage system, and traditional society. Each party branch ought to support women by organizing women's groups that will work for the liberation of women and their participation in the national revolution."[41]

In Hunan, these women's associations prospered. The Liling county women's association, for instance, reportedly had fifty branches and a membership of more than 6,000.[42] What is significant about the process of female mobilization in Liling is that the ideological message contained in the association's literature was heavily tinged with May Fourth feminist concepts. Much stress was laid on the oppressive nature of the patriarchal family system, which was blamed for inhibiting the development of women's individual character (*ren'ge*), an important May Fourth theme, and for propagating the practice of polygamy.[43]

These women's associations in many areas evoked an immediate and overwhelming response. They were inundated with pleas from women who desired to escape arranged and abusive marriages, prostitution, and servitude. Xie Xueqin, for instance, complained that she had only come out of hiding and agreed to marry Zeng Songnian after he had arranged for soldiers of two local Guilin warlords to intimidate her classmates and her parents. After three years of this "intolerable" marriage, she had fled to Guangzhou and appealed to the Communist-sponsored Guangdong Women's Liberation Association and the Guomindang Women's Department for assistance in divorcing her husband.[44] Another case handled by the Guangdong Women's Liberation Association involved a woman named Feng Xiujuan, who was humiliated on her wedding night when the bridegroom suddenly began to yell that she was not a virgin. His friends poured into the couple's bedroom and deluged her with verbal abuse and then seized the possessions that she had brought into the marriage. It was only through the services of the Guangdong Women's Association that she was able to seek redress for the loss of her property and reputation. Ultimately, she obtained a favorable court judgment, which ordered the Li family to pay her one hundred yuan.[45]

As this revolution in gender relationships and roles began to ripple through south China, it provoked its own counter social movement. In many cases, the backlash was as strong as the original impulse for change. Women workers who had become political activists were warned by their families to desist from their assumption of self-assertive roles or they would be disowned or encouraged to commit suicide.[46] Rural parents in certain communities refused to allow their daughters to attend school in order to shelter them from contact with radical ideas. The reputation of a Communist-sponsored women's association in Meixian was impugned when it agreed to help a woman gain a divorce. Thereafter it was commonly referred to as a "high-class brothel." This trend was much stronger in more socially conservative provinces like Henan, which a writer for the women's journal *Light* described as one of the worst places for women in the country.[47] By the time the Northern Expedition reached Henan, foreign correspondents reported that the very presence of women accompanying the troops caused such opposition among the local populace that the women had to be withdrawn. What these examples illustrate was the growing opposition of other mobilized groups in the revolutionary coalition to female agency that was explicitly feminist in orientation.

This counter-movement against the mobilization of women put additional strain on the alliance between the Guomindang and Communist parties. Local elites in many areas pressured the Guomindang to stem the social revolutionary tide. In one case, a Guomindang official in Xinxing county, Guangdong, refused to decide in favor of a woman seeking a divorce from a wealthy member of the local gentry who was in charge of the local militia because her husband's family had rallied strong support among the influential families in the community. Afterward, supporters of the husband, whom the Communist Youth League journal labeled "disciples of Confucius," began to join the Guomindang party in order to enhance their political clout in the area. Thus, the case began to take on the appearance of a conflict within the United Front, with the Communist Youth League and women's association supporting the wife and the right-wing Guomindang officials supporting the husband.[48]

The backlash also effected Communist efforts to unite different segments of the independent women's movement into one national organization. The Guangdong Women's Rights Alliance, for instance, accused Communist women organizers of trying to split the Chinese women's movement by manipulating "muddled, mindless peasant women." Such concerns prompted the Guangdong Women's Rights Alliance to verbally attack Communist women for "infiltrating" the Guomindang Women's Department for their own political purposes.[49] As a result of such accusations, the influence of Communist women in the Guomindang was curtailed.[50]

Conclusion

The alliance between the Guomindang and the CCP erupted in bloodshed in April 12, 1927, due to a host of political and social tensions of which the women's mobilization campaign generated only one small segment. A general terror was unleashed throughout the land, and Communists were hunted down. Women's associations were brutally suppressed and many women were targeted for torture and mutilation just because of their bobbed hair. The vengeance unleashed against women and the particularly savage way in which many of them were killed correlated with the danger they were believed to pose to the social order. Still a further indication of the intensity of the backlash against those seeking to change gender relations was the sexual violence many women were subjected to before their deaths. It sent a clear signal to social revolutionaries that the defenders of the patriarchal kinship system were determined to maintain the status quo in social relations.

The violent nature of this counter-revolution against the women's mobilization campaign was encouraged and exacerbated by Guomindang officials who decided that it was politically useful to seize on this issue of wholesale gender reform in order to differentiate themselves from the Communists. They started a propaganda war in which women organizers were characterized as promiscuous and immoral. In such an environment rumors proliferated about Communist iniquities. It was alleged that Communist men shared wives and that they had even held a naked women's parade in Wuhan, where male officials were allowed to choose the women who were most physically suited for display.[51] The net result of such allegations was to weaken the nationalist underpinnings of feminist goals and to cast aspersions on the cause of women's emancipation as an organized social movement. Although the Guomindang government that was set up in Nanking in 1928 enacted legislation that extended legal rights and the vote to women, it dismantled the Guomindang Women's Department and propagated traditional values about female roles in the family and society.

Pushed out of the cities into the Chinese hinterland, the CCP decided to revise its women's program dramatically. This change of policy was first reflected in 1928 in its Sixth Party Congress "Women's Revolution," which condemned its United Front policy in women's work as having knuckled under to bourgeois feminism. More explicit statements disassociating the Communist movement from its feminist phase included denunciations of the women's movement as reformist, counterrevolutionary, and bourgeois.[52] Although the CCP adopted the standard vocabulary of European and Russian Communists to explain the disastrous consequences of its women's mobilization campaign, in essence it was declaring that the party could ill afford to persist in a women's policy that challenged patriarchal powerholders who were participating in their revolutionary coalition. During the next twenty years, the gap between the Communist ideological formulations on women's emancipation and its concrete women's program continued to grow. Peasant women living in Communist base areas, for instance, were encouraged to support the civil war against the Guomindang by producing badly needed clothing and nursing wounded soldiers, but they were rarely encouraged to challenge gender hierarchal power relationships in the family.

In this swift reversal of fortunes and policy, Communist women survivors were confronted with difficult personal and political choices. Many simply retired from revolutionary and public life into the security of their families. Some chose to become martyrs for the cause, patterning themselves on a traditional model of female heroism that had been deeply imbedded in Chinese culture for centuries.[53] Such instances of self-sacrifice were intended to serve as a moral indictment against the execu-tioner. Xiang Jingyu's decision to remain in Wuhan, which had been a major center of Communist organization in the first half of 1927, was tantamount to a sacrificial act, and thus revealed the influence of tradi-tional ideals on her behavior. Like Qiu Jin, the most celebrated female martyr of the 1911 revolution, Xiang was easily captured by her adversaries and was executed on May 1, 1928. For those Communist women who plunged into the countryside, the formidable task of igniting a rural revolution overshadowed their desire to see a continuation of a feminist-oriented women's program. Clearly they had decided that the harsh histor-ical lessons of the social revolution of 1925–27 had revealed the great risks involved for any political party in a frontal assault on patriarchy.

Notes

1. See, for example, Kay Ann Johnson, *Women, the Family and Peasant Revolution in China* (Chicago: University of Chicago Press, 1983), pp. 40–41. The materials that I have drawn on for the analysis in this article came from libraries in the People's Republic of China that were not open to American scholars when Kay Johnson was conducting her research.

2. See, for example, Sue Gronewald, "Recent Scholarship on Chinese Women," *Trends in History* (1986).

3. No monograph in English, Chinese, or Japanese exists on this topic. The best English accounts are contained in Elisabeth Croll, *Feminism and Socialism in China* (New York: Schocken, 1978), pp. 117–52; Leslie Collins, "The New Women: A Psychohistorical Study of the Chinese Feminist Movement from 1900 to the Present" (Ph.D. diss., Yale University, 1976); and Johnson, *Women, The Family and Peasant Revolution in China*, ch. 2.

4. Certain feminist ideas had in fact been present among Chinese scholars and writers for many centuries, but they did not crystalize into a distinct ideology until the late nineteenth century. Hsiung Ping-chen has put forward an interesting hypothesis on the origins of indigenous feminist ideas in China in her unpublished paper, "The Rela-tionship Between Women and Children in Early Modern China," presented at the Seventh Annual Convention of the National Women's Studies Association in Seattle Washington, June 19–23, 1985. Another insightful view on the emergence of feminist ideas in Qing China can be found in Paul Ropp, "The Seeds of Change: Reflections on the Condition of Women in the Early and Mid Ch'ing," *Signs* 2, no. 1 (1976): 5–23.

5. For a discussion of Liang's ideas about women's emancipation, see Collins, "The New Women," pp. 239–40.

6. Chen Duxiu, "The Confucian Doctrine and Modern Life," *Xin qingnian* (New Youth) 2, no. 4 (December 1, 1916); reprinted in Zhonghua quanguo funü lianhehui funü yundong lishi yanjiushi (Research Department of the All-China Women's Federation on the history of the women's movement), eds., *Wusi shiqi funü wenti wenxian* (Beijing: Sanlian shudian, 1981), pp. 101–2.

7. Chen Dongyuan, *Zhongguo funü shenghuo shi* (History of the Life of Chinese Women) (Taibei: Tawian Shangwu Yinshuguan, 1975), pp. 336–7.

8. Some examples of women's journals and New Culture Movement periodicals that carried articles by early male Communists on women's issues were *Funü zashi*, *Xin funü*, *Juewu*, *Xiaonian Zhongguo*, *Xin qingnian*, *Funü pinglun*, and *Jiefang yu gaizao*.

9. Shen Zemin, perhaps more than any other Chinese Communist, expounded on Engels'

notion that prostitution was analogous to the institution of marriage. His writings on the subject evoked an extremely hostile response from one woman, who in her letter to the editor condemned such ideas as constituting an insult to womankind. See Zemin, "Hanying nüshi gei Zemin xiansheng de yuanxin ji qi fuxin" (The Original Letter of Miss Hanying to Mr. Zemin and His Reply), *Funü pinglun*, no. 26 (February 1, 1922): 1.

10. For an in-depth exploration of the disparities in the expostulation and the practice of gender equality for one May Fourth male feminist who became a Communist, see Vera Schwarcz's unpublished paper, "Libertine or Liberationist: Zhang Shenfu's Views of Women During the May Fourth Era," presented at the Thirty-Seventh Annual Meeting of the Association of Asian Studies, March 22, 1985.

11. Tan Sheying reported that three women, Wu Jiaying, Zhou Tianpu, and Wang Chang-guo, were elected to the Hunan Provincial Assembly. However, other sources confirm the election only of Wang Changguo (Tan Sheying, *Zhongguo funü yundong shi* [A History of the Chinese Women's Movement] [Shanghai, 1936], p. 108).

12. Jingyu, "Minguo huiyi yu funü (The National Convention and Women), *Funü zhoubao*, no. 64 (December 14, 1924); reprinted in Xu Rihui, ed., *Xiang Jingyu wenji* (A Collection of Xiang Jingyu's Writings) (Changsha: Hunan Renmin Chubanshe, 1980), p. 163.

13. Chen Duxiu, "Funü wenti yu shehuizhuyi" (The Woman Question and Socialism), *Guangdong chunbao*, January 31, 1921; reprinted in *Wusi shiqi funü wenti wenxian*, pp. 80–83.

14. For a biographical sketch of Miao Boying, see Ceng Changqiu and Zhou Jianchun, "Miao Boying," in Hu Hua, ed., *Zhonggong dangshi renwu zhuan* (Biographies of Personages in Chinese Communist Party History) (Xian: Shaanxi Renmin Chubanshe, 1985), vol. 24, pp. 132–46.

15. For young Chinese radicals who broke away from the conventional marriage practices during the first few decades of the twentieth century, a free-choice marriage meant that the decision to marry was made by the couple themselves and a social celebration would be held to mark the occasion. By contrast, no party was held by those couples choosing to enter into a consensual union. As no legal registration was required at that time, in the public eye, the first type of marriage was considered legitimate; the second, immoral. One of the most famous writers of the era to enter into a consensual union was Lu Xun.

16. Wang Huiwu, "Zhongguo funü wenti—quantao jiefang" (The Chinese Woman's Ques-tion—Liberation from a Trap), *Xiaonian Zhongguo* (Young China) I, no. 4 (October 1919): 6 and 9.

17. Wang Huiwu's role in the early CCP is revealed in the memoirs published in Zhongguo Gongchandang diyici daibiao dahui qianhou ziliao xuanbian, eds., *"Yida" Qianhou* (Before and After the First Party Congress), vol. 2 (Beijing: Renminchubanshe, 1980).

18. This view was stressed in articles carried in *Funü pinglun* (The Women's Critic), a journal edited by Communists. See, for example, I.C.E., "Duiyu zhengzai gaige zhong de nüjie lianhehui xianyi" (A Suggestion on Reforming the Women's Association), *Funü pinglun*, no. 16 (November 16, 1921): 1.

19. Pan Yun, "Yige nüzi yin beipuo hun tuoli jiating" (A Girl Who Leaves Home Because She was Forced to Marry), *Funü pinglun*, no. 67 (November 15, 1922): 4.

20. Interview with Wang Yizhi, October 15, 1979.

21. An interview with Cai Bo, son of Cai Hesen and Xiang Jingyu, on July 23, 1983, confirmed that neither party historians nor close family members knew the introducers of Xiang Jingyu. In contrast, those of Cai Hesen are known. When weak admittance procedures prevailed, such as in the case of Li Lisan, who was admitted unilaterally by Chen Duxiu, this information was generally known among members of the Shanghai branch. Such knowledge does not exist for Xiang Jingyu, although she was viewed as a member.

22. See, for instance, "Gongchandang di'erci quanguo daibiao dahui" (The Second National Congress of the Chinese Communist Party), *Renmin ribao*, May 28, 1981, p. 3.

23. For a different view on Xiang's attitude toward recruiting students, see Suzette Leith, "Chinese Women in the Early Communist Movement," *Women in China: Studies in Social Change and Feminism* (Ann Arbor: University of Michigan Press, 1973), p. 42.

24. Xu Rihui, *Xiang Jingyu wenji*, p. 90.

25. Ibid., pp. 213–14.

26. Gu Ci, "Xiang Jingyu," p. 75 and Claude Cadart and Cheng Yingxiang, *Mémoires de Peng Shuzhi: L'envol du communisme en Chine* (Paris: Gallimard, 1983), p. 365.

27. Xu Rihui, *Xiang Jingyu wenji*, p. 216.

28. Ibid., p. 125.

29. Ibid., p. 103.

30. Ibid., pp. 125, 111, and 105.

31. Ibid., pp. 125–26.

32. Ibid., p. 163.

33. Yizhi, "Zimeimei kuailai gan nüquan yundong ba" (Sisters, Quickly Undertake the Women's Rights Movement), *Funü pinglun*, no. 60 (September 27, 1922): 1.

34. Chen Wangdao, "Kanle nüquan yundong tongmenghui xuanyan yihou" (After Reading the Proclamation of the Women's Rights League), *Funü pinglun*, no. 63 (October 18, 1922): 1.

35. Junyu, "Nüquan yundongzhe yingdang zhidao de" (What Those in the Women's Rights Movement Ought to Know), *Xiangdao zhoubao* (The Weekly Guide), no. 8 (November 1922): 65.

36. Xu Rihui, *Xiang Jingyu wenji*, pp. 216–17.

37. Ibid., pp. 209–11.

38. Ibid., p. 216.

39. Dai Xugong, *Xiang Jingyu Zhuan* (A Biography of Xiang Jingyu (Beijing, 1981), p. 175.

40. Nationalist themes were stressed, for instance, in an article by Xia Songyun, the first chairperson of the Guangdong Women's Liberation Association, entitled "Funü yundong he guomin geming" (The Women's Movement and National Revolution), *Guangming*, pp. 14–16.

41. "Chao Mei Hai Lu Feng daibiao dahui dangwu yijue an" (Resolutions on Party Affairs Passed at the Representative Congress for Chao, Mei, Hai, Lu, and Feng Counties), *Guohua* (National Flower), n.d. (approximate date April 1926).

42. "Women's Liberation in the Hunan Peasant Movement," *China Reconstructs*, March 1975, p. 40.

43. Pamphlet put out by the Liling Women's Association, dated 1927. This material was kindly provided by Delia Davin, who acquired it from the Revolutionary History Museum in Beijing.

44. Xie Xueqin, "Xie Xueqin (yuanming Huiying) jiechu qiangpo huyin yu Zeng Songnian duanjie guanxi xuanyan" (A Proclamation by Xie Xueqin [original name Huiying] Terminating Her Forced Marriage with Zeng Songnian), *Guang ming*, no. 8 (June 30, 1926): 58–62.

45. Interview with Li Jie and Mai Jingwan. In Shanghai during the 1900s a family of four required a minimum living wage of 21.34 *yuan* a month. As the cost of living in Shanghai was quite high, possibly several times more expensive than in the rural areas of Guangdong, one hundred *yuan* would have been sufficient to provide basic necessities of a small family for a year. Jean Chesneaux, *The Chinese Labor Movement, 1919–1927* (Stanford: Stanford University Press, 1968), p. 98.

46. Yang Zhihua, "Zhongguo funü yijiu erliu nian Shanghai sichang nügong bagong yundong zhong zhi ganxiang" (Thoughts on the Strike Movement of Female Silk Workers in Shanghai in 1926), *Zhongguo funü* 16 & 17 (June 30, 1926): 7.

47. You Yi, "Henan funü zhuangkuang" (The Situation for Women in Henan), *Guangming*, no. 8 (June 30, 1926): 18–21.

48. Liang Xinzhi, "Xinxing xian de yige nüxing panni zhe" (A woman rebel in Xinxing County), *Xiaonian xianfeng* (Youth Vanguard) II, no. 18 (March 21, 1927): 263–64.

49. "Benhui wei hu dang jiuguo xuangao" (The Proclamation of Our Organization on Protecting the Party and Saving the Nation), *Guangdong funü* (Guangdong Women), no. 9 (July 1927): 11.

50. Interview with Lu Jingqing, official in the Guomindang Women's Department 1926–27, in Shanghai in January 1983.

51. Anna Louise Strong, *China's Millions* (New York, 1928), pp. 23–24.

52. "Sixth CCP Congress Resolution on the Women's Movement," *Chinese Studies in History* 4, no. 4 (Summer 1971).

53. For a similar account of the influence of traditional heroines on Chinese women revolutionaries, see Mary Rankin, "The Emergence of Women at the End of the Ch'ing: The Case of Ch'iu Chin," Margery Wolf and Roxane Witke, eds., *Women in Chinese Society* (Stanford: Stanford University Press, 1975), pp. 39–66.

Part 3
The "Woman Question" in Third World Revolutions

The "Woman Question" in Cuba: An Analysis of Material Constraints on Its Resolution

Muriel Nazzari

Participants in the Cuban revolution shared the belief that the advent of a socialist society would solve the "Woman Question." The classic writings on socialism—which inspired their view of future society—were clear that under socialism women would gain equality before the law; they would enter socially useful production on a par with men; private domestic economy would be transformed into a public enterprise through the socialization of housework and child care; and the personal subjection of women to men would end.[1]

Soon after the triumph of the Cuban revolution, the Woman Question began to be addressed. As early as 1959, Fidel Castro spoke about the need to free women from domestic slavery so that they could participate widely in production to the benefit of women themselves and of the revolution.[2] Over the next twenty years the government increased women's educational opportunities and labor-force participation while providing more and more services to lighten domestic chores for those who worked outside the home. In the early 1970s Cuba went one step farther than any other socialist nation by enacting the Cuban Family Code, which makes husband and wife equally responsible for housework and child care.[3]

Despite these positive developments, the consensus in Cuba today is that full equality for women has yet to be achieved. A frequent explanation is that sex prejudice and *machismo* persist in Cuban society. According to one scholar, these attitudes remain because of the inevitable time lag between structural and ideological change.[4] Important though ideological change may be for achieving women's equality, it must be evaluated in the context of the material constraints that limit social change within Cuban society. This essay accordingly analyzes the position of women in the context of the larger struggle surrounding the economic strategies adopted during Cuba's transition from capitalism to socialism. In it, I argue that Cuba's adoption in the early 1970s of a system of distribution based on material incentives and the requirement that enterprises show a profit perpetuates women's inequality in the home and in the workforce.

My argument rests on the fact that childrearing requires both labor and resources. Marxist-feminist theory has stressed the social importance of women's labor for reproducing the workforce, both generationally (through biological reproduction and the socialization of children) and on a day-to-day basis (through housework and emotional nurturance).[5] If we assume that the labor involved in the daily care of a worker (housework) is a given in any society and could conceivably be performed by workers for themselves, then the variable that determines women's position in the home and society is generational reproduction, that is, childbearing and childrearing.

I take this argument one step further, however. Women's position is determined not only by the institutional arrangements that apportion the labor of childrearing to women but also by the institutions that determine how children gain access to means of subsistence. In developed industrial societies, both capitalist and socialist, most children receive their means of subsistence from the wages of one or both parents. Wage labor, however, cannot usually be performed simultaneously with the labor necessary to raise children. The resulting contradiction historically led to a specific division of labor within the family, the father working outside the home for a wage, the mother doing housework.

The theoretical answer to the Woman Question was to change this division of labor by socializing child care and housework so that married women and mothers could engage in production on an equal basis with men. In practice, socialist countries have thus far found it impossible to eliminate all aspects of privatized household and family maintenance.[6] Cuba has sought to compensate for this shortcoming by passing a law requiring men to share housework and child care.

My analysis of the Cuban case makes it seem evident that both strategies (the socialization of domestic chores and child care and the equal apportionment of the remaining tasks between husband and wife) are necessary but not sufficient conditions for achieving full equality between women and men. Although both address the issue of the allocation of labor for childrearing, neither considers that raising children also requires access to resources. A full solution to the Woman Question must therefore address the issue not only of the labor but also of the income needed to raise children. Power relations within the family are affected by whether that income comes from the father, the mother, both parents, or society as a whole. The issue of systems of distribution therefore has a direct impact on Cuba's attempts to solve the Woman Question.

The Choice of Systems of Distribution in Cuba

The Cuban revolution moved quickly toward the implementation of a socialist society. In the early 1960s it effected a general redistribution of income by raising wages while lowering rents and prices. Meanwhile, it nationalized all means of production except for small peasant holdings and small businesses. To manage the nationalized productive units, the new government had to develop and institute nationwide systems of management and choose a system of distribution of goods, services, and income. Because the revolution was committed to guaranteed employment for all, it also had to design a system of work incentives to replace the fear of unemployment that motivates workers in capitalist economies.

The problem of work incentives in a socialist society is linked to the choice of a system of distribution. In capitalist economies, income distribution is carried out principally through the wage and through the profit that accrues from ownership of the means of production. In socialist economies, private ownership of the means of production is largely abolished, and private profit disappears as a source of income. When Marx envisioned this ideal society he proposed that distribution be carried out by the formula "From each according to his ability, to each according to his need." He called this the communist system of distribution. Under this system people would be expected to work to contribute to society, but not for wages, because goods and services would not be bought or sold, and needs would be met as they arose. Marx believed it would be impossible to implement a communist system of distribution during the transitional stage from capitalism to socialism. For a time, distribution would have to follow a different formula: "From each according to his ability, to each according to his work." This formula is called the socialist system of distribution, and under it needs are primarily met through remuneration for work, that is, through the wage. After the triumph of the Cuban revolution, the question was whether it would be possible to use a combination of both the socialist and the communist systems of distribution.[7]

During the early 1960s ideological struggles took place within the Cuban Communist Party over this issue as well as the related issue of incentives—a problem embedded in the formula of distribution according to need.[8] In all historical eras people have worked to satisfy their needs, either directly through access to the means of production or indirectly through wage labor. But if a socialist society satisfies needs independently of work, what will induce people to labor? While Cuba never completely abandoned the wage as a system of distribution or work incentive, throughout the 1960s the revolutionary government emphasized moral over material incentives and promoted nonwage volunteer labor.

During that period Castro expressed the belief that Cuba could utilize both systems of distribution simultaneously. In 1966 he declared that as soon as possible society must use its resources to provide for all essential needs, including health, housing, adequate nutrition, physical and mental education, and cultural development. The state was already providing free education, health care, sports, recreation, and meals in schools and workplaces. Castro stated that the government intended to supply housing and day care without charge as soon as possible.

In the same speech Castro discussed the problem of family dependents. Should the earning power of a son determine how an elderly parent lives, or would it not be preferable for society as a whole to ensure that the old have all they require? In the case of children, he contended that the "shoes and clothing they receive, as well as their toys, should not depend on whether the mother has ten children and can do little work, but rather on the needs of the child as a human being."[9]

These statements indicate that Castro envisioned a society in which the means to satisfy basic needs would be freely available to everyone and children would receive their subsistence from society itself rather than depend on relatives' wages for support. Although this ideal solution was never fully implemented in Cuba, much of the initial redistribution after the revolution was evidently carried out according to need, unrelated to recipients' work in production.

Initial Effects of the Cuban Revolution on Women

Many Cuban women have claimed that women were the greatest beneficiaries of the revolution. Are they right in their assessment? Did women gain more from the revolution than men?

Differences in the ways women and men were affected by the revolution can be traced to their traditional roles. Most Cuban women were housewives, not wage workers. The initial measures of redistribution brought about a change in their living and working conditions, but the class lines that divided Cuban women caused them to experience these changes in very different ways.

Middle- and upper-class women experienced a loss, since they shared with their male relatives a certain reduction of income. The nationalization of productive enterprises and banks abolished dividends at the same time as lower rents decreased landlords' profits. Many emigrated, but of those who remained in Cuba, women experienced greater hardships than men. Men from these classes retained their status because their skills as entrepreneurs and professionals were valuable to the revolution. In contrast, the status of middle- and upper-class women (except for those who were themselves professionals) had formerly been defined by the large amount of leisure they enjoyed, which was a function of their ability to avoid performing menial labor by hiring others to do domestic chores. After the revolution, these women lost servants, chauffeurs, and nannies, and due to rationing they had to stand in line to buy products that had previously been plentiful for those who could afford them.

Conditions for lower-class housewives, on the other hand, improved dramatically during the first five years. All the initial measures of re-distribution resulted in positive changes within the lower-class home, with the most spectacular differences evident in rural areas where prerevolutionary poverty had been greatest. Agrarian reform eliminated rural rents and evictions by giving tenants, sharecroppers, and squatters free title to the land they were farming. All large estates were nationalized and transformed into collective farms to be worked by landless agricultural workers, resulting in permanent incomes and adequate housing for the remaining rural families.[10]

The urban reform program slashed rents and electricity and telephone rates by half. These redistributive measures meant a 15–30 percent rise in the purchasing power of the poor at the same time that prices for other essentials were also being lowered.[11]

Lower-class housewives could feed and clothe their families better. Consumption of foods that a majority of Cubans had rarely eaten before, such as milk, eggs, and meat, soared. Until production could be increased to meet the expanded purchasing power, rationing was instituted to guarantee everyone a certain amount of these products. At the same time, better clothing became available through a program that brought young women to Havana from all over Cuba to learn to sew. The first thousand took free sewing machines back to their rural homes; each committed herself to teach at least ten other women how to cut and stitch.[12]

During this early period housing was also upgraded, for before the revolution, only 43 percent of the population had lived in more or less acceptable conditions.[13] Urban housing was redistributed by transforming large old residences abandoned by their former owners into apartments. New buildings were constructed for the agricultural collectives, latrines were added to existing rural dwellings, cement replaced dirt floors, and many people had running water and electricity for the first time. New roads in rural areas made buses available to previously isolated families.[14]

The most spectacular accomplishments of the Cuban revolution—the literacy campaign and the institution of free education and health care for all—also had an effect on the working conditions of lower-class housewives. Education revolutionized both immediate opportunities and future expectations for them and their children. Free health care combined with lessons in hygiene and an improved standard of living to yield a decline in the infant mortality rate from 43.6 per one thousand live births in 1962 to 15.0 in 1984.[15] By the early 1970s, 98 percent of all childbirths were medically attended.[16] Polio, diphtheria, and malaria were eradicated, and life expectancy rose to seventy years. Since women were the ones who traditionally cared for the ill, they especially benefited from these improvements in health.

Much of the early redistribution in Cuba was undoubtedly effected through the formula "to each according to his need." Rural inhabitants were not given cement floors because of their ability to pay for them, nor were they allocated housing because their individual jobs were important. Rather, people learned to sew and read and received health care solely because they needed these skills and services. Yet not all distribution was carried out according to this formula. During the same period, a large portion of people's needs was still met through the wage. The improved purchasing power of the wage, however, was not due to wage earners' efforts or productivity but to deliberate policies framed by the revolution in accordance with the formula of distribution according to need.

This lavish initial redistribution was made possible only by drawing on existing reserves such as nationalized land and capital, formerly unused resources in equipment and land, and underutilized sectors of the labor force such as women and the unemployed.[17] But these reserves were not inexhaustible. To achieve economic growth, hard work and increased productivity became necessary.

Economic Growth and Work Incentives

To meet these economic imperatives, in the mid-1960s the government adopted a mixture of moral and material incentives and experimented with different strategies for growth. One strategy involved industrialization through import substitution and agricultural diversification. By 1963 a crisis in the balance of payments prompted a shift in economic policy. From 1964 to 1970, the government returned to sugar production as the principal source of foreign exchange, stressing investment in production for export and the acquisition of capital goods at the expense of the production of consumer goods.[18] Meanwhile, such services as education, health care, public telephones, sports, and child care continued to be furnished at no cost. The income gap between workers with the highest wages and those with the lowest narrowed, as did the gap between urban and rural incomes.[19] By the end of the decade the combination of ample wages and free services with rationing and the restricted production of consumer goods put money in people's pockets but gave them nothing to spend it on. Absenteeism at work reached a high point.

People began to think that moral incentives do not work. This assumption is belied by the Cuban example itself, for women put in 41 million hours of volunteer work in the sugarcane harvest of 1970. And in all societies throughout the centuries housewives have worked for only moral incentives. It was material incentives that were not working in Cuba. The wage did not function as an incentive to work when there was not enough to buy and many goods and services were provided at no cost.

At the same time, economic problems were multiplying, leading to an increased awareness of general inefficiency and low productivity. In response to these problems, massive readjustments of Cuba's social, economic, and political structures took place after 1970, culminating in 1975 with the First Congress of the Communist Party. This restructuring addressed several areas of concern. A deflationary monetary policy corrected the imbalance between money in circulation and the amount of available consumer goods. A reorganization of the managerial system and the substitution of material for moral incentives responded to the problems of low productivity and inefficiency. Union reforms, moves to strengthen and broaden the Communist Party, and the creation of People's Power (the new government administrative system) sought to structure channels for carrying negative feedback to the central planning bodies.[20]

All these measures increased the efficiency of Cuba's planned socialist society, but the first two (the monetary policy and the new system of management) involved a change from a commitment to carry out as much distribution as possible according to need to an ever greater reliance on the socialist formula. Distribution became tied principally to the wage, and enterprises were expected to show a profit. Since the wage, material incentives, and production for exchange are also the mainstays of capitalist societies, these measures represented a decision not to go as far in revolutionizing society as initially planned.

This was a conscious decision. The Thirteenth Congress of the Confederation of Cuban Workers, which took place in 1973, extensively debated the two systems of distribution and the issue of moral versus material incentives. Castro maintained that the development of productive forces had been hindered because Cuba had been too idealistic in the use of moral incentives and distribution according to need. The congress concluded that Cuba must adopt distribution according to work, since the productive forces would have to develop much further to reach the state in which all distribution could successfully be carried out according to need.[21]

The effects of these policy decisions on the condition of women in Cuba become clear when we compare the situation of women in the labor force and the home before and after the shift in systems of distribution.

Women in the Workforce, 1959–69

Because the Batista regime left a legacy of 700,000 unemployed and 300,000 underemployed men, one of the first goals of the revolution was full male employment. By 1964 this goal had been achieved, and it affected not only the men involved but also the women and children who depended on the men's wages.

Despite the priority placed on achieving full male employment during the first five years, the government did not entirely ignore the issue of women's participation in the workforce. Rather than try to incorporate all women into paid work, it concentrated on women who were already working by providing child care and other services to assist them. Night schools and boarding schools were set up for the large number of women who had been domestic servants or prostitutes at the time of the revolution. These institutions functioned until the women learned new jobs, becoming typists, secretaries, bank tellers, and bus drivers. [22]

Recognizing the need to involve those women not in the wage labor force, the government created the Federation of Cuban Women to mobilize them for building the new society. The federation organized day-care centers and started schools to train day-care workers, formed sanitary brigades to supplement professional medical care, and became the backbone of the campaign to eliminate illiteracy. [23]

Women's participation in voluntary organizations required their liberation from the patriarchal norms that had traditionally confined them to the home. Individual men often resented this change. One woman recalled, "It was husbands who were most limiting, and the rest of the family, too, because they were used to seeing women as the center of the home, the ones who solved all problems, and they didn't understand that women could solve problems outside the home, too." [24] Going from the home to the street, from solving the problems of a family to resolving issues in the larger community, profoundly altered women's lives and perceptions of themselves.

As soon as full male employment was achieved, a demand for getting more women into the workforce developed. In May 1966, Castro called for the addition of a million women to the labor force, remarking that if each woman created a thousand pesos of value per year, a billion pesos of wealth would be produced by women annually. And he indicated that the government was building more and more nurseries and school cafeterias to make it easier for women to work outside the home. [25]

Yet only nine months later, Castro's emphasis had shifted. Women were still needed in production, but the government was finding it difficult to provide the thousands of facilities that would make it possible for a million women to work. He pointed out that, to liberate women from all the activities hindering their incorporation into the workforce, society had to create a material base. In other words, Cuba had to develop economically.

This means that at the same time Castro was asking women to work, he was also informing them of material constraints that prevented the government from providing the costly social services that would free them for wage labor. When government planners had to decide between alternative investments, day-care centers frequently came in second. Castro noted that the establishment of day-care centers was slowest in regions where the greatest number of roads and buildings were being constructed. Nevertheless, this speech was a rousing call to women. In it Castro claimed that the most revolutionary aspect of Cuba's transformation was the revolution taking place among Cuban women.[26]

During the rest of the decade the Federation of Cuban Women responded valiantly to his appeal. It mobilized thousands of women for volunteer work, especially in agriculture, and continued to pursue its objective of incorporating 100,000 women per year into the paid workforce, also conducting a search for women to run the countless small businesses nationalized in 1968.

By the early 1970s, however, it was obvious that recruiting women into wage work was an uphill effort. Seventy-six percent of the women who joined the labor force in 1969 left their jobs before the year was out.[27] As the Cuban government modified its policies to address inefficiency and low productivity, analysts began to explore the causes behind women's impermanent tenure in paid occupations.

Diagnoses and Solutions

In 1974 the Federation of Cuban Women reported that the high turnover among women workers could be attributed largely to "the pressure from housework and family members; the lack of economic incentive; and the need for better services to aid working women."[28] The federation also organized a survey to investigate why there were so few women leaders in government. In the trial run of People's Power held in the province of Matanzas, women constituted only 7.6 percent of the candidates and 3 percent of those elected. Both male and female respondents to the survey believed that if women had not been nominated, had refused nomination, or simply were not elected, it was due to family responsibilities.[29]

These disturbing trends at the national level posed the question of whether the problems that prevented women from participating in government were the same as those that kept women from joining or remaining in the labor force. Another study was conducted comparing the free time available to working women with that available to working men and nonworking women. It found that housework occupied nine hours and fourteen minutes of the daily time budget for housewives, four hours and forty-four minutes for working women, but only thirty-eight minutes for working men. In the words of the study's authors, "The time society and especially women dedicate to housework is at the center of all discussion having to do with the struggle toward women's full equality."[30]

I would argue, in contrast, that the issue in the struggle for women's equality is not housework per se but child care and the additional housework the presence of children requires. In this respect the research mentioned above has a serious defect, since it averages time spent performing housework and child care without establishing how many women in the sample had children. A survey of mothers alone, as opposed to women in general, would have revealed much less free time. Thus we must deduce that the "family problems" cited to explain why few women were nominated or elected to People's Power in Matanzas must have referred not to housework, which can usually be postponed, but to child care, which cannot.

In response to these and other studies, the federation made many suggestions that were later implemented to help correct the problems women experienced. Day care was restricted to children of working mothers. Those children were also given priority access to boarding schools and to day schools that served meals. Stores lengthened their business hours so women could shop after work, and a plan was devised to give working women precedence at food markets. Employed women received better laundry services, some provided at the workplace.[31] These measures helped, but they did not eliminate women's double work shift. The conclusion ultimately reached by Cubans was that men and women must share housework and child care. As one woman worker argued in one of the many popular debates about the Family Code, "If they're going to incorporate us into the work force, they're going to have to incorporate themselves into the home, and that's all there is to it."[32] In 1975 this belief was made into law with the adoption of the Family Code, which gave women and men equal rights and responsibilities within the family.

This law can be seen as a change in the locus of the solution to the Woman Question, as it approached the problem at an individual rather than a social level. The first solution attempted, socializing child care and housework, tried to move women toward equality by transferring their family duties to social institutions without disturbing men's lives or roles.[33] Cuban economists calculated that for every three women who joined the workforce, a fourth must be employed in institutions supplying supportive services to facilitate their incorporation.[34] The great cost of this solution meant that it had to compete with other investment needs in the national budget, especially those that would more obviously aid economic development. The Family Code, on the other hand, provided a solution to the Woman Question that did not need to come out of the national budget. It would take place within the home without affecting the rest of society. It did, nevertheless, require a change in individual men's lives, and men resisted.[35] However, as we shall see, other factors operating in the Cuban context indicate that the difficulties encountered in achieving equality between men and women within the family cannot be attributed solely to men's recalcitrance.

Inequality Within the Home

To discover what factors make the equality proclaimed by the Family Code difficult to achieve, we must analyze the situation of wives and mothers. Housewives constituted three-fifths of the adult women outside the workforce in 1972, and married women were only 18 percent of women employed.[36] A possible conclusion to draw from these data would be that housework and child care discouraged married women from taking paid employment. Yet the same set of data shows that the largest category in the female labor force was divorced women (43 percent, followed by single women, 30 percent, and ending with widows, 9 percent). Since divorced women are just as likely as married women to have children to care for, the variable determining their incorporation into the workforce must have been divorce itself. Conversely, the variable permitting married women to remain outside the workforce must have been access to a husband's wage. Under a system of distribution according to work, the needs of the wageless housewife are met only through her husband's labor, reinforcing his power and her dependence.

The dependence of children also continued under the socialist system of distribution. The Family Code held parents rather than society responsible for the support of minors.[37] This section of the new law provoked no objection when the code was debated throughout Cuba, possibly because similar statutes prevail in most modern nations. But tying the fulfillment of children's needs to the wages of their parents directly contradicted Castro's 1966 statement that a child's subsistence should be determined solely by the "needs of the child as a human being." In this sense the Family Code itself was a step away from distribution according to need toward distribution according to work.

While the Family Code was being elaborated and discussed in the early 1970s, the Cuban government was making important economic changes related to the full implementation of the socialist formula for distribution. The government instituted price increases that were explicitly intended to reduce the amount of money in circulation and to act as an incentive to individual productivity.[38] The goal of abolishing house rents was postponed indefinitely. Prices for long-distance transportation, cigarettes, beer, rum, restaurant meals, cinemas, and consumer durables rose. Free public telephones were abolished, and people were now charged for canteen meals, water, and electricity.[39] By 1977 day care was no longer free, forcing mothers to bear part of the cost of providing the conditions that enabled them to work.

In the face of higher prices and fewer free services, the nonworking mother's increasing dependence on her husband's wage might lead her to avoid pressing him to share housework and child care. Whether the working mother would do so would depend on the degree of parity between her wage and her spouse's. If the husband's income were much greater, making the well-being of the children more heavily dependent on the father's wage than the mother's, a woman might perform the extra labor associated with child care so as not to hinder her husband's productivity. This would allow him to work overtime, join the Communist Party, or be elected to People's Power as ways to augment his earning capacity. Unless the wages of husband and wife were equal, we would therefore expect a system of distribution tied to the wage to exacerbate inequalities between men and women in the home. What is the current situation in Cuba?

Women in the Work Force, 1970–84

There does not appear to be a gap between the national average wages of male and female workers in Cuba. Cuban law establishes that men and women must be paid an equal wage for equal work, and no statistics are compiled comparing men's and women's earnings. Yet the General Wage Reform of April 1980 shows a difference between the minimum wage set for office and service employees, $85 per month, and that of industrial workers, $93.39 per month.[40] In 1980 only 22.1 percent of the female workforce held industrial jobs, while 41 percent were in service occupations.[41] We could tentatively conclude that, at the level of minimum-wage work, women's average wage is lower than men's due to the concentration of female labor in the service sector. This is partially confirmed by data on day-care workers, an exclusively female occupational group, who were the lowest-paid workers in 1973, receiving only 77 percent of the national average wage.[42] Yet not all those who earn the minimum wage in the service sector are women, for in 1980 women were 84.4 percent of the clerical workforce, while they only held 62.6 percent of the manual labor service jobs.[43]

The fact that women are overrepresented in the service sector does not necessarily mean that women as a whole earn less than men, since a large proportion of female workers are professionals and middle-level technicians, 30 percent in 1980.[44] For example, by 1984, 68.9 percent of the employees at the Ministry of Public Health were women, and 39 percent of these were professionals in positions of authority.[45] Women constituted 33 percent of the doctors and 95 percent of the nurses. Some nurses in Cuba can earn more than some doctors, for doctors' salaries range from $231 to a maximum of $450, while nurses with university degrees earn between $198 and $280.[46] The maximum salary for teaching personnel is $450, like that of doctors, judges, and attorneys, and in 1984, 43 percent of university professors were women. Women also made up 53.8 percent of all technicians.[47] The high proportion of women in better paid positions means there may not be a gap between the national average wages of men and women.

There is, however, a general inequality between Cuban men and women that proceeds from the way the constitutional principle of guaranteed employment has been interpreted. In practice, only males and female heads of household are guaranteed jobs. The antiloafing law, passed in the early 1970s, makes work compulsory for all males (but not females) over seventeen who are not students or military personnel. In a way, this law recognizes the social value of housework, since only adult males who do not work are considered parasites, thereby implying that women who are not employed do work that is necessary to society.

Nevertheless, the result of these policies is that housewives in Cuba are used as a labor reserve, which has different effects for women under each system of distribution. During the 1960s when Cuban women provided much unpaid voluntary labor, the lack of a wage did not make women so dependent on their relatives, since a large number of needs were met at no cost. In contrast, once the satisfaction of needs became tied principally to the wage, to go without a wage for volunteer work or to have difficulty finding employment made housewives, and adult single women, more dependent on their male relatives.

Being part of the labor reserve results in lower annual wages for female cyclical contract workers in agriculture. Although contracts protect these women from uncertain employment, and the women also receive full maternity benefits even when childbirth occurs outside the work period, their wage and pension rights are apportioned according to work accomplished.[48] Because they work only part of the year as seasonal laborers, their annual income and pension rights will necessarily be smaller than those of male counterparts who work year-round.

There are also indications of a lack of sufficient employment for Cuban women. An important function of the Federation of Cuban Women is to coordinate information about job vacancies for female applicants. In 1980, even women trained as technicians were reported to be having difficulty finding jobs.[49]

When full male employment is viewed against the shortage of jobs for women, it appears that women are hired only as needed. This was confirmed by Vilma Espin, who noted that the proportion of women in the workforce grew from 23 percent in 1974 to 30 percent in 1979 but added that expansion of the female labor force would not be able to continue at this pace because women's participation in employment depends on the "requirements of the economic development of the nation."[50] Linking women's job opportunities to national economic needs adds an insecurity to the lives of Cuban women that Cuban men, with guaranteed employment, do not experience.

The economic development of the nation has continued, however, and women's participation in employment has increased. The number of employed women grew 40 percent in five years, going from 800,000 in 1979 to 1,142,000 in 1984, representing 37 percent of the workforce.[51]

The principal problems still encountered are a resistance to hiring and promoting women.[52] It appears evident that these problems are the consequence of the new system of management adopted in the 1970s, which established that enterprises must show a profit by producing over and above inputs. This profit is different from profit in capitalist societies, which goes to shareholders and owners. In Cuba, since all enterprises belong to the state, the largest share of the profit goes to the national budget by way of a large circulation tax. The remaining profit is distributed by the worker's collective of each enterprise for three purposes: (1) to improve the technical and productive capacity of the enterprise; (2) to improve the sociocultural level of employees; and (3) to provide material and monetary rewards to individual workers, including management, in proportion to results achieved.[53]

But an emphasis on profit includes a concern with cost. Under the new system of economic management, any extra expense entailed in the employment of women would logically result in prejudice against hiring them. There is evidence of both the cost and the discrimination.

One cost encountered by enterprises employing women is tied to the maternity law. This excellent law provides that pregnant women receive a fully paid leave of six weeks before and twelve weeks following childbirth. The new social security system passed in 1984 frees the enterprise from paying the mother's salary during her leave, but the need to hire substitutes or rearrange work loads when a woman takes maternity leave remains.[54] It is safe to assume that, given the choice between hiring women who might become pregnant and hiring men, any enterprise required to show a profit would prefer to hire men.

The most constant cost of employing women workers lies in their higher absentee rate, which is due to family obligations. In his speech to the Third Congress of the Federation of Cuban Women, Castro remarked that a certain amount of absenteeism had practically become legalized so that women could perform duties they could not carry out after hours, such as taking children to the doctor.[55] Castro's comments confirm that, despite the Family Code, men had not assumed family responsibilities that interfered with their wage labor. This may be partly due to resistance in the workplace. If we accept the existence of a cost to the enterprise in women's conflicting duties at work and at home, it becomes evident that it would require major readjustments in the workplace if males, almost two-thirds of the workforce, were to perform an equal share of domestic tasks. These conflicting responsibilities tend to continue to be identified as "women's problems."

Discrimination against hiring and promoting women has therefore continued. A report to the Third Congress of the Federation described the prejudice that has led managers to choose men instead of women to occupy jobs, "because men can spend all the time that is necessary on their work."[56] In a 1984 interview, the late Vilma Espín declared that women were repeatedly denied political and administrative promotions to avoid subsequent difficulties related to their family responsibilities. She denounced the persistence of this prejudice.[57] But denunciations alone cannot be effective so long as such prejudice has a material basis in the actual cost to the enterprise of finding solutions to the "problems" of women workers.

Cubans are aware of these contradictions and there has been at least one advance in this respect. A regulation that permitted women but did not permit men to ask for leave to accompany sick children or other relatives while they were in the hospital was extended to men in 1984. Though the State Committee on Labor, Wages, and Social Security had expressed concern that this new regulation might lead to breaches of discipline or pretexts to be absent, it was passed because the prohibition discriminated against men and hampered the promotion of women in the workplace.[58]

Conclusion

Material constraints on the solution of the Woman Question in Cuba originate in the drive for socialist accumulation and the development of the country's productive forces. These concerns have led the state to make policy decisions that preserve women's inequality in the labor force, perpetuate the personal dependence of women on men, and thus work against the equal sharing of housework and child care decreed by the Family Code.

The Cuban constitutional guarantee of employment for all has been transformed in practice into guaranteed male employment, backed by a law making work compulsory for men. Underlying these measures is the assumption that adult women will be supported by their husbands or other male relatives. In accordance with this premise, the government feels free to use women for seasonal agricultural labor and as a labor reserve. Though efficient at the national level, at the individual level these practices reinforce male power at women's expense.

The Cuban state's endorsement of the socialist system of distribution and material incentives has also contributed to women's continued subordination. Distribution through the wage, combined with higher prices and fewer free goods or services, makes wageless or lower-paid wives more dependent on their husbands than they were during the period when distribution according to need was also in effect. For mothers this dependence is compounded by concern for the well-being of their children. The requirement that enterprises show a profit contributes to discrimination in hiring because women's "family problems" increase operating expenses. Since they constitute a labor reserve and cannot always find employment, individual women who realize they may not be economically self-sufficient all their lives may rely primarily on relationships with men for financial support. The degree to which women's access to resources is more limited than men's in an economy where distribution is tied to the wage and children rely on parental support thus constitutes a material barrier to any final solution of the Woman Question.

Because the socialist formula for distribution based on material incentives acts as a brake on women's increasing equality with men, women would seem to have an even greater stake than men in the eventual implementation of a communist system of distribution. Such a system would allow people to work according to their abilities and reward them on the basis of their needs. Household maintenance and child care would be counted as work. Inequalities would disappear between manual and intellectual labor, between service providers and industrial workers, between individuals who raise children and those who do not, and between women and men. This ideal society appears to be very far in the future.

In the meantime, besides subsidizing day care and maternity leaves, the Cuban national budget could subsidize other expenses related to women's employment in the paid labor force, so that enterprises have no reason to discriminate against women. Further plans could also be made at a national level to restructure enterprises so that men can fully assume their share of family responsibilities. Lessening the individual mother's dependence on her husband's wage would involve carrying out what Fidel Castro envisioned in 1966: society as a whole must provide the means of subsistence for children, so that not only parents but all workers share in their support.

Notes

This is an updated version of an article that originally appeared in *Signs: Journal of Women in Culture and Society* 9, no. 2 (Winter 1983). © 1983 by University of Chicago. All rights reserved.

1. *The Woman Question: Selections from the Writings of Karl Marx, Frederick Engels, V. I. Lenin, Joseph Stalin* (New York: International, 1951).
2. Fidel Castro, "Speech to the Women" (Havana, 1959), p. 9.
3. Marjorie King, "Cuba's Attack on Women's Second Shift, 1974–1976," in Eleanor Leacock et al., ed., *Women in Latin America: An Anthology from Latin American Perspectives* (Riverside, CA: Latin American Perspectives, 1979).
4. Lourdes Casal, "Revolution and Conciencia: Women in Cuba," in Carol Berkin and Clara M. Lovett, eds., *Women War and Revolution* (New York: Holmes & Meier, 1980).
5. For example, see Isabel Larguía and John Dumoulin, "Aspects of the Condition of Women's Labor," NACLA *Latin America Empire Report* 9, no. 6 (September 1975): 2–13.
6. A review of the problems socialist countries have encountered trying to implement this solution can be found in Elizabeth J. Croll, "Women in Rural Production and Reproduction in the Soviet Union, China, Cuba and Tanzania: Socialist Development Experiences," *Signs: Journal of Women in Culture and Society* 7, no. 2 (Winter 1981): 361–74.
7. Castro explained both systems to the Thirteenth Congress of the Confederation of Cuban Workers. See "XIII CTC Congress: A History Making Event," *Cuba Review* 4, no. 1 (July 1974): 15–25.

8. See Bertram Silverman, *Man and Socialism in Cuba* (New York: Atheneum, 1971).
9. Quoted in Martin Kenner and James Petras, eds., *Fidel Castro Speaks* (New York: Grove Press, 1969), p. 213.
10. Edward Boorstein, *The Economic Transformation of Cuba* (New York: Monthly Review Press, 1968), pp. 42–54, 78–79.
11. Archibald R. M. Ritter, *The Economic Development of Revolutionary Cuba* (New York: Praeger, 1974), p. 107.
12. Laurette Séjourné, ed., *La mujer cubana en el quehacer de la historia* (Mexico: Siglo Veintiuno, 1980), pp. 124–33.
13. Claes Brundenius, *Revolutionary Cuba: The Challenge of Economic Growth with Equity* (Boulder, CO: Westview Press, 1984), p. 86.
14. Séjourné, ed., *La mujer cubana*, pp. 121, 128.
15. Fidel Castro's speech to the Fourth Congress of the Federation of Cuban Women, Havana, March 24, 1985.
16. *Economia y desarrollo*, September–October 1974, p. 198.
17. Boorstein, *Economic Development of Cuba*, pp. 81–83.
18. Ritter, *Economic Development of Revolutionary Cuba*, pp. 128–270.
19. Jorge I. Dominguez, *Cuba: Order and Revolution* (Cambridge, MA: Harvard University Press, Belknap Press, 1978), pp. 227–28.
20. Ibid., pp. 243–49, 271–79, 306–40; Ritter, *Economic Development of Revolutionary Cuba*, p. 250.
21. Castro, "XIII CTC Congress." The adoption of the socialist system of distribution was incorporated into the constitution of 1976. See *Constitution of the Republic of Cuba* (New York: Center for Cuban Studies, n.d.), ch. I, article 19.
22. Ramiro Pavon, "El empleo femenino en Cuba," *Universidad de Santiago*, December 1975, p. 123.
23. Ministerio de Justicia, *La mujer en Cuba socialista* (Havana: Editorial Orbe, 1977).
24. Séjourné, ed., *La mujer cubana*, p. 193; my translation.
25. Kenner and Petras, eds., *Fidel Castro Speaks*, p. 207.
26. *Bohemia* (December 16, 1966). Day-care centers continued to be built, providing three meals a day and laundering clothes worn at the center. There were 433 centers in 1970 and 782 in 1978 (Federation of Cuban Women, "La mujer cubana, 1975–1979", Havana, n.d. mimeo., p. 10.
27. Ministerio de Justicia, *La mujer en Cuba*, pp. 252–57.
28. Ibid., p. 252; my translation.
29. Primer Congreso del Partido Comunista, *Sobre el pleno ejercicio de la igualdad de la mujer*, 3d thesis, p. 5.
30. Marta Tribo Marabotto, ed., *Investigaciones científicas de la demanda en Cuba* (Havana: Editorial Orbe, 1979), pp. 96–101, esp. p. 101; my translation.
31. Carollee Bengelsdorf and Alice Hageman, "Emerging from Underdevelopment," in Zillah Eisenstein, ed., *Capitalist Patriarchy and the Case for Socialist Feminism* (New York: Monthly Review Press, 1979).
32. Margaret Randall, *Afterword* (Toronto: Women's Press, 1974).
33. Edmund Dahlstrom, *The Changing Roles of Men and Women* (Boston: Beacon Press, 1971), p. 175.
34. Pavón, "E empleo femenino," p. 115.
35. Magaly Sánchez, "Rights and Duties Go Together," *Cuba Review* 4, no. 2 (September 1974):13–14.
36. Juceplan, *Aspectos demográficos de la fuerza laboral femenina en Cuba* (Havana, 1974), pp. 32, 44.
37. Ministry of Justice, *Family Code* (Havana: Editorial Orbe, 1975), articles 33, 122.
38. Domínguez, *Cuba*, p. 170.
39. Carmelo Mesa-Lago, *Cuba in the 1970's* (Albuquerque: University of New Mexico Press, 1974), pp. 42–48.

40. *Granma Review*, April 6, 1980.
41. Isabel Larguía and John Dumoulin, "Women's Equality and the Cuban Revolution," in June Nash and Helen Safa, eds., *Women and Change in Latin America* (South Hadley, MA: Bergin and Garvey, 1986), p. 367.
42. Domínguez, *Cuba*, p. 501.
43. Larguía and Dumoulin, "Women's Equality," p. 357.
44. Ibid., p. 367.
45. Vilma Espín, in *Bohemia*, November 23, 1984.
46. Salaries in *Bohemia*, June 4, 1982.
47. Castro, Speech to the Fourth Congress.
48. For maternity provisions, see Ministerio de Justicia, *La mujer en Cuba*, p. 130; for pension and wage apportionment, see Vilma Espín in *Granma*, March 7, 1980.
49. Espin, *Granma*, March 7, 1980.
50. Ibid.
51. Castro, Speech to the Fourth Congress.
52. Vilma Espín, *Granma*, August 23, 1985.
53. Fidel Castro, *Report of the Central Committee of the Communist Party of Cuba to the First Party Congress* (Havana, 1977), p. 159; Raul Martell, *La empresa socialista* (Havana: Editorial Orbe, 1978).
54. Enterprises, not employees, contribute to the social security system, which includes payment of maternity leaves. Código de Trabajo, 1984, ch. XIII, articles 267–69.
55. Fidel Castro in *Granma Review*, March 16, 1980.
56. Maria S. Morales, ed., *Memorias del 3er Congreso de la Federación de Mujeres Cubanas* (Havana: Editorial de Ciencias Sociales, 1984), p. 40.
57. Espín, *Bohemia*, November 23, 1984.
58. Castro, Speech to the Fourth Congress.

Women's Role in the Nicaraguan Revolutionary Process: The Early Years

Maxine D. Molyneux

The course of the Nicaraguan revolution in its first decade posed the question of the relationship between social transformation and its effects on women in a particularly acute form. On the positive side, the revolution had a major mobilizing impact on Nicaraguan women, and they in turn played a significant part in it, both in the overthrow of the Somoza dictatorship and in the consolidation of the postinsurrectionary regime. In the insurrection itself, women fought in the guerrilla army, comprising some 30 percent of the combat forces of the Sandinista Liberation Front (FSLN) and providing some of its leading commanders. The political support organization for women, the Association of Women Confronting the National Problem (AMPRONAC), had up to 8,000 supporters at the time of the Sandinista victory, which was a significant response from the adult female population.[1] After 1979, women were involved in a series of programs designed to strengthen the revolutionary state and broaden its impact: in the party and mass organizations, in the social and economic reforms, and in the auxiliary security forces, the militia, and the neighborhood surveillance and defense groups. The Sandinistas both before and after the seizure of power made the mobilization and emancipation of women important and sustained goals.

This process of mobilizing women, and of Sandinista commitment to their emancipation, was, however, severely constrained by a number of factors. Taken together, these limited the degree to which the overthrow of the political dictatorship, and the accompanying social change, simultaneously challenged the prevailing forms of gender inequality. In the first place, Nicaragua remained an extremely poor country, and with effective U.S. pressure (financial and military), sources of foreign capital were reduced to a trickle by 1984, and the economy was in severe crisis by 1986. The material resources available for realizing a program of radical social change—to provide education, welfare, jobs, housing, and child-care facilities—were therefore scarce at the beginning and even scarcer thereafter, as the effects of the war bit deeper. At the household level, the shortages of goods in the market, a factor that particularly affects women, had become acute by 1983 and worsened with inflation of over 700 percent after 1985. Second, the pressures of the counterrevolutionary war took their toll on programs to emancipate women. Not only material resources, but also time, thought, and effort were diverted to other priorities. Third, the decisiveness of the political revolution that ousted the Somoza regime was not matched by a comparable change in attitudes or social structures. The increasingly oppositional conservative wing of the Catholic church, with its institutional weight and ideological hold, was a particularly powerful obstacle to any program to emancipate women. A complementary cultural dimension was the pervasive *machismo* of Nicaraguan life, a value system in part underpinned by the widespread internal migration system under which men traditionally had relations with several women simultaneously and left them to bring up the children. The social situation of the majority of Nicaraguan women at the onset of the revolution also allowed of no easy solutions: illiteracy of well over 50 percent, concentrated in the rural areas, employment in the least remunerative and stable jobs, together with widespread legal discrimination, combined to render the double oppression of women, on class and gender grounds, particularly acute.

Yet the difficulties faced by a program of women's emancipation were not confined to these objective obstacles of the history and circumstances of Nicaragua. For the ambiguity of women's role in the Nicaraguan revolution was inscribed within the very momentum of the revolution itself and of the organization of the FSLN. The Sandinista Front's victory came about in a two-phase process: guerrilla war by a revolutionary vanguard in the period up to 1978, and mass and often spontaneous uprisings in the final months. The success of this process could not automatically overcome the problem it encapsulated: of an alliance between the Front and the population that was preliminary, one that needed consolidation by substantial political work in the postinsurrectionary period. This general issue was equally pertinent to women: many had rallied in the insurrections and had supported the revolution with their courage and their lives. But whether the revolution would continue to command their loyalty remained to be seen. If, to this preliminary nature of support for the Sandinistas, one adds the fact that women, of different classes, interests, and capacities, would respond to the revolution in different ways, then the question of their support for, and benefits from, the revolution becomes even more complex.[2] As with all social groups, the links between women and the revolutionary process, the Front, and the state were something that had to be created, reproduced, and developed at each stage of the revolution.

The FSLN and the Woman Question

This political issue of the relationship *between* the Front and women was compounded by a question internal to the Front itself, namely its own conception of the program of women's emancipation. The commitment to this general principle in the 1969 FSLN Program was repeated in the "Statute of Rights and Guarantees of Nicaraguans" of September 1979, which proclaimed the full equality of men and women with respect to citizen's rights and duties, juridical personality, work, wages, and family relations, and pledged the state to "removing all obstacles" to achieving that equality.

But this commitment was a conditional one, especially in the initial period; in the FSLN's terms it located the goal of women's emancipation within "the context of Nicaraguan reality" and within the broader strategy of the FSLN. This meant that policies for advancing the cause of women's emancipation would be pursued so long as they contributed to, or did not detract from, the realization of other, broader goals. Nora Astorga, a founding member of AMPRONAC (and at the time deputy foreign minister), said in 1982: "In Nicaragua we cannot conduct a struggle of a Western feminist kind. This is alien to our reality. It doesn't make sense to separate the women's struggle from that of overcoming poverty, exploitation and reaction. We want to promote women's interests within the context of that wider struggle."[3]

Although this conditionality necessarily narrowed the scope of the campaigns for improving women's position, the FSLN was careful to acknowledge the irreducibility of women's oppression and the need, in particular, to confront the issue of ideology among both men and women. In an important speech on the occasion of the third anniversary of the women's organization, in September 1985, Tomás Borge made this position clear:

> Economic development on its own is not enough to achieve the liberation of women, and neither is the mere fact of women organising. There must be a struggle against the habits, traditions and prejudices of men and women. We must launch a difficult and prolonged ideological struggle, a struggle equally undertaken by men and women.[4]

The FSLN, like comparable revolutionary governments elsewhere, was therefore concerned both to improve the position of women and to encourage their participation in the three main areas of revolutionary consolidation and reconstruction—economic development, political activity, and national defense. It was in order to accomplish these tasks while advancing the cause of women's emancipation that AMPRONAC was transformed in September 1979 into the new mass organization for women, AMNLAE (the Luisa Amanda Espinosa Association of Nicaraguan Women).[5] The restructuring of women's social position envisaged in the FSLN program was therefore one that was clearly defined: politically, in that the women's organization was to work in close collaboration with, and under the general direction of, the FSLN, and theoretically, in terms of the way in which this restructuring was to be achieved. At its Constitutive Assembly, at the end of 1981, AMNLAE defined its role as one of "giving women an organic instrument which would permit them to integrate themselves as a decisive force in the program of the revolution; and moreover, express in an organized manner, both their concerns and their social, economic, and cultural aspirations." By 1982 AMNLAE was transformed from a mass organization to a more broadly based movement that depended upon a core group of activists to advance its program. But the next few years were ones that are now seen by AMNLAE as rather unfocused; the "integrationist" approach, as it was referred to, was neither reaching large numbers of women, nor addressing their different needs, ones which varied according to class and ethnicity.

In 1985, in response to growing dissatisfaction with AMNLAE's role, and in preparation for its Second Congress, a major debate on policy developed both within the Sandinista organizations and in the public realm. AMNLAE held 600 open assemblies in Managua, with more than 40,000 women meeting in small groups to debate issues and priorities. The AMNLAE leadership was surprised to discover how critical its constituency was of their failure to address such issues as domestic violence, *machismo*, abortion, rape, and contraception.

The meetings and criticisms resulted in a number of positive outcomes. In the first place, AMNLAE included various demands previously considered "too feminist" in its submission to the commission set up to draft the new Constitution. These included proposals to equalize divorce and to leave the possibility open for the legalization of abortion. The second outcome was a shift in the official attitude of the FSLN toward the "Woman Question." The FSLN policy document presented at AMNLAE's Third Congress in 1987 placed the struggle for women's liberation on a new footing. It stated that the struggle against "women's discrimination" would not be "put off " or separated from the question of defense of the revolution. *Machismo* and other forms of discrimination against women "inhibited the development of the whole society." The statement denounced male supremacy in no uncertain terms: "*Machismo* holds up a supposed male superiority, excludes women from work and activities thought of as "for men," claims that men have a right to abuse women . . . and (to) rights women can't enjoy." Overall, this was a declaration that women's issues had been taken on board by the party, a fact given further public affirmation by the presence at the Congress of four members of the (all male) National Directorate.

Women's Emancipation: Assigning Priorities

While the priorities for AMNLAE's work have not changed in form since its founding Constitutive Assembly, the emphasis as among priorities and the manner in which the issues have been tackled have varied over the years. The 1981 Assembly defined the six main areas of activity in which AMNLAE would seek to promote the full participation and improve the position of Nicaraguan women as follows:

1. Defending the Sandinista revolution;
2. Promoting women's political and ideological consciousness, and advancing their social, political, and economic participation in the revolution;
3. Combating legal and other institutional gender inequalities;
4. Promoting women's cultural and technical advancement, and their entry into areas of employment traditionally reserved for men, combined with opposition to discrimination in employment;
5. Promoting respect for domestic labor, and creating child-care services for working women;
6. Creating and sustaining links of international solidarity.

These goals did not represent the full extent of AMNLAE's involvement in programs to improve the participation and situation of women, nor did they represent the entire range of Sandinista activities that had positive implications for women. Other initiatives in the areas of public welfare, health, housing, and education provided the wider context within which these specific goals were advanced. Indeed, it is important to note that in many cases the impact of the welfare programs affected women from the poorer classes more profoundly, at least until the economic policy changes of 1984–85, than some of AMNLAE's more specific and woman-centered goals.

Nonetheless, the first five of these goals were the main focus of Sandinista activity with regard to women *per se* and embodied certain important principles that informed other areas of policy. The discussion that follows, therefore, considers the efforts AMNLAE made under each of the five main headings during the early years of the revolution.

1. Defending the revolution

Security was the priority of the FSLN from the moment of the Sandinista triumph and became an even more absorbing activity with the intensification of the counterrevolutionary war in the period after 1982 and especially after 1984. It was a priority for AMNLAE too because the safeguarding of the revolution was, as the resolution stated, "the political guarantee for the achievement of women's emancipation."[6] The fact that women participated so actively in the insurrection meant that there was a fund of experience and commitment on which the Front could draw in the new military confrontations it faced. Yet the manner in which women participated in the defense of the revolution differed from that in which they contributed to making it.

The central instrument for defending the revolution was the Sandinista People's Army, the *Ejército Popular Sandinista* (EPS). After the victory women made up almost 40 percent of its forces and 6 percent of its officers. Six women (as well as some thirty men) were awarded the rank of Comandante Guerrillera in recognition of their combat role in the revolution and some of these women continued to train army and militia recruits. But the postrevolutionary period saw a gradual transfer of women from combat roles to backup positions. Of the women who fought in the FSLN forces up to 1979, only a quarter were still in combat units by 1981. Subsequently, more women were moved into administrative positions, while others were reallocated to civilian government positions and to the police force.[7] By 1987 there were few women in regular combat roles, and no women above the rank of captain in the army. However, women did occupy senior positions in auxiliary activities as technicians and intelligence operatives.

This redeployment of women away from combat roles was met with a mixed response. In Estelí, on the war front, it was vigorously resisted by women soldiers who complained of not being taken seriously by their male comrades, and of being expected to combine their combat duties with traditional female tasks such as cooking for the troops. In 1981 AMNLAE's general secretary in the region, Martha Mungía expressed the sense of injustice felt by many women: "We can't limit our participation in defense to secondary roles because we would be leaving empty the place in the front line which was filled by the women who died for their country (in the war against Somoza)."[8]

But other women in the Front saw the move as inevitable. In the words of Gladys Baez, the first woman to join the guerrilla forces and to endure the fighting in the mountains: "Women have proven themselves to be heroic, combative, courageous, and able. But we *are* less tough, we march slower, and above all we have children. You can't have a regular army poised for instant mobilization based on a floating population."[9]

AMNLAE nonetheless put up a spirited defense of women's right to be treated as equals, even in military matters. In the event, a compromise was reached and in January 1981 the first all-woman reserve unit was established in Estelí on the orders of Edén Pastora, at that time in charge of defense. By 1982 there were half a dozen all-women reserve battalions, but over the next two years these were gradually dissolved into mixed battalions.

The exclusion of women from active service remained an issue. When the decree concerning conscription was debated in the Council of State in 1983, AMNLAE delegates opposed it because, again, it exempted women. Magda Enriques, an AMNLAE delegate to the council, recounted what happened:

> We raised one and a half problems for them. The mandate from our grass roots was to struggle to the end to get equal status so we called two general assemblies in Managua to discuss the whole issue. We demanded scientific, not emotional, explanations for the exclusion of women.

> There was a national debate in the media. In the end they agreed to accept women volunteers into active service, which was something of a victory. Of course we AMNLAE delegates were the only ones to vote against this resolution because it still did not settle the issue of principle. [10]

However, other efforts to incorporate women into security activity were pursued with a considerable degree of success. The militia, a part-time force based partly on the workplace and partly on the mass organizations, was open to everyone between the ages of sixteen and sixty. Not all recruits were trained for combat, but they were deployed on guard duty and were prepared for the possibility of having to take over and run factories, installations, and offices in the event of all-out war. In their role as guards in the regions where the contra war was being fought, militia women have been involved in combat. Women were said to make up as much as a fifth of the nonregular combat forces overall.

Civil defense provided a separate, and increasingly important, area of security, one in which women also played a vital part. Two associated efforts were organized in this field: the Sandinista Defense Committees (CDSs), part of the CDRs, organized on a neighborhood basis to oversee the running and resolve the problems of particular locations; and Revolutionary Guard Duty, a system of local guard duty operating day and night. By 1983, about 50 percent of the membership of the CDSs were women and four years later 67 percent of "active members" were reported to be women. A further 80 percent of those on guard duty were said to be women and there have been reports of more than 50,000 women guards in the country, 20,000 of them in Managua alone. [11] The demands of the increasingly tense security situation obviously contributed to this mobilization of women, and considerable efforts went into preparation for what the future might hold, in terms of air attacks, sabotage, and invasion. But these civil defense organizations were also involved in reducing crime and coping with natural disasters. During the Managua floods of 1982, the emergency committees set up to deal with the effects of the disaster worked under the slogan "AMNLAE in the front line of civil defense." Women were therefore present, and increasingly mobilized, throughout the organizations of revolutionary defense in Nicaragua: In the EPS, militia, CDS,

Revolutionary Guard Duty, and the Voluntary Police. Many of those most active in these bodies were also AMNLAE members, and AMNLAE had a role in organizing some of this activity.

AMNLAE was also involved in the defense of the revolution in a less direct manner, through its political role in mobilizing support for the FSLN and through local organizations such as the Association of Mothers of Heroes and Martyrs. The association sought to invest motherhood with a positive political and combative connotation, as well as to provide emotional support for the bereaved, and those anxious about relatives posted to the war front. Overall, however, this mobilization of women for national defense was double-edged. Insofar as women were placed in a predominantly supportive role in the Sandinista military system, they lost an element of the equality they had won in the revolution itself; and the relentless strains of national defense, although leading to an increase in women's participation, inevitably distracted the efforts of the Front and AMNLAE, as well as of Nicaraguan women as a whole, away from the tasks of transforming women's socioeconomic position along more egalitarian lines. This led to strains within AMNLAE itself, as debates went on over how far to tackle the specific causes of women's oppression in such conditions. Yet as the contra war intensified in the mid-1980s, and support among some groups declined, the participation of women in the revolution was greater than at any time since 1979.

2. Promoting political and ideological awareness and greater participation

The central organization for promoting political mobilization and education was the FSLN, within which women made up a sizeable minority. There are no figures on membership but in 1984 women were said to comprise 22 percent of the total, and it was officially claimed that they made up over a third, or 37 percent of the leadership cadre.[12] By 1987 female membership had risen slightly, to 24.3 percent, with 38.1 percent of most recent appointments to positions of responsibility comprising women. Although there were no women in the nine-member National Directorate that constituted the core of the FSLN leadership, the post of vice president of the Council of State was held by a woman, as was the head of police, and women assumed positions of responsibility in the party at a regional level. On three occasions between 1979 and 1985, women filled ministerial posts.[13] In 1987 the official figure for the number of women occupying responsible posts in the government was 31.4 percent.

Beyond the Front itself there were the mass organizations, some of whose members were also in the Front, but the majority of whom were not. These organizations acted as two-way transmission systems between the FSLN leadership and the population through which the wishes and complaints of the membership were relayed to the top. Mass organizations or "movements" (as AMNLAE came to be called) were responsible for both politicizing their constituencies and representing their interests. Among other functions, they publicized the aims, policies, and achievements of the revolution and encouraged participation in its campaigns. Apart from the CDSs women were also well represented in the Sandinista Youth Organization, where they made up around 50 percent of the membership. But they remained a small minority in the trade unions and until a campaign was undertaken to redress the situation during 1983–84, they were virtually absent from the associations of agricultural workers. However, as a result of this campaign, from mid-1984 women made up over 40 percent of the membership of the Association of Farmworkers (ATC), and this rose to 56 percent by 1987, with women taking an active role in policymaking for the first time.[14]

AMNLAE's own organizational capacity grew steadily. At its Constituent Assembly in 1981 a seven-woman National Directorate was elected, headed by a general secretary, with other secretaries responsible for Organization, Health, International Relations, Information and Education, Defense, and liaising with the Council of State.[15] A similar structure was duplicated at departmental and municipal levels. From 1981 onward, AMNLAE encouraged the establishment of Work Committees, comprised of three to five members, which were set up in factories, plantations, places of learning, state and private institutions, markets, and hospitals. They were charged with "promoting fuller participation of women, political and ideological clarification, co-ordinating with other organizations to promote the tasks of the revolution." These Work Committees were also designed to ensure that the trade unions and employers observed the laws prohibiting discrimination against women, and tried to promote women's interests as they were defined at sectoral level. By 1983 in Managua alone there were 211 Work Committees, with more than 8,000 affiliates.[16]

A major initial focus of AMNLAE's activities was the specific campaigns launched around social issues. Women participated in considerable numbers in the mass literacy campaign of 1980 and the health campaign of the following year. The literacy campaign mobilized a large number of women teachers—60 percent of the total—and some 12 percent of those teaching in it were AMNLAE members. Another 20 percent of AMNLAE's members entered the literacy classes. One hundred and ninety six Committees of Mothers for Literacy were formed to undertake housekeeping and other tasks for the crusade participants. Many women benefited substantially from the campaign: 196,000 became literate as against a total of 210,000 men. This was proportionally less than the percentage of illiterates (60 percent) that women accounted for, but it nevertheless represented a considerable opportunity for educationally deprived women.[17]

A similar picture of female mobilization and benefit could be seen in the health campaign of 1980–81 and in the continuing program of health initiatives, such as health teach-in days (Jornadas de Salud). Over 77,000 people joined the health brigades organized by AMNLAE and other mass organizations to carry out basic preventive health and education, and women made up the great majority of those involved in such campaigns: 80 percent of the health brigade activists, and 75 percent of the "health multipliers" or practical teachers.[18] Overall women's participation in activity of this kind and related forms of voluntary work was high. In the immediate postrevolutionary period it was women who cleaned up neighborhoods and helped reorganize community life, a commitment to local political involvement which was reflected in their active participation in the CDSs.

After the reappraisal of AMNLAE's role began in 1985, it was considered necessary to change the structure and character of the organization to reflect its new orientation. At the Third Congress the three-member executive was replaced by an expanded National Committee of (initially) nine members. This was designed to reflect a wider range of interests, to overcome what some activists had seen as a leadership that was "too urban, too theoretical, and too middle class." Henceforth, the executive, with Lea Guido (former health minister) as general secretary was to follow FSLN guidelines and to include representatives of the trade unions and other mass organizations. Each of these sectors would participate in debating and in defining the needs of women and these would then define the agenda for AMNLAE's work. According to the FSLN statement issued at the Congress "AMNLAE should not attempt to be a mass organization of women parallel to the other existing mass organizations. On the contrary [it] must promote the incorporation of women in trade unions [and other organizations]." Those who supported the move felt that in this way women's issues would not be left to AMNLAE alone to deal with; by becoming integrated with sectoral interests, women's needs would be more adequately met. Those who opposed the reorganization feared that feminist issues might be displaced or diluted in the new structure. However, the dominant feeling in 1987 was that a decisive turning point had been reached with the FSLN's public support for campaigns to promote greater equality between the sexes. As Heliette Elhers, the ATC representative on AMNLAE's restructured leadership, said when visiting London in 1987, "We have had a lot of problems with male comrades telling us to shut up about feminism and concentrate on defending the revolution. But now that the national leadership has come out and said that position is wrong, it is the men who have to shut up!"

3. Combating institutional inequalities and discrimination against women

Within a few weeks of coming to power the FSLN initiated measures to alter the legal position of women. In response to one of the demands of

AMPRONAC, Article 30 of Decree No. 48 banned the media's exploitation of women as sex objects. This swift action highlighted the fact that the FSLN considered the law to be an instrument for equalizing relations between the sexes, as well as being a site of conflict between revolutionary and prerevolutionary values. Whereas other reform measures led to an improvement in the political and material conditions of women, along with other subordinated groups, legal reform confronted traditional relations between the sexes directly, by removing certain male privileges and challenging some of those that remained.

AMNLAE spearheaded the campaign to reform the legal status of women. The organization's permanent representative on the main legislative body, the Council of State, was responsible for drafting, circulating, and presenting new legislation for ratification. Following the passing of the law against media exploitation of women, several other laws relating to women and the family were approved by the Council. In some cases, old laws, already on the statute books but not implemented, were revived and reaffirmed. One such law embodied the principle of equal pay for the same work. This was implemented to women's advantage in many state enterprises and cooperatives, sometimes against the wishes of male workers. Other measures allowed for the reduction of the working day where this was particularly long, as in the case of rural workers and domestic servants. Health and safety provisions of industrial workers were also improved, and steps were taken to ensure that women workers in some enterprises received their entitlement of four weeks maternity leave on full pay before childbirth, and eight weeks afterward.

The position of women workers in the rural sector was radically improved in 1982 by a decree based on a provision in the 1979 Statute of Rights under which wages were no longer paid only to the male head of family but to all workers over age fourteen on an individual basis. This enabled the contribution of women workers to receive greater social recognition while providing them with their own income. Two other new laws aroused considerable controversy, and it was these which addressed male-female relations directly. The first, the Law of Relations between Mothers, Fathers, and Children of 1981, aimed "to regulate equality of rights and duties between men and women with respect to (their) common children". The law sought to remove men's special privileges over custody in divorce settlements (known as *patria potestad*), and recognized the legal rights of illegitimate children.

The second, the Provision Law drafted in 1982, was even more controversial. This attempted to redefine family responsibilities more broadly than the existing legislation, which stipulated only a parental obligation to provide children with the basic necessities of life. This law was important not only for the reaction it aroused, but also for what it revealed about Sandinista thinking concerning the emancipation of women. It was designed to fulfill two goals that were seen as complementary: on the one hand, to promote greater family cohesion, and on the other to redress some of the injustices from which women suffered. Policies on the family were formulated within a perspective that defined the family as a "basic institution of society," entitled to the support and protection of the state. AMNLAE saw its role as helping to strengthen the Nicaraguan family, and this was considered necessary for two reasons. First, as an institution the family had suffered from the erosion of kin ties and from the historical prevalence of male out-migration. Second, given the lack of resources available for public welfare, the family, and in particular the extended household, could be encouraged to meet some of these needs. In this spirit the Provision Law therefore aimed to promote "greater family reciprocity and responsibility" by making all adult members legally liable for maintaining the family unit. This meant that all income earners should contribute financially and share in the household tasks.

The second aim of the Provision Law was to improve the position of both women and children by giving them a more secure financial base within the family. This was intended to offset the effects of the high rate of male desertion, migrancy, and serial polygyny which left women as the sole providers for their children: with a total fertility rate of 6.3, Nicaraguan women bore large numbers of children and this, coupled with the fact that 34 percent of Nicaraguan households were female headed (and 60 percent in Managua), was a major constituent of female poverty.[19] The new law sanctioned a practice already established at the Welfare Ministry (INSIBBI) which made it possible for a woman to claim aid from the father of her children provided he accepted paternity. It thus gave the state increased powers to ensure that such aid was provided and specified that this could be in cash, kind, or even in the form of housework, a novel feature of the Provision Law.

When the law came up for public discussion in 1982 it generated considerable controversy. AMNLAE convened over 100 Popular Assemblies to discuss its provisions and these were attended by trades unionists, market women, CDS members, and public sector employees: fewer men than women attended, as they were said to feel threatened by AMNLAE and its campaigns of law reform. There was also a lively debate in the national press about the place of women's emancipation in the process of revolutionary consolidation, which was repeated when a somewhat modified law was presented to the Council of State in October 1982.

To charges by members of the Council of State that it was waging a "sex war" by setting women against men, AMNLAE argued that its principal aim was to strengthen the family and thereby provide better conditions for the nation's children by giving them a more secure environment. The law was criticized on the grounds that it was not realistic in calling for changes in the difficult area of male-female relations, particularly at that time.

Some critics were more straightforward in expressing the fear that it could polarize relations between the sexes and so weaken the struggle against the main enemy, the counterrevolutionary forces. The law was referred back to AMNLAE for redrafting to meet some of these objections. The revised law was approved by the Council of the State in November 1982, but by 1987 it had still not been ratified by the National Directorate, although some of its clauses were embodied in the new Constitution.[20]

Beyond the conjunctural question of the relation between women's emancipation and defense of the revolution there lay a deeper problem, namely whether the law adequately identified the causes of the weakness of the family, specifically the marked gender inequalities that prevailed and that privileged men in certain ways. It was therefore doubtful whether the family could be strengthened without tackling the roots of these privileges, and confronting the issue of *machismo*, and thereby questioning the basis of male-female relations. Merely making men legally responsible in the financial realm was not adequate to the task of what Tomás Borge had called "humanizing social relations."[21] Yet even such mild proposals as these opened AMLAE to vigorous attacks from both conservative and staunchly revolutionary sectors. Magda Enriques, a member of AMNLAE's National Directorate, maintained: "These were issues of common concern to men and women. By improving the position of women we also helped to remove from men the burden of their own oppression."[22]

The Constitution of 1986 embodied many of the proposals advanced by AMNLAE's legal advisers, and gave weight to some of the previous legislation. The Constitution guaranteed women's right to enforce men's responsibility for their children, whether born in or out of wedlock; established absolute equality of rights within the family; allowed marriage to be dissolved by the will of either party; and established the principle of unconditional equality between the sexes with respect to political rights. Yet issues that threatened to divide the people along religious or gender lines would continue to be treated with caution. In a situation where priority was given to national defense, and the revolution's survival was seen as the only guarantee for any process of women's emancipation, progress in establishing real, rather than simply formal, equality between the sexes was likely to be slow.

4. Improving and extending women's economic and social position

Women's entry into productive activity was considered by AMNLAE to be both an important precondition for women's emancipation and a contribution to the national development effort. AMNLAE consequently sought to increase women's training and employment opportunities, although this proved difficult in the prevailing conditions of capital scarcity and industrial decline. After the victory, women played an increasingly important part in the Nicaraguan economy. Whereas in 1971 they formed only 17.21 percent of the Economically Active Population (EAP), this had increased to at least 34 percent by 1987.[23] This made female participation rates in Nicaragua almost double the average for Latin America as a whole, and even if some allowance is made for different accounting methods, a substantial increase nonetheless appears to have taken place particularly in the agrarian sector following the occupation of men's jobs by women as a result of the war. However, most women workers were still concentrated in areas where incomes were low.[24] In the urban centers many women worked in the large and expanding informal sector; in 1982 two-thirds of the urban labor force were outside permanent wage employment and women comprised 70.1 percent of this category, which grew even further after 1985.[25] Work conditions were sometimes better in formal sector urban employment, but women accounted for at most 15 percent of the workforce here and were chiefly concentrated in the conventional areas of female employment—textiles, chemicals, and foodstuffs. High rates of inflation from the mid-1980s and the downward spiral of real wages led to many workers leaving the formal sector to work in the informal economy.

From the outset AMNLAE focused its efforts on alleviating the situation of the most deprived women, and to this end it took three main initiatives. In the first place, both jobs and training in semi-skilled occupations were provided through the establishment of production collectives. This program began in 1980, and small enterprises were established at the same time to produce low-cost utilities such as clothing and pottery. By 1983 there were over fifty collectives in which AMNLAE participated, eighteen of them entirely run by the women's organization. Four years later AMNLAE was involved in more than a hundred projects of this kind. Some of these functioned as rehabilitation centers that trained ex-prostitutes in skills such as sewing and tailoring.[26]

The second component of this program began in August 1982 and involved a campaign to promote the cultivation of family plots. The official aim was, once again, "to integrate women into production." AMNLAE undertook to provide seeds of basic staple vegetables and helped in planning cultivation. The campaign was considered to be a great success: only a year after it began, over four hundred individual plots, and twenty-three communal ones, had been established. In the following year, the number of plots worked under this scheme more than trebled and in the conditions of increasing scarcity further expansion in some areas of the city has occurred.[27]

The third campaign initiative was directed specifically at the rural areas, where from 1983 AMNLAE made its priority the alleviation of the situation of rural women, a particularly deprived group. The redistribution of land under the provisions of the Agrarian Reform—to private, cooperative, and state cultivation—brought a substantial number of women into production for the first time, and the 1981 Law of Agricultural Cooper-atives included as one of its stated objectives the greater involvement of women in both production and related administrative activities. By 1987 more than 50 percent of cooperatives had some women members, but overall, women constituted only 6 percent of membership. The pattern of increased female productive activity varied, however, according to region: one reason for this was the different degrees of effort devoted to mobilizing and integrating women, and the other was that recruitment of men for the defense of the revolution was uneven. In some cases the demands of the war on the male labor force produced changes in the traditional division of labor, with women taking over jobs previously performed by men and becoming the principal agrarian producers. Perhaps the most affected regions were those of Matagalpa and Jinotega, where by the mid-1980s women made up as much as 45 percent of the rural workforce.[28]

Finally, AMNLAE encouraged women to acquire technical and voca-tional training in areas from which they were traditionally excluded. This was assisted to some degree by a general rise in female enrollment at school and the complementary rise in the number of women in higher education after the revolution. Only five years later, women accounted for over 40 percent of university students, an increase of almost 100 percent on 1979 figures, and one which rose even further in the next few years.

However, there was also a need to redirect young women into more challenging and socially necessary roles in the public realm.[29] In 1984 high school students were given a series of seminars in vocational training and a special effort was made to encourage girls to enter areas such as agricultural engineering and technology. With support from AMNLAE and the FSLN, some women began to enter areas previously closed to them. The most striking advance in this respect was the graduation of five women pilots by 1984. The first of these, Saida González, became a fighter pilot and was killed in 1984 while on duty near the war front.

5. Promoting respect for domestic labor and creating child-care services for working women

From its inception AMNLAE devoted considerable efforts to changing and improving women's position in the home. Its papers, first *La Voz de la Mujer* (Woman's Voice) and later *Somos AMNLAE* (We Are AMNLAE), founded in 1982, published both political and theoretical articles on the need to free women from the burden of domestic responsibilities, as well as proffering advice on making housekeeping, sewing, and cooking easier.[30]

AMNLAE's view was that domestic labor should not only be made a "category of socially recognized work but also be shared by all adult household members." Moreover, child-care should not devolve solely upon women but should be equalized within the household, with the state providing appropriate support systems that would also help to improve the care of children. However, it was only in 1982 that these issues came to the forefront of public discussion when the Provision Law was debated. Article 1.2 of that law stated: "Domestic labor is one of the pillars on which the family rests, and to which all members who are able and have the opportunity to do so must contribute, regardless of sex." At the Popular Assemblies held in 1982 to discuss the draft law, this clause received considerable attention from AMNLAE officials and substantial support from the women present.[31] Despite some opposition to it as "impractical," the clause remained in the final version of the Provision Law: yet it was noticeable that public discussion, and hence stimulation of awareness, on the issue had significantly declined by 1983. AMNLAE's Legal Office, established on March 8, 1983, assumed responsibility for explaining the provisions of the law to individuals wishing to invoke it. After the Second Congress there were also radio announcements at meal times for a while urging husbands to help with cooking and cleaning up. But in the absence of a popular and sustained campaign around this issue, the law could do little to alter the division of labor between men and women in the domestic sphere.

If progress on equalizing domestic labor was therefore limited, more public attention focused on the social and economic dimensions of the household, especially as a result of prevailing shortages, which the counterrevolutionary war had exacerbated by late 1983. AMNLAE conducted a number of campaigns designed to increase women's awareness of the implications of their housekeeping practices for the economy as a whole, and to point out how women, through their own individual efforts, could help to stretch the family income and thus reduce the pressure on wages, as well as help to conserve scarce or expensive resources. In 1982, named the Year of Austerity and Frugality in the Family, AMNLAE called on women to be better housewives in order to preserve national resources and help the rationed basic foodstuffs go further. AMNLAE's argument was that domestic labor had a different significance under socialism than it did under capitalism: if in the latter it benefited the capitalist, in the former it protected the resources of the revolution. A publicity campaign called on women to save imported glass bottles for recycling and so reduce the foreign exchange bill. Such campaigns were designed to serve a dual function: a strictly economic one, whereby changes in housekeeping practices alleviated the burden on the national economy, and a broader political one, of mobilizing women and increasing their consciousness of the revolution through their participation in such campaigns.[32] The Family Plot campaign was also conceived with similar ends in view.

Positive as they were in some respects, such mobilizations of women around domestic issues reflected a deeper ambiguity in the FSLN's policies toward women; while these were concerned to challenge traditional female stereotypes in the public arena, less attention was given to the private, domestic sphere. The most resilient and indeed powerful of female representations, that of motherhood, remained unassailed by the changes that had taken place in other areas. This was to be expected in a society where motherhood received religious confirmation, but it also acquired official support in the public emphasis on Mothers' Circles, Mothers' Demonstrations for Peace, and Mothers' of Martyrs masses. While these encouraged the more heroic aspects of revolutionary motherhood, they nonetheless retained a more traditional perception of women's reproductive duties. The conservative Catholic church's opposition to contraception and abortion and celebration of motherhood as women's primary role, provided the ideological underpinning for Nicaragua's high birth rate. The Sandinistas were as a result unable to legalize abortion (outlawed in the Penal Code of 1974), or make contraception widely available. Increasing numbers of abortions were carried out in conditions that endangered the health and lives of many women. One official source states that 27 percent of maternal deaths in the mid-1980s were due to illegal or badly performed abortions.[33] Lea Guido, when minister of health, summed up the dominant view within the FSLN's leadership until the mid-1980s: "While we don't have a problem of over-population (far from it) abortion and contraception are a human right. We want to make these available but since there is opposition to it, we must be careful how we proceed."[34] There is hope in some official quarters that abortion may be decriminalized in coming years; but in the meantime AMNLAE stresses preventative measures, especially sex education programs in schools.

More progress was registered in the field of child care, although the limited resources available, and the reluctance of men to play their part, meant that this remained an obstacle to women's greater participation in extra-domestic activities, in both the rural and urban areas. While the state's provision of childcare facilities continued to fall short of demand, their numbers steadily increased over the years following the triumph. By 1986, 26 Child Development Centers, catering for 3400 children were established in the urban areas, while in the countryside, 41 Rural Infant Services absorbed over 3,000 children. By 1987 the number of centers had risen to 182, with a corresponding rise in the number of attenders to over 7,000. These comprehensive systems, which combined child care with educational, health and nutrition needs, could not be greatly expanded because of financial constraints. Instead more attention was focused on increasing the number of Children's Lunchrooms, which aimed to provide working children and those from the poorest families with a main meal each day while encouraging them to attend school. About 80 of these, involving some 15,000 children, were in existence by 1984, and this figure had doubled in the three years that followed.[35]

Conclusion

The evidence suggests that in the period after 1979 women continued to participate in large numbers in the revolutionary process, as combatants against counterrevolution, organizers of welfare programs, and workers in the various branches of the economy. Many women, and especially those from the more disadvantaged groups, also benefited from the welfare policies implemented by the Sandinista state as well as from AMNLAE's specific programs. They gained more access to health, education training, and housing; at least until 1984 their basic provisions, although rationed, were heavily subsidized. These benefits, a direct product of the priorities and policies of the state, had a particular significance for women, who by virtue of their place within the sexual division of labor were disproportionately responsible for the provision of basic needs.

Some progress was also made in equalizing gender relations and in tackling the causes of women's subordination, especially through women's greater participation and prominence in social life, but also through legal reform. For many women the revolution raised their expectations and fundamentally changed their lives. Judged by their own goals the Sandinistas had achieved a substantial amount in a relatively short period of time. Yet they were not complacent about the results, nor could they be.[36] The limits of the process were also clear. By 1988 most women were still located in the least rewarding jobs and in areas such as the informal sector where they had traditionally predominated; daily provisioning became acutely difficult after 1986 with steep rises in inflation owing to the war; the legal measures designed to equalize the burden of domestic labor remained largely ineffective in the absence of a sustained campaign to combat entrenched attitudes; and women had not gained reproductive freedom. In 1984 Magda Enriques expressed what many must have felt:

> When we look back and see how much we have achieved we are very proud. But when we see how much there is still left to be done that's when we feel angry because there is so much more we could be doing that we are not able to do because of the War. But women are defending the gains of the revolution; they know it offers the only opportunity and the only guarantee for improving their lives.[37]

There can be little doubt that, whatever the shortcomings of the process were, the revolution had nevertheless introduced major, positive, reforms in the position of women, and that the survival of the regime was a precondition for the maintenance and continuation of these changes. The example of Grenada, where the military intervention of October 1983 was immediately followed by the public reemergence of prostitution, the ending of welfare programs, disbandment of the National Women's organization, and mass unemployment, demonstrated this link all too clearly.

The fate of women in Nicaragua in the first decade and beyond was conditioned to a greater degree than usual by external forces. These limited the capacity of the government and organizations such as AMNLAE to implement a far-reaching reform program, let alone maintain an acceptable standard of living. Yet the paradox of the war was that while it certainly divided many women, not only along class lines, it nevertheless created the conditions in which women were increasingly mobilized in support of the revolution's gains. The spontaneous mobilizations of women in the prerevolutionary period were therefore to a considerable extent transformed into an organized and institutionalized defense of the regime they themselves had helped to bring to power.

Notes

I would like to thank Hermione Harris, Irene Vance, and friends in and from Nicaragua for their help in the preparation of this article, as well as the Nuffield Foundation (which sponsored the research undertaken in Nicaragua) and the Fuller Bequest of the Department of Sociology, Essex University.

1. For accounts of women's role in the anti-Somoza struggle see M. Randall, *Sandino's Daughters* (London: Zed, 1981); S. Ramirez-Horton "The Role of Women in the Revolution," in T. Walker, ed., *Nicaragua in Revolution* (New York: Praeger, 1982); H. Harris, "Women in Struggle: Nicaragua," *Third World Quarterly*, 5, no. 4 (1983); and E. Maier, *Nicaragua, la Mujer en la Revolución* (Mexico, 1980). This and other accounts do not deal with the specific situation of ethnic minority women; for a discussion of this issue and for testimonials by ethnic minority women see A. Angel and F. Mackintosh, eds., *The Tiger's Milk* (London: Virago, 1987).
2. This question of the heterogeneous nature of "women's interests" and of their support for and benefits from the revolution is critically evaluated in my article "Mobilization Without Emancipation? Women's Interests, the State, and Revolution in Nicaragua," *Feminist Studies* 11, no. 2 (1985), updated and reprinted in R. Fagen, C. D. Deere, and L. Coraggio, eds., *Transition and Development* (New York: Monthly Review Press, 1986).
3. Author's interview, Managua 1982. Nora Astorga, who died in 1987, was awarded the title of Comandante Guerrillera for her role in the guerrilla struggle. She was appointed ambassador to the United States in 1984 but the U.S. government refused to allow her to take up the post. (The reason given was her part in the assassination of Perez Vega, one of Somoza's close advisers.) She became ambassador to the UN in 1986.
4. Speech by Cdte. Tomás Borge, one of the leaders of the revolution, published in *Barricada*, October 4, 1982.
5. The name commemorates the first woman combatant (a seamstress) to be killed by Somoza forces.
6. AMNLAE, *Documentos de la Asamblea Nacional* (Managua, 1982).

146   Third World Revolutions

7. J. Deighton et al., *Sweet Ramparts* (London: War on Want and the Nicaraguan Solidarity Campaign, 1983).
8. AMNLAE, *Mujer, Revolucion*, July 19, 1981. Martha Mungía was elected to AMNLAE's national leadership in 1987.
9. Author's interview, London, March 1984.
10. Author's interview, London, March 1984. Magda Enriques was the member of the Secretariat responsible for Education and Information.
11. *Somos AMNLAE*, July 1983. There are no official figures on defense matters at the time of writing (1987), and statistics on other areas of female participation are hard to come by. Many must be taken as broadly indicative.
12. Oficina de la Mujer, the bureau that coordinates FSLN and AMNLAE policy, provided these figures. See P. Perez and P. Diaz (1986) *Informes: 10 Ános de investigación sobre la mujer en Nicaragua (1976–1986)*.
13. These were Lea Guido, minister of health; Daisy Zamora, deputy minister of culture; and Nora Astorga, deputy foreign minister. Ctde. Dora Maria Téllez was the vice president of the Council of State. See *Pensamiento Propio*, April 1987, pp. 9–11 for more recent details of women's distribution in government.
14. The ATC set up a Women's Secretariat, which works to make women's issues an integral part of union policy. The ACT since 1986 has been committed, among other things, to nursery provision, and integrating men into domestic responsibilities.
15. In 1982 Glenda Monterrey assumed the role of general secretary from Gloria Carrión, a move that was seen to coincide with efforts to make AMNLAE "more responsive to the needs of working class women." In 1986 Lea Guido, former minister of health, took over as general secretary.
16. *Barricada*, September 29, 1983.
17. *Una Mujer Donde Esté Debe Hacer la Revolucion*, AMNLAE pamphlet 1982, Managua.
18. *Somos AMNLAE*, no. 1, May 1982.
19. According to MIPLAN statistics for the early 1980s, in the poorest income earning sector in Managua there were 354 women for each 100 men.
20. The situation was legally ambiguous since the law did have some force through the invocations at tribunals of "common law."
21. Borge, in *Barricada*, October 4, 1982.
22. AMNLAE pamphlet *Una Mujer Donde Esté*.
23. Official sources for 1987 give women as comprising 36 percent of the EAP with a female participation rate of 42 percent. Oficina de la Mujer. Other sources put the percentage of economically active women as high as 44.1.
24. Deighton et al., *Sweet Ramparts*, p. 65.
25. In 1982 women made up 70 percent of the urban labor force outside permanent wage relations. In the same year, 85 percent of female heads of households went out to work; ibid., p. 64. This figure no doubt rose in the period after 1982.
26. Prostitution was made illegal after the victory, although it remained an important survival strategy for poor women. The Sandinistas tried with comparatively little success to provide alternative income generating projects for ex-prostitutes. See Deighton et al. *Sweet Ramparts* for an account of these prostitution rehabilitation centers.
27. Interview with Magda Enriques, March 1984.
28. A CIERA survey of 1981 found that women represented 36 percent of the cotton harvest workers and at least 28 percent of the coffee harvest workers. See C. D. Deere, "Co-Operative Development and Women's Participation in the Nicaraguan Agrarian Reform," *American Journal of Agrarian Economics*, December 1983. The figure of 45 percent is based on research carried out by the ATC.
29. Despite the increase in participation, the female drop-out rate remained high. In order to

counter one of the reasons for this, AMNLAE organized seminars in sex education for final year high school students.

30. *Somos AMNLAE* also ran a series of articles designed to teach readers about reproduction and family health.
31. This was evident in the seven assemblies I attended.
32. Author's interview with Glenda Monterrey, when general secretary of AMNLAE, September 1982.
33. In 1985 one Managua hospital was admitting an average of twelve women a day as a result of illegal abortions. See Deighton et al, *Sweet Ramparts*, p. 154; *Barricada*, November 1985 *(passim)*; and my article "The Politics of Abortion in Nicaragua," *Feminist Review* 29, (May 1988).
34. Author's interview, Autumn 1982. Although a criminal offense abortion cases have only rarely been brought before the courts.
35. Figures provided by the Oficina de la Mujer, and by the Minister of Social Welfare Services, Raimundo Téfel. (Interview published in *Critical Social Policy*, Spring 1988.)
36. Tomás Borge alludes to this in the speech cited above; see *Barricada*, October 4, 1982.
37. Author's interview, March 1984.

Ambiguous Transformations: Women, Politics, and Production in Mozambique

Sonia Kruks and Ben Wisner

This paper sets out to describe the situation of peasant women—the vast majority of women—in Mozambique, and to discuss how it has and has not changed since independence was achieved in 1975. We focus our postindependence analysis on three areas: the relation of women to the political process, domestic social relations, and woman's place in non-domestic relations of production. We have sought to show in what ways rural women have become less oppressed in these areas, but also to pinpoint and evaluate the chief constraints on their further emancipation. While some of these constraints are specific to their situation as women and specific to understanding of that situation by the ruling party, the Mozambique Liberation Front (FRELIMO), we will argue that some other constraints suggest certain difficulties in FRELIMO's concept of and relation to the peasantry as a whole.

However, at present, those constraints on women's emancipation that have arisen from inadequacies in FRELIMO's analyses and policies are wholly overshadowed by the problems posed by a massive crisis of destabilization. Since the early 1980s, a South African backed and supplied terrorist organization has escalated brutal attacks on the civilian population and engaged in the destruction of social infrastructure. It has now caused such a level of disruption in many parts of Mozambique that most agendas for social transformation—including the question of woman's emancipation—are virtually in abeyance. At the most optimistic, the present struggle to survive as an integral nation state has put Mozambique's agenda for a socialist transformation largely "on hold." Thus, in what follows we will discuss primarily the policies that were being implemented in the late 1970s and early 1980s—the policies of that small window between the war against colonialism and the present war against South African destabilization, when "building the bases for the transition to socialism" did not seem a wholly unrealistic dream.

We have chosen to focus in our discussions mainly on conditions in the southern third of Mozambique—the "Sul do Save." This is because our own knowledge is greatest of that area and because more research has generally been carried out there.[1] However, while the political economy of this region has some distinctive features (arising primarily from the use of the area as a labor reserve for the South African mines), we assume that the critical points we make concerning FRELIMO's analysis of women and the ways in which policies are likely to impinge on women are also, in general, relevant for the rest of Mozambique.

The Situation at Independence

At independence, in 1975, FRELIMO took power over a society deeply marked by the effects of a particularly long and abusive colonial rule. At least 80 percent of the population was rural, yet subsistence agriculture had been so distorted by Portuguese policies of forced labor and forced cultivation, by taxation policies and an emphasis on exportable cash-crop production, that malnutrition and disease were rife.[2] Since the Portuguese had not intended to decolonize but had encouraged poor Portuguese to come to the colonies as small traders, artisans, clerical workers, and so on, education and training for the African population had been minimal. At independence the illiteracy rate was about 90 percent, and must have been nearer to 100 percent for women.[3]

All colonial states are politically repressive, but given the lack of internal traditions of liberalism in fascist Portugal and the more intense degree of exploitation Portugal required of its colonies to compensate for its own economic backwardness in the European context, Portuguese rule was particularly vicious. Local administrators were virtually unchecked in the methods they used to obtain taxes, crops, and men to fulfill forced-labor quotas. In most areas Portuguese administrators, with the aid of their own local police force, ruled the population directly. In some areas indirect rule through compliant local chiefs was used. Either way, there were no forms of political participation open to the bulk of the African population.

The period immediately following independence (1975–77) was that in which FRELIMO attempted to make its control of the state more than formal. Control over the police and transformation of FRELIMO forces into a national army proceeded fairly smoothly, but control over the central state apparatus was—and still is—more difficult to achieve, in part because of FRELIMO's need to rely on skilled personnel who had not come up through the party's ranks but had been educated and politically formed by the Portuguese. In the rural areas, because of political problems with administrators who remained from colonial times and a general shortage of government officials, the party has tended to overlap a good deal with the main administrative bodies. Positions such as locality administrator and locality party secretary are frequently vested in one person.

The transition to state power was made the more difficult by the chaotic economic situation provoked by the mass exodus of Portuguese and mismanagement by the remaining foreign firms (including practices that shaded over into economic sabotage). The exodus caused a profound collapse of the commercial infrastructure in the entire country, since the small country stores that had provided the supply and marketing framework had been owned and operated by the Portuguese colonial pettybourgeoisie. Simultaneously there occurred a depression in the construction industry in Maputo and the nearly simultaneous collapse of South African mine employment opportunities for many of the men in the southern third of Mozambique.[4] FRELIMO's response to these massive, many-sided problems was to try to keep as much of the colonial economy ticking as possible: abandoned settler farms were managed as "blocks" of hastily planned state farms; bankrupt plantations and food-processing industries were managed by "administrative commissions"; marketing and supply was attempted through a network of "people's shops" (lojas de povo). Many of these immediate responses have subsequently proven too costly, wasteful, and unmanageable. A further major effect of such a pattern of planning by crisis management has been to divert attention from the needs of the mass of the rural producers—the women. The squeaky wheel gets the oil and, as we will show below, the voice of the female peasantry was neither loud nor clear during this critical transition period.

By early 1977 the worst initial problems of independence were sufficiently resolved for FRELIMO to hold its Third Congress, at which policies and directions for the future were laid down in considerable detail. For the first time FRELIMO declared itself openly to be a Marxist-Leninist party and asserted that socialism had to be the long-term goal for Mozambique. However, given the colonial heritage, it was argued that Mozambique had to go through a preliminary stage, catching-up period, known as "Popular Democracy," in which would be created "the political, ideological, technical, and material bases" for the later development of socialism.[5]

At the congress the decision was announced to turn FRELIMO from a broad front into a Leninist vanguard party. Membership was to be open only to militants who successfully fulfilled a period of candidacy, while the broad mass of the population was to be incorporated into the political process for the first time and given contact with the party through the "mass democratic organizations," under the control and tutelage of the party. One of these was to be the Organization of Mozambican Women (OMM).

The notion of the vanguard party not only involved questions of organization. It was linked to an analysis of social classes in Mozambique in which FRELIMO's original emphasis on the peasantry in the rural north of the country as the main force in the anticolonial struggle was replaced by an analysis of it as the less dynamic partner in a "worker-peasant alliance" led by the party. This analysis was initially developed by the Central Committee at its eighth session, the year prior to the Third Congress of FRELIMO. While granting that the war had been fought primarily with the support and participation of the peasantry, it argued that the peasantry could not now play the leading role in the new phase, the struggle to create the "bases" for the transition to socialism. Although the peasantry had shown, even in the nonliberated zones, a strong nationalist sentiment and a resistance to colonialism, a number of prominent farmers whose basis lay in traditional feudalism had been encouraged by the Portuguese to develop forms of capitalist organization. Thus it was concluded that it must fall to the proletariat to be the "leading class" in the "worker-peasant alliance."

However, the proletariat in Mozambique is both numerically small and lacking in political experience. It must play the leading role in the worker-peasant alliance, but it is ill-equipped to do so. If it is destined to grow into the leading class, it is not yet so. In the meantime, and as an aid to the development of the proletariat, revolutionary leadership must remain the task of the vanguard party, whose members may be of any class origin, but whose proven revolutionary practice and grasp of revolutionary theory permit them to unite and lead the masses.

Vanguard theory in Mozambique, as elsewhere, also embraces the theory of "democratic centralism." This implies not only that once decisions are taken at the higher levels they are binding on lower levels, but also that lower levels of the party should make contributions to the decision-making process. Since most people are not in the party, FRELIMO has also emphasized the role of the mass democratic organizations in the process of policymaking. The organizations were characterized by the Third Congress as "the contact point between the party and the people."[6] In practice, however, democratic centralism in Mozambique has had a tendency to operate more from the top down than the other way around—a problem that is of considerable significance for the situation of women, who are not given sufficient consideration as a group by the predominantly male leadership.

On the economic front, emphasis at the Third Congress was placed above all on increasing the level of production. Indeed, the "battle for production" was said to have replaced the battle for national liberation as the main struggle. Plans for eventual industrialization were posited on raising production both of food crops and exportable cash crops. To these ends, policies for cooperative agriculture were elaborated, linked to the resettlement of the rural population in communal villages. In addition, it was decided to develop the state farms sector on large abandoned estates, using fairly high technology, in order to normalize and increase the urban food supply as soon as possible and to provide export crops to bring in foreign exchange.

Communal villages were to be not only more efficient production units, but equally centers for political and social advancement. They were to serve as a basis for political organizations, as centers for the location of such services as health and education, and as the nodal points in an urgently needed new network for commerce. However, the movement of the population into villages has not been as fast as hoped for, and the development of cooperative agriculture within them has been even slower. In spite of criticisms made as early as 1978 that too much investment was going to the state farms, the Central Committee reported to FRELIMO's Fourth Congress, in 1983, that only 2 percent of the agricultural investment had gone to the cooperative sectors, while "in practice support to the family sector was virtually nonexistent" between 1977 and 1982. Only 37,000 people were said to be members of agricultural cooperatives by 1982, although 1,800,000 people lived in villages.[7] The relationship between state farm, cooperative, and individual family agriculture and the amount of encouragement and assistance each should receive continues to be debated.[8] How this debate comes to be resolved will be central to the question of women's liberation.

Rural Women Before Independence

Mozambique contains a great number of ethnic groupings, but even so, some broad generalizations can be made on the treatment of women.[9] Except in the north, most groups are patrilineal and most are polygamous; bride price, known as *lobolo*, appears to have been ubiquitous and was often paid in livestock in the south. Women were often promised in marriage in infancy and in some tribes child marriage was common. It is still rare among rural women for a woman to have a say in her marriage partner. Initiation rites, often painful or demeaning, are still widespread.[10]

Once married, a woman came under the authority of her husband and led a rather privatized existence within his household. She lived in a house that he constructed and that she had to leave in the event the marriage broke up. Her access to land was usually through her husband's ownership of it. Although men were responsible for some agricultural tasks, notably clearing new land and plowing, their main activities within the traditional division of labor were hunting, warfare, care of cattle, and construction. Colonial rule changed male activities primarily to migrant wage labor and cash-crop production, but women still maintained—and continue to maintain—their traditional role: the production of the family food supply. Normally, a woman controls the land she works, in the sense of making the decisions about how and when to plant, and she has the right to sell any surplus she can produce. Thus, although women are confined within a rigidly defined domestic sphere, it is a sphere that includes their own and their children's means of subsistence.

In addition to agriculture, women are exclusively responsible in most instances for an entire range of domestic tasks. Food preparation involves not only cooking but preparation of grains through pounding and the time-consuming tasks of fetching water and firewood. Washing, cleaning, and childcare are additional demands on their time. Studies conducted in other sub-Saharan countries suggest that women's working day is considerably greater than that of men, often stretching from before dawn until after dark.[11]

Colonialism added to these burdens. The increase in malnutrition caused by a diversity of colonial policies falls hardest on women, who spend much of their adult life in a state of pregnancy or lactation. In addition, policies that forced men into migrant wage labor increased the labor burden on women. Work that men would traditionally have done— such as clearing new ground, plowing, and even house repairs—was taken over increasingly by women. The effects of male migrant labor, especially to the South African mines, were also to give men access to cash income and to the workings of the so-called modern sector, which were denied to women. As a result of such processes, women generally came to be regarded by colonial administrators as even more "backward" than their men. They were even ignored in agricultural extension efforts, although they were the main agricultural producers.

This combination of negative influences on women in southern Mozambique has been reconstructed and poignantly evoked in a series of studies by Sheryl Young.[12] She documents how diet worsened while women's work burden and vulnerability to epidemic disease, flood, and drought increased during the beginning of the late colonial period (1890–1920). However, what is striking is that women were not reduced to a thoroughly passive condition by such horrendous conjunctures. There are numerous examples of innovative response to crisis. Women were the first to make cashews edible and to market them, and the first to grow cotton and groundnuts for sale on a large scale. Women's knowledge of "bush foods" and other products of a gathering economy was important in limiting deaths during famine periods. Of even greater importance, women took over ritual and broader sociopolitical functions during these crisis periods.

Although at its founding congress in 1962, FRELIMO had already resolved to promote the involvement of women in the struggle and to establish a women's organization, it was not until 1967 that any formal women's organization was established.[13] In the meantime (as in any rural guerrilla war), FRELIMO had had to rely on support from women, who provided food, shelter, and assistance with transport. Some of the leadership argued quite early for formal women's participation in the war, but were opposed by the more traditionally minded, warfare being seen as an exclusively male domain. When in 1967 women were admitted, it was as full military members: the organization of the Women's Detachment reflected the general radicalization of FRELIMO and the dominance within the movement of those who saw the struggle as one to build a wholly new society and not simply to end colonialism.

The Women's Detachment, however, remained small and women did not progress from it into the top FRELIMO leadership. Although militarily trained, members of the detachment were used primarily for mobilizing and for "social service" tasks such as health, education, and care of war orphans.[14] As its members lived on a military base and traveled extensively, few married women joined it. Later an organization in which women with families could be mobilized more easily was founded. This organization, the OMM, had its initial conference in 1973, but it appears to have remained rather small and fragmentary until after independence. It is important to point out that although there was a certain amount of pressure from women for both the Women's Detachment and the OMM to be established, neither was in any way a spontaneous women's movement; they were created by decision of the male FRELIMO leadership, in order to carry out tasks defined as important by that leadership.[15]

At the first OMM conference FRELIMO's president, Samora Machel, gave an analysis of the sources of women's oppression, of why it was necessary for FRELIMO to struggle for women's emancipation and of the ways that this should be done, an analysis that still provides the basis for policies concerning women in Mozambique.[16] In many ways Machel's prescriptions for the emancipation of women were similar to those of other Marxist-Leninist movements, following the orthodox position that identifies private property as the root of women's oppression. Machel argued that political mobilization and involving women in production *outside* the household are the main keys to emancipation. He also followed orthodoxy in seeing the mothering role of women as "natural," although in need of improvement through education since women are the teachers of the next generation of socialists. However, in spite of the economistic and productivist bias of the analysis, the policies that FRELIMO (through the OMM) has pursued most clearly and consistently toward women since independence have been—and continue to be—mainly to do with family structure and sexuality. Indeed, there has been a noticeable *lack* of clear thinking or policies on the question of the relation of women to production outside the family sphere. It is to the period since independence that we now turn.

The OMM and Women's Political Participation

FRELIMO sees privatization and isolation, leading to general political backwardness, as major effects of both the traditional and the colonial treatment of women. Thus entry into the political process is seen as a prerequisite for their emancipation: isolated rural women at least have to be *reached* by the state and the political organizations before such issues as illiteracy, polygamy, or anything else can be dealt with. Women are more likely to be contacted and mobilized directly by the OMM than by the party itself. The OMM was created "as our longest arm, the arm that would organize women farthest from our country, that would reach women in the most remote, most forgotten regions of our country."[17] For those women whom the OMM has contacted, what has been its impact?

As we have seen, OMM is not intended to be an autonomous women's movement, but is supposed to provide a channel for informing women of FRELIMO's policies and involving women in carrying them out. The most common way the OMM goes about contacting and incorporating women is through campaigns around specific events or issues. Mobilizing for specific events seems to be quite effective. For example, when a mass vaccination campaign was conducted, the OMM mobilized women to come and bring their children with considerable success.[18] What appears to be harder—not surprisingly, given the demands on women's time—is to mobilize women in a more continuous manner. Of the continuous campaigns, the adult literacy campaign has been one of the most important. Few illiterates speak the national language, Portuguese, and it is only in literacy classes that most women can obtain the language skills that permit them access to and participation in the political system. According to 1979 figures, over 40 percent of those attending literacy centers were women.[19] In comparison with colonial times, there is a vast increase in women's literacy.[20]

Other continuous campaigns the OMM conducts have been to involve women in collective agriculture and campaigns against bride price and other "social problems" affecting women. These problems were the subject of a national special OMM conference in May 1984, in preparation for which local-level meetings took place from July 1983. The official summary of the preparatory meetings shows an acute awareness at the grass roots of the disadvantaged economic role of women, but the OMM's strategy does not get beyond prior calls for "integration of women into production."[21] The descriptive material collected in the first part of the report does not inform the "strategic" conclusions of the second part.

For instance, it is quite clearly said of the unorganized rural woman (*a mulher camponesa*) that she is the principal producer of material goods in Mozambican society although she is not recognized as such (p. 34). Numerous concrete problems were documented by the OMM "brigades" that toured the country: difficulties in selling farm produce and finding basic necessities in shops (p. 35); refusal of men in the north of the country to accept women as members of agricultural cooperatives (p. 35); absence of maternity leave or child-care facilities even in cooperatives where women are in the majority (p. 36); conflict between women's domestic work load and the demands of cooperatives (p. 36). But the document does not take up such specific economic problems in its discussion of strategy, not even to formulate on behalf of women the *implied demands* for minimum preconditions for effective production.

Virtually the entire last third of this major OMM document, which laid out the empirical information from which new approaches to the actual condition of women could be developed, is concerned with the educating/nurturing role of women and family relations, *not* women's role in production. On the contrary, in one revealing passage (p. 53) the authors clearly accept the received colonial census category "active female population" according to which fully 58 percent of adult Mozambican women are not considered "economically active" *despite* a previous assertion by these same authors that women are the principal producers in the countryside! What the OMM authors have received uncritically (together with the National Statistical Service) from colonial statisticians is a systematic misunderstanding/devalorization of women's daily productive labor in the countryside (subsistence farming, carrying firewood and water, caring for children, cooking, providing health care). There is more here than a quibble with the definition of a census category. Where the OMM document *does* take up women's "integration into production" again, it simply leaps over the list of rural problems discussed earlier and concerns itself with why more women are not employed in industry (pp. 53–56).

OMM leaders seem more comfortable with campaigns that have aimed to educate women to be better mothers and housekeepers. Here, both the inadequacies of FRELIMO's analysis of women's situation and the very real conflicts in priorities of the present emerge. For example, given the high infant mortality rates, the OMM campaign to get mothers to give their children three meals a day makes sense from a public health point of view. However, given the work involved in food preparation, it is demanding a great deal of additional domestic labor from women at a time when many other new demands are also being put on their time; and, of course, it is further reinforcing the view of women as uniquely responsible for the well-being of their children.

Yet, having pointed out these problems, one also has to say that at the present time a campaign to involve fathers in the additional labor would not be successful, and the organizational structures for communal child feeding are not developed, so that this campaign, which is in some ways detrimental to women, would still seem to be justified if it succeeds in reducing infant mortality. It is clearly inevitable that there will be such conflicts in the complex and multifaceted social transformation FRELIMO is attempting. The main problem is that FRELIMO does not appear to confront them face on, but simply assumes that all that is good for the revolutionary transformation must also be good for the emancipation of women.

On perhaps a more positive note, it is clear that OMM activity and campaigns are encouraging women to leave their traditionally privatized domestic role and participate increasingly in the general running of their communities. For example, in the first postindependence elections to state assemblies, held in 1977, 28 percent of representatives of "locality" assemblies (the lowest level) were women, while even at the highest level, the People's Assembly, over 12 percent of those elected were women.[22] In the 1980 elections to locality assemblies nearly 25 percent of the representatives were again women.[23] Although no general figures are available on party membership, about 15 percent of delegates present at the 1983 Fourth Congress were women and some women serve in law courts, the police, and popular militia.[24] Given that women rarely spoke in public before independence, their entry into political life, even though it remains mainly at the local level, must be seen as a great achievement.

The OMM is not intended only to mobilize women: it is also supposed to make an input to the policymaking process with regard to women. It is in this area that the organization is undoubtedly at its weakest. Monthly meetings are held between the national OMM leadership and the party at which suggestions and initiatives are supposed to pass in both directions. But when asked in an interview in 1983 what policies OMM had suggested to FRELIMO, the secretary general of OMM had considerable difficulty in answering and reportedly could only come up with one example.[25] Policy regarding women is clearly determined in the party. This is to say, a predominantly male leadership is deciding what are—and are not— "women's issues" and which are the most pressing issues, without that input of women's opinion from the grass roots up which the OMM theoretically channels to the party.

There are several reasons for OMM's lack of initiative. Some of these are connected to the general top-down tendency of democratic centralism in Mozambique and the position of the peasantry in FRELIMO's analysis, which have already been described. Others, however, relate more specifically to the history of OMM. Before independence, the OMM was run by members of the Women's Detachment, peasant women from the liberated zones in the north. But with independence, OMM headquarters moved south to Maputo and few of its leaders moved with it. A new leadership developed, which was primarily urban and middle class and lacked an understanding of rural society. This leadership was criticized and largely purged by FRELIMO in 1976. The present leadership is still mainly urban, though it now includes some working-class women. Many of them feel intellectually insecure in relation to FRELIMO, and there may well be a fear of a repeat purge if they fail to understand FRELIMO's policies and are branded as counterrevolutionary. Between their fears and genuine lack of understanding of rural life, a lack compounded by poor communication between local OMM branches and the center, it is not surprising that the OMM leadership fails to act as advocates of women's needs to the party.

If in the long run better communication develops between rural OMM and its national headquarters, and if in time OMM develops a leadership drawn from peasant women, it might begin to formulate and propose policies that articulate the interests of peasant women. Were this to happen, the "sex-blind" nature of vanguardism could well emerge as an issue. It is possible that there would be pressure to establish a women's section of the party, to raise the implications of proposed economic and social policies for women from within the core of the vanguard itself, or perhaps there would be a challenge to the present way in which the relations between "mass democratic organizations" such as the OMM and the party are articulated. Either way, peasant women's leaders would have to develop structures that would enable them to define "women's issues" more broadly and to enter more fully into general policy formation than they can do at present. Such a possibility would require some modification of FRELIMO's present style of vanguardism.

Domestic Social Relations

In his speech to the first OMM Conference in 1973, Samora Machel gave the issue of altering family life a low priority. Again in 1976, opening the second OMM conference, he insisted that the liberation of women depended on their involvement in the "main transforming task" of society, which was now the battle for "production," the prerequisite for constructing "the material and ideological base" for socialism.[26] Yet the actual resolutions passed by the conference had virtually nothing to say about the means of involving women in production and dealt primarily with matters of family life and sexuality instead. Why this was so is not clear, but one might hypothesize that it was to do with FRELIMO's lack of sustained thinking on the problems of involving women more in nontraditional production relations: it was perhaps very hard to come up with practical resolutions on production and easier to devote attention to the apparently more clear-cut issues of women and the family. In fact, even these issues are not as clear-cut as they appear and are inseparable from issues of women's labor and, therefore, of production.

The conference resolutions on "social problems in the rural areas" dealt with the following matters: initiation rites, premature and forced marriage, forced and hereditary marriage, *lobolo*, polygamy, adultery, and divorce. This is essentially the same list that still appears in the OMM's Special Conference report some eight years later. In general, education and propaganda were seen as the main "means of combat" against these practices, though in the case of polygamy stronger disincentives were applied in the form of a prohibition on FRELIMO membership and other public positions for those entering new polygamous relations. The economic foundations of polygamy were also recognized, (though many of the implications of its economic basis were not), in the recommendation that OMM should encourage communal villages since, "through collective work, the situation in which enslaved women feel obliged to share their husbands will be eliminated."[27]

Since the 1976 conference a new Family Law has been drafted. The Family Law embodies the ideal of the egalitarian, "militant," monogamous marriage that FRELIMO espouses as the alternative to polygamy. Property is to be jointly owned, place of residence a joint decision. The Family Law also permits divorce, though it can only take place after reconciliation efforts have been tried and have failed.[28] Clearly, much of the Family Law is simply not enforceable in the majority of cases at present. Even so, the formal statement of women's equality and rights within marriage is a useful advance on the colonial situation.

It is hard to assess the present impact of FRELIMO's policies on the traditional family structure. Provincial OMM sections reported major declines in polygamy and other practices after 1976. But more recent visitors to communal villages report that close questioning brings forth admissions that new polygamous marriages are taking place.[29] The preparatory report for the May 1984 OMM conference discussed earlier is clear that in all provinces most of the rural population is still firmly in support of such traditional practices as *lobolo*, polygamy, and initiation rites.

One significant point about polygamy, which was already noted in the documents of the 1976 OMM conference but which reemerged in the more recent discussions in the countryside, is that it is often women who encourage and even help their husbands to take another wife (in the south often a younger relative from their own family).[30] This is not done through blind traditionalism but, as was noted, for essentially material reasons: it is not only the man who stands to benefit from the increased labor supply that a second wife represents. For the first wife, a second represents not only more agricultural labor for the household but possibilities also of reducing domestic labor, for example by taking turns in cooking or collecting wood. There are certain "economies of scale" in domestic labor in the polygamous household that women recognize and value, even if in other ways many find the institution detestable.[31] Polygamy is not simply a "social problem of women": it is also a relation of production.

If this is the case, might not the policy of attempting to abolish polygamy be detrimental to women in some ways? Undoubtedly polygamy is an institution that permits the male exploitation and oppression of women. But it is also part of the complex and delicately balanced social organization that enables an impoverished peasantry to subsist, by reducing domestic labor time, and also possibly by spreading out risk. What is clear is that its abolition will be of value to many women *only* in the context of a full reorganization of the relations of production and reproduction in which both agriculture *and* domestic labor relations are transformed. While

FRELIMO is clear about the need for the former, there appears to be little serious consideration of the need for the latter. Clearly the monogamous family, if it is instituted, will increase domestic labor-time loads for women yet further unless it is accompanied by a new organization of household and child-care tasks—either through the extensive socialization of such tasks or through a new division of such tasks within the family so that men share them.

Socialization of domestic labor—day-care centers, public laundries, eating places, and so forth—has been part of the classic Marxist solution to the "Woman Question" from Engels and Bebel onward. But such a "solution" requires a development of forces of production and a social surplus that Mozambique is not likely to have for many decades. Although a day-care center is supposed to be provided in each communal village, it is not surprising that few exist and many of those that do exist have problems in functioning.[32] Even if they were more widespread, their existence would still leave most of women's domestic labor burden untouched.

A new division of domestic labor within the household would seem to be a more feasible solution in terms of the economic constraints that operate. But the socioeconomic and ideological obstacles to it are enormous—bride price and polygamy being of course integral to the problem. Yet to attempt to end the polygamous household and to encourage women to enter public production without *simultaneously* attempting to define a new division of domestic labor within the family is to demand of rural women an even more extensive "double day" than they have now. It is also effectively to say that in an economic strategy that depends on accumulation from peasant production to finance industrial and urban development, rural women are going to have to contribute a greater proportion of the labor than are the men.

This is an issue FRELIMO has not seriously addressed. There have been the odd exhortations to men to "help" their wives, but no suggestion that this in fact should be their *responsibility*; women have rather been warned *not* to demand the participation of their men in household tasks, but to hope that their own example of hard work will encourage their husbands to assist.[33] The fact that the 1984 OMM conference again focused on "social problems of women" without addressing the concrete implications of substituting new family forms for those under attack points to a continuing weakness in FRELIMO's analysis of not only the question of women's liberation but of the very nature of peasant production relations and the implications of attempting to transform them.

Non-Domestic Relations of Production

The allocation of resources between state farm, cooperative, and family production is of key importance for women's incorporation in nonfamily production. The state farms employ a wage labor force that is overwhelmingly male, since men were the existing labor force when abandoned Portuguese estates were transformed into state farms. However, this situation is likely to be perpetuated, given that the top priority in the state farms is immediate productivity; for men are already experienced in the discipline of wage labor and trained in the use of mechanical equipment. In addition, there seems to be a firm prejudice by men workers against "their" women doing permanent wage work and leaving the domestic sphere—those women who do seek wage work are usually single mothers. In all, the integration of women would require major shifts of values and priorities on the part of both workers and management on the farms.

Cooperative production in communal villages, on the other hand, clearly provides better possibilities for the integration of women into nonfamily production. Cooperative agriculture is much more flexible than wage work. Both the duration and timing of work hours can be more easily geared to the needs of women. However, in many cooperatives where there are men as well this has also posed a problem: women tend to work fewer hours in the cooperative, as they still devote time to their traditional role as family food producers on individual plots. The result is that the men not only receive more money when the crop is sold but also take over most of the leadership positions. Even so, the fact that women are members of the cooperatives in their own right, can work full or part-time and receive a cash income that is their own, means that cooperative agriculture must be seen as the form most conducive to the incorporation of women into increasingly socialized relations of production. [34]

No matter what might be said about the positive potential of cooperatives for rural women, the fact remains that at the present time the vast majority of women practice isolated family production. Mozambique's national population census of August 1980 suggests that 83 percent of the workforce (adults over twelve years) were engaged in agriculture, and 93 percent of these were engaged in *family* agriculture. These census data allow a conservative estimate of 2.5 *million* adult rural women engaged in isolated production as opposed to at most 25,000 organized in cooperative farming (out of the approximately 250,000 women presently resident in the newly formed communal villages). [35]

How is one to interpret such orders of magnitude? The most obvious point is the very limited success to date in mobilizing the female peasantry for nonindividualized rural production: at most one in every hundred rural women is involved in cooperative production. Yet even this modest success is significant, given that only 2 percent of agricultural investment went to cooperatives during the period 1977–82. [36] Given the very limited role women had in the monetized economy under colonialism and given the severe crises that have accompanied the first years of independence (not only internal economic and environmental crisis but also regional destabilization and international capitalist recession), possibly 1 percent would be significant. On the other hand, if both FRELIMO and our analyses are correct in pinpointing women's involvement in nondomestic production as the key to their liberation, there has either been considerably less dedication to the cooperative sector than FRELIMO's rhetorical commitment to women's liberation would imply, or—despite a genuine commitment—some severe constraints on and/or errors in implementation have blocked this key pathway for women's advancement.

The individual family farming sector remains, then, central to the production of most of the food eaten in rural Mozambique. In the transitional period 1973–75 such subsistence production appears to have increased slightly while the amount of peasant production marketed fell dramatically—by about 60 percent—as Portuguese controls were relaxed.[37] As FRELIMO recognized at the Fourth Congress, the family sector is in crisis. Yet it remains the sector within which FRELIMO must mobilize the peasantry if socialization of agricultural production is to continue. It is also therefore the primary sector within which women have to be reached, and to mobilize this sector successfully note will surely have to be taken of the fact that most family production is carried out by women.

What are the main problems of this vast family sector and what are the specific problems faced by the attempt to draw it into cooperative production?[38] First, this sector has become widely dependent on cash income for the renewal of its means of production (oxen, plows, hoes, wells). Thus it has been severely weakened, especially in the south, by the dramatic reduction in migrant mine labor and other sources of wage employment since independence. However, except in the cases of flood or other major disruptions of production, peasants are not likely to move voluntarily into communal villages or into cooperative production *unless* they can be convinced that cooperative labor will yield an income comparable with that obtained by wage labor. At present, as we have seen, cooperatives remain undersupported and inefficient. In one example studied, cooperative members received the equivalent of less than two-fifths of the daily wage paid at a nearby state farm.[39]

A second major problem area concerns marketing and the availability of those commodities previously purchased with wages—not only hoes, plows, and the like, but such household necessities as salt, oil, soap, and cloth. A profound breakdown in rural supply and marketing networks accompanied the Portuguese exodus and FRELIMO has not been able effectively to organize an alternative network. By the early 1980s, it appears, a vicious circle had developed, in which lack of commodities to purchase has acted as a disincentive to peasants to produce a marketable surplus and the lack of surplus has in turn meant that Mozambique is unable to feed its cities and to export sufficient goods to be able to purchase abroad such items as hoes or cloth that it still cannot produce itself.[40]

Given the failure of the state farms also efficiently to produce a surplus, and the compounding of the problems described above by recent drought and cyclones and the disruption caused by the terrorists, it is hard to see the way out of this circle.

FRELIMO's response to this multifaceted crisis was, at the Fourth Congress in 1983, to criticize the previous concentration of agricultural assistance on the state farm sector and to call for more support for family agriculture and the private sector, as well as for more political decentralization.[41] While one can see the immediate and practical imperatives for supporting family farming in the present crisis, some major questions remain unaddressed: first, while the Central Committee report also talks of support for cooperatives "in the priority districts," the swing toward supporting family agriculture is likely to leave the cooperative sector as unattended as it has been in the past.[42] Second, if the peasantry in the south of the country is induced to provide significant marketable surpluses, this will involve persuading men to turn to cash-crop production instead of seeking a wage. The implications of this (*if* it can be done) for domestic relations of production and power would of course be enormous: its effects would surely consolidate male power in the peasant household and lock women more firmly into their traditional subordinate role. Supporting family agriculture to solve the immediate crisis might be a reasonable short-term policy—but it is hardly a policy that will help to resolve the "social problems of women," which, as FRELIMO itself has recognized, can only be resolved in the context of communal production relations.

Theory, Practice, and Crisis

In spite of the economistic nature of Machel's analysis of women's oppression and the exhortations to involve women in socialized production, especially within communal villages, little concrete thought has been given to the constraints on involving women in production, or to ways of alleviating these constraints. One reason is the lack of analysis or theoretical contribution by the OMM. This is compounded by the dominance of men in the national planning processes and the fact that "women's problems" continue to be conceived primarily as those relating to the family. Thus when a decision is made on an aspect of social policy or an economic project is planned, its impact on women is not usually considered.

For example, when a new state farm project or a village is being planned, comments will be made by officials not only from the ministries of agriculture and public works, but also from the ministries of health and education; the problem of water supply, the possible need for a new school, and so on, will be discussed. But there is nobody responsible for considering the impact on women: there is not a ministry for women and the only structure that might in theory consider the impact of the plans on women, the OMM, is not as far as we know consulted.[43] It is striking that the "Economic and Social Directives" of both the Third and Fourth Congresses of FRELIMO, which lay down detailed goals for both economic and social development, do not include a section on women. Equally striking is the absence in the Land Law of 1979 of any reference to traditional land tenure systems or any other statement that would establish, clarify, and reinforce women's rights to land.

The problem of essentially writing women out of development plans has been exacerbated by the very centralized nature of planning in Mozambique. Were plans for, say, a new communal village developed more at the "locality" level, possibly in some areas the OMM, or women in local assemblies, would be able to have an input. They might suggest, for example, that a day-care center or easy access to firewood should be a priority.[44] Planning could become more decentralized in the future as the party is consolidated nationwide and as more planners and technicians are trained and do not have to be concentrated in the capital. Certainly decentralization is an issue being discussed, and the Fourth Congress (in 1983) emphasized "small-scale" projects and local initiative, suggesting a shift—in policy if not yet in practice—toward decentralization. Indeed, one reading of Fourth Congress views on decentralization is that they are partly responding to the de facto split up of communal villages in the north of the country, which was well advanced by 1980.[45]

Decentralization has been hampered by the activities of the South African-backed National Resistance Movement (MNR; also called RENAMO), whose sabotage and massacres of civilians, a problem by 1981, have massively increased since 1984.[46] In the most fundamental way, where there is no production, planning is meaningless. This unfortunately is the case in many parts of the country where in early 1988 more than 4 million people (nearly one-third of the population) cannot farm due to disruption caused by these armed gangs. Apart from the direct destruction, economic loss, and disruption (making the implementation of planning even more difficult than it has generally been since independence), the level of violence has necessitated militarily informed—hence centralized—decisionmaking taking precedence over local decisions. For example, many new villages have recently been created, but apparently to make the population more defensible, not as part of local initiatives toward communal living and production.[47] The 1984 Nkomati accords with South Africa did nothing to reduce MNR disruption.[48] Thus with the rural economy paralyzed, implementation of Fourth Congress resolutions on decentralization (as well as the program of a ten-year plan launched in 1980 to "overcome poverty" by 1990) is on hold. One must also conclude

that significant advance toward including women in the economic planning process is also on hold.

Concluding Observations

In our discussion of Mozambique since independence we have focused
on three areas: political participation, domestic social relations, and nondomestic relations of production. In all three areas we have described some
limited successes in the struggle for women's liberation and we have also
pointed out major stumbling blocks for future progress. However, it is not
sufficient simply to draw up a "balance sheet" of successes and failures.
Women's liberation is not simply a matter of adding to a checklist of rights
or capacities that women have attained. Rather, what is involved is a
transformation of *social relations* in the broadest possible sense: not only a
transformation of the social relations of production, but also of family
relations and relations of political power.

It is clear that the present crisis in the Mozambican countryside makes it
hard for FRELIMO to opt for policies that will benefit women. However,
it would not do to conclude from this that women's liberation will just have
to wait. For a crucial point is that the crisis of peasant production is in large
part a crisis of *women's* production. Thus one essential prerequisite for any
resolution to the crisis of peasant production must be for FRELIMO to
develop a wider theoretical analysis of the Woman Question, an analysis
that will not dwell on women's ideological backwardness and passivity, or
identify women's problems primarily as those of traditional family relations. Rather, what is needed is an analysis that focuses on women *as
producers*, as well as reproducers, and on family relations and the political
and planning processes as they affect women *as producers*. The crisis of the
peasantry and the problems of rural women in Mozambique are not
separate issues, to be addressed on two separate agendas; they are two
aspects of one and the same totality.

Unfortunately, the results of our research suggest that male-dominated
(and urban-biased) FRELIMO thinking about these issues seriously oversimplifies. The issue of woman's labor—of woman as producer—seems to
have been collapsed into that of woman as possession, as the victim of
bride price and polygamy. This oversimplification springs, we believe,
from the tendency to view the past as "feudal" (as does much orthodox
Marxist-Leninist thought about the third world). This tendency has led
FRELIMO to oversimplify two other related issues. First, the issue of land
seems to have been collapsed into that of "landlordism," thus missing the
significance of interhousehold relations and woman's access to resources
within that context.[49] Second, the positive importance of interhousehold

support networks has been misunderstood, and the party's emphasis has been on such negative aspects as nepotism and bride price. By focusing on a narrow program of socialist "modernization," aimed at stamping out what it sees in all these cases as feudal relations, FRELIMO has failed to appreciate the magnitude of changes in the daily subsistence struggles of millions of rural people that will be required before alternatives for traditional social relations are viable. We have argued this case in some detail earlier in regard to polygamy, but the case could also be made for the survival value of other "evils" such as clan-based access to land, bride price, and interhousehold networking.

Given sufficient time the OMM could gain the self-confidence to assert the importance of these broader issues. At present, however, the Woman Question, however defined, is on hold together with every other "question" bar sheer survival. Destabilization of Mozambique at the hands of South African–sponsored terrorists clouds every planning and policy issue. At the end of February 1988, some 5.9 million Mozambicans (out of a population of 12–13 million) were dependent on food aid; 600,000 were refugees in surrounding countries. The MNR had destroyed 1,800 schools, 720 health posts, 44 factories, and at least 1,300 trucks. Some 1.1 million people are living in camps as displaced persons in their own country because of MNR attacks.[50]

When one considers the scale of violence in this undeclared war of South Africa against Mozambique, it is truly amazing that so poor and beleaguered a country has still had the political will to carry on development work at all. Yet Mozambique has devoted from 12 percent (1981) to 8 percent (1984) of its national budget to health care, training 573 midwives/ MCH nurses by 1984 and some 1,369 village-level health workers.[51] In general there is a political commitment to "adaptation without basic retreat" in the policy of building popular democracy.[52] In administrative terms there is a commitment to "holding the line" in such ministries as health and education. Throughout the worst of the terror, a program of providing women in communal villages with labor-saving facilities such as water points and grain mills has continued.[53]

There is much in such institutional behavior under the greatest stress that augurs well for renewed consideration of women's situation if and when the pressure of South African aggression is removed. Even while people live temporarily as refugees and displaced persons, it is possible the OMM will be able to assume a role in shaping the future agenda. While no one would wish to live in a refugee camp, it *is* possible to make the most of such a sojourn by providing educational services, small industries, and outlets for skills and production.[54] The next challenge for the OMM would therefore seem to be that of articulating woman's interests in these camps. Successes in this role would add to the OMM's self-confidence and make it more likely that the Woman Question is placed squarely on

FRELIMO's agenda in a uniquely Mozambican, nonorthodox form in the future.

One hesitates to speculate any further. The struggle of Mozambican women has been punctuated by unique developments for over one hundred years, since the time when women began to take over men's activities in the face of male migration to the South African mines: the experience of women in the armed struggle, the disruptions and policy shifts of immediate postindependence, the assertion of rural and working-class women's interests through election to local assemblies. All these moments of women's struggle have emerged with an element of unpredictability. So too the next phase, whatever its form, will carry the stamp of Mozambique's unique and painful history of decolonialization.

Notes

An earlier version of this paper was published as "The State, the Party and the Female Peasantry in Mozambique," *Journal of Southern African Studies* 11, no. 1 (October 1984): 106–27.

1. Unfortunately, our firsthand knowledge ceases in 1980 and we have had to rely on information from other people in our account of what has taken place since then. We are particularly grateful to Stephanie Urdang, author of *And Still They Dance: Women, War and the Struggle for Change in Mozambique* (New York: Monthly Review Press, 1988), who has traveled extensively with workers in the Mozambican women's movement and who has shared her observations with us. In addition, we gratefully acknowledge the unpublished results of several studies began under the direction of Ruth First in the Centre of African Studies in Maputo involving Bridgit O'Laughlin, Ursula Semin-Panzer, Martha Madoerin, Maureen Mackintosh, and Helena Dolny. The best single source for background on the South of Mozambique remains Ruth First's *Black Gold: The Mozambican Miner, Proletarian and Peasant* (Sussex: Harvester Press, 1983).
2. Male life expectancy in the late 1970s was 42 and female 44. Infant mortality rates ranged between 75 and 150 per 1,000, depending on area (UNICEF/WHO, *Country Decision Making for the Achievement of the Objective of Primary Health Care: Report from the People's Republic of Mozambique*, 1980). Because of destabilization by South Africa, infant mortality is probably twice as high in 1988. See Note 46 below.
3. *Relatório do Comité Central ao 3 Congresso* (Maputo: Frelimo, 1977), p. 65.
4. This consensus view of the economic crisis at independence began to crystallize in the late 1970s in the Centre of African Studies at University Eduardo Mondlane: see Marc Wuyts, "Peasant and Rural Economy in Mozambique," Discussion Paper, Maputo, CEA/UEM, 1978, and First, *Black Gold*. The analysis of growing crisis has been summarized by Barry Munslow, *Mozambique: The Revolution and Its Origins* (London: Longman, 1983) and by David Wield, "Mozambique: Late Colonialism and Early Problems of Transition," in Robin Murray, Christine White, and Gerald White, eds., *Socialist Transformation and Development in the Third World* (Sussex: Harvester Press, 1983). The continuing crisis, exacerbated by the global recession, has been explored by B. Egerö and J. Torp, "What Kind of Socialist Transition in Capitalist Recession?" in J. Carlsson, ed., *Recession in Africa* (Uppsala: Nordiska afrikainstitutet, 1983), and by Bertil Egerö, *Mozambique: A Dream Undone* (Uppsala: Nordiska afrikainstitutet, 1987).
5. *Programa e Estatutos* (Maputo: Frelimo, 1977), p. 8.
6. *Relatório*, p. 107.

7. *Out of Underdevelopment to Socialism: Report of the Central Committee* (Maputo: Frelimo, 1983), p. 28.

8. A concise overview of agricultural policy debate through the Fourth Congress is provided by O. Roesch, "Peasants and Collective Agriculture in Mozambique," in Jonathan Barker, ed., *The Politics of Agriculture in Tropical Africa* (Beverly Hills: Sage 1984), pp. 291–97; by Joseph Hanlon, *Revolution Under Fire* (London: Zed Books, 1984), pp. 93–132, and by Phillip Raikes, "Food Policy and Production in Mozambique Since Independence," *Review of African Political Economy* 29 (July 1984): 95–107.

9. The standard ethnography of southern Mozambique is still the detailed two-volume work by Henri-A. Junod, *Usos e Costumes dos Bantos* (Maputo: Imprensa Nacional de Moçambique, 1975).

10. *Documentos da 2 Conferência da Organização da Mulher Moçambicana* (Maputo: OMM, 1977), pp. 90–91. See also Junod, *Usos e Costumes*, pp. 170–76.

11. Barbara Rogers, *The Domestication of Women* (New York: St. Martin's Press, 1980), ch. 7.

12. Sheryl Young, "Changes in Diet and Production in Southern Mozambique 1855–1960" (Paper presented at the meeting of the African Studies Association of the United Kingdom, 1976) and "Fertility and Famine: Women's Agricultural History in Southern Mozambique," in R. Palmer and N. Parsons, eds., *The Roots of Rural Poverty in Central and Southern Africa* (London: Longman, 1977).

13. *Datas e Documentos da História de FRELIMO* (Maputo, Frelimo, 1975), p. 25.

14. Information given by old-time OMM members interviewed in 1979 in Cabo Delgado. B. Isaacman and J. Stephen. *Mozambique: Women, the Law and Agrarian Reform* (Addis Ababa: United Nations, Economic Commission for Africa, 1980), p. 15.

15. Eduardo Mondlane, *The Struggle for Mozambique* (London: Penguin, 1969), p. 186; Isaacman and Stephen, *Mozambique*, pp. 14–15.

16. "The Liberation of Women Is a Fundamental Necessity for the Revolution," in *Sowing the Seeds of Revolution* (London: Committee for Freedom in Mozambique, Angola, and Guinea Bissau, 1974).

17. Samora Machel, "Defining Woman's Enemy" (speech to the OMM in 1976), in Barry Munslow, ed., *Samora Machel: An African Revolutionary* (London: Zed Books, 1985), p. 170.

18. As much as 95 percent of the population participated in some provinces—a remarkably high figure. See G. Walt, "Commitment to Primary Health Care in Mozambique: A Preliminary Review," *Rural Africana* 8–9 (Fall 1980–Winter 1981): 91–98.

19. Isaacman and Stephen, *Mozambique*, p. 103.

20. For a fuller discussion of women's literacy campaigns see Stephanie Urdang, "The Last Transition? Women and Development," in John Saul, ed., *A Difficult Road: The Transition to Socialism in Mozambique* (New York: Monthly Review Press, 1985), pp. 373–379. There was also an explosion in school education for girls—1979 figures give over 42 percent of primary level students and over 20 percent of secondary school students as female (Isaacman and Stephen, *Mozambique*, p. 98). As with certain health advances mentioned earlier, terrorist attacks have probably eroded some of this educational progress. By 1988 some 1,800 schools had been destroyed; see footnote 46 below.

21. OMM/Gabinete Central de Preparaçao da Conferéncia Extraordinária, *Análise da Situaçao Social da Mulher e Proposta de Estratégia de Luta Pela Sua Emancipaçao* (Maputo: OMM, 1984).

22. Isaacman and Stephen, *Mozambique*, p. 35.

23. *Relatório da Comissão de Eleições* (Maputo: Inprensa Nacional, 1980). Reference supplied by Bertil Egerö.

24. "Report of the Credentials Commission," in *Building Socialism: The People's Answer* (Maputo: Inprensa National, 1983), p. 40.

25. Personal Communication from the interviewer, Stephanie Urdang.
26. 2 Conferência, p. 23.
27. Ibid., pp. 96–97.
28. Isaacman and Stephen, Mozambique, pp. 53–54. The law also stipulates that the well-being of a child should be the main criterion for deciding which parent should have custody. This overturns the traditional assumption that children automatically belong to the father and go to his relatives in cases of separation.
29. Urdang, "The Last Transition?," pp. 381–83.
30. The 1976 document noted that "in the majority of cases it is the wife herself who procures other wives for her husband, with the object of increasing the labor force to help her with family production" (2 Conferência, p. 96). This was noted also by Stephanie Urdang, who traveled with the brigades in late 1983.
31. Urdang, "The Last Transition?," pp. 382–83. There has even been a suggestion that under some circumstances African children have better nutritional status where polygamy is practiced; see Loretta Brabin, "Polygyny: An Indicator of Nutritional Stress in African Agricultural Societies?" Africa 54, no. 1 (1984): 31–44. We should not, however, give the impression that the OMM is wholly incapable of treating polygamy in a situated way. For instance, a member of the OMM National Secretariat, Anabella Rodriguez, noted in an interview in 1979 that "in areas like Cabo Delgado, many of the men served in the armed struggle and now live in other provinces. In some areas we find 1,750 women and only 300 men. How can we combat polygamy in this situation?" See "Mozambican Women After the Revolution," in M. Davies, ed., Third World, Second Sex: Women's Struggles and National Liberation (London: Zed Books, 1983), pp. 127–34.
32. Isaacman and Stephen, Mozambique, pp. 76–77.
33. Urdang, "The Last Transition?," pp. 385–86.
34. Membership in cooperatives is by individual worker and not by household, according to the official guidelines. However, Isaacman and Stephen found that in some villages wives were in fact incorporated into the same brigade as their husbands and that the total remuneration was then given to the man ("Mozambique," p. 88, note 39).
35. Estimates are calculated from 1980 census data published during 1982 in Tempo (Maputo). The figure 25,000 is a very liberal estimate of women in cooperatives since the Report of the Central Committee to the Fourth Congress gives total membership in producer cooperatives in 1982 (both men and women) to be 37,000. This was up from a total of 25,000 in 1977. The figure for population resident in communal villages at about the time of the population census in 1980 was taken from data discussed in a 1981 session of the People's Assembly (8th Session) and the proportion of adult women in this communal village population estimated. The People's Assembly data is cited in O. Marleyn, D. Wield, and R. Williams, "Notes on the Political and Organizational Offensive in Mozambique and its Relationship to Agricultural Policy," Review of African Political Economy 24 (1982): 118. It should be noted that the difference in two years between the numbers presented to the People's Assembly and those reported in the Report of the Central Committee to the Fourth Congress is quite striking: the 1981 source has 70,000 people involved in cooperative production in a communal village population of 1 million; the 1983 report claims only 37,000 in cooperative production in a communal village population of 1.8 million.
36. Report of the Central Committee, p. 28.
37. Wuyts, "Peasants and Rural Economy," p. 30.
38. We draw in the following discussion on Centre for African Studies, "Sumário preparado à pedido da Direcção Nacional de Habitação para ser utilizado na preparação prévia do Seminário sobre Aldeias Comunais de 1979–80," Universidade Eduardo Mondlane, Maputo, 1979.

39. Lawrence Harris, "Agricultural Cooperatives and Development Policy in Mozambique," *Journal of Peasant Studies* 7, no. 3 (1980): 345.
40. Frelimo dates the decline in gross agricultural production as starting in 1981–82, *Report of the Central Committee*, p. 26.
41. In fact such criticism began to appear much earlier; see, for instance, J. Hanlon, "Does Modernization = Mechanization?" *New Scientist*, August 24, 1979.
42. See Frelimo, *Report of the Central Committee*, p. 59.
43. The arrangements for "social impact analysis" of projects in Mozambique are fragmented and complex. It is not clear that planning would reflect women's views *even if* the OMM were a forceful and omnipresent advocate of the interests of women (which it is not); see Ben Wisner, "Social Impact, Socialism, and the Case of Mozambique," in W. Derman and S. Whiteford, eds., *Social Impact Analysis and Development Planning in the Third World* (Boulder, CO: Westview Press, 1985), pp. 262–83.
44. In reality there is a complex, ever-shifting interplay between national and local interests in a "decentralized" development process. See M. Mackintosh and M. Wuyts, "Accumulation, Social Services and Socialist Transition in the Third World: Reflections on Decentralized Planning Based on Mozambican Experience," The Open University, *Development Policy and Practice*, Working Paper 9, November 1987.
45. Egerö, *Dream Undone*, pp. 150–65.
46. Bands of terrorists roam the countryside kidnapping, murdering, and mutilating the population and sabotaging infrastructure. They have made no attempt to occupy territory and win support among the people. On the contrary, since their creation by Rhodesian and former Portuguese intelligence officers in the last years of the Zimbabwean war of national liberation, they have been solely concerned to disrupt and destroy. With independence in neighboring Zimbabwe in 1980, control of these so-called freedom fighters passed to South Africa. By 1985 they had destroyed 1,800 schools. By 1986 they had destroyed a third of the health service in the country: 213 health centers destroyed, another 382 looted. UNICEF estimates that 325,000 children have died as the result of attacks and sabotage. Infant mortality nearly doubled between 1981 and 1986. By 1986 some 350,000 Mozambican refugees had fled the terror into neighboring countries. The history of the MNR is traced by A. Isaacman, "Historical Introduction," in L. Magaia, *Dumba Nengue: Run for Your Life: Peasant Tales of Tragedy in Mozambique* (Trenton: Africa World Press, 1988), pp. 1–14, and Joseph Hanlon, *Beggar Your Neighbor* (Bloomington: Indiana University Press, 1986), pp. 139–42. Documentation of these atrocities is given by UNICEF, *Children on the Front Line* (New York: UNICEF, 1987); Julie Cliff and A. Noormohamed, "Impact of South African Destabilization on Health in Mozambique" (Maputo, 1987); and U.S. Committee for Refugees, *Refugees from Mozambique: Shattered Land, Fragile Asylum* (Washington, DC: U.S. Committee for Refugees, 1986).
47. Hanlon, *Revolution Under Fire*, ch. 13.
48. Hanlon, *Beggar Your Neighbor*, pp. 149–150, summarizes documentary evidence of continued South African support for the MNR.
49. Strong feelings of attachment to "clan" lands were cited by Egerö, *Dream Undone*, pp. 155–165, as one of the reasons why a communal village in the north split up.
50. "Latest Figures on Emergency," *Mozambique Information Service News Review*, no. 125 (March 17, 1988): 9.
51. Julie Cliff, N. Kanji, and M. Muller, "Mozambique Health Holding the Line," *Review of African Political Economy* 36 (September 1986): 7–23.
52. Egerö, *Dream Undone*, p. 93.
53. Stephanie Urdang, *The Impact of Rural Transformation on Peasant Women in Mozambique* (Geneva: ILO, 1984).
54. For instance in the case of refugee camps in Somalia discussed by Hanna Christensen,

Survival Strategies for and by Camp Refugees (Geneva: UNRISD, 1982). The more general experience of such positive or developmental uses of the refugee situation is discussed by G. Kibreab, *African Refugees* (Trenton: Africa World Press, 1985), and by B. Harrell-Bond, *Imposing Aid: Emergency Assistance to Refugees* (Oxford: Oxford University Press, 1986).

Vietnam: War, Socialism, and the Politics of Gender Relations

Christine Pelzer White

> If mass revolutionary action has a relatively brief history, female revolutionary politics is a mere flicker in its midst. A new consciousness is a laborious thing. Now we are like babes thrashing around in darkness and unexplored space. The creation of an alternative world and an alternative culture cannot be the work of a day. But we cannot afford to waste time while reaction consolidates itself.
> —Sheila Rowbotham, *Woman's Consciousness, Man's World*

Socialism is a Process, Female Identity is a Process

The idea of socialism has been around for a little over a hundred years—a moment in terms of world history. The term "socialism" should be understood as process and potentiality. Socialism is not just a set of political and economic institutions and development policies. Most importantly, socialism aims at transforming the world as it is presently structured by neocolonialism, capitalism, patriarchy, racism, and sexism into a better world characterized by political self-determination by producers and equality between the sexes. The strength of the resistance to this enterprise, as well as the tenacity of deeply ingrained traditions of inequality, have led to many distortions of the socialist ideal as socialist and communist individuals, parties, and nations attempt to carve out for themselves a domain of relative autonomy in a wider hostile and more powerful world. The gender relations characterizing "actually existing socialism" should not be confused with what might have been if social alternatives had been allowed to develop in peace.

Over one hundred years ago Engels, in what has become the classic Marxist-Leninist text on the "Woman Question," had this to say about gender relations in a future socialist or communist society:

> What we can now conjecture about the way in which sexual relations will be ordered after the impending overthrow of capitalist production is mainly of a

172

negative character, limited for the most part to what will disappear. But what will there be new? That will be answered when a new generation has grown up: a generation of men who never in their lives have known what it is to buy a woman's surrender with money or any other social instrument of power; a generation of women who have never known what it is to give themselves to a man from any other considerations than real love or to refuse to give themselves to their lover from fear of the economic consequences. When these people are in the world, they will care precious little what anybody today thinks they ought to do; they will make their own practice and their corresponding public opinion about the practice of each individual—and that will be the end of it. [1]

Although the vocabulary may be archaic ("surrender" is now considered an old-fashioned term in the battle of the sexes), the egalitarian economic and social transformation has yet to be achieved. The basic preconditions for the emergence of new men and women envisaged by this founding father of the communist movement include material abundance and an egalitarian system of distribution. At the present time, the Socialist Republic of Vietnam, as one of the poorest countries in the world, is far from meeting even the most basic prerequisite for human development: sufficient food to feed its population. Nguyen Thi Dinh, one of the most influential women in the Vietnamese Communist Party, former deputy commander-in-chief of the armed forces of the National Liberation Front of South Vietnam during the American war, now president of the Women's Union, member of the Central Committee, and delegate to the National Assembly, addressed these grave concerns for the future of Vietnamese socialism to the Sixth Party Congress:

The young people who will build socialism . . . in Vietnam in the early years of the twenty-first century are the children who are now in kindergarten and child-care centers today and the children who will be born in the next five to ten years. The malnourished children, the small, underweight newborns and the retarded children we see today are a cause of great concern. [2]

Vietnam was made to pay a terrible price for the decision of its anti-colonial leadership to embrace Marxist-Leninist ideology and to reject the nearly universal pattern in the third world of postcolonial integration into the Western-dominated capitalist world system. As is well known, the United States went to extraordinary lengths to prevent Vietnam from becoming a socialist, unified country under the indigenous communist leadership, headed by Ho Chi Minh, which had led the nation's anti-colonial war of independence against the French. Except for nuclear weapons (which hung over Vietnam as a threat), every weapon in the U.S. arsenal was used extensively. Three times the volume of bombs used in World War II were dropped on the socialist portion of Vietnam, the Democratic Republic of Vietnam (DRV). The U.S. government incrementally and incredulously escalated the violence in the belief, in the words of presidential adviser Henry Kissinger, that "North Vietnam could not be the only country in the world without a breaking point." In the words of the U.S. commander, General Westmoreland, "We'll go on bleeding them until Hanoi wakes up to the fact that they [sic] have bled their country to the point of national disaster for generations."[3]

The apparent victory for socialism and third world liberation in Vietnam in April 1975 soon seemed a mirage dispelled by intractable economic problems and the postwar war between socialist neighbors: China, Pol Pot's Democratic Kampuchea, and Vietnam.[4] In retrospect, a number of American scholars have claimed the Vietnam war as an American "success story," pointing out, for example, that the United States had demonstrated to would-be revolutionaries throughout the world that "the cost of successful revolution against a determined foe is very great."[5] The United States has yet to end its undeclared war on Vietnam: there are no diplomatic relations and an economic embargo is strictly enforced.[6] While the United States once waged war on Vietnam in the name of stopping the spread of Chinese communism, since 1979 the United States is cooperating with China to support the military attempt of the genocidal Khmer Rouge to overthrow the government of the People's Republic of Kampuchea which is backed by Vietnamese troops.[7] Vietnam has now lost as many men in Kampuchea in an attempt to secure a friendly government on its border and prevent the return to power of Pol Pot's Khmer Rouge as the United States lost during the Vietnam war.

The U.S. war, the continuing war in Kampuchea, and the tensions on the Chinese border, have resulted in a society seemingly permanently mobilized for national defense. This obviously has a profound impact on the roles of women and on gender relations in socialist Vietnam. The large number of men killed in the war has created an imbalanced sex ratio. With continued mobilization of men into the military, it is women who make up the overwhelming majority of the labor force. In agriculture, the most important economic sector, women make up over 60 percent of the labor force according to official statistics.[8] In fact, in many villages the percentage of women workers is much higher. In many rural families, there is no male labor power; women do everything from child care to agricultural labor. According to recent sociological investigations, in agricultural cooperatives only about 54 percent of households have two main workers, one male and one female; 23 percent of households have only one, a woman. Where cooperative land is subcontracted to households rather than farmed collectively, the imbalance is greater: in 50 percent of households surveyed the main worker was a woman.[9]

In precolonial times, a peasant proverb summed up the division of labor: "the husband plows the land, the wife transplants the rice seedlings, the water buffalo pulls the harrow." The Vietnamese word for the verb "to farm", *cay cay*, literally means to plow and to transplant. The close rhyme of these two words expresses the symmetry and balance that existed between male and female labor in agriculture. Male and female cooperation was essential for production as well as reproduction, in order to produce children and rice, the core of the traditional way of life. However, this interdependence was limited to the household sphere, and women's economic productivity did not give them a political voice. Only male household heads could play a role in village political life, and public office on the national level was strictly limited to men.

This traditional way of life has changed for better and for worse. Many Vietnamese women now play an active role in political life. Although there are no women in the leading Political Bureau of the Communist Party of Vietnam, there are women ministers and vice-ministers, women ambassadors, and women on the Central Committee. At the local level as well, women play a role in political leadership. However, for many women in the countryside, decades of war have caused a marked deterioration compared to the situation before Western colonialism and Western military occupation. In some parts of the country peasant women have no option but to pull the plow themselves. [10] With the husband either killed in the U.S. war or fighting on the Kampuchean front, the water buffalo dead and tractors too expensive, women have to farm on their own. The traditional division of labor, with a husband to guide the plow and a buffalo to pull the plow and harrow, would seem preferable to the situation in many Vietnamese rural families today where there is no division of labor and women have to do everything: the women's work, the men's work, and the buffalo's work. In this context, the Leninist route to women's emancipation by drawing women into productive labor seems a cruel joke, a formula for total exhaustion rather than for liberation. There are increasing appeals for policymakers and administrators to pay more attention to the needs of the female labor force in agriculture; one article points out "the rational use of male labor in agriculture is of great importance for the emancipation of women." [11]

We do not yet know what women could become if socialism were allowed to flower in Vietnam and elsewhere without the distortions caused by war and poverty, just as we do not know what men could become. [12] All that can be done here is to detail the relationships, in twentieth-century Vietnamese history, between the struggle for gender equality and those for national liberation and socialist development.

Socialism, Women's Liberation, and National Liberation

"If women are not free, half of the nation is not free"—Ho Chi Minh

An account of the introduction of socialist ideas to Vietnam must begin with Ho Chi Minh, known in his youth as Nguyen Ai Quoc (Nguyen the Patriot). Rebuffed in his attempt to plead Vietnam's case to U.S. President

Wilson at the Versailles Conference in 1918, Nguyen Ai Quoc found a sympathetic hearing among French socialists and became a founding member of the French Communist Party in 1920. In *French Colonialism on Trial*, an early anticolonial pamphlet, Nguyen Ai Quoc wrote: "It has been said: 'colonization is theft.' We add: rape and assassination."[13] In 1926 his training course for young Vietnamese revolutionaries in Canton included a long section on the Women's International directly after his description of the Third International and before the sections on the Workers' International (i.e., the communist federation of trade unions) and the Youth International.[14] This reflected the great importance attached to the Woman Question in the international communist movement at that time.

A number of young Vietnamese women joined the revolutionary movement from the outset. In any society, but especially in Confucian cultures, to rebel is "unfeminine." For women to become involved in anticolonial activities meant to break with the neo-Confucian cultural values promoted by the collaborating Nguyen court which barred women from participation in political life and taught them subservience within the confines of the family. Women were to submit to male authority in the family throughout their lives: to their fathers, then to their husbands, and finally, in widowhood, to their eldest son—the "three submissions."

Ideas of political and social revolution went hand in hand, and freedom from parental control of the choice of marriage partners was a youth liberation issue in the wave of modernization of which the communist movement was a part.[15] For communists, as for others influenced by modern Western ideas, traditional marriage practices such as child marriage, polygamy, and forced marriage were reprehensible "feudal" practices to be eliminated and replaced with monogamous marriage with equal rights for husband and wife. However, for most Vietnamese of the time, the idea of basing marriage on love alone and advocating free choice of partners without prior approval by parents was scandalous. Discussions of Engels' ideas of marriage based on love and of the freedom of young men and women in the Soviet Union to meet socially at cultural and sporting events were controversial within the party itself and were seized upon by Vietnamese conservatives to prove that communists advocated "free love" and "jungle behavior."[16]

French conquest dealt a blow to the Confucian patriarchal system which rested on mutual reinforcement between the absolute authority of the emperor as ruler of the nation and the father as ruler of the family. Imperialism and colonialism smashed the power of the emperor and family heads. Colonial rule was not rooted in patriarchal relations, that is, not based on the power of man qua husband or father, but rather on man qua colonial administrator, officer, or soldier. This radical rupture between absolute power in the state and in the family was one of the most revolutionary effects of colonial rule. French colonialists soon realized the subversive impact of this development and tried, along with conservative Vietnamese collaborators, to shore up the traditional family and patriarchal authority, but it was too late. The rupture between family and state authority helped create a space for women to enter the political arena. [17]

Most of the young men and women who joined the budding communist movement in its formative stage were literate in a primarily illiterate society, "intellectuals" with several years of education in the French colonial school system that exposed them to modern ideas. In attracting women from this strata, protocommunist leftist parties had competition from other nationalist parties, most notably the Quoc Dan Dang (modeled on the Chinese Guomintang), as well as from bourgeois women's organizations and publications. One such journal was *Phu Nu Tan Van* (Women's News) launched in Saigon in 1929 with the financial backing of a major Saigon importer, wholesaler, and retailer who was the husband of the publisher. The modern young women who read this weekly were exposed to ads for the commercial products that symbolized a new, Western way of life for women: cigarettes, Citroën automobiles, and (already at this early date) Nestlé's condensed milk. Participants in the weekly's regular contests had a chance to win prizes such as a hardwood liquor cabinet which would enhance their bourgeois lifestyle. [18]

In the first full Communist Party program in October 1930 the leadership found it necessary to distinguish the party's position from the views of "bourgeois feminism." [19] The program advocated "equality between the sexes on the basis of women's conscious participation in state management" and called for freeing "women" from bourgeois ideas, something which would obviously not be a problem if women party members were from peasant or worker backgrounds.

What did the term "bourgeois feminism" mean in Vietnam at the time? One example taken from *Phu Nu Tan Van* after a radical (but not communist) editorial takeover in 1933 was a critique of "feminism" as the tendency of women with schooling or financial means to separate themselves from their sisters and act in an individualistic, selfish manner. The alternative was to work for socialism, in other words for a fundamental restructuring of the economic system so that peasant and proletarian women (as well as men) could benefit. On the other hand, a conservative male writer accused *Phu Nu Tan Van* of encouraging women to abandon their families and caricatured the liberated Vietnamese woman as desiring equality with men in gambling, extramarital sex, and conspicuous consumption. [20] Caught between rigid Confucian morality on the one hand and strictures against bourgeois individualism and feminism on the other, socialist women were more constricted by public opinion in their behavior than were their male comrades.

On September 2, 1945, Ho Chi Minh declared Vietnam's independence as the Democratic Republic of Vietnam (DRV, which at that time referred to the entire country, north to south). Equality between men and women was adopted as a principle in the first constitution in 1946. The text specified women's right to vote and to stand for election, equal pay for equal work, and stipulated that in the new system "women have the same political, economic, cultural, social, and family rights as men."[21] At the time this was in advance of the law in several European countries, but standard for countries with socialist consitutions.

Despite the significance of foreign influences, the ideas current in the communist movement about equal rights for women were not just Comintern and Western imports. The peasant population that made up the mass base of the revolutionary struggle which exploded in 1945 was not as deeply affected by Confucianism as was the communist intelligentsia from relatively well-off backgrounds. The folk culture included remnants of the greater equality between the sexes which is believed to have existed in pre-Confucian Vietnam. While rich peasants and landlords were generally polygamous and did not have to work but gave orders to their wives, concubines, servants, and children, the poor peasant household was monogamous, relatively egalitarian, and interdependent in its division of labor.[22]

Pre-Confucian Vietnamese heroines of earlier national liberation struggles against Chinese invaders were invoked as role models by the revolutionary movement. The most famous were the Trung sisters who led a rebellion against Chinese domination in the first century A.D., and Trieu Thi Trinh (Ba Trieu) who did the same two centuries later. The fact that they were actually military commanders who led male as well as female troops into battle against the Chinese has been interpreted by Vietnamese Marxist scholars as one indication of an earlier period of matriarchal social organization along the lines outlined by Engels. If oral tradition can be accepted as evidence, Trieu Thi Trinh's reply to advice that she should get married could be counted among the world's earliest recorded feminist declarations (circa 250 A.D.), predating Mary Wollstonecraft's *Vindication of the Rights of Women* by about 1500 years: "I would rather ride strong winds, tread mighty waves, and drive out the Wu [Chinese] invaders to reconquer our land, recover our independence and break the yoke of slavery, than bend and be a maid-servant of man."[23]

Although Ba Trieu was a role model in fighting against foreign invaders, the Vietnamese communist movement never rejected the idea of marriage. Rather, marriage was to be transformed into an egalitarian institution in which the wife would combine the virtues of both tradition and modernity by being loyal but not subservient. While advocacy of equal rights for women as workers and as citizens was revolutionary in the Vietnamese context, the Communist Party's conception of the interests of women as women stressed women's traditional roles as wives and mothers. The 1946 constitution specified: "the State protects the rights of mothers and children. The State protects marriáge and the family." Communist ideas on women's roles were thus a mixture of foreign and indigenous, as well as modern and traditional, views.

During the anticolonial revolutionary upsurge of 1945, platoons of women guerrillas were formed. The most famous of these, the women's self-defense platoon of Bac Giang, under the command of a twenty-year-old woman, succeeded in destroying many enemy posts. However, during the resistance war against French colonialism (1946–54), women's primary role was to "replace men on the home front" (a Woman's Union slogan), producing rice and becoming guerrillas in defense of their villages, particularly in liberated areas where all the able-bodied men had joined the resistance forces. Women made up two-thirds of the porters carrying food and ammunition for the Vietminh army, leaving their homes and villages in large numbers for months at a time.[24]

Women's role in the second Indochina war, the U.S. war, was even more important. In accordance with the Geneva Agreement of 1954, revolutionary troops south of the seventeenth parallel regrouped to the north of that line, leaving their wives and children behind, pending elections for national reunification which were to be held two years later. The revolutionary forces had good reason to believe that they would win free elections due to the popularity of Ho Chi Minh and his anticolonial movement, but the elections were never held. Instead, the United States replaced the French in the south (the regroupment zone for French troops according to the Geneva Agreements) and created an anticommunist government in Saigon, which launched a campaign to arrest or obtain the recantation of those who had been involved in the anticolonial struggle. Since Vietminh military forces from the south had gone north, women left behind—for example, the younger sisters of Vietminh soldiers—played an unusually important role in both political and armed struggle in the years that followed.

The role of women in national liberation struggle was also very important on the symbolic level. Woman as revolutionary is a powerful symbol of the potential for apparently weak and powerless peoples subordinated in the international world order to fight back against apparently overwhelming forces and take their destinies into their own hands. The photo of a tiny North Vietnamese militia woman with a rifle trained on a towering but subdued U.S. pilot appeared on posters of the anti-war movement in the West as well as on DRV postage stamps.[25] This simultaneous reversal of two power relationships—imperialist/third world and man/woman—created a potent and internationally recognizable image of revolution.

The same symbolism was acted out on an international diplomatic level during the years when Nguyen Thi Binh served as foreign minister of the Provisional Revolutionary Government (PRG) of South Vietnam and its leading negotiator at the Paris talks. Her position at the talks underlined the grotesque power inequality in the Vietnam war. Just as a woman is vulnerable to rape but is physically incapable of raping a man, Vietnam, the country that was being subjected to the heaviest and most concentrated bombing in history was physically incapable of bombing a single American city.

Vietnamese men took pride in the role that their women played in standing up to the enemy but preferred to picture them in a traditional service role in their relationship to their male comrades, as the following poem by the male PRG poet Luu Thong Lu illustrates:

> Nguyen Thi Dinh
>
> In the assault you command a hundred squads.
> Night returns, you sit mending fighters' clothes.
> Woman general of the South
> You've shaken the brass and steel of the White House.

Who but a woman general would be praised for staying awake after battle to mend her soldiers' uniforms! While in the lineage of Trieu Thi Trinh in terms of her military role, Nguyen Thi Dinh is no iconoclast on the subject of marriage, and is deeply influenced by Confucian tradition. In her autobiography she recalls listening, with her family and neighbors, to the nineteenth-century Vietnamese Confucian classic "Luc Van Tien." She recalls her father's words: "This story teaches people all the virtues they must have in life: humanity, kindness, filial piety, courage, determination, and loyalty."[26] Cultural attitudes within the revolutionary movement on the subject of women's roles were a contradictory mixture of new and old attitudes. In fact, one important aspect of the anti-imperialist struggle was to defend Vietnamese traditions against what were seen as corrosive Western influences.[27]

The image of the revolutionary Vietnamese woman as fearless in challenging the enemy while also fulfilling her traditional female obligations is pervasive in Vietnamese writings, but not all militant women were as traditional in their attitudes as Nguyen Thi Dinh. The biography of a South Vietnamese guerrilla of a younger generation from the same province, Ta Thi Kieu, An Heroic Girl of Ben Tre, shows a complex mixture of acceptance and rejection of traditional female roles and values.[28] The text is a nonfiction account of the struggle of a young woman against sexist attitudes on the part of both relatives and local underground party leaders to be allowed first to participate in the revolution, then to initiate, plan, and execute political and military actions against the Saigon military post that had been set up to control her formerly Vietminh village. Her parents were afraid that, a mere girl, she would give away revolutionary secrets if arrested, since even many men had given in under torture. Also, they needed her labor power in the fields, since they were old and their sons had regrouped to the north with the Vietminh army after the Geneva Accords. They were also afraid that she might dishonor the family in unchaperoned contact with men in the course of night-time revolutionary duties. Ly (Ta Thi Kieu's nickname) responded by working long hours in order to combine revolutionary activities with helping her parents, and indignantly affirmed her commitment to defending her own honor.

Ly's revolutionary commitment stemmed first from family tradition, but she was also radicalized by the savage rapes of young relatives and neighbors by soldiers from the local Saigon army post who felt free to do anything to "Viet Cong," as former Vietminh were being called. One of her first revolutionary initiatives was to propose the assassination of a young man named Hon, the son of the commander of the Saigon military post in the village, who "thought it his right to have any woman he wanted and if the victim resisted she would be accused of being Viet Cong, and brought to the post where tortures of the worst kind awaited her."[29] The underground male party secretary initially rejected this suggestion, but Ly was so insistent that he finally agreed, but the execution of the rapist was entirely in her hands. At that point the village revolutionary movement had no weapons; Ly felled Hon with a bamboo stick through the wheel of his imported motorbike while he was speeding along a deserted road. The news quickly spread through the whole region that the son of the chief of An Phong post "had been caught and killed by the liberation army*men*"![30] Ly's next targets were the chief and deputy chief of a local group of Saigon government militia who had committed many rapes of women and girls in Vietminh families. Still without any arms, Ly next figured out a way to take over the local militia post and capture its U.S.-supplied weapons and ammunition. This action, and the attack by Nguyen Thi Dinh on another post in the same province of Ben Tre, were among the first military engagements of the Vietnam war. It was this grass-roots process of village women and men seizing U.S.-supplied weapons from the Saigon army that was at the origin of the armed struggle against the Saigon government, not "invasion from the North."

Capitalist and Socialist Transformations of Gender Relations

Because of Ly's acceptance of the traditional values of chastity and obligations to her parents, most of the students in a recent class I taught on Women, Revolution and Socialism were adamant that she was "not a feminist," and that her only commitment was to the socialist revolution.

Their identification of feminism with sexual freedom and the rejection of family obligations would earn them the label of "bourgeois feminists" and "individualists" in the eyes of most Vietnamese socialist men and women. I believe that the militancy with which Ly and other women like her defended women against the U.S.-sponsored Saigon government's rapists in uniform deeply affected the nature of the revolutionary movement in southern Vietnam. It is noteworthy that on two occasions Ly, a teenager and a woman, disagreed with a senior male Communist leader and won the argument. I think we need a less ethnocentric definition of "feminism" which appreciates the realities of the third world where village women need protection against sexual violence and where sexual liberation is constrained by the unavailability of affordable or safe birth control methods as well as by traditional morality.

While revolutionary men and women in the south Vietnamese countryside fought to preserve Vietnam's traditional values against the onslaught of militarization, war, and consumerism, Saigon and other urban areas underwent rapid social and cultural change which included, after large-scale American military intervention in 1965, the wholesale transformation of hundreds of thousands of Vietnamese women into prostitutes.[31] This development can be seen as an extreme case of capitalist-style "liberation" of women from traditional patriarchal controls in the third world; there are now even more prostitutes in Thailand than there were in Vietnam during the war. Freed of traditional patriarchal controls on her sexuality, a third world woman can sell herself (rather than be sold by her father) on the job, marriage, or sex market.[32]

To be "modern" young women in the third world want to wear cosmetics and sexy clothes. In effect, they are buying commodities to enhance their attractiveness on the marriage market, since presenting themselves as sex objects is a necessary self-marketing strategy when marriages are no longer arranged—but to traditionalists they just look like loose women.[33] If "revolution" means radical change, there is no doubt that it is capitalism rather than socialism which has caused the more revolutionary changes in women's roles in the third world. However, this leads to a new form of subjugation and should not be confused with women's liberation. In the capitalist or "free world" countries of Asia rural women who are "freed" from the traditional pattern of control by their parents of both their labor power and their sexuality are not likely to find feminist fulfillment as self-determining and autonomous women. Instead, many become fodder for short-term employment by multinational corporations, prostitutes servicing local or foreign men, or sell themselves on the international marriage market as "correspondence brides."[34] New cultural phenomena such as pornographic photographs and films and the increasing incidence of rape establish new forms of male supremacy which are based not primarily on patriarchy within the family but on the more "democratic" principle of the dominance of all men over all women.

Within weeks of the "fall" or "liberation" of Saigon in April 1975, pornographic literature was burned in a campaign carried out by students to rid the city of imperialist and culturally decadent books and magazines from the era of U.S. military occupation.[35] The Saigon government's plans to promote sex tourism as a source of foreign exchange came to an abrupt end. In an attempt to end prostitution, schools were set up to try to turn prostitutes into "new women."

On a research trip to Vietnam in September 1979 I was taken to visit a reform center for prostitutes in Saigon, one of the centers for the Restoration of Women's Dignity.[36] When my guides explained that the young women were taught that they were not a commodity for sale, I countered: "Any commodity must have a buyer as well as a seller—what measures do you take to reeducate the buyers?" The reply surprised me: they had thought about the problem and measures were taken to reform male clients. First there would be private discussions in the place of work or residential area; if that did not work, the shame of a public reprimand followed. For those men with formal employment in the socialist economic sector, there was some leverage to discipline them with fines or dismissal from their job if the initial attempts at persuasion failed. However, since the socialist sector was still relatively small and unemployment high, most clients were outside the range of such pressure.

Although Vietnam has taken vigorous measures to try to eliminate prostitution, the problem of economic and power imbalances along class and gender lines still remains. Despite radical measures to reduce social inequalities, Vietnam is still a society with significant differences in economic, social, and political power stemming from the legacy of the prerevolutionary system, the postrevolutionary political and economic role of the male-dominated vanguard party, and the emerging sexual division of labor in the existing socioeconomic system which draws more men than women into modern and better-paid economic sectors. Men in positions of political, managerial, or economic power in Vietnam as elsewhere can take advantage of their position in their sexual relations. This has been exacerbated by the marked imbalance in the number of men and women due to the war, which has undermined full implementation of the socialist marriage law legislating monogamy.[37] Engels' vision of the transformation of gender relations from the realm of necessity to that of pure love is obviously still a long way off in Vietnam.

In Vietnam marriage-and-the-family is still very much an economic institution. Official attitudes in Vietnam to the economic role of the family have been ambiguous and in flux. One of the aims of the first stage of socialist transformation—cooperativization and the socialization of factories—was to eliminate the economic role of the family as owner of the means of production and organizer of labor power. However, the household retained an important economic role in agriculture through the institution of the 5 percent land or "private plots" and has been given an expanded economic role in recent economic reform measures.[38] In the orthodox conception of socialist development, the family was to lose the dominant economic role it plays in precapitalist and capitalist societies but remain the "social cell of society." While theoretically the new socialist family should do away with feudal remnants, in practice some aspects of Confucianism have been encouraged by the socialist state, particularly women's traditional responsibility to care for her husband's parents, since this liberates men to leave their villages to serve in the army or in modern economic sectors. Despite these limitations, and the fact that Vietnam is far from having achieved ideal gender relations according to either socialist or feminist ideology, there are positive lessons to be learned from Vietnam's attempts to reverse the wholesale transformation of female sexuality into a commodity and to coordinate socialist development with women's emancipation.

The Impact on Women of Socialist Development Strategies

Following established formulae for socialist economic development, Vietnam's socialist transformation initially emphasized state-controlled economic development—state accumulation and state planning to increase productivity in a more egalitarian framework than that of precapitalist or capitalist society.[39]

Orthodox socialist thinking on development since the time of Lenin has stressed the importance of building heavy industry. In the late 1950s and early 1960s, as the only former colony in the socialist world, the Democratic Republic of Vietnam benefited from a sizeable influx of aid and was something of a showcase for socialist industrialization in the third world. (The war, of course, smashed Vietnam's leading edge in this regard.) The proudest achievement of this period was the Thai Nguyen iron and steel complex, built entirely with external aid.[40] The conception of women's emancipation was linked to the development strategy: women workers in heavy industry were seen as models for women's new role under socialism. A number of young women of peasant origin were recruited as steel workers for the Thai Nguyen plant, and one of Vietnam's leading novelists, herself a woman, Le Minh, spent several months at the plant living and working with these young women and interviewing them for two novels on what was seen as the young woman of the future. The rather macho image of the emancipated woman as steel worker and tractor driver could be found in the pages of *Vietnam*, a typical socialist bloc glossy pictorial.

These capital-intensive jobs dealing with machinery are considered the vanguard of socialist development; however, most of them are filled by men, while the majority of women remain the traditional economic sector in nonmechanized agricultural production that is starved of investment funds under a conception of socialist development which gives priority to the modern sector.

In orthodox Marxist-Leninist analysis, the route to women's liberation involves freeing women from the drudgery of housework by socializing child care and housework as well as mobilizing women for social production on the same footing as men. There have been attempts in Vietnam to put this concept into practice with an extensive day-care system for infants and preschool children. For example, at a model factory, the March 8 textile mill in Hanoi factory, spacious nursery and day-care facilities enable mothers to work in a large factory, with short breaks for breastfeeding infants. However, at a large factory like this it takes time to walk from the workplace to the nursery, and babies are not machines that can be turned on to nurse exactly when the mother rushes in during her break, so the arrangement is far from satisfactory.[41]

This approach to women's emancipation—full employment plus day care—has been criticized in studies of women in socialist countries. No matter how many socially provided facilities such as day-care centers exist, there will always be work involved with child care and housekeeping; it cannot be completely socialized. It has been argued that many women, whether in socialist or capitalist countries, have experienced mobilization into the formal workforce as a double workload rather than "emancipation."[42]

A number of solutions have been proposed to the universal problem of the working woman's double day, most notably (1) the equal sharing of housework and parenting by men and women, and (2) a redefinition of "work" rejecting the male-oriented model of the separation of social production from the household.[43] The Vietnamese experience can throw some interesting light on the process of implementing these solutions. The social process of achieving equal male participation in housework is one that begins with the differential socialization of male and female children. In societies where women are expected to be housewives, girls are trained for this role but boys are discouraged or actually prohibited from doing "female" household tasks and are socialized by full-time housewife mothers to expect to be served by women.[44] In my experience, young men who grew up in the socialist north with working mothers are accustomed to doing housework, unlike young men from Saigon.[45]

However, with the continued mobilization of men into the military, many husbands are absent for years. In this context, equal sharing of housework and parenting is not possible. What is on the agenda now in Vietnam is the second of the above proposed feminist solutions: flexible work arrangements that make it easier for women to combine their work in production and reproduction.

The new policy direction is part of a larger change. In 1979 the economic situation forced a reevaluation of the continued stress on large-scale industrialization. New policies promoting the production of consumer goods and exports were introduced. The reforms involve a new openness to small-scale organization of production on the household or small group level, whether in light industry, handicraft production, or agricultural production. With small-scale production, including both small workshop and household production, redefined as compatible with socialism, women can more easily coordinate production (e.g., making rugs for export or conical hats for the local market, to cite two cases I looked at during a research trip in 1979) with their other work. Depending on their household situation, women can either work in small handicraft and light industry workshops in their village or urban neighborhood or do outwork at home.

The village and urban handicraft production cooperatives I visited in 1979 and 1983 in the north seemed to me far more congenial work environments than the large model March 8 textile factory where the din of the machines in a single huge workhall not only made conversation impossible but must damage workers' hearing as well. The handicraft workshops provided work on a human scale in a sociable atmosphere. However, some women with small children prefer outwork. For example, during one household interview in Quang Nap cooperative, Thai Binh province, I saw a pile of half finished conical hats in a corner of the room identical to one stage of the work process in the workshop I had just visited. They were being worked on by the married daughter of the widow who owned the house: by working there she could get away from the crowded conditions in which she lived with her in-laws, husband, and children, work in a quiet environment, and visit with her mother, a widow living on her own because her two sons were killed in the war.

One scholar, Maria Mies, is very critical of current Vietnamese policy, which includes mobilizing women's labor for producing luxury goods such as carpets and embroidery for export to the Soviet Union and Eastern Europe.[46] She analyzes this as a strategy using the labor of subordinated housewives for capital accumulation in a way that is essentially no different from the "housewifization" promoted by international aid agencies in capitalist third-world countries.[47] Mies notes that "housewives are atomized and isolated, their work organization makes the awareness of common interests, of the whole process of production, very difficult."[48] I found that this was certainly true in Nepal, where I evaluated UNFPA-funded income-generating cottage industry projects for women which were based on what Mies calls the "housewife" model. There had been no provision for workshops; widows were working in their own homes where they were isolated and did not have adequate lighting.[49]

However, the social organization of production in Vietnam is decidedly not "housewifization." In Vietnam the preferred form of handicraft production is precisely not working in the seclusion of the household but rather in workshops which provide a sociable environment for married as well as unmarried women.

In Vietnam, economic reform measures introduced since 1981 have encouraged and legitimated an expansion of the economic role of the family, particularly in agriculture. However, this is neither "housewifization" nor *a priori* bad for women. The overwhelming majority of the agricultural labor force is made up of women, and after the end of the war in 1975 female cooperative cadres promoted during the war years were by and large replaced with veterans, because officers in particular would have felt it a slight to their wartime service if they had to work under the managerial control of women cadres. In the late 1970s *Phu Nu Vietnam*, the Women's Union weekly newspaper, carried several complaints from cooperative level women's union branches about the postwar exclusion of capable women with managerial experience from ballots for cooperative management committees as well as complaints about mistreatment of women workers by cooperative management. The most frequent complaint was that women were fined for absenteeism without sufficient consideration for their circumstances and needs. Rural women appear to have welcomed the policy since 1981 of subcontracting cooperative land to households. Women peasants are now allowed to sell their surplus products at market prices. With so many husbands either dead in the war or still absent in the military, the partial resurrection of household agriculture has not led to "housewifization." This is in marked contrast to China where similar reforms have led to a reemergence of patriarchal controls of female labor power.

The major priority during the period of building socialism is surplus accumulation for development. While the orthodox socialist accumulation strategy which was implemented in socialist Vietnam for twenty years, from the late 1950s to the late 1970s, stressed accumulation at the central, national level, with egalitarian rations and other basic entitlements providing a welfare floor for the population, Vietnam is now in transition to a reformist economic policy which allows more freedom for accumulation and investment at basic levels of production, including factories, workshops, and peasant households, and which stresses material incentives for productivity rather than egalitarian entitlements. What has been the impact of these two successive models of development on women's lives? Can it be argued that one or the other system is more advantageous for women?

The short answer is that this depends on which women one is talking about. As is discussed at length in the literature on women and development, "women" must be differentiated not only by class, earning power, and profession, but also by their situation in the family as mother, mother-in-law, wife, or daughter. The orthodox model of socialist development, the egalitarian, centrally planned model, provided a social welfare floor for women in economic difficulties such as old mothers who had lost sons in the war and young wives with small children to support whose husbands were absent in the army—not an insignificant group in Vietnam. If state and cooperative-supported egalitarian social welfare measures are cut back, more of the burden of caring for relatives injured during the war falls on their working wives, mothers, and daughters, a fact which is of particular concern for the Women's Union. On the other hand, in the traditional Vietnamese sexual division of labor, men tend to dominate in the political sphere, and women in the marketplace. Despite some significant changes in gender roles in socialist Vietnam, this pattern has continued. The sellers in socialist Vietnam's marketplaces are overwhelmingly women, while the great majority of the party cadres and government officials who dominate both political and economic life, as well as the policemen at the checkpoints which control the circulation of goods, are male. The market liberalization of the recent reform policy gives Vietnam's peasant women—who are the mainstay of the rural economy—more freedom to exchange their products or become full-time traders without bureaucratic impediments.

Vietnam's dilemma now is that the economic situation is so desperate that it is difficult to make any system work. The increasingly difficult economic situation has contributed to a cynicism about socialism and even a crisis in morale in the party. Within the party corruption has become a major concern for the first time. During the first years of the transition to socialism in the late 1950s and early 1960s, the population of the Democratic Republic of Vietnam experienced a rising standard of living. But since the end of the war, following the cut-off of U.S. and Chinese aid to Vietnam, the standard of living dropped precipitously. During the war, U.S. aid in the south and Chinese commodity aid in the north had provided a supply of material goods which was suddenly cut off after the end of the war.

Vietnam's enormous postwar welfare problems make it more difficult to implement reformist measures to give more incentives to able-bodied and productive workers. Vietnam's development dilemma was summed up in an interview in 1979, at the beginning of the reform period, by Nguyen Huu Tho, agricultural editor of the party newspaper *Nhan Dan*:

> We are a poor country, and the problems of distribution can even arise within a family at the most basic level. Imagine a family with only one fish for a meal. One son is the only full-time worker in the family; another was

wounded in the war and cannot work. The family income is dependent on the strength of the former, but it is the latter who has made the greatest sacrifice for the independence of his country. How should the fish be divided? All our problems lie in this question . . . The war lasted thirty years, but it will take another twenty years before we will be able to overcome the legacy of problems it has left.[50]

Changing the gender of the able-bodied worker to female, a reality articulated in the pages of the Women's Union's newspaper, *Phu Nu Vietnam* (Vietnamese Women), adds to the complexity of the dilemma.

The theory of socialism, now tarnished, is a vision of a future society in which all people, regardless of gender, class, or race equally enjoy prosperity, the right to meaningful work, the right to eat, the rights to health care and education. It is the vision of a society in which people's labor power is not a commodity, women's bodies are not commodities, where food, the means of life, is not a commodity, and where photographs of women as sex objects are not used to sell commodities. This vision, which is shared by socialists all over the world, deeply shapes Vietnamese socialist thinking. However, it is a vision that presupposes material abundance and peace. Unfortunately, there are few signs at the end of the 1980s that these conditions will be allowed to Vietnamese women or men in the foreseeable future.

Notes

1. Friedrich Engels, *The Origin of the Family, Private Property and the State* (London: Lawrence and Wishart, 1972), p. 145.
2. Nguyen Thi Dinh, "Contributions to the socio-economic strategy in the initial stage of our country: some matters to which attention must be given in the mobilization of women." *Tap Chi Cong San* (Hanoi) 7, (July 1986): 50–54, translated in JPRS SEA 86–193, pp. 61–66.
3. Quoted in David Chandler, "Post Mortem on the Wars in Indo-China: A Review Article," *Journal of Asian Studies* 40, no. 1, (November 1980): 78.
4. See David G. Marr and Christine P. White, *Postwar Vietnam: Dilemmas in Socialist Development* (Ithaca, NY: Southeast Asia Publications, 1988), pp. 1–13; Grant Evans and Kelvin Rowley, *Red Brotherhood at War: Indochina Since the Fall of Saigon* (London: Verso, 1984), and Nayan Chanda, *Brother Enemy: The War After the War* (San Diego: Harcourt Brace, 1986).
5. Douglas Pike and Benjamin Ward, "Losing and Winning: Korea and Vietnam as Success Stories," *The Washington Quarterly* 10, no. 3 (Summer 1987): 81.
6. Joel Charny and John Spragens, Jr., *Obstacles to Recovery in Vietnam and Kampuchea: U.S. Embargo of Humanitarian Aid* (Boston: Oxfam, 1984).
7. Eva Mysliwiec, *Punishing the Poor: The International Isolation of Kampuchea* (Oxford: Oxfam, 1988).
8. In 1975: 61 percent, in 1979: 62.69 percent. *Women of Vietnam: Statistical Data* (Hanoi: Vietnam Women's Union, 1981).
9. Hoang Tuong Van, "Female Labor in Agriculture," *Vietnam Courier* 2 (1988): p. 19.
10. Nguyen Thi Dinh, "Contributions . . ." For eloquent interviews with Vietnamese

women denouncing the heavy work burden they must bear, see Mai Thu Van, *Vietnam, un peuple, des voix,* (Paris: Pierre Horay, 1983).

11. Hoang Tuong Van, "Female labor," p. 19.

12. The phrase "female identity is a process" is from Judith Gardiner, "On Female Identity and Writing by Women," *Critical Inquiry* 8, no. 2, (Winter 1981).

13. Ho Chi Minh, "French Colonialism on Trial," in *Selected Works*, Vol. 2 (Hanoi: Foreign Languages Publishing House, 1961), p. 114.

14. Ho Chi Minh, "Duong Cach Mang" (The Revolutionary Road), *Toan Tap* (Collected Works), Vol. 2 (Hanoi: Su That, 1981), pp. 217–19.

15. David G. Marr, *Vietnamese Tradition on Trial, 1920–1945* (Berkeley: University of California Press, 1981), pp. 199ff.

16. Nguyen Thi Kim Anh, *Van De Phu Nu* (The Woman Question) (Cholon, 1938) includes a summary of Engels' *The Origins of the Family, Private Property and the State.* For discussion see Marr, *Vietnamese Tradition*, pp. 237–40.

17. The Vietnamese Communist attitude to Confucianism has been to reject and criticize some aspects (e.g., the "three submissions") while affirming the value of other aspects (e.g., the nonreligious emphasis on social organization, the virtues of courage and loyalty, etc.). One leading Vietnamese communist intellectual has even emphasized the similarities between Confucianism and Marxism (without reference, however, to gender dimensions). Nguyen Khac Vien, "Confucianism and Marxism in Vietnam," in *Tradition and Revolution in Vietnam* (Berkeley, CA: Indochina Resource Center, 1974).

18. Marr, *Vietnamese Tradition*, pp. 220–22.

19. Mai Thi Tu and Le Thi Nham Tuyet, *Women in Vietnam* (Hanoi: Foreign Languages Publishing House, 1978), p. 116.

20. Marr, *Vietnamese Tradition*, p. 227.

21. Quoted in Mai Thi Tu and Le Thi Nham Tuyet, *Women in Vietnam*, p. 149.

22. Mai Thi Tu, "The Vietnamese Woman, Yesterday and Today,." *Vietnamese Studies* (Hanoi) 10, (1966): 12–16. On the subject of the relatively egalitarian Vietnamese tradition compared to Chinese Confucianism or Nguyen dynasty neo-Confucianism, see Ta Van Tai,"The Status of Women in Traditional Vietnam," *Journal of Asian History* 15, no. 2, (1981), John Whitmore, "Social Organization and Confucian Thought in Vietnam," *Journal of Southeast Asian Studies* 15, no. 2, (September 1984), and Insun Yu, "Law and Family in Seventeenth and Eighteenth Century Vietnam," Ph.D. diss., University of Michigan, 1978.

23. Cited in Mai Thi Tu and Le Thi Nham Tuyet, *Women in Vietnam*, p. 313.

24. For this period see ibid., pp. 146–63.

25. There is a reproduction of the DRV stamp in Arlene Eisen-Bergman, *Women of Vietnam* (London: Zed Books, 1984), p. 173.

26. Mai Elliott, translator, *No Other Road to Take: Memoir of Mrs. Nguyen Thi Dinh*, data paper #102 (Ithaca, NY: Southeast Asia Program, Cornell University, 1976), p. 25.

27. For a sensitive discussion of the contradictory interaction of tradition and revolution— reform and preservation of the cultural heritage—in an NLF area in South Vietnam see David Hunt, "Village Culture and the Vietnamese Revolution," *Past and Present* 94 (1982).

28. Phan Thi Nhu Bang, *Ta Thi Kieu, An Heroic Girl of Ben Tre* (South Vietnam: Liberation Editions, 1966).

29. Ibid., p. 25. This was not the first time Ly had disagreed with the party secretary, Bay. Earlier he had proposed the execution of two spies in the village, a very poor couple. Ly had argued that they were only spies because they had no other source of livelihood and successfully appealed to a number of villagers who supported the revolution to donate a small amount of land to the couple. Shamed before public opinion with the exposure of their activities and grateful for the land, they swore never to spy again. The different priorities and proposed courses of action suggested by Bay and Ly in these two cases

reflected their different interests and situations: for the underground cadres, spies were
the greatest threat, while for Ly and her young women friends the greatest danger to their
safety and integrity was sexual harassment.

30. Ibid, p. 26 (emphasis added).

31. Eisen-Bergman, "Mass Production of Prostitutes," in *Women of Viet Nam*, p. 80–91.

32. In the precolonial patriarchal world of the early nineteenth-century Vietnamese literary
    masterpiece *The Tale of Kieu*, it was assumed that it was a daughter's duty to sacrifice her
    life and happiness for her father and family. Kieu volunteers to be sold to pay her father's
    debts. Nguyen Du, *The Tale of Kieu* trans. Huynh Sanh Thong (New Haven: Yale
    University Press, 1983).

33. Probably the best detailed description of this process is by a scholar who draws on both
    Marx and Foucault: Aihwa Ong, *Spirits of Resistance and Capitalist Discipline: Factory
    Women in Malaysia* (Albany: State University of New York Press, 1987).

34. Following short-term employment in multinational corporations, young women become
    socialized into new cultural values and accustomed to cash employment; as a result
    many go into prostitution; see Aihwa Ong, "Industrialization and Prostitution in South-
    east Asia," *Southeast Asia Chronicle* 96 (January 1985); on correspondence brides see
    John Krich, "Here Come the Brides," *Mother Jones* 2, no. 11 (February–March 1986):
    34–37; 43–46.

35. Tiziano Terzani, *Gai Phong: The Fall and Liberation of Saigon* (New York: St. Martin's
    Press, 1976), p. 209.

36. For more information on these schools, see Eisen, *Women and Revolution in Viet Nam*,
    pp. 229–36.

37. At the end of the war in 1975 there were an estimated 2 million more females than males
    in Vietnam; women made up 52.1 percent of the population (24,821,000 females to 22,
    817,000 males). By 1979 the disparity had reduced slightly due to new births (51.5
    percent females in the population), but the discrepancy among adults remained. Viet-
    nam Women's Union, *Women of Vietnam/Femmes du Vietnam* (statistical data) (Hanoi,
    1981), p. 11.

38. In agricultural producer cooperatives 5 percent of the cultivatable land was divided
    among member households for their private use, while the rest of the land was cultivated
    collectively.

39. For an overview of Vietnam's development strategies, see Melanie Beresford, *Vietnam:
    Politics, Economics and Society* (London: Pinter, 1988). For their impact on women, see
    Christine Pelzer White, "Socialist Transformation of Agriculture and Gender Relations:
    the Vietnamese Case," in *IDS Bulletin* 13, no. 4 (September 1982): 44–51; Christine
    Pelzer White, "Collectives and the Status of Women: The Vietnamese Experience,"
    Ceres 16, no. 4 (July–August 1983), and Nancy Wiegersma, *Vietnam: Peasant Land,
    Peasant Revolution: Patriarchy and Collectivity in the Rural Economy* (New York: St.
    Martin's Press, 1988).

40. Jacques Charrière, "Socialism in North Vietnam," *Monthly Review*, February 1966, pp.
    19–41.

41. Visit to factory in March 1983 in connection with joint Institute for Development
    Studies (Sussex, UK)-Social Sciences Commission (Hanoi) colloquium. Christine Pel-
    zer White, "Women, employment and the family: report on a colloquium comparing
    the women's movement and government legislation for gender equality in Britain and
    Vietnam," *IDS Bulletin* 15, no. 1 (1984): 57–61.

42. See e.g., Elisabeth Croll, "Socialist Development Experience: Women in Rural Produc-
    tion and Reproduction in the Soviet Union, China, Cuba, and Tanzania," *Discussion
    Paper 143*, IDS, Sussex; Maxine Molyneux, "Women in Socialist Societies: Problems of
    Theory and Practice," in K. Young et al, eds., *Of Marriage and the Market* (London:
    CSE Books, 1981). For an example from a nonsocialist third world country, an Indone-
    sian national slogan for women promotes women's "double role" *(peran ganda)*; Indone-

sian women comment that this really means "double load" *(beban ganda)*. Thanks to Ron Witton for this comparison.

43. The argument has been made that men and women were more equal in European history before the industrial revolution removed production from the home to the factory; C. Hall, "The Butcher, the Baker, the Candlestick Maker," in *The Changing Experience of Women* (Oxford: Martin Robertson, 1982), and I. Pinchbeck, *Women Workers and the Industrial Revolution* (London: ??, 1981).

44. For example, during a visit in an Indonesian household I saw a little boy burst into tears because he was not allowed to help serve snacks to the guests like his sisters.

45. I saw this when I was teaching in the mid-1970s in Australia, where there were students from both north and south. A young woman from Hanoi who studied in Great Britain in 1982 told me an amusing story along the same lines. During breaks in her English class the students, all from third world countries, would drink tea or coffee until the few female students declared that they would no longer wash all the cups. Except for one male Vietnamese student from Hanoi, all of the male students decided that rather than wash their own cups they would prefer not to drink anything.

46. Mies, *Patriarchy and Accumulation*, pp. 188–94.

47. Ibid., pp. 112–35.

48. Ibid., p. 116.

49. Getting women into debt was also an integral part of the program which provided the women with imported Japanese knitting machines and imported yarn which were then considered loans repayable with interest. The women's eyesight had suffered and they had no way of repaying the loans as the state trading store had stopped accepting their products. The official report of the evaluation of this project is in *Report on the Evaluation of UNFPA-Assisted Women, Population and Development Projects in Nepal* (New York: United Nations Fund for Population Activities, June 1985), pp. 17–24.

50. Christine P. White, "Interview with Nugyen Huu Tho," in *Journal of Contemporary Asia* 2 no. 1 (1981).

Legal Reform and Socialist Revolution in South Yemen: Women and the Family

Maxine D. Molyneux

In November 1967 the national liberation forces of South Yemen gained independence from Britain and established the People's Republic of South Yemen, later renamed the People's Democratic Republic of Yemen (PDRY). In accordance with its egalitarian principles and its commitment to the revolutionary socialist transformation of state and society, the new government introduced a set of legal reforms, which were subsequently embodied in the new Constitution in 1970. The Constitution is pledged to advancing the cause of women's emancipation, and the policies adopted by the government to further this goal have much in common with those of other socialist states in their emphasis on legal reform and in their attempts to redefine family relations.[1] The PDRY differs from most of these states, however, in being a Muslim country and thereby inheriting prerevolutionary legal codes that were derived from the dominant religion, Islam. This is a situation that has proved, in other contexts, to be highly resistant to secularizing change.

Democratic Yemen therefore occupies an interesting, and distinctive, place in the discussion of socialist legal reforms and their implications for women and the family. In common with the Muslim republics of the Soviet Union and with Albania, it is a Muslim society that has experienced a substantial period of rule by governments committed to "scientific socialism."[2] In its espousal of Marxist doctrine and in its economic policies, the PDRY differs from those other Muslim countries—Eygpt, Algeria, Syria, Iraq, and Libya—that have also proclaimed themselves to be "socialist." In these latter cases the ruling governments made clear that *their* socialism was an essentially local or "Arab" variant and distinct from that of other regions. When this specificity was defined by Nasser, or by the Ba'ath, "Arab socialism" was held to be based on two main characteristics: it was derived from the principles of Islam, and it tried to avoid, through an appeal to nationalism, what Nasser called "class strife." Moreover, despite an expansion of the state sector, capitalist social relations prevailed in these states and marked inequalities of wealth persisted.

The PDRY has challenged this definition of socialism in the Arab world. The ruling party, formerly the National Liberation Front (NLF), and known since 1978 as the Yemeni Socialist Party, describes itself as "the vanguard of the Yemeni working class," and its official doctrine is not derived from the teachings of Islam, but bears the explicit influence of the writings of Marx, Engels, and Lenin. While according to party documents the country is not yet socialist but is "socialist-oriented," it is scientific socialism that provides the theoretical underpinnings of government policy, and the word "scientific" is implicitly contrasted to the word "Arab."[3] For these reasons the legal system that has emerged in South Yemen is distinctive in the Arab context and its laws, taken as a whole, are arguably the most radical in the non-Soviet Muslim world. Despite several outbreaks of intra-regime conflict, the most recent and violent being in January 1985, the underlying policy orientation has been constant since the late 1960s.

South Yemen

In November 1967 the National Liberation Front came to power after five years of guerrilla fighting and terminated 128 years of British colonial rule in South Yemen. Aden, the region's principal city and main port, had been ruled by the United Kingdom as a colony since 1839, and by the 1930s formal control was gradually extended over the twenty-four ministates in the hinterland to encompass the region that became known as South Arabia—with an area of around 114,000 square miles, but a population of only 1.6 million in 1967. The last two decades of colonial rule were marked by an unsuccessful attempt to forge a single state, a Federation of South Arabia composed of Aden and these smaller units of the interior. It was the defeat of this project and of a rival guerrilla grouping, FLOSY, in an armed struggle that lasted for four years that brought the revolutionary National Liberation Front to power.[4] In March 1968 the Fourth Congress of the NLF laid down its guidelines for government policy. The main decisions were influenced by the left of the party and committed it to destroying the old state apparatus and developing, in its place, "people's power," creating a revolutionary people's army, implementing measures against foreign capital, adopting an anti-imperialist foreign policy, and carrying out radical land reforms.[5]

However, little was done to implement these measures by the first NLF government headed by Qahtan Al Sha'abi. It was not until a more radical faction came to unchallenged power in the "corrective move" of June 1969, over a year and a half after independence, that serious efforts to transform the economy and society along socialist lines were made, and the early guidelines began to be translated into policy. All foreign trading and banking concerns were nationalized in late 1969. A redistributive land reform was decreed in 1970. The first three-year plan of 1971–74 embodied the party's earlier nationalist objectives but went some way further. It stressed the urgency of stimulating the rapid development of the economy to overcome the extreme poverty and underdevelopment of the country, to raise per capita income (estimated in 1968 at $82 p.a.), and effect a policy of redistribution in favor of the most deprived sectors of the population. The state was to assume a leading role in economic life, the main sectors of the urban economy were to be nationalized, industrialization given maximum support, and foreign trade brought under government control. The agrarian sector was to be transformed following the expropriation of the larger private holdings, through the rationalization of production and, where possible, through the establishment of state farms and cooperatives. In broad outline, the policies amounted to the construction of a planned economy with a strong state sector (80 percent of production in 1983) and considerable government intervention at the level of prices, wages, distribution, and production—a model emulated in most of the countries within the pro-Soviet socialist bloc.

The "destruction of the old state apparatus" and transformation of the relationship between state and people was formalized by the Constitution of 1970, which was the embodiment of what Soviet theorists call "basic laws." Among other things, it outlined the government's political principles, the organization of the powers of the state, and the rights and duties of citizens and their representative organizations. The Constitution was drawn up with the collaboration of East German jurists and it laid the basis for the establishment of a state and legal system similar to that which was first developed in the USSR and which has since spread to other countries in the socialist bloc, such as Vietnam, North Korea, Cuba, and China.[6]

As in these countries, state power in the PDRY was formally vested in "the working people" and according to the Constitution it was exercised through their representatives in the Supreme People's Council, initially a 111-member body charged with enacting laws and approving state policies. The new state, according to the Constitution, was to be "democratic" both because it represented the interests of the working people and because state power was to be devolved through greater popular participation in decisionmaking, especially through the mass organizations, and at middle and local levels of state power.[7] In establishing a new state form, the 1970 Constitution, embodying what was now party policy, also redefined the legal system and the place of law in society. It pledged the government to introduce new legislation in the areas of employment, the family, and criminal law, and these measures were defined in accordance with the egalitarian principles laid down in the Constitution. In the new legal system, the separation of the juridical and executive powers of the state was rejected on the same grounds as those advanced by Soviet constitutional theorists. Since in theory state power was based on popular sovereignty and state policy originated from popularly elected representative bodies, the delegation of legislative power was considered to be in violation of the principles of the socialist political order.[8] The institutions, practice, and content of the law were henceforth to respond to the requirements of the "national new Democratic Phase" of the revolution, and to the needs of "the broadest sectors of the population."[9]

On gaining power, the NLF had to administer an area that had no unified national economy or political structure, let alone a common legal system. The newly independent state, which became the People's Democratic Republic of Yemen, comprised the former Aden colony and the formerly independent states of the interior. The hinterland had been constitutionally separate from Aden, and was politically and economically fragmented as a result of tribal segmentation and the local autonomy hitherto enjoyed by ruling sheikhs, sultans, or emirs. In general the area outside Aden colony was characterized by a marked division between town and country, and by a preponderance of precapitalist relations of production, ranging from the nomadic pastoralism characteristic of the Bedouin tribes to the more diversified class structure typical of the towns. Some areas, such as the Hadramaut, were characterized by a many-tiered caste system, which had survived amid decades of migration, increasing commercialism, and social differentiation in the wealthier inland areas.[10] This variety of social forms and the relative autonomy of regional potentates was reflected in the varying degrees of local legislation and practice incorporated within the prevailing legal systems. Religion provided the fundamental unity of these different regions and systems, however, and established the main principles and practice of the law, as laid down in the Koran and interpreted by the Shafei school of jurisprudence.[11]

Before discussing the reforms that have affected the position of women, two general points can be made about the changes in the PDRY's legal system. First, it is clear that this process involved fulfilling what the bourgeois revolutions achieved in Europe: namely, creating a unified, state-administered legal system by extending the central legal authority into rural areas where religious, customary, and tribal law prevailed. Moreover the creation of a new legal system and new laws was part of the process of constructing a national entity, in the course of which efforts were made to dissolve the old ties of allegiance, chief among them being tribalism. The new areas of regional jurisdiction, the governorates and districts, were especially designed to cut across tribal divisions and provide a different principle of regional identification.[12] Second, and following from this, in common with other socialist states, party leaders have seen legal reform not just as an accompaniment to the process of social transformation, but also as an important instrument in achieving it. The official texts have therefore justified reform in terms of three main arguments— that the previous legal order served colonial and feudal interests and therefore had to be abolished; that it was undemocratic in failing to respond to the needs of the broadest sectors of the population, and that new legal instruments had to be created in order to "deepen and accelerate" the revolutionary process.

The conception of the law embodied in the new system is therefore one that sees law not merely as a reflection of existing social relations, favoring certain class interests over others, but as a means of intervention in the process of transition, with the capacity to further this process through some measure of popular participation. It is obvious that the transition from a free-market economy to one based on centralized planning, and from private to state control of productive property, crucially affects concepts of ownership, possession, and property, as well as definitions of the obligations of state functionaries and citizens in this regard. The relationship between the law and the plan, and between civil and economic law, had to be redefined in order to provide the conditions of existence of the new social relations, and their institutional forms. Collective property had to have legal recognition, if only in order that the state could allocate resources to it and enter into contract relations.[13]

In the PDRY, as in other socialist states, changes in the law were also seen as a means of accelerating or deepening the struggle of social forces that were to benefit from the government's policies—peasants, women, and the industrial working class, for example. The passing of the 1970 land reform was followed in 1970–72 by peasant uprisings against landlords and the seizure of their lands. The embryonic state lacked the means of effecting this popular transfer of resources without the mobilization of the rural workforce, itself spurred on by party activists. The legal reform was important for this process in two respects: it provided the legitimation for class struggle and at the same time withdrew state and juridical support from the previous system of ownership. Its effectivity, however, crucially depended on the capacities of its beneficiaries and opponents to achieve their different aims.

Legal Reform, Women, and the Family: Socialist Priorities

Legal reform affecting women and the family has been seen by most government planners in the socialist countries as a necessary part of their principled support for women's emancipation. But it is also considered to be important in securing more general policy objectives. In the context of underdeveloped societies, such as Democratic Yemen, the fulfillment of government development programs depends on bringing about social changes of a major kind. The prerevolutionary social order, which is seen as an obstacle to economic development and social reform, needs to be transformed and replaced by a new social order, one more suited to the demands of economic development. The development strategies usually pursued by socialist states have a number of implications for women, both as to how women will be affected by them and as to how government planners perceive the part women are to play in the process. Revolutionary governments consider the mobilization of women in the period of social and economic transformation as helping to accomplish at least three goals: (1) to extend the political base of the regime; (2) to increase the active labor force; and (3) to help "modernize" the family and harness it more directly to state goals. Legal reform is of fundamental importance in all three cases.

The first of these considerations is to help consolidate the power of the state by drawing women into political activity—into such organizations as the women's union, the party, neighborhood associations, and other mass organizations. In South Yemen, women had been an active but small minority in the NLF during the national liberation struggle, and it was therefore a question of maintaining and extending that support in the postindependence period. This kind of participation was only possible, however, if kin control over women was challenged, along with the practice of seclusion.[14] As part of this process of encouraging women's entry into the political realm, women were given the vote for the first time in 1977, when universal suffrage was implemented. A special effort was made to ensure that some women candidates stood for election.

The second way in which the mobilization of women was regarded as important was more directly relevant to the economy. The education of women and their entry into employment increases and improves the available labor supply, a process that is a necessary concomitant to any successful development program. In the period after independence the preexisting scarcity of labor in the PDRY was exacerbated by the departure of some 20,000 skilled and professional workers, and by the large-scale out-migration of men to the oil-producing states. The World Bank estimated in 1980 that there occurred a loss of one-third of the men in the 15–35 age group or 18 percent of the total workforce.[15] Faced with this situation, the government was dependent on women to make up the shortfall in labor supply. The five-year plan of 1981–85 included among its principal objectives the promotion of women's participation in economic and social activities, and the emphasis was on mobilizing "housewives" into economic activity to help meet the goal of a 3.61 percent annual increase in the labor supply. By 1984 women still made up only one-fifth of the EAP; this low rate of participation results partly from the fact that there is a stigma attached to women performing income-generating activities, especially if these involve working outside the home.[16] These cultural

disincentives to women taking up paid employment were further reinforced by the legal authority invested in male guardians, which gave them
the power to prevent their female custodians from breaking the rules of
seclusion.

This latter concern is one that also lies behind the third objective, family
reform. For, as we have seen, if women are to become politically active and
enter wage employment, they must be freed from traditional familial and
cultural constraints. But there are two other social policy objectives that
family reform addresses. One of these is the attempt to hasten the transformation of the economy by eroding preexisting social relations and practices. Women's subordination is an integral part of the reproduction of
many forms of peasant and tribal property systems. The control of marriage alliances by kin groups, for example, as well as systems of inheritance
that discriminate against women frequently do so in order to preserve the
integrity of the property system concerned.[17] Economic planners in socialist states have long recognized this coincidence of the goal of women's
emancipation and socialist modernization, and the Family Laws they
promote soon after coming to power have their simultaneous achievement
as one of their explicit aims.[18]

The family is an important site of state intervention for a further reason.
Seen as the "basic cell of society," it is considered to be responsible in
helping to form the next generation of "patriotic, socialist" subjects. By
promoting greater equality between the sexes, family reforms are seen as
laying the basis for a new egalitarian socialist family. Such a family should
be stronger not only because it is more harmonious, but also because it is
better equipped to perform the roles assigned to it by the state.[19]

In Democratic Yemen, according to the preamble of the Family Law,
the "traditional" or "feudal" family is "incompatible with the principles
and program of the National Democratic Revolution," because its "old
relationships prevent it from playing a positive role in the building up of
society." The role of the reformed family is envisaged in terms of educating
the young into the ideals of the revolution so that they can participate in
constructing and defending the new society. Women's role in this process is
regarded as crucial, since it is they, as mothers and educators, who have
primary responsibility for the care of the young. Family reform is therefore
seen simultaneously as a precondition for mobilizing women into economic and political activity and an indispensable adjunct of both economic change and social stability.

These more general considerations about the value of legal reform, in
helping to secure policy objectives as well as address issues of principle, are
shared by most socialist governments. What was distinctive and especially
problematic about the process of legal reform in the PDRY was that
improvements in women's social and legal status involved reforming codes

that were derived from Islam and were considered to be of divine inspiration.

Islam and Gender Relations

It is a commonplace that women's legal rights and social position in Muslim societies are worse than in most other regions of the world. Comparative studies of religion have led to speculation about the part played by Islam, as a system of belief, in the perpetuation of gender inequality.[20] However, it would be facile to attribute women's subordination in the Arab world solely to the influence of Islam. Women in non-Muslim regions of the third world suffer from many of the forms of discrimination that Muslim women are subjected to. Such customs as polygyny, bride price, and child marriage are by no means confined to the Muslim world, or even to the third world; they are linked more generally to certain precapitalist property forms and economic systems that have existed in both East and West.[21] In Muslim countries, moreover, the ideology of women's inferiority and the customs within which it is articulated are usually a fusion of religious and customary or tribal laws, some of the latter denying the rights given to women by the Koran and other sources, especially in the *Hadith*, the "sayings" of the Prophet.

Similarly, as Islamic reformers have been concerned to point out, the explicit religious content within this ideological ensemble is generally made up of selective and interpretive readings of the Koran and the *Hadith*. Such interpretations have tended to disregard some of the more humanitarian provisions of the sacred texts, particularly in the matter of women's rights.[22] Others have read ambiguous statements as clear mandates and have legislated as if they were such. For example, although the Koran sanctions polygyny and divorce by repudiation, it nonetheless attaches certain humanitarian conditions designed to bestow some rights on women. These are frequently ignored in practice. And although the strict seclusion of women is not compulsory for believers any more than are clitoridectomy, veiling, and other customs found in some Islamic societies, phrases and verses from religious doctrine that might be seen as favoring these practices have often been interpreted as making them mandatory.[23] It is therefore a matter of some dispute as to how far the sexual inequalities enshrined within the traditional legal codes and practices derive from Islamic doctrine itself, and how far they derive from a particular interpretation of it.

Despite these qualifications, there can be little doubt that the ideological ensemble that articulates women's inferiority in many Muslim societies *claims* a religious derivation and on the basis of this derivation establishes its legitimacy. Moreover, while the Koran was in advance of most of the other world religions in according women any rights at all, these were never equal to men's. In certain passages, the Koran and the *Hadith* represent women as inferior to men and this inferiority is institutionalized in the orthodox legal codes and practices. These give women only half as much as men in property rights[24] and define women as juridical minors, in a subordinate position to men and requiring male guardians. At the same time, men are accorded a place of privilege and authority; the Koran states categorically that "men stand superior to women in that God hath preferred the one over the other."[25] Elsewhere women are characterized as less responsible and more susceptible to distraction. This often provides the rationale behind the exclusion of women from positions of social responsibility, whether in the economic, social, or political spheres, and forms the basis for the injunction in *Shariah* law to consider women's testimony as worth only half that of a man's.[26] Similarly, in the traditional divorce procedure known as *talaq*, a man's judgment on the matter of divorce is unquestioned and he need only pronounce the formula "I divorce thee" three times to secure a divorce, while a woman must press her case in the courts and produce witnesses to substantiate it. Thus, juridical inequality and the ideology of female inferiority, together with the practice of seclusion, ensure that women are often excluded from positions of responsibility in civil society.

For these same reasons, women are also restricted in their participation in economic activities. The exceptions have arisen in conditions of extreme poverty or where such participation was mediated through and subordinate to men, as, for example, when rural women worked on familial land or tended flocks.

The impact of religious orthodoxy on the juridical realm, in particular on the Family Laws, or laws of personal status as they are sometimes known, is a factor of the utmost significance: it is precisely within these religious codes that the position of women is defined as legally and socially subordinate to that of men. The religious influence and derivation of the codes has allowed the subordinate status of women to be legitimized in terms of divine inspiration and doctrinal orthodoxy and has made it especially difficult to bring about reforms in this area.[27] Yet given the marked gender inequality in many Muslim societies and the role of Islamic orthodoxy in sustaining it, no government that was genuinely committed to the emancipation of women could leave the *Shariah* and *urf* (customary) codes intact.

This problem is reflected in the history of legal reform in the Muslim world. Turkey was the first Muslim country to take the path of legal reform, and despite recent moves in some countries to reverse the process (Iran, Pakistan, Sudan, Algeria), Muslim societies underwent a gradual loosening of the ties between religion and the state from the mid-nineteenth century onward.[28] This was a slow and uneven process both across and within countries; but while there were differences between them in points of detail, most Muslim countries experienced a process of gradual secularization, wherein the institutions of the state, education, and the law have acquired some measure of independence from the religious authorities, involving varying degrees of reform. Following the early example of the Ottoman reforms, many Muslim countries secularized that part of their legal systems pertaining to commerce, finance, and criminal and penal law.

There are several explanations for this, but an important factor influencing the Ottoman reforms in matters pertaining to finance was the desire to remove the traditional and religious restrictions on commerce, usury, and trade to enable the "sick man of Europe" to compete with his rivals on equal terms. Other Islamic states such as Egypt followed suit for similar reasons. The reforms in the penal and civil codes (and these included some improvement in the position of women) were inspired by different considerations and were brought about largely as the result of a desire to abolish unduly harsh practices thought incompatible with "modernizing civilized societies."[29] Within this rubric, reformers in many Muslim countries pressed for an improvement in women's legal rights. Ataturk went furthest, in abolishing the *Shariah* altogether in Turkey.

However, while some changes along these lines were also made in Egypt, family law remained the most resilient redoubt of orthodoxy throughout virtually all the countries of the Muslim world until the period after the mid-1950s. It was only then, under both internal and external pressure to modernize, that some Muslim states began to see the practical advantages of liberating women from some of their traditional constraints. The more radical family law reforms were generally passed by governments committed to female social participation in their countries' development programs. Some of them, too, proclaimed a commitment of principle to greater social equality. The Tunisian Law of Personal Status brought into effect in 1957 (amended in 1959) was the first and most far-reaching of these attempts to improve women's status (again excluding Soviet laws), and it is this which is instanced by South Yemen's jurists as providing the main inspiration for their own Family Law of 1974.

The introduction of this law in the PDRY as elsewhere involved challenging both the power of the Muslim clergy and orthodox interpretations of Islam. After 1969 the government sought to curb the institutional and economic base of the traditional clergy and transferred its responsibilities to agencies of the state. This process began during the liberation struggle when the revolutionaries moved against the *Sada* (an elite caste) and other religious leaders in the areas around Radfan where they were based, expropriating their lands without compensation and forcing the more conservative elements into exile. After the revolution, *waqf* (religious) lands were placed under state administration and those religious leaders who did not leave the country were given the option of either surrendering their posts or continuing to occupy them as employees of the state. At the same time, religious education in schools was scaled down and made the responsibility of lay teachers.

Yet the program pursued by the PDRY was one of reform rather than of *abolition* of the old codes along the extreme lines of Albania in the 1960s and 1970s or Turkey in the 1920s under Ataturk. Islam remained the state religion; religious belief, observance, and holidays were respected. The government refrained from adopting a confrontationist or provocative stance, although it sought to reduce the influence of orthodox beliefs and practices by redefining religious discourses so that more progressive readings were emphasized. The legal reforms that were introduced were often legitimized, where possible, in terms of the canons of Islamic jurisprudence and carried out with the cooperation of prominent religious jurists before being debated in public meetings.

The NLF and Women's Emancipation

We can now turn to consider the legal measures taken to improve the position of women in the PDRY. Within the NLF it was the left-wing radicals who were chiefly concerned with women's rights, and it was after they came to power in 1969 that more concerted efforts were made to encourage women to participate in and benefit from the revolutionary process.[30] The Constitution of 1970 outlined the government's policies toward women and provided the framework within which the ensuing legal reforms would be inscribed. The proposed reforms were phrased in the familiar language of other socialist countries and embodied many of the same provisions.[31] Women were referred to in terms of two main roles envisaged for them by the revolutionary government: as "mothers" and as "producers." Article 7, which described the political basis of the revolution as an "alliance among the working class, the peasants, intelligentsia, and petty-bourgeoisie," went on to add that "soldiers, *women*, and students are regarded as part of this alliance *by virtue of their membership of the productive forces of the people*" (emphasis added). Women were thus recognized as forming part of the "working people," and the Constitution, in giving all citizens the right to work and in regarding work as "an obligation in the case of all able-bodied citizens," called on women not yet involved in "productive work" to do so. This was part of the attempt to promote acceptance of identities based on economic function rather than on more traditional kinship or religious referents and in particular to transform the legal and social identities of women. Moreover, calling on women to enter productive work implicitly challenged both the restrictions of seclusion and the male authority through which it was enforced. At the same time, the Constitution promised to "strengthen the family status and [to] protect mother and child" (Article 29). Lest this concern to preserve the family and encourage women to enter social production be thought contradictory, certain provisions were to be made specifically for the working mother: Article 36 promised that "(the) state shall also ensure special protection for working women and children by granting paid leave to expectant mothers [and]. . . . shall establish nurseries and kindergartens and other means of care and custody [of children]."[32]

These statutes and provisions marked a considerable advance on previous government policy in a number of respects, but it was the article declaring juridical and political equality for all citizens that provided the context for even more profound changes in the legal position of women. Article 34, which stated that "all citizens are equal in their rights and obligations . . . [and] all are equal in the eye of the law," represented a break with previous laws and customs under which women had rights inferior to those of men, and did not have a full legal personality, being treated as minors and regarded as having male custodians. Constitutional reform in this case implied at the very least a radical change in legal status if only, as yet, a formal one. Article 36 went some way toward making it more than merely a formal commitment by affirming that "the State shall guarantee equal rights for men and women in all fields of political, economic and social scope [sic] and shall provide in a progressive manner the conditions necessary for realizing that equality." Among the conditions provided for in the Constitution were the expansion of the General Union of Yemeni Women (which in 1984 claimed 8,000 members) in order to assist women in gaining their new rights, the extension of education and literacy programs to women, the encouragement of women's political participation, and their mass entry into social production. In short, the Constitution embodied the conventional socialist program for the emancipation of women and provided some of the legal preconditions necessary for its realization. As yet, however, there was no specification of the forms of enforcement that would make them effective.

The 1970 constitutional reforms, and the progressive extension of new penal and civil codes to the hinterland, brought some immediate gains for women. Whereas in the past crimes against women were frequently regarded as family or tribal affairs and harsh punishment could be meted out to disobedient daughters or wives by men who were never themselves brought to trial, women gained not only new rights, but also official support in demanding these rights from the mass organizations. Moreover, the fact that this formal equality was inscribed in the Constitution gave legal support to women's demands for equality in the face of opposition from their families and the traditional social milieu.[33] The state and its goals thus became a higher authority than the kin group, even above religion, in matters pertaining to women's status. However, it was not until the promulgation of the Family Law in 1974 that significant progress was made in transforming women's legal position within the home.

The Family Law

The Family Law, like the Constitution, was discussed in the press and in open meetings around the country before being promulgated. The draft law was drawn up in 1971 and over a period of three years amendments were incorporated into it on the basis of the popular response and on the advice of the mass organizations and legal practitioners. In the manner of its adoption it was similar to the family laws passed in Cuba and Somalia a year later, in 1975.

The text of the law contained the official justification for the reforms: it began by denouncing "the vicious state of affairs which prevails in the family," the ending of which opened up the possibility of unleashing "vast [areas] of creative work and equal revolutionary relations which lead to the increase of production, development, and innovation." The law also proclaimed the end of some of the traditional inequalities in marriage: "Marriage is a contract between a man and a woman who are equal in rights and duties, and is based on mutual understanding and respect with the object of building up the cohesive family which is regarded as the foundation stone of the society."

The specific reforms introduced by the law included the following:

(1) The principle of free-choice marriage was established. Families were henceforth forbidden to agree to engagements without the consent of the parties concerned. Although this was stipulated in one of the *hadiths* or sayings of the Prophet, it was almost never observed, and its reincorporation into the Family Law marked an attempt to end kin control of marriages.

(2) Whereas there had previously been widespread child marriage in the countryside, the minimum legal age was fixed at sixteen years for women, and at eighteen for men. (In 1984 this was under review and was to be raised to eighteen and twenty years respectively.) In a further move to prevent the marriage of young women to much older men, the age difference was limited to twenty years for women under thirty-five.

(3) Whereas under the *Shariah* codes men had previously been allowed to marry up to four wives, the Family Law now stipulated that men could have only one spouse, except in certain exceptional circumstances, such as barrenness or incurable disease.

(4) In order further to reduce family control over marriage, the amount of the brideprice or *mahr* was limited to 100 Yemeni dinars (about twice an average white-collar monthly salary). In this way it was hoped to remove a

conventional form of class control over marriages while at the same time making it easier for women to escape from a bad marriage by repaying the brideprice herself. The preamble to the law stated that women in the previous situation had been "in the hands of the highest bidder." Officials justified this control by referring to the *Hadith*: they recalled Mohammad's remark that his daughter could marry for a "mere ring of iron."

(5) Whereas men were expected to be the main breadwinners, article 17 of the new code stipulated that both spouses must bear the cost of supporting the family's economy. This clause, along with that on custody (below), finds no authority in the Islamic codes and derives from the government's commitment to egalitarian principles. [34]

(6) Under the new law unilateral divorce was prohibited and all divorces had to be processed through the courts. The grounds for divorce were, with some minor differences to be discussed later, now applicable to both men and women.

(7) Whereas on divorce, men previously had greater rights of custody, male children were henceforth to remain with their mothers until the age of ten years and female children until the age of fifteen years. In all cases the courts reserved the right to decide the outcome in terms of the best interests of the children.

The Family Law therefore established the basis for a quite different family structure and sought to alter the relations within it. It attempted radically to change existing forms, reducing both the husband's authority and the control of the natal families over marriage. The new Yemeni family was to be monogamous and egalitarian, and the preferred institutional form was no longer the extended but the nuclear family. [35] It was hoped that this family form would be a more stable institution and thus perform its social functions as the "basic cell of society" more efficiently. However likely this was in the longer run, the immediate consequence of the passing of the law had the opposite effect, namely a steep rise in the divorce rate.

Divorce rates were always high in South Yemen, but in the past these were mainly initiated by men;[36] after 1974 women began to form an increasing proportion of those suing for divorce. [37] Among the main reasons were women's greater financial independence and desertion by emigrant husbands who had remarried abroad and abandoned their families back home. The trend to divorce grew even stronger after 1978, when a civil law bill was passed that awarded the marital home to the wife on divorce if there were children from the marriage. This led to a steeper rise in the number of women petitioning for divorce and caused the Supreme People's Council, the legislature, to revise the article to give the courts more scope in deciding these matters. The People's Defense Committees were also requested to play a role so as to arrive at a more equitable solution to the allocation of accommodation.

To curb the rising incidence of marital instability in the 1970s the government made divorce more difficult to obtain for both men and women. Potential divorcees were obliged to wait between several months and a year before their case was heard, in order to allow them time to reconsider whether they should continue to press their suit. In the meantime the Women's Union or the People's Defense Committees acted as marriage guidance counselors and tried to reconcile the couple. Before a case even went to court these bodies had to be persuaded that the litigant had a reasonable case; otherwise it did not go forward. But according to Yemeni legal practitioners this did not result in any significant fall in the number of women petitioners. This was striking in view of the fact that alimony was granted for only one year and was in practice difficult to enforce. After that the chances of support from the state, although theoretically possible, were minimal; husbands were then under no further obligation, and a divorced woman (unless she was a wage earner) generally had to rely on the beneficence of her kinfolk, who, foreseeing this, were likely to try to dissuade her from divorcing in the first place. The kin network thus joined the government bodies in discouraging the breakup of the family.

Despite the radical changes in the law, it is worth noting that, even after the 1974 reforms, certain inequalities between men and women persisted as relics of Islamic and customary practices. A man, for example, could take a new spouse under exceptional and certified circumstances such as barrenness, while a woman could not do so on grounds of impotence. Similarly, a woman could be divorced for barrenness but nothing was said in the law as to whether a man could be divorced for impotence, although the courts would be likely to give a sympathetic hearing to a case brought on such grounds. A divorced woman was still prohibited for the stipulated period (known as *iddat*) of ninety days from remarrying, an Islamic injunction designed to protect men from the loss of an heir who might have been conceived before the divorce and who, if the woman remarried, would be considered to belong to her new spouse. Although arranged marriages were outlawed, the brideprice remained, albeit with a lower upper limit. Finally, as far as property transmission was concerned, *Shariah* law continued to prevail, and the discrimination against women that it embodied therefore persisted.[38] On the occasion of the tenth anniversary of the passing of the Family Law in 1984, a symposium was called to discuss its adequacy. Although this was largely a celebrative occasion, there was a move by some women present to have the *mahr* abolished and more egalitarian inheritance laws introduced. These proposals were quashed, however, and the existing law approved.[39]

The Law and Islamic Society

The retention of certain provisions influenced by the Islamic codes must be understood in the regional context as well as in relation to the government's domestic policy on religion. As noted earlier, the official concern was to avoid provoking opposition on religious grounds, but even so, the reforms that have been introduced have provided the government's adversaries with ammunition. Yemeni exiles in Saudi Arabia, and during periods of hostility between the two countries the Saudi state itself, tried to provoke internal opposition by beaming hostile radio broadcasts into the PDRY.[40] They accused the government of "godlessness," and pointed in particular to the efforts to emancipate women as proof of the PDRY's contravention of religious customs. Further evidence of the "degeneracy of the regime" was said to be the appointing of women as judges; this was claimed to be in violation of the Koran, which stipulates that "masculinity" is among the ten qualities required of judges. Other conservative Arab states such as Kuwait have in the past reportedly joined Saudi Arabia in condemning the PDRY for encouraging gender desegregation and have repeatedly called on them in Pan-Arab congresses to resegregate their educational establishments. While the dangers of a traditional and religious backlash are ever present, especially in the context of growing popular support in the Muslim world for fundamentalist movements, government officials insist that it should not be exaggerated, both because the reforms have been genuinely popular in many quarters and because traditional religious feeling in South Yemen has never been as strong as in some other Arab states. Be that as it may, the PDRY is vulnerable to pressure from both inside and outside and for this reason has been at pains to demonstrate its continued adherence to Islam, and its tolerance of at least some of its social practices. Yet the growth of an underground opposition, organized by the Muslim Brotherhood and receiving funds from Saudi Arabia, was causing considerable concern by the mid-1980s.

These considerations help to explain why the government refrained from using the law to intervene in certain social practices associated with women's subordination, such as veiling or for that matter clitoridectomy (khitan). As far as the latter was concerned, the official view was that it was not a serious problem since it was not widely practiced in the PDRY. Where it did exist it was thought that it would soon die out, with the extension of medical facilities to the rural areas and the erosion of the power of traditional doctors (hakimi).[41] Male circumcision was, as would be expected, still encouraged as an acceptable, even desirable, Islamic custom.

Veiling and the seclusion of women were similarly tolerated on the grounds that, as the then head of the women's organization put it, they were "merely anachronisms," which if left to objective forces would soon disappear.[42] Between 1970 and 1972, with the intifadhat or peasant uprisings following the land reforms in the interior, women were reported to have marched through the streets proclaiming the end of veiling, and while the government gave some support to this campaign, it later preferred to discourage veiling in a more indirect manner. Certainly stringent measures against the veil such as those adopted in Soviet Central Asia in 1927, in Turkey under Ataturk, or in Iran under Reza Shah were never adopted. The policy again was to avoid provoking hostility by refraining from directly confronting the issue.[43] Indirectly, tacit support was given to eroding the practice by encouraging the wearing of school and workplace uniforms; many government officials and Women's Union cadres also went about their tasks in the urban areas unveiled, but wearing scarves and long-sleeved blouses as a token observance of the Islamic injunction to wear "modest" dress.

As far as the issue of juridical reform is concerned, two main problems confronted the government: that of popularizing the law, and that of enforcing the new legislation; merely to promulgate laws was no guarantee that they would be effective. In drafting and circulating the new laws for discussion, an effort was made, as in Cuba during a comparable period, to diffuse knowledge of the laws through public meetings and to encourage some measure of popular participation in their formulation. Even a decade after the promulgation of the laws, work went on to inform people about their rights and obligations through public meetings, newspaper coverage, and television and radio broadcasts. In this way the government hoped to further the voluntary acceptance of the new codes through persuading people of their role in formulating laws and of the superiority of the new over the previous system.

Yet evasion of some of the new rules of conduct was common, especially in the rural areas where traditional and familial authority remained strong and where customary modes of procedure continued to be favored. The payment of high *mahrs* continued, along with arranged marriages, often with legal minors.[44] Likewise, although marriages were supposed to be registered by the state, and individuals were under no official obligation to undergo religious ceremonies, Yemenis in many regions continued to do so.

However, the government occasionally resorted to severe measures against those who violated the law, as was illustrated by an episode that took place in the Fourth Governorate in 1978.[45] A young girl from a prominent *Sada* family in Haban refused to marry the man her grandfather had chosen for her. Instead she eloped with a man of inferior caste. Her grandfather tracked her down, and had her murdered and secretly buried; but some local people who suspected that a crime had been committed reported their suspicions to the authorities; they mounted a search for the young girl's body, and found it. The villagers, on hearing of the crime, seized the old man and dragged him through the streets in a procession; he was eventually brought to trial and sentenced to death. The whole episode was well publicized in the media and at public meetings so that appropriate lessons could be drawn. The attitude of the authorities and of the villagers was significant in that it marked a radical change in mores as much as in understandings of legality; a few years earlier such a murder would have gone unpunished and would indeed have been regarded as the natural prerogative of an elder whose will had been disobeyed by a woman, [46] and whose family honor was put in jeopardy.

As this episode suggests, some of the reforms may have been popular, at least among the poorer and disadvantaged sectors of the population. This was reportedly the case with the attempt to lower the *mahr*. But it is clear that there was some organized resistance to them as well, although it is not known on what grounds, by whom, or how widespread it was. As already indicated, there has been some opposition on orthodox religious grounds, although the government claims that this was minimal and largely stimulated by outside sources.

Conclusions

The transformation in the structures and practices of legality that have been brought about in the PDRY have had far-reaching implications for women, as well as for some other social groups. This is so despite the fact that the substantive impact of the legal reforms has varied as between the specific laws themselves and as they have affected different categories of social agents. As far as women are concerned the legal reforms may be considered modest, but their radical significance is given by their regional context and by the place they occupy within the wider process of social transformation.

The case of Democratic Yemen, like that of other socialist states, demonstrates how the law was conceived of by the government as providing some of the conditions of existence of new forms of ownership and control, as well as constituting a form of intervention outside the economic realm to meet certain social policy objectives. Our main concern here has been to show how legal reform has assisted in the social, political, and economic repositioning of women. In summary, five related but discrete forms of such legal intervention to achieve this can be identified.
(1) Relations between the sexes were redefined by conferring on women new rights and providing them with new capacities. For example, women could now divorce, refuse arranged marriage, work, and vote; they could seek the assistance of the mass organizations and the state in actualizing these rights. By the same token men have lost certain rights and privileges that they previously enjoyed (polygyny, *talaq*).
(2) Kin, class, and tribal control over women were outlawed and to some degree delegitimized. This was in part designed to meet the social policy objective of redefining the structure and affiliations of the family by

reducing the incidence of polygyny and promoting the nuclear family form.

(3) The legal authority of orthodox Islam' and customary law was challenged and the state became the higher legal authority, bringing under its control certain ceremonial and juridical functions previously in the hands of religious entities (marriage), or voluntary agencies (divorce).

(4) The law functioned to assist in the demarcation of a realm of legitimate struggle between women and traditional repositories of power over them. (This redefinition also occurred in the case of peasants through the provisions of the land reform.)

(5) Within the realm of public law, women were interpellated in new ways (as workers, national subjects, political subjects) in order to help construct less private, traditional, identities. In this sense, as well as in that of the first point, they acquired new legal personalities. Legal reforms also made it more possible concretely for women to operate in these areas, as evidenced by women's entry into the legal profession and into political life.

The substantive impact of these juridical changes on women was of course contingent on the degree to which they were matched by transformations in their material circumstances, on popular acceptance of the new codes, and, failing that, on women's willingness and capacities to struggle for their observance. While there was a marked increase in the participation of women, particularly urban women, in the areas of education and employment, much remained to be achieved before women were able to attain anything approximating an independent and equal place in a male-dominated society. Attitudes toward the reforms are more difficult to assess, especially since they were introduced "from above" and as far as we know in the absence of any demands for legal change from below. While there was opposition to some of them on a variety of grounds (religious, practical), the available evidence seems to support the government's claims that with some exceptions the new codes were popular among many women, if less so among men. Official observers present at meetings called to discuss the draft laws reported that women generally exhibited more enthusiasm than men and in many cases called for more radical measures than those proposed by the original law.[47]

One index of the popular acceptance of new laws is the degree to which they are used. In many Islamic countries it is common to find that most rural women have little knowledge of their legal rights and even if they are aware of them they rarely initiate legal action to attain them. In the PDRY, partly as a result of the efforts to publicize the reforms, women in most areas made use of their new rights and brought their complaints to the courts within a few years of the passing of the Family Law. The sharp rise in female-initiated divorces was the clearest indication of this. It is nonetheless likely that some women may have perceived the increase in personal freedom and responsibility entailed by the law as a threat to their security, particularly if the kinship system of responsibility was eroded and the gap was not filled by satisfactory alternatives.

In spite of these qualifications, the changes that were introduced can be recognized as important without exaggerating their overall impact or their contribution to "women's emancipation." Their limits in this latter respect are evident enough, and it is worth remembering that even where legal reform is considerably more advanced and effective than in Democratic Yemen, the rules of jurisprudence do not by themselves define the entire spectrum of power relations that prevail to women's disadvantage. In the PDRY, legal reforms affecting the family have helped to weaken some of the traditional loci of power and inequality, whether these were based on gender (patriarchy) or on kinship and class. By most standards of historical change this process has been an accelerated one; in the West such power relations suffered some erosion through protracted and extensive changes in the economy in some cases centuries before legal reforms were introduced. The opposite has occurred in the PDRY, with economic change accompanying and in some cases *following* the legal reforms. These transformations have been seen by the government as a necessary part of constructing a socialist society, yet this is a process that itself has barely begun. According to official party policy, efforts in this direction can only remain at the stage appropriate to the "national democratic" phase of development. The elementary forms of democratic participation have not as yet acquired a meaningful influence on the political life of the country, and until they do the PDRY's reforms are best understood as attempts from above to promote "socialist modernization."

Notes

Thanks are due to Fred Halliday for his comments and help with translations from the Arabic and German, and to the numerous South Yemenis, juridical practitioners and otherwise, who provided much of the information on which this article is based. The material was gathered on two field trips, one in 1977, the other in 1984, and supplemented by interviews in London.

1. The term "socialist" is used here for the sake of brevity to refer to those states that broadly adhere to Marxist doctrine, have socialized a substantial proportion of the economy, and have effected policies of social redistribution. They are of course not socialist in the strict sense of the term as they have not implemented socialist democracy.
2. PDRY, *Programme of the Unified Political Organisation, the National Front* (Nottingham: Russell Press, 1977).
3. PDRY, *Proceedings of the 1st Congress of the Yemeni Socialist Party* (Moscow: Progress Publishers, 1979).
4. See F. Halliday, *Arabia Without Sultans* (Harmondsworth: Penguin, 1974), for a detailed account of the history of the revolution and its aftermath.
5. F. Weidnitzer, "Grundzuge der Enticklung der politisch—staatlichen Verhaltnisse im revolutionaren V.D.R.J.," *Asien, Afrika, Latein-amerika* 8, no. 6.

6. W. Butler, *Soviet Law* (London: Butterworth, 1983); and R. Stookey, *South Yemen: A Marxist Republic in Arabia* (London: Croom Helm/Westview, 1982).

7. The East German writer Frank Weidnitzer, although from a sympathetic perspective, comments that by 1980 this process had not proceeded very far ("Grundzuge").

8. Butler, *Soviet Law*.

9. PDRY, *The Political Report Presented by Comrade Abdul Fattah Isma'il* (Aden: Government Press, 1975).

10. A. Bujra, focusing on the Hadramaut region, provides the only sociological analysis of the social relations in the South Arabian Protectorate; see *Politics of Stratification: A Study of Political Change in a South African Town* (Oxford: Oxford University Press, 1971).

11. The Shafei school of jurisprudence is within the Sunni branch of Islam, one to which 95 percent of South Yemenis belong. For a more detailed discussion of the colonial and postcolonial legal infrastructure, see Maxine Molyneux, "Legal Reform and Socialist Revolution in Democratic Yemen: Women and Family," *International Journal of the Sociology of Law* 13 (1985).

12. F. Halliday, "The P.D.R.Y.: The 'Cuban Path' in Arabia," in G. White, R. Murray, and C. White, eds., *Socialist Development in the Third World* (Sussex: Wheatsheaf Books, 1983).

13. Butler, *Soviet Law*; and P. Q. Hirst, "Law, Socialism and Rights," in P. Carlen and M. Collison, eds., *Radical Issues in Criminology* (Oxford: Martin Robertson, 1980).

14. Interviews with women activists revealed this to be the focus of considerable struggle. Some recalled being locked out of their homes by irate fathers after returning from political meetings (M. Molyneux, "State Policy and the Position of Women in South Yemen," *Peuples Méditérranéens* 12 (July/September 1980).

15. World Bank, *The P.D.R.Y.: A Review of Economic and Social Development* (Washington, DC: World Bank, 1979); and idem, *Development Report 1980* (Oxford: Oxford University Press, 1980).

16. For a detailed study of women and work in the PDRY, see M. Molyneux, *State Policies and Women Workers in Democratic Yemen: 1967–1977* (Geneva: ILO, 1982).

17. M. Molyneux, "Women's Emancipation Under Socialism: A Model for the Third World?" World Development 9, no. 9/10 (1981).

18. G. Massell, *The Surrogate Proletariat* (Princeton: Princeton University Press, 1974); and J. Stacey, *Patriarchy and Socialist Revolution in China* (Berkeley: University of California Press, 1983). Chinese and Soviet theorists are perhaps the most explicit about this relationship.

19. L. Liegle, *The Family's Role in Soviet Education* (New York: Springer, 1975).

20. L. Beck and N. Keddie, *Women in the Muslim World* (Chicago: University of Chicago Press, 1979); and N. Youssef, *Women and Work in Developing Societies*, Population Monograph Series No. 15 (Berkeley: University of California Press, 1973).

21. J. G. Peristiany, ed., *Honour and Shame: The Values of Mediterranean Society* (London: Weidenfeld and Nicholson, 1965).

22. N. Anderson, *Law Reform in the Muslim World* (London: Athlone Press, 1976).

23. N. El-Saadawi, *The Hidden Face of Eve: Women in the Arab World* (London: Zed Books, 1979); and F. Mernissi, *Beyond the Veil* (New York: John Wiley, 1978).

24. The Holy Quran, trans. and commentary by Abdallah Usuuf Ali (London: The Islamic Foundation, 1975), 4:9–12.

25. Ibid., 4:58.

26. Anderson, *Law Reform*.

27. Beck and Keddie, *Women in the Muslim World*.

28. N. Coulson, *Conflicts and Tensions in Islamic Jurisprudence* (Chicago: University of Chicago Press, 1969).

29. Anderson, *Law Reform*.

30. General Union of Yemeni Women, *Documents of the G.U.Y.W.* (Aden: Government Press, 1976).

31. Most of these were formulated at the Second Congress of the Comintern in 1920 and have since formed the basis for pro-Soviet governments' provisions and policies on women.

32. By 1984 there were twenty "kindergartens" in the PDRY.

33. As one factory worker expressed it to me: "If my father forbids me to go out to work I can tell him he is acting against the law. If he still stops me, I can get the Women's Union to make him leave me alone. After all I am in the right and he is in the wrong."

34. Anderson, *Law Reform*; and I. Ghanem, "A Note on Law No. 1, Concerning the Family, Peoples Democratic Republic of Yemen," *Arabian Studies* 111 (1976): 191–96.

35. Nuclear families were considered by officials and many interviewees in the urban sector to represent the ideal of modern living, free from parents and in-laws. After the revolution modern apartments were usually built with this ideal in mind. See Molyneux, *State Policies and Women Workers*, for factory workers' attitudes toward family size and composition.

36. *Aden Colony Census Report* (Aden: Government Press, 1955).

37. As written sources on the PDRY are extremely rare, this information is based on interviews with the then minister of justice in 1983, and with senior legal practitioners in the PDRY in 1984.

38. In the laws of 1957 and 1975, respectively, Iraq and Somalia tried to equalize inheritance between the sexes but with limited success and determination owing to the strength of religious opposition; see Anderson, *Law Reform*.

39. The case for maintaining *shariah* inheritance was said by a woman advocate to rest on the fact that it is customary for men to bear the financial responsibility for aged parents and infirm relatives. As women are not expected to nor wish to assume such responsibilities, they are generally allocated a smaller share of the inheritance. Defenders of the *mahr* pointed out that in some regions, this payment was to the bride and remained hers as an insurance against divorce.

40. BBC Summary of World Broadcasts ME/3568/A/5, December 21, 1970.

41. Medical practitioners claim that the practice of *khitan* is more pervasive and enduring than official policy implies, and they are skeptical about the belief that it will die out. In the Sudan the professionalization of medical services has been accompanied by the spread of female excision and infibulation. There, despite the illegality of the practice, trained nurses are often prepared to perform the operation for payment.

42. Molyneux, "State Policy."

43. The same is true with regard to abortion and contraception. These practices have no legal status and the government's official view is that they can be justified where necessary on the grounds that Islam does not expressly forbid them.

44. Interview by the author with officials of the General Union of Yemeni Women, 1977, in Dhaleh in the Fourth Governorate.

45. The death penalty is in force and applies *inter alia* to cases of rape where the victim dies as a result of the attack. It was reportedly resorted to infrequently.

46. Author's interview with party officials in the Fourth Governorate, 1977.

47. Author's interview with an official rapporteur appointed to monitor the proceedings of the public meetings called to discuss the Family Law. His account was corroborated by other observers.

Democratic Centralism in the Home and the World: Bengali Women and the Communist Movement

Amrita Basu

"We see the CPI(M) as our family. Like our family it protects us."
—Purna Das, executive member of the West Bengal Democratic Women's Association

"The essence of Stalinist communism," argues Ronald Tiersky, "is its monolithic internal politics, and Stalinism is the attempt to make *all* politics into internal politics."[1] Imagine then the possibilities of extending the realm of internal communist party politics when democratic centralist principles are already prefigured in the private sphere. Like the Communist Party of India (Marxist) (CPI[M]), the Bengali Hindu family is organized along strictly hierarchical lines: the men who occupy its highest rungs exercise the most power. Yet the family, like the party, mystifies such inequality and projects itself as a solidaristic unit whose members share identical interests. Democratic centralist principles in the home fortify the CPI(M) in the world, at the cost of perpetuating sexual inequality.

The CPI(M) has ruled intermittently in West Bengal, one of India's most important states, since the late 1960s. It presently heads the Left Front government, which was first elected in 1977 and returned to office for a third term in 1987. The CPI(M)'s electoral success as a parliamentary communist party at the subnational level is not only unprecedented within the Indian context but virtually unique among communist parties in liberal democracies. As such, it provides an important test of the implications for women of parliamentary socialism.

West Bengal, the birthplace and principal home of the Indian communist movement, provides an ideal context in which to examine the CPI(M)'s approach to gender. A major source of its repeated electoral success seems to be its identification with Bengalis' pride at their unique literary, artistic, and political heritage, their fear of domination by the Hindi heartland, and their desire to achieve greater autonomy from the center. Yet this regionalization of the party is linked to its growing reformism with respect to class and gender.

215

If the CPI(M) in West Bengal now accepts women's subordination within the family, the communist movement has not always done so. Based on a brief historic overview, I argue that communists' adherence to democratic centralist principles in the home and the world have developed simultaneously. I then assess the CPI(M)'s approach to women's issues since 1977, and contend that its conservatism with respect to gender is closely linked to its reformist approach to class and caste.

The sources of Bengali women's political quiescence are rooted in the CPI(M)'s democratic centralist principles of organization, electoral preoccupations, class reductionist ideology, and extension of women's private roles into the public arena.[2] The CPI(M) appropriates and reproduces, in its ideology and practice, certain features of Bengali Hindu culture. It thereby employs the notion of women as repositories of tradition to limit the extent and forms of political change.

The Romance of Bengali Communism

Two facets of Bengali women's political participation are of key significance. On the one hand, given the formidable barriers they had to overcome, communist women were more audacious in the 1940s then they are today. Moreover, they clearly struggled harder to resolve contradictions between their public and private lives. Yet the bleaker reality is that communist women have never been as active as men, the party has never seriously attempted to eradicate sexual inequality, and the problems of poor rural women have always been marginalized.

The account that follows is based on reminiscences of the first generation of Bengali communist women.[3] Virtually all of those who were interviewed spoke of the risk and romance entailed in becoming a Communist Party of India (CPI) member between 1939 and 1942. Most of the young women who joined the CPI during this period were from wealthy, conservative families. Many had been active in the so-called terrorist movement, a militant anti-imperialist struggle in the first two decades of the twentieth century. Consider the account of Bani Dasgupta, who joined the CPI Student Federation in 1939.

> It is difficult to describe my sense of excitement when some students told me about the party. You see my father was from a big *zamindar* [landlord] family. I used to hear laborers screaming with pain when they were beaten for being lazy and dishonest. . . . Here was a party which would put an end to such injustice. I began to attend the student meetings. When my relatives found out they locked me in my room at night. When they realized that they could not stop me, they drove me out of the house—beat me with shoes—because they said I was an insult to the family.[4]

Dasgupta arrived in Calcutta in 1941 with a letter of introduction to party leaders and the two rupees she had left after paying her train fare. Like many other young, middle-class women who had left their homes to work for the party in Calcutta, she moved into a communally organized home that was headed by Manikuntala Sen, the senior-most woman in the CPI at the time. The fifteen men and women who shared the house lived in an extremely egalitarian fashion; meager incomes were shared as were household responsibilities. Dasgupta recalled that often they could not afford to eat for several days at a time. At the suggestion of the party, she gave up graduate studies to work as a full-time party member for a monthly salary of twenty rupees (a dollar and a half).

The first generation of Bengali communist women did not question the party's neglect of gender issues. Having taken the radical step of severing ties with their parents, they sought camaraderie and protection from male comrades. Many were financially dependent on the party. But the more important explanation for their silence was that they considered the CPI the major fount of opposition to women's oppression.

Communist men and women attempted to organize their personal lives in an emancipated fashion. Breaking with traditional practice, they rejected arranged marriages, lavish weddings, and the dowry, and often married across religious and caste lines. In some areas where the communist movement was strong, party members consecrated marriages with an exchange of garlands rather than through religious ceremonies. In striking contrast with the present, communist men tended to marry women who were full-time political activists. Although these women were primarily responsible for housework and child care, their husbands encouraged them to be politically active.

One can only speculate about why the chasm grew between party members' private and public lives. The CPI seems to have increasingly absorbed dominant cultural values once it became incorporated into the formal political arena. In Gita Mukherjee's view, from the 1950s the CPI reduced the autonomy of mass organizations among women and other groups by relying upon them for electoral mobilization. However, even in its heyday, the CPI was ill-equipped to challenge gender inequality, particularly among poor rural women. There was a deep cultural abyss between urban, educated, upper-caste, upper-class communist leaders and the rural poor. The rift was compounded by the CPI's alienation from indigenous cultural traditions, in part because of its close links with the Soviet Union.

The period 1944–48 represents the high-water mark of communist mobilization in West Bengal. During this period, the communist movement closely identified itself with a renaissance in Bengali theater, film, and literature. It also created a number of mass organizations, including the Mahila Atma Raksha Samiti (MARS or Women's Self-Defense League) in 1943. MARS' first major contribution was to assist in rehabilitating poor rural and urban women during the tragic Bengal famine. It was especially active because women were the worst victims of the famine. Needless to add, women's organizations were the first to engage in charitable social work.

MARS' second major activity was antifascist organizing. The CPI's declaration when Germany attacked the Soviet Union that the "imperialist war" had become a "people's war" was doubly ironic: the CPI's refusal to challenge British imperialism alienated it from the Congress-led nationalist movement, which was mobilizing peasant men and women on an unprecedented scale. Moreover, opposition to Nazi Germany had little meaning to poor rural women. Because of its reluctance to criticize the Allies, the CPI did not even expose British complicity in creating the famine.

Today some CPI members, such as Bani Dasgupta, informally criticize the CPI's stance on this issue. But Kanak Mukherjee, also a long-standing communist and one of the foremost CPI(M) women leaders, adamantly defends the CPI's position: "You cannot judge the correctness of a party line by whether the people are behind you. Otherwise we would always be running after the people."

The activities of MARS were heavily centered in Calcutta. Thus MARS played a relatively insignificant role in organizing peasant women during the militant Tebhaga movement (1946–47). Under the aegis of the communists' peasant organization, sharecroppers demanded two-thirds of the harvest from landlords, often using confrontational tactics. Bimla Maji, the foremost woman leader in Midnapur, reported that MARS encouraged peasant women to provide activists who had gone underground with food, shelter, and medical supplies. At this time, Maji reports, women spontaneously protested sexual harassment both by landlords and by their own husbands. MARS was a passive spectator to these activities.

One of the bedrock obstacles to the development of feminist consciousness among communist women was their dependence on the party, which inhibited recognition of the transcendent nature of women's oppression across class, caste, and party lines. During periods of sectarianism, the male party leadership would rein in its mass organizations and thereby undermine the gains they had achieved. For example, until 1949, communist women participated in the Congress Party-affiliated All India Women's Conference (AIWC), which comprised a broad cross-section of women. Vidhya Munshi described it as an important national forum in which communists could disseminate their ideas, make contacts with otherwise inaccessible women, and influence relevant legislation. Thus communist women were able to fight in parliament for the passage of the Hindu Code Bill, which was designed to give women legal rights to divorce, remarry, and inherit property. However, communist women left the AIWC in 1949 because they felt that it was an elitist organization. They thereby relinquished an important resource.

When the CPI emerged from its sectarian phase, it formed the National Federation of Indian Women (NFIW) in 1954. The NFIW poured its energies into establishing contacts with communist-bloc women's organizations. Such activities do not appear to have advanced the women's movement within India. In fact, Bengali communist women seem to have become even more isolated from the rural poor.

More damaging yet to communist women's organizing efforts were rifts within the CPI. Although dissident Communist Party members formed the CPI(M) in April 1964, women members of the two parties worked jointly in the Paschim Bangla Mahila Samiti (PBMS) until 1971. Relations between them became estranged as a result of the downfall of a CPI(M)-led United Front government in 1971 and attendant strains between the two parties. The PBMS remained affiliated with the CPI while the Paschim Bangla Ganatantrik Mahila Samiti (PBGMS) was established as a separate organization, linked to the CPI(M).

The PBGMS, born of the split, was more sectarian than its predecessor. The contrasts between the two communist women's organizations became particularly marked after the Left Front government was elected in 1977. The CPI was not a constituent of the Left Front coalition at this time; it had been severely discredited because it had supported the Congress Party's declaration of a national emergency in the period 1975 to 1977. Its marginalization from the formal political arena freed the CPI-affiliated PBMS, unlike the official PBGMS, to join feminist groups in struggles against women's oppression.

PBGMS influence on the CPI(M) further declined during the Left Front government's tenure in office. The CPI(M) increasingly used the PBGMS as a vehicle for securing electoral support. Because the Left Front government was responsible for maintaining law and order, the CPI(M) discouraged the PBGMS from organizing agitational movements. Furthermore, the CPI(M) became less responsive to women, who now constituted only one part of a large and heterogenous constituency. In short, added to the CPI(M)'s earlier economic reductionism was its growing political reductionism: its tendency to narrow the scope of confrontational activities because of supposed electoral imperatives.

Women Under the Left Front Government

If the undivided Communist Party created a counter-community for a small group of urban, middle-class women in the 1940s, the CPI(M) has replicated its efforts, this time for peasant women in the 1980s. Indeed, one of its major achievements is to have imparted some sense of dignity to poor rural women. This intangible gain is apparent at Left Front government rallies in Calcutta. The women who arrive in party-sponsored buses from the surrounding villages clearly attend these demonstrations for their entertainment value. But equally unmistakable is their new-found sense of solidarity, political efficacy, and pride that "their" government is in office. Their sense of dignity grows out of a political context that is relatively free from police repression, ethnic conflict, and violence against women. For example, in contrast to north Indian states in which the incidence of dowry deaths is high and rising, the Left Front government has helped prevent their escalation by appointing dowry prohibition officers in all the districts.

The Left Front government has brought about a number of small but significant improvements in the conditions of rural women. It has expanded the scope of the West Bengal Social Welfare Advisory Board (SWAB), which is financed and staffed jointly by state and central governments. There are three categories of SWAB activities: social work, rehabilitation programs, and vocational training. The board also sponsors thirty-four women and child welfare programs that organize nonformal education, nutrition classes, nursery schools, and craft centers in the villages. SWAB has formed village committees, each of which includes a female *panchayat* (local, elected councils) member and a woman who organizes programs for rural women.

With central government assistance, the West Bengal government has recently provided poor rural women loans to promote income generating projects.[5] Since the Left Front government assumed office in 1979, it has opened a number of centers in Midnapur district, which provide women with supplies as well as outlets for their goods. The Legal Aid Department provides free legal services to widows, destitute women, and prostitutes.

With respect to education, the Left Front government provides free tuition up to the twelfth grade, textbooks to the fifth grade, and, on an experimental basis, midday meals. According to Kanti Biswas, minister of education, since 1977 the government has opened 12,000 schools and appointed 46,000 teachers; it has increased the proportion of school age children attending school from 69 percent to 96 percent. As a result, literacy rates increased from 34 percent to 40 percent between 1971 and 1981.

Overall, however, when compared with the efforts of autonomous women's organizations and socialist governments elsewhere, the CPI(M) has scarcely attempted to restructure women's economic, political and social roles.

The sphere of production

Ironically, the CPI(M) has been insufficiently Marxist in ignoring the links between women's propertylessness and sexual inequality. Thus it has not questioned women's limited inheritance rights under Hindu law and Bengali social custom. Moreover, it has redistributed land (acquired from landlords whose holdings exceed land ceiling laws) only to household heads, who are generally male. Its most striking failure with respect to women is its major achievement with respect to men: tenancy reforms.

It should be noted, by way of background, that the Left Front government has focused attention on the agrarian sphere: the state government is constitutionally prohibited from legislating major urban reform, three-fourths of West Bengal is rural, and peasants form the CPI(M)'s major constituency. The government's major reform involves guaranteeing tenants' rights to land and three-fourths of the harvest from landlords. In 1978 it launched "operation barga," a campaign designed to encourage share-croppers to register their names on land records. Land Reforms Minister Benoy Chowdhury estimates that only 275,000 sharecroppers were bold enough to register before 1977; by December 1984, 1,300,000 of the 2 million sharecroppers in West Bengal had registered.

Shortly after the government had initiated "operation barga," an independent women's organization, the Center for Women's Development Studies (CWDS), organized a workshop for rural women in Bankura district. At this meeting, a landless tribal woman rose and spoke: "Babu, it is all well and good to give *puttas* [land titles] to our husbands. But if they leave us, we become landless again." A participant in the workshop, D. Bandopadhyaya, then land reforms secretary to the West Bengal government, persuaded the central government to include the principle of joint *puttas* in the seventh five-year-plan. New Delhi left the initiative for implementing this proposal to state governments. Yet by early 1988, the West Bengal government was registering only the names of household heads, who are generally men, on land records.

Resistance to joint *puttas* clearly emanates from upper-caste Hindu and Muslim men who fear increasing women's economic independence. But given the fact that tribals and scheduled castes (untouchables), who do not share such prejudices, are the major recipients of land titles, the more significant obstacles must be sought elsewhere. Although Bandopadhyaya encouraged the PBGMS to mobilize peasant women around this critical issue, it simply submitted a memorandum to the government. Ironically, PBGMS members themselves often opposed joint land titles. Kanak Mukherjee commented, "If we give *puttas* in women's names, next children will be demanding land in their names. And what will happen if the couple separates? The land will become even more fragmented."

By bestowing land titles on household heads, the CPI(M) exacerbates economic disparities between men and women and buttresses male domination. Since Hindu norms permit men but not women to divorce and remarry, women whose husbands leave them are often destitute. The problem is compounded by the government's failure to significantly increase credit facilities and employment opportunities for women. Nor has the PBGMS demanded that women should be recognized as sharecroppers in their own right, although such a designation is legally permissible. Shymali Gupta, the PBGMS secretary, did not believe that people would accept the notion that women work as hard as men. Yet women often toil alongside their husbands on leased land at a range of cultivation tasks.

Rural women's economic dependence is compounded by their inability to secure loans for cultivation and self-employment. The Left Front government has neither provided women with credit facilities nor helped them secure central government loans. In 1984–85 only 5 percent of the beneficiaries of Indian Rural Development Program (IRDP) loans (the major central government assistance to the rural poor) were women. Although the proportion of female beneficiaries increased to 10.4 in 1985–86 and 14.4 in 1986–87 it still fell far short of the central government target of 30 percent. Far from setting a precedent among India's twenty-two states, West Bengal was one of the ten states whose performance was poorest with respect to providing IRDP loans for women.

Despite its rhetorical claim that the key to women's emancipation lies in their incorporation into social production, the PBGMS has not seriously attempted to increase employment opportunities for women or to improve their working conditions. It has not challenged the displacement of women in industry as a result of plant closings, nor in agriculture, as a result of mechanization. It has not brought female agricultural laborers under the purview of labor legislation. Nor has it experimented with intermediate technology that could increase women's productivity and alleviate their work load. The government's only significant achievement in this domain is the attainment of equal wages for male and female agricultural laborers in a few scattered areas within West Bengal.

The Left Front government's attitude toward women's work reflects its conservative conception of female roles. The major employment opportunities it has sought to create for women are in such home-based forms of production as knitting, sewing, and weaving. This poorly paid work contributes to the notion that women work for "pocket money" rather than stable wages, that women's work is an extension of their housework, and that paid manual labor is degrading to women. The CPI(M) thus imposes on peasants implicitly middle-class conceptions of what constitutes women's work.

That women can greatly profit from employment in nontraditional jobs is evident from the experience of tribal women in eastern Bankura district. Few employment opportunities were available to men or women in this arid, drought-prone region during most of the year. In 1980 the CWDS organized a number of income-generating activities that utilized local materials, such as manufacturing disposable plates from pressed leaves. Women's cooperatives were responsible for all stages of the production and marketing process: manufacturing the items, managing the accounts, and corresponding with distributors in Calcutta. Women's roles as the principal income earners increased their stature within the family. Yet although the project achieved enormous material and moral gains for women at little financial and organizational cost, it held little interest for most government officials.

The political world

In the political realm, women have similarly been invisible and confined to narrow, sex-linked roles. There were only two women in the previous Left Front government (1982–87), both low-ranking ministers responsible for "soft" portfolios: a minister of relief and social welfare and a minister of state for education. In the present government, only one of thirty-two cabinet ministers is a woman—Relief Minister Chayya Bera, who heads one of the weakest ministries in the government. Women's underrepresentation in the cabinet is especially striking, for an unprecedented number of women were elected to the Legislative Assembly in 1987. (The Left Front nominated sixteen women; fourteen were elected, twelve on the CPI[M] ticket and two from other parties.)

Unlike many socialist and communist governments, the Left Front government has not created a women's ministry. Manjuri Gupta, the president of the national women's organization affiliated with the CPI(M), opposed "artificially separating the problems of women and of men." Other PBGMS members felt that the Social Welfare Ministry could adequately address issues concerning gender; they denied that this perpetuated women's sex-linked roles.

Nor has women's political representation been much greater at the local level.[6] As with "operation barga," this failure is especially glaring because the government's major political reform was to overhaul the *panchayats.* Despite central government opposition, the Left Front government allowed political parties to contest the *panchayat* elections for the first time in 1978 and once again in 1983 and 1988. The CPI(M) secured a majority of seats in both elections. In the process it replaced the dominant classes, which had traditionally controlled the *panchayats,* with schoolteachers, middle peasants, and, to a lesser extent, poor peasants and agricultural laborers.

In a path-breaking move, the Left Front government decreed in 1978 that at least two women must serve on each village *panchayat.* If they were not elected in the general balloting, the government was empowered to nominate them. As a result of criticisms of partisanship in selection of candidates, the government later decided that the dominant political party in each *panchayat* should nominate women who were not elected.

Yet according to Prasad Rai, director of the *panchayats,* women remain greatly underrepresented, particularly in the lowest rungs of the three-tiered *panchayats.* Given a total of 3,305 *gram panchayats* at the village level, at least 6,610 women should have become members after the 1983 elections; instead the total female membership of the *gram panchayats* was 4,300. At the block level, in West Bengal's 339 *panchayat samitis* the female membership was 600 rather than 678. At the district level *zilla parishads*, women occupied no more than 10 seats. After the 1987 elections, women constituted only 49 out of 5,420 elected officials in the *gram panchayats*, 11 out of 1126 officials in the *panchayat samitis*, and 4 out of 98 officials in the *zilla parishad*.

Antipathy to women's political representation is further evidenced by the fact that a large proportion of women who serve on the *panchayats* are nominated rather than elected. It is widely believed that sexism among the electorate is greatly reinforced by the failure of the CPI(M) and other leftist parties to sponsor women candidates. Shymali Gupta admitted that local party cadre often openly opposed women's candidacy. It seems likely that the appointed female *panchayat* members are more malleable than those who contest the elections.

The West Bengal government's State Planning Board has recently introduced further decentralization reforms. Committees at the district, sub-divisional, and block levels now coordinate the activities of elected officials, technical advisers, and state and central government bureaucrats. These committees play a major role in planning economic development programs. Although including women would seem an important aspect of ensuring wider representation, A. K. Ghosh, the chairman of the board, admitted that no mechanism had been created to include women. He concluded pessimistically that the underrepresentation of women was inevitable in a patriarchal society.

Not surprisingly, few women are included among the upper echelons of CPI(M) leadership. At the national level, there are no women in the Politbureau and only four women are on the Central Committee. In West Bengal's State Committee, five of the ninety-seven members are women. A few of the district committees include female members but in most cases women constitute only two or three of the thirty to forty members.

When asked about women's invisibility in the political sphere, CPI(M) women often dismissed the problem. "Women's political participation should not be measured by counting heads," Kanak Mukherjee quipped. "The more important question is: How active are women in political struggle?" Sarla Maheshwari commented, "We had a woman prime minister for fourteen years and it did nothing for the majority of women. More women in our ministry would not automatically improve the status of Bengali women." Although Maheshwari's observation is indisputable, it simply underlines communist women's disinterest in women's rights. Nor have the men who run the CPI(M) and Left Front government been attentive to women's interests. Most of those interviewed treated the question with levity and scorn; several asserted that since the family was an indivisible unit, the issue was irrelevant.

While it is indisputable that women who occupy political office need not *automatically* represent women's interests, female representatives visibly manifest the existence of women as social actors. Moreover, the CPI(M)'s anti-feminist perspective raises questions about how the notion of "women's interests" should be defined. If CPI(M) male and female leaders hold similar views, peasant men and women do not. Thus even the most subjugated women who were interviewed expressed grievances at women's limited life chances. Nor should culturally relativist perspectives be employed to deny inequality. That Bengali women eat less nutritious and smaller quantities of food than their husbands may be customary but is also unjust.

The cultural domain

In both private and public spheres, the CPI(M) has accepted as natural the prevailing sexual division of labor and thus perpetuated women's sex-linked roles. For example, the government has sacrificed both the quality and the scope of girls' education. Kanti Biswas, minister of education, reported that the government had introduced mandatory vocational training programs in schools for boys in carpentry, woodwork, and agriculture, and for girls in needlework and handicrafts. In his view, girls were more manually dexterous than boys. Although he recognized that textbooks might contain slurs on religious minorities (indeed, he had appointed a commission to review textbooks in order to remove incriminating material), he considered it inconceivable that they might contain sexist material. Nor did he see any value to including women's history in textbooks. Biswas reported that the government had created 8,000 new schools for boys and only half that number for girls. He proudly added that West Bengal has a ratio of 34:66 female to male teachers, which was higher than the ratio of 30:70 for India as a whole!

The CPI(M) has also failed to question women's subordination in the family, as manifested through the taboos surrounding divorce, widow remarriage, and women's infertility. It has not attempted to educate rural women about the everyday forms of sexual inequality they experience and reproduce: restrictions on their physical mobility, the practice of women eating only after they have served their families, and their exclusion from major religious rites.

Nor has the PBGMS investigated the extent of violence against women. It has ignored newspaper reports of a few families who have performed sex-selection tests in order to abort the female fetus. It has only recently begun to protest the large numbers of dowry deaths in Calcutta: women murdered by their in-laws so that the husbands can remarry and obtain another dowry. (The CPI-affiliated PBMS has been much more active around this issue.) The PBGMS could combine struggles against the dowry with demands for women's land rights. But it has failed to do so.

The fact that women are generally exclusively responsible for housework and child care has seriously constrained their political activism. Shymali Gupta noted that women's political consciousness lagged far behind that of men for women had so little time to devote to reading, study groups, and party activity. As a result very few of those were active in the PBGMS felt that they were in a position to criticize party policy.

The Sources of CPI(M) Sexism

Which facets of the CPI(M)'s ideology, organization, and strategy have fostered its tendency to ignore, underrepresent, and even disparage women's interests? At the simplest level of analysis, male and female leaders are often oblivious to the varied manifestations of sexual inequality. When the issue was raised with CPI(M) men, they were so amused that it allayed their anxieties about being interviewed. They simply could not consider women's issues serious political issues.

The CPI(M) leadership's theoretical justification for the party's passivity is its interpretation of Engels: women cannot be emancipated until socialism is achieved, at which point their liberation is assured. It also justifies inaction by appealing to another Marxist tenet: the notion of class conflict as the motor force of history. Aarti Dasgupta, the most prominent female leader in the CPI(M)-affiliated Center for Industrial Trade Unions (CITU), argued: "As trade unionists we work for the laboring class as a whole and do not make invidious distinctions between men and women; to do so would be wrong and anti-Marxist." The CPI(M) opposes reserved seats and special quotas for scheduled castes and tribes on the grounds that a leftist government should privilege class over caste. "As long as there is no legal bar on women's participation there is no question that they will come up in political life and there is no need for reservation," Kanak Mukherjee argued. Yet, as the Congress government recognized in instituting the system of reserved seats, competition for positions in education and employment is not governed by meritocratic principles. Nor, as we have seen earlier, is the Left Front government's own composition free of gender bias.

More significant than the CPI(M)'s economic reductionism is its political reductionism. As the CPI(M) has become increasingly committed to the exercise of power, its relationship to women has become highly instrumental: women should be seen, particularly on election day, but not heard! Electoral considerations also contribute to women's political marginality. When asked why the CPI(M) did not nominate more female candidates, several party members responded that women were less likely than men to be elected.[7] As noted above, those women who are appointed to political office often project women's nurturing roles. Given a patriarchal context, the CPI(M) doubtless fears male opposition if it were to bestow land titles on women. Given an environment charged with religious conflict, it doubtless fears being voted out of office if it proposed far-reaching reforms of the family, which is governed by religious law.

At the level of organization, democratic centralism is the major source of the CPI(M)'s sexism. Democratic centralist principles explain: (a) the subordination of the PBGMS to the CPI(M), (b) inequalities between urban, middle-class PBGMS leaders and poor rural women, and (c) female CPI(M) members' subordinate position within the party hierarchy.

If growth is an indication of strength, the PBGMS has flourished since the Left Front government attained office. According to Shymali Gupta, PBGMS membership grew from 250,000 in 1979 to over 1,250,000 in 1987.[8] Yet the more it has grown, the more dependent it has become on the CPI(M). Whereas in the past, Gita Mukherjee and others noted, the women's organization included noncommunists, today the PBGMS consists entirely of CPI(M) members and supporters. The close relationship between the CPI(M) and its mass organization is best exemplified by the fact that CITU, the PBGMS, and the All-India Kisan Sabha (AIKS), the CPI(M)-affiliated peasant organization, occupy the same building complex in Calcutta.

The worlds of male and female activists are inextricably intertwined, for the wives of CPI(M) male activists usually participate in the PBGMS. Once again we observe the interplay of democratic centralism in the home and the world: PBGMS members are unlikely to challenge the CPI(M), since doing so would require them to question both the party and their own families.

The CPI(M) has also weakened the PBGMS by siphoning off its most talented leaders. Interviews revealed an inverse relationship between members' skill and their commitment to the women's organization. The most talented women could devote the least time to women's issues because they were preoccupied with party and government responsibilities. Chayya Bera, minister of relief, described herself as responsible for her department as a whole, not for women's particular concerns. Kanak Mukherjee's presidency of the PBGMS has become virtually an honorific position since she became a member of parliament.

The PBGMS in turn reproduces democratic centralist principles when organizing poor rural women. Through close consultation with party officials, PBGMS leaders in Calcutta generally decide which issues to raise throughout the state. They then convey directives to the district level women's organizations, which in turn convene meetings at block and village levels with local women leaders. Nando Rani Daal, president of the

Midnapur district women's organization, reported that the major demands of demonstrations between 1980 and 1985 included greater state autonomy vis-à-vis the center, higher prices for agricultural produce, equal wages, reduced inflation, and global peace. With few exceptions, rural women thus have little opportunity to organize around the problems they confront in their daily lives.

Democratic centralist principles further buttress female seclusion. For example, women can generally become active in CPI(M) activities only with their husbands' consent. Thus, virtually all the husbands of the married women who were CPI(M) members or supporters were involved in party activity themselves. But even then, politically active women are suspect in the eyes of the public. Chayya Bera noted, "A serious disadvantage for women is that they can be maligned and gossiped about more easily than men. When I was contesting the election this time [1987], Congress-I made up a lot of unspeakable, slanderous stories about me. People like to believe such stories about women."

The CPI(M) is hardly in a position to create greater public acceptance for women when it upholds their traditional roles in both the party and the family. CPI(M) members often tolerate glaring contradictions between their public and private lives. For example, while publicly denouncing the dowry system, many party members participate in it. The PBGMS has not challenged the dowry system through political education and mobilization.

One explanation for the CPI(M)'s sexism may be its adaptation to Bengali social values. Because Hindus consider women the repositories of tradition, the CPI(M) can demonstrate its indigenous character by upholding female seclusion and subordination. Numerous CPI(M) leaders took great pains to dissociate themselves from feminism, which they believed was a Western import. The CPI(M)'s domestication of Marxism has protected it from a widespread criticism of the pro-Soviet CPI: that it is alien. However, its interpretation of Marxism does not radically challenge class, caste or gender inequality.

The Consequences of Democratic Centralism in the Home

The CPI(M) seems to assume that issues concerning women are "social" while issues that concern men are "economic." Such a distinction underlies the division of labor between the PBGMS and CITU, the CPI(M)-affiliated trade union. The PBGMS attends to "social" issues that are of little relevance to women from working-class and agricultural laborer families. Conversely, CITU attends to "economic" matters, primarily among male workers, thereby neglecting female workers and men's "social" concerns.

Such distinctions mystify the intimate relations among social, economic, and political spheres. They also falsely imply that the CPI(M) could radically challenge class inequality but adopt a conservative approach to gender. To the contrary, the CPI(M)'s acceptance of sexual inequality provides a key to explaining its conservatism in other spheres. Two examples are illustrative. The PBGMS distances itself from the rural poor by upholding middle-class conceptions of women's roles. Conversely, CITU's neglect of gender is linked to its narrow conception of class.

The PBGMS tends to project an image of womanhood that is based on upper-caste, upper-class norms. Its assumption that women are economically dependent, socially secluded, and politically inactive is reflected in its emphasis on home-based income generation projects and sex-linked constructive activities. This urban, elite ideal ignores the relative independence of women from lower castes and classes in the rural areas. Many female agricultural laborers who were interviewed had little time for what they considered recreational activities, given their need to engage in wage labor. Thus the Communists' reactionary views of gender roles are closely linked to their conservatism with respect to class.

Conversely, CITU is weakened by its underrepresentation of women. CITU restricts itself to the organized sector of the economy, in which male workers predominate. But workers in the informal sector, in which women are concentrated, are especially in need of trade union support, for wages are abysmally low, working conditions are wretched, and labor legislation is largely absent. Moreover in neglecting to organize in the informal sector, CITU weakens its own potential for expansion and fails to tap incipient militance among workers who have experienced extreme exploitation.

In a twist on Lenin, economistic tendencies do not arise spontaneously among workers and peasants but are imparted from without by CITU. Underrepresenting women and their specific concerns reinforces CITU's tendency to focus on short-term material gains for economically defined classes, rather than noneconomic quality of life issues such as child ca.e, maternity leave, and sexual harassment at the workplace. Thus CITU neglects some of the most vital and complex matters regarding the reorganization of relations of production and of the larger society. Similarly, the AIKS' lack of female membership and inattentiveness to women's problems narrows its focus to wages, land, and tenancy, to the neglect of issues concerning the relation between production and social life.

The economism of CITU and the AIKS reflects the approach of the CPI(M) and Left Front government. Just as the CPI(M) opposes autonomous women's movements, it considers tribal aspirations for greater regional autonomy to be antinational and secessionist. The CPI(M) has thereby failed to harness tribal militance. Instead, as the growth of the Jharkhand movement and Gurkha agitation suggest, minorities have become increasingly hostile to the Left Front government.[9]

Conclusion

What is the balance sheet of progress for women under the Left Front government? What are the implications of the CPI(M)'s approach to gender for its broader political strategy?

I have argued that despite some notable achievements—above all, women's increased sense of efficacy, material security, and freedom from repression—the CPI(M) has generally neglected women's interests. Indeed, inequalities within the family have grown as male household heads have gained landownership, credit facilities, and agricultural technology. The PBGMS perpetuates the sexual division of labor within the home and the world by confining its demands to incremental, sex-typed reforms and accepting its subordinate role within the communist movement.

The CPI(M)'s preoccupation with electoral success and its democratic centralist principles of organization have been especially damaging for women. But the influence between party strategy and female subordination is not unidirectional. The CPI(M)'s obliviousness to gender inequality and sex-typing of women's roles narrows its approach to class inequality and contributes to its overall conservatism.

The fact that the CPI(M)'s approach corresponds so well to structural conditions in West Bengal might suggest that the CPI(M) has had no choice but to concede defeat in face of overwhelming odds. Yet structural conditions may be more malleable than the CPI(M)'s perspective suggests. It is particularly noteworthy that Bengali communist women's activism was more extensive and that sexual relations were more egalitarian in the 1940s than they are today. Such shifts cannot be explained with reference to altered structural conditions.

Yet one should not assume, in a politically determinist fashion, that the CPI(M) is incapable of innovation. From its creation in 1964 when it sought an independent trajectory from the international communist movement, through the 1970s when it carved out a rural base, the CPI(M) has demonstrated great capacity to translate constraints into opportunities.

Moreover, Bengali conservatism should not be exaggerated. West Bengal has long been India's progressive cultural capital. One of the greatest achievements of the early communist movement was to draw upon and enrich this vitality in order to challenge conservative traditions. Such a legacy has created a greater climate of tolerance and scope for experimentation in West Bengal than exists in most of India.

Nor is there one monolithic, internally consistent cultural paradigm in West Bengal. Women's freedom increases as one moves down the caste and class hierarchies. Thus instead of imbibing *bhadralok* (elite) values, which are heavily laden with upper-caste snobbery, disdain for manual labor, and male chauvinism, the CPI(M) and PBGMS could appropriate the sexually egalitarian traditions of scheduled castes and tribals.

When CPI(M) leaders assert that women lack political consciousness, Bengali society is tradition-bound, and feminism is alien, they ignore their own responsibility in creating this situation. For example, by fostering PBGMS dependence on the party, the CPI(M) further reduces the effectiveness of the communist movement in representing women's interests. Rather than helping women to recognize and overcome structural constraints, the CPI(M)'s ideology and organization have reinforced women's passivity and dependence. The male-dominated bureaucracy and party are poor instruments for consciousness-raising, and the CPI(M) has inhibited more creative grass-roots mobilization among women.

Perhaps the CPI(M) has discouraged autonomous women's mobilization for fear of a spiraling of feminist activity. Women's attainment of joint *puttas* could lead them to demand equal rights to inheritance and other forms of property ownership. This in turn could free women from their dependence on the family. To understand why the CPI(M) is reluctant to undertake such reform, we must shift our attention from structural to political constraints. The prospect of women's economic independence could prove costly to the CPI(M) in electoral terms. Even more disturbing to some, might "decentering" the family eventually threaten the edifice of democratic centralism in the world?

Notes

1. Ronald Tiersky, *Ordinary Stalinism* (London: Allen and Unwin, 1985), p. 47.
2. I often refer interchangeably to the CPI(M) and its women's organization, the Paschim Bangla Ganatantrik Mahila Samiti, for their approaches to women's issues are virtually indistinguishable. Moreover as the discussion that follows suggests, even their membership is the same at the highest ranks of each organization.
3. Interviews were conducted with Manikuntala Sen, Gita Mukherjee, Vidhya Munshi, Kanak Mukherjee, Bani Dasgupta, Renu Chakraborty, Bella Bandopadhyaya and Vimla Ranadive, among others, about their experiences in the CPI from the 1930s on. These and other interviews cited in the text were conducted by me and in some cases by Bella Bandopadhyaya and Shreemati Chakrabarti in Calcutta between 1985 and 1988.
4. The romance of the Communist movement finds resonance cross-culturally. For a moving account of its manifestations in the United States see Vivian Gornick, *The Romance of American Communism* (New York: Basic Books, 1977).
5. Of the central government rural development schemes—National Rural Employment Program, Rural Landless Employment Guarantee Program, Drought Prone Areas Program, etc.—only one, the Development for Women and Children in the Rural Areas (DWCRA) is geared toward women. So far the central government has released very limited funds for DWCRA and implemented the program in only fifty districts nationwide.
6. This pattern contrasts with that of many socialist states in which women's political representation is much greater at the local than at the national level. However, it conforms to the all-India pattern in which elite women of middle-class, upper-caste backgrounds have extensive opportunities to enter the national political arena and are readily accepted when they do so. Until political parties overcome the electorate's reluc-

tance to elect women candidates, women will remain greatly underrepresented at the local level.

7. However, this form of "political reductionism" overlooks the possibilities for using electoral means to educate and mobilize women to defend their interests. The CPI(M) in West Bengal might learn from its sister party in Kerala, where young militants developed imaginative campaign techniques around gender and other nonclass-based issues when campaigning for the 1985 parliamentary elections.

8. In 1981 the CPI(M) created a women's organization at the national level, the All-India Democratic Women's Association (AIDWA) which has a membership today of 2,100,000.

9. The Left Front government's neglect in recognizing and supporting tribal aspirations for autonomy has fueled the Jharkhand movement in Midnapur, Bankura, and Purulia districts. More recently and seriously, the Gurkha agitation in Darjeeling illustrates the Communists' insensitivity to the "nationalities question."

Chicken Little in China: Women After the Cultural Revolution

Marilyn B. Young

There were three of them, all in their late 20s, all Han Chinese and all in Beijing for a two-year course of study before a mandatory return to middle school jobs in a remote province. XX was clearly their leader. Tight jeans, red shirt, a wide, ready, terribly eager smile, a strutting walk that was positively startling in the Beijing context. "Beijing is paradise," XX said. "And Beijing compared to America must be like my home is to Beijing." Her friends nodded rather depressed agreement. "At home I would be stoned in the street for dressing like this." "I was jeered at for less," one of her quieter friends broke in. What did they think of Jiang Qing? "She was great," XX burst out. "Maggie Thatcher too! They make men afraid." There was a silence then, as the three women took in the somewhat stunned expression on their American friend's face. "Of course Jiang Qing was also very bad," XX added. "Very bad," her friends chimed in.

The title of this essay draws on two tales, one Western, the other Chinese. In both the sky is understood as something solid; in both it is subject to falling down. In the Western story an overexcited and misinformed chicken alarms the barnyard with a false rumor that the sky is about to crash down on everyone's head. The Chinese tale is more static: once upon a time women were said to hold up half the sky. I want to explore the nature of the Chinese story, a favorite during the Cultural Revolution, and think about it in relation to the period after the Cultural Revolution when, looking around at women and then up at the sky, one might begin to wonder if Chicken Little had a point after all.

The starting place for any discussion of women and Chinese socialism is the premise of the Chinese revolution itself and the promise held out to women: that the liberation of women would be an integral part of the proletarian revolution. And that has indeed been the case. Initially, the revolution in power, no more imaginative than its Soviet avatar, relied on the mobilization of women in "social production," that is, waged labor, as a necessary, ideally sufficient first step. But, as Phyllis Andors has per-suasively argued, state policy toward women in China is an intimate variable of the overall revolutionary process.[1] The mobilization of women into—and also out of—the labor force followed not only, nor perhaps even primarily, the vagaries of the labor market but more centrally the debate within the leadership over the direction, speed, shape, and duration of the revolution itself. At times women were the *named* subject of particular policy endeavors (efforts to socialize women's work during the Great Leap Forward—the supercharged 1958 campaign for increased production in industry and agriculture—or the periodic encouragement to women to retire to the household in a becoming socialist manner); sometimes they were explicitly *unnamed* (as in the Cultural Revolution, which, among other things, declared that it was *not* about a "sex" revolution). Always, of course, the effect of policy was gender-specific, whether or not it was framed with gender in mind.

Women, in China as elsewhere, comprise a double or even a triple category of analysis. There is gender, of course, but then as well class and race or ethnicity. Women *embody* social contradictions. They are workers, or the wives of workers, middling or ruling class (by marriage or kinship rather than in their own persons), members of racial or ethnic minorities. No single line of analysis will cover their case. Frequently, when writers talk about "workers" they mean, really, male workers—and women work-ers become invisible. Or, from another analytic perspective, when "women" are discussed, their membership in a particular social class is forgotten.

In a country that defines itself as a dictatorship of the proletariat, the contradiction of women's doubled identity (and often consequent invis-ibility) makes their relationship to the state of vital importance. Uniting with the men of their class almost always means the disappearance of those concerns that are specific to their gender. Uniting with women of other classes on the basis of gender ignores real class divisions and is, or in any case was, ideologically suspect. Unable, then, to marshal sufficient social force to act on their own behalf, without independent power or leverage, women are placed in the position of depending on what Judith Stacey has called the "public patriarchy"—the state and the party—to a greater extent than other groups in the society. In a survey conducted by the journal *Women in China* several years ago, an older woman doctor asserted that women could achieve many things if they were *actively* supported by the state. "You see," she explained, perhaps adapting one of Mao's most familiar quotations, "state support is essential for women, just as water is indispensable for fish."[2] Thus in China, the withdrawal or modification of strong central government support for women has a major impact on their welfare. And in launching a massive central government campaign, such as the Cultural Revolution, the state put into high relief the inherently contradictory position of women, as well as the contradictions that inhere in women.

Kay Ann Johnson in *Women, the Family and Peasant Revolution in China* succinctly summarizes the interpretive framework within which policy on women was set during the Cultural Revolution.[3] First, the barrier to full equality between women and men was located in the superstructure—bourgeois ideology and/or remnant feudal ideas. Second, the slogan "politics in command" meant, with respect to women, a conscious, ongoing effort to expand their public political roles as well as their economic ones. Yet finally, since class was the primary analytic category for understanding all social problems, the ideological attack on inequality left structural issues untouched.

In a largely unchanged rural setting what this could mean in practice was an unplanned consonance between traditional "feudal" mores with respect to women and leftist denunciations of "bourgeois" individualism and personal freedom. Not that it need always mean that. In at least one South China village, young people intent on marrying within the village in defiance of traditional exogamous practice successfully accused disapproving elders of "feudal attitudes" and got their way.[4] But on the whole, Johnson argues, the emphasis on class made things worse for women. It meant a tendency to deny considerations of gender and to repudiate manifestations of feminism, which anyway were always high on classic Marxism-Leninism's enemy list. Thus, with perfect consistency, the Women's Federation was abolished in 1966 on the logical ground that, since class struggle was what it was all about, a separate organization for women made little sense.

Yet precisely *because* of its insistence on gender neutrality, the Cultural Revolution pushed women into the public realm as no movement since the Great Leap Forward had done. As Johnson writes again, "the Cultural Revolution . . . witnessed the most vigorous affirmative action efforts since 1949 to recruit larger numbers of women into political organizations."[5] At the same time, the firm refusal to acknowledge structural constraints on the position of women meant that public responsibilities, as well as work in the factory or on the collective farm, were simply added on to domestic burdens. A woman was expected to put her revolutionary work first and then tend to her husband and children. No one in China could ever have publically remarked, as did the late female Nicaraguan ambassador to the United Nations, "The truth is, with a revolution and kids, you don't have much time for a husband."[6]

What gender neutrality meant in fact was the requirement that women work harder than ever before—and the standard for achievement remained resolutely male. The Iron Girls, whose production in heavy agricultural labor rivaled that of men, are a case in point. Enormously appealing in their energy and effort, their claim to equality was simple: they could work as hard as or harder than men (and even then only rarely for equal work points). Therein lay their honor; and, from a feminist standpoint, therein lay their failure.

The proletarian woman, Mao told Malraux in 1965, man to man, was yet to be born.[7] Meanwhile her prototype during the Cultural Revolution was finally, under all the banners, a remarkably familiar figure: the uncomplaining working mother, ready to retire or join the workforce as needed. Indeed the Cultural Revolution, for all its heady rhetoric, in this regard merely worked out to its logical conclusion one tendency in Marxist approaches to women, an approach Marxism shares with many liberal ideologies. Many liberals and Marxists reject all notions of biological determinism; both embrace a concept of universal humanity. For both, as well, the universal human is male—a class-conscious revolutionary for the one, an autonomous individual for the other, but in neither case a woman.

Liberals and Chinese Marxists share another characteristic—a conviction, born of their common belief in human agency, that social change can be the product of the transformation of "attitudes." If then the definition of the problem facing women is that they are *seen* as women, the solution seems fairly evident. At the level of material reality, of course, they will continue to bear and rear children and be responsible for their usual chores. At the ideological level, however, this implicit aspect of their identity can be put aside. In the public realm they are to be *seen* as men. Standing in the way, however, are "feudal attitudes" that restrict women's movements and participation in the world of work and politics and "bourgeois attitudes" that lead women selfishly to focus on their own small family responsibilities. With sufficient effort, both attitudes can be overcome and the path cleared for the new woman, a kind of socialist androgyne; for public purposes a man, at home a loving wife and mother; genderless in public, chaste wife and selfless mother in private. Moreover, in China this division is consonant with much more ancient cultural constructs, in which gender is firmly tied to role rather than to biological sex. A woman active in the public realm must be sexually invisible. Indeed the most effective way to delegitimize a woman exercising political power is to insist on her sex—as Jiang Qing was to discover.

Some of the misunderstanding that arises between Chinese and Western feminists is a result of cultural misreading. Tani Barlow, watching a play in which an uppity wife is brought into a properly submissive relationship to her husband—part of a Woman's Day celebration in 1981—was astonished when her Chinese hosts said the play had nothing to do with male/female antagonism but was rather a conflict over rank.[8] The 1962 movie *Li Shuangshuang* and the 1982 movie *The In-laws* have radically different representations of women.[9] In the earlier movie, Li Shuangshuang is a leading force in the Great Leap Forward in her village, hampered at every turn by her small-minded husband; the 1982 movie heroine, by contrast, turns out to be a dutiful daughter-in-law. To any Western audience the movies are *about* women and the changes in representation since the 1960s. Yet Chinese discussions focus instead on the issues of production in one case and intergenerational conflict in the other. Moreover, an analysis of how the camera works in both films reveals, once more in direct contrast to Western cinematography, that the audience is in effect *blocked* from taking a gender-identified point of view. As Chris Berry explains: "The place of the viewing subject [i.e., audience] only becomes gender-identified . . . at negative points in the text, points of transgression, failure and collapse." We cannot be surprised then, Berry writes, "if a discourse of sexual difference concerned with the individual interests of one gender versus the other is absent from discussion of the films. . . ."[10] Here Chinese socialism and Chinese culture are braided together, collectivism reinforced by feudalism, an anti-individualist class perspective by an older vision of fixed social estates.

Nevertheless there remains a profound and instructive difference between *Li Shuangshuang* and *The In-laws*. The former may indeed be understood by Chinese audiences as being about production, but the clear message of the movie is that production, a central national goal, is sabotaged by Li Shuangshuang's backward husband. The message of *The In-laws* is that private familial harmony is sabotaged by a selfish daughter-in-law. Both movies reject bourgeois individualism, but what they reject it *for* makes a considerable difference and in that difference lies the history of the last two decades, including the history of women as such.

The Cultural Revolution, in its effort to salvage the vision of revolutionary possibility Mao had earlier vested in the Great Leap Forward, encouraged policies of radical mobilization and mass participation that, as Phyllis Andors has written with respect to the Great Leap, created "a more favorable atmosphere and generated forces in which all kinds of inequality—including that of women—could be effectively challenged."[11] Moreover, the 1973 campaign to criticize Lin Biao and Confucius, which the Chinese would now date as falling within the period of the Cultural Revolution, was explicitly focused on women's issues, publicizing the efforts of rural women to gain equal work points, stimulating research into the ideological origins of women's subordination, publishing hagiographies of women rebels, and linking anyone who opposed the equality of women to such villains as Liu Shaoqi, Lin Biao, and, of course, Confucius himself. Revolutionary committees, at that time the governing body in factories, schools, and government agencies, were instructed to "pay greater attention" to the role of women and to make sure that in "organs of political power at all levels and in mass organizations, there should be a certain number of women representatives and in actual work their opinions should be listened to seriously and with respect."[12] Women, the campaign trumpeted, held up half the sky and could certainly do whatever men did. And yet, even in the most favorable assessment of its impact, the campaign's focus on ideology left structural and cultural problems untouched. The conflict between gender and class was never effectively confronted.

I want now to shift the focus of analysis. Instead of thinking about Chinese women in this period in terms of various categories relating to revolutionary processes, I want to place them in a different, comparative context. If we take the experience of mass mobilization as central to the period, then it might be illuminating to look at the Chinese experience in the light of the mobilization of women in other times and places.

In both the United States and Great Britain (and very differently in Japan and Germany) the years of World War II required a shift in gender ideology and practice in order to mobilize women into the workforce for the war effort.[13] Although in both countries efforts were made to retain prewar gender roles in the face of changing practice, the actual *experience* of women during the war profoundly disturbed the status quo. Women were more mobile than they had been, often moving to places where jobs in war industries were available; they did jobs previously defined, and jealously maintained, as male. Many women found themselves independent, economically and socially, in ways they had not anticipated and for which they had no political language. There was no feminist movement as such during the war. But national exigencies transformed the lives of women in ways a later feminist movement could and would raise to consciousness.

While the war thus brought women everywhere unprecedented mobility, they were not everywhere mobilized in the same way. In the West they were mobilized on the basis of gender and patriotism; in China on the basis of class and revolution. Nonetheless, the fact of mobilization itself may be more significant than this difference.

For Chinese women, the experience of the Cultural Revolution could have a particularly powerful effect because of the peculiar fluidity of their ideological situation. The early promises of liberation through incorporation into socially productive labor had posited an explicitly antifeudal conception of women's roles. For most women this was, at best, only fitfully possible. However, during the Cultural Revolution, state-sponsored insistence on the participation of women in the public realm inevitably unsettled the status quo of gender relations or, more basically perhaps, the given hierarchy of power and authority, and encouraged women to take action against it.

The hierarchy at issue was, in addition to its other features, *generational*. Perhaps one way to understand the reports of the quite stunning ferocity of female middle-school students against figures of authority (up to and including beating people to death) is as a rebellion against the weight of prior social repression, as well as a means to extirpate old stereotypes of feminine behavior. Criticized as bourgeois for having worn a dress, Li Xiaochang went to school the next day in trousers, then joined a Red Guard organization and participated in a range of violent activities she describes with considerable vigor (and some chagrin) today: "We caught the members of street gangs too, like the 'Nine Dragons and a Phoenix.' They sounded frightening, but when we caught them, we beat them until they begged us 'Red Guard ladies' for mercy."[14]

In these actions, as in their participation in the exchange of revolutionary experiences or the movement to "go down to the countryside," young women were physically sprung loose from a home, school, or work environment that, until then, they may not have consciously felt to be oppressive. Listening to one Chinese friend recount a series of Cultural Revolution horror stories, I was surprised to find her smiling broadly as she remembered being left entirely on her own when she was thirteen or fourteen, her parents and elder siblings having been scattered around the country. "That must have been awful," I said sympathetically. "Oh no," she insisted. "You don't understand. I was free. I could do what I wanted. It was wonderful."

Many other women, none of whom intended to praise what they all agreed had been largely a personal and national disaster, talked enthusiastically about specific aspects of their time in the countryside. "Because I did the work better than anyone, better even than any of the men, I was made team leader," a woman whose life in almost every respect had been thoroughly devastated by the Cultural Revolution told me. "And that meant I sat," and she gestured at her kitchen table, "*there*, in the seat of authority, of the most respected person, where no woman had ever sat before." Another recalled riding horses in Inner Mongolia. "I rode at night," she said proudly. "All the boys were frightened to do that, but I loved it. And fast. I rode very fast." Which is not to deny that many young women found separation from their families terrifying, nor that an unknown number of urban female students suffered varieties of sexual abuse in the countryside—from peasants or from their male comrades. Thus Li Xiaochang remembers what it was like to learn to ride a horse really well. "I began to appreciate the great outdoors. Riding slowly across the great grasslands was beautiful. If now I have a sense of wonder, or of powerful, indefinable nostalgia, if I have an understanding for melancholy and quietness, it all goes back to those days." But later, in that same place, where the herdsmen who taught her to ride had also become her friends, she was raped. "The whole family was there and they helped him." Her urban-educated male comrades charged her with seduction and invited her to do a self-criticism. "There was no question of bringing a case against the boy," she concludes. "They were national minorities and this was their custom."[15] Yet for some there was sexual pleasure as well as danger, the possibility of experimentation that both the material and the ideological conditions at home precluded.

It is worth noting the frequency with which female figures in current literary and film treatments of the Cultural Revolution are depicted as especially venal, or authoritarian, or brutal. "Marxist Grannies" are figures of fun, but the antiheroine of Liu Binyan's *People or Monsters* is far more threatening.[16] A play popular in Beijing in 1985 featured a truly loathsome girl Red Guard leader who seemed to be the only Red Guard in her neighborhood. Her voice was shrill, she had the most sympathetic characters in the play beaten and arrested—an altogether evil child who, in the last act of the play, grows up to be, in the context of the current reforms, a corrupt, quarrelsome, and self-seeking woman. These examples are, of course, contemporary reconstructions intended for current consumption. But they may, as well, contain a measure of truth. Perhaps the behavior of women in power should be understood as a reaction against long-established constraints on women. Given the possibility of some portion of power, they seized it, exercised it with maximum force, even relished it, not as power to do something, but, in a manner hardly peculiar to women, as power over others.

Finally, whatever else might be said of the Iron Girls or their epigones in hundreds of feature magazine articles on women pilots, high-tension wire workers, and boat crews, women in nontraditional jobs broke standard gender stereotypes. They were tokens, to be sure, but a token signs a promise; eventually it becomes a sign of the breach of the promise.

The aftermath of the Cultural Revolution in China and the war in the United States and Great Britain was in part marked by the difference in the ideologies that had mobilized women at the outset. Women in the West were eased out of the workforce into the home with relative ease, as consumers, as the stipulated bearers of harmony and stability, as essential reproducers, literally and figuratively, of the cold war social order. Some women, though hardly all, put by their wartime experience and welcomed a return to "normalcy." The ideology of gender roles remained essentially hegemonic and difficult to resist.

In China, normalization required a direct attack on Cultural Revolution ideology. Women were not fired, though since the early 1980s there has been considerable pressure to persuade, or even force, them to take lengthy maternity leaves and earlier retirement.[17] Neither in the West nor in China was this a matter of conscious conspiracy, and certainly women were complicitous in it. But it is necessary to discriminate between what was self-generated, by women themselves, and what was externally imposed. Neither in China nor the West do women fully possess the power of self-definition.

In China, after the fall of the Gang of Four in 1978, among the early expressions of rejecting the past was a movement by women to define for themselves what it meant to be a woman with needs and goals different from those of men. Freed of an imposed asceticism, women sometimes could find no better expression of pleasure in their difference than to get their hair permed in astonishing numbers; in the newspapers there was an explosion of fashions, cosmetics, beauty tips.

At a more political level, in the 1980 local election campaign in Beijing, a woman candidate opened her campaign with a big character poster on the subject of "Oriental Beauty." She was attacked for such a nonpolitical choice and, in response to posters criticizing her, she wrote one called "Women are human beings too." The text is a tangle of contradictions that, however, clearly reflect the legacy of recent Chinese cultural instructions to women. "Women," it argues, "are human beings too. Why should their specific attributes, their interests, their development as a sex and many other aspects of their womanhood not be important questions?" Women must be allowed to develop their own personalities, their point of view can "widen and reinforce the overall understanding of things." Through struggle, women will "acquire the right to be human beings and the right to take up responsibilities and the honours that flow from them."[18]

Here two things are going on simultaneously: an appeal to women's special attributes and point of view while the definition of the normative human being remains male. The double bind is familiar, a consequence of the fact that women's identity *is* doubled in any modern or modernizing society. We are dealing here with what can only be called the dialectic of female identity, within which different terms are stressed depending on the larger social situation. Ironically, the Cultural Revolution delivered women into the modern era by wrenching them free of feudal models, proposing instead their dispersion and dissolution into society at large. But women *cannot* be made to disappear in this way. In modern society their identity is of necessity both individual and generic. The feminist argument here is compelling: the secret of modern equality is the suppressed inequality of women. Women's special attributes are exactly what make them unfit to be human in a male sense. Responsible for children, they can no more fulfill the goals of the four modernizations equally with men than they could those of the preceding revolutionary period.

Of necessity then, post–Cultural Revolution reform and restoration has had to make the subject of women's place central. There are two simultaneous aspects to the ongoing construction of female gender roles. First, the explicit repudiation of the past. Iron Girls Brigades are the subject of comic clapper talks, critical discussions in the press, snide side comments. In a style familiar to women elsewhere, the idea that one can somehow lose one's very sex by behaving inappropriately is regularly deployed. Iron Girls were unwomanly, unmarriageable, unattractive, in short, "false boys." At a recent symposium attended by sociologists, legal scholars, literary critics, and philosophers in Beijing, it was pointed out that "young men want women to have a pretty face, a nice figure, be good at housework and have a gentle disposition."[19] The higher a woman's educational attainment, the harder it is for her to find a suitable mate. Women with "strong career interests" are not considered desirable wives—a strong echo of the traditional notion that a woman without talent is virtuous. Indeed, unmarried women over the age of twenty-eight constitute a social problem that is much worried over. Sometimes the women are blamed for being "too picky."

But on other occasions men themselves are criticized for ignoring the value of an older woman. Several men who married women three years older than themselves wrote of their satisfaction in a popular youth magazine—such women were socially experienced, capable housewives, and wonderfully supportive of their husbands' work (one young man marveled gratefully that he had written twenty articles since his marriage). While the Beijing forum was very critical of many of the current attitudes described, the men who participated (described by the reporter as being the "more voluble" participants) were uniform in their denunciation of "iron women" and "fake boys." "A woman who becomes masculine is a mutant. Capable women should be different from men. They have their own special charm, for example exquisiteness and depth of emotions, and well-developed imagistic thinking. Women's own latent abilities should be called forth."[20]

In thus rejecting the approach set forth by the Cultural Revolution, which attacked the notion that biology was destiny but only by holding out to women the promise that they could be like men, the participants in the Beijing forum embraced a different but no less unequal view of women. Here biology *is* destiny—but a pleasant one. Women and men are complementary, gender polarity is to be honored, and women are, as they had been all along, instrumental to the realization of Chinese development— whether Maoist revolutionary or Deng Xiaoping reformist.

In dramatic writings about the "ten years of turmoil," as the Cultural Revolution is routinely described, women in political roles are universally depicted in the most negative way. Perhaps it is easier to focus anger on the women who carried out policy than to attack directly the men who actually made it. Perhaps, as in prerevolutionary China, women characters are again the vehicles through which male writers express social criticism. But it matters that abuse of power is most easily denounced when it has been feminized.[21] Evil itself has been feminized and the message to women is clear: there is something in the natural order of things that does not love a woman exercising public power.

The slogans of the past, as they relate to women, are emphatically rejected. That women can do what men can do, I was told by Women's

Federation cadres in two different cities in 1985, is a "reactionary" idea, which ignores their actual physical weakness compared to men. A popular play in Shanghai referred to the part of the sky that women held up as "less weighty" than the half sustained by men. The sexually undifferentiated style of dress and manner urged on women during the Cultural Revolution has been overwhelmingly rejected and women's magazines feature careful diagrams of instruction on how to sit down, stand up, and walk in an appropriately female fashion. And if your body is insufficiently feminine to meet current needs, you can reform it, even revolutionize it. The inside back cover of a recent issue of *Zhonguo funu* (Women of China) is entirely devoted to an advertisement by the Silver Star Plastic and Color Printing Factory of Jiangmen City, Guangdong, which in the patriotic pursuit of "eliminating the flaws in female development" has invented and is currently marketing a "Rapid Healthful Beauty Bust Enhancer." Consisting of a rubber cup and a small length of hose, this wondrous mechanism will stimulate the "secretions of the pituitary glands in the chest, expand the spongeability of the breasts," and allow "flat breasts to become full and protruding in a short period of time." Testimonials from satisfied users claim that the device will also "promote blood circulation in the breasts, prevent breast cancer, guard against neurasthenia, make both breasts a uniform size" and, especially important in a country that considers them a major defect, "cause freckles on the face to disappear naturally." A satisfied user, Kuang XX, reported it cured her insomnia as well.[22]

There is a small industry of essay writers generating lists of female as opposed to male characteristics. In one typical article the author asserts that "the thinking of male classmates is comparatively broad and quick. They have wide-ranging interests, a strong ability to get to work, and they like to think things out for themselves; but sometimes they are not careful or thorough enough. Female classmates often have stronger memory and language ability, are more diligent and meticulous. But they have one-track minds, do not think dynamically enough, have a rather narrow range of activity, and easily become interested in trivial matters. Their moods fluctuate easily, they are shy, and they don't dare to boldly raise questions." Another account notes that the "nervous system of females is not as stable as that of males. . . . Women are highly sensitive, so much so that the slightest misfortune can make a woman cry. Men, in contrast, only shed tears on extremely tragic occasions." Moreover, women can quickly stop crying but "a crying man finds it difficult to calm down." The same is true of other emotions. "Women's laughter for the most part is like a light breeze; it sweeps past and is gone. The laughter of men is not often heard, but is very infectious." In a version of the dialectic that would have made Mao Zedong weep long (or laugh infectiously) the writer concludes that the two sexes "must form two aspects of equal value that unite into a whole. Conversely, without differences, combination would be an unsuitable goal."[23] (Mao always did insist that "one breaks down into two" rather than two combining into one.)

A 1985 *Life Handbook for the Contemporary Woman* has a convenient checklist of characteristics reminiscent of those tests one used to take at the back of Western women's magazines. If you're a girl you love to talk, are very refined, understand other people's feelings, are devout, pay attention to your appearance, are neat, clean, quiet, need security, love art and literature, and easily express "gentle feelings." If you're a boy, on the other hand, you are aggressive, independent, not influenced by others, dominating, not troubled by trivia, vigorous, risk taking, decisive, not dependent on others (which is apparently different from being independent), and pay little attention to your appearance.[24]

All these messages are contradictory, reflecting an ongoing inconclusive debate. Women should learn the arts of adornment, but refrain from their undue exercise; women should be filial toward parents and in-laws, but modern, independent, antifeudal; women should certainly follow the dictates of state population policy and are of course the primary child-rearer, but they must learn, from professional experts, how to avoid spoiling the single child; women should fully participate in the drive to realize the four modernizations (in agriculture, industry, science and technology, and defense), but they might just want to take three, four, or even ten years maternity leave as well. Romantic love is an acceptable socialist notion, but women are responsible for controlling their own and male sexual behavior and sex itself should be indulged in only after marriage and strictly within its confines. Struggling to understand how it is possible, under a social system "that guarantees equal rights for both sexes legally, economically, politically and educationally," that women nevertheless fall behind, one author sorts through both objective and subjective causes. The objective causes are that the "weaknesses of women ideologically and educationally, shaped in the course of centuries, give many the reason to persist in considering them inferior." Not surprisingly, this objective situation has a decidedly negative sujective impact, giving young women an "inferiority complex" and leading them to be dependent on others. A final subjective factor is that girls are "near-sighted and complacent." Confined to a smaller circle of friends than boys, "girls are apt to discuss clothes and make-up and other such immediate concerns rather than bigger social issues."[25]

Gender roles and family organization, Foucault has suggested, are not objects of social policy but the necessary instrument through which the policy is expressed and enforced. In China today, a release of individual energy, deemed necessary to fuel the four modernizations, must nevertheless be constrained so that it remains amenable to centralized control. A stable nuclear family, maintained by women who are at the same time as available for paid labor as the developing economy requires, has proven historically the most efficient form of social and personal organization to achieve such a controlled empowerment of individuals—with one requirement: that nuclear families be induced to restrict the number of their children. But given China's population problems, the restriction needs to be drastic: preferably to one child per family. For families to be satisfied with one child, the status of women must become more nearly equal to that of men—else the preference for high-status sons continues; couples whose first child is a girl will be radically dissatisfied. Yet in most of the countryside, young women continue to marry into the husband's family, which usually means into another village altogether. A son at home is the only guarantee most peasants have that they will be cared for in old age. Even in the cities, ongoing unemployment (disproportionally female), lower wages for women's work, the push to retire women early, all militate against a more relaxed attitude toward the sex of a perhaps one and only child. It becomes more and more difficult for the regime to hold out to women the old promise of socialist liberation—that their equality will devolve from their integration into the paid workforce and the socialization of household chores and childrearing.

One possible and tempting solution, as I have suggested above, is to revive a gender ideology that stresses the "natural" differences between women and men, limits the notion of socialized housework to improved domestic technology (the liberation of women, *pace* Mao Zedong, *is* about the manufacture of washing machines), and condemns "iron women." Thus "modern" ideas about women in China are once again conveniently consonant with traditional views and the new in turn reinforces the old. "Socialist spiritual civilization" is invoked to control such unwanted results of the open door as prostitution and pornography. The contents of that civilization are rarely spelled out in any detail. Sometimes, with respect to women, socialist spirituality sounds remarkably like traditional Confucian morality: both subordinate the interests of the individual to that of the family. And the family is, in both, the province of the male head of household. The current Confucian revival—the renaissance in Confucian studies, the refurbishing of the sage's birthplace, the feature articles on his direct descendants and praise for their unbroken filial piety despite the ravages of revolution—is more broadly an effort to revitalize a cultural heritage that is uniquely Chinese in the face of the erosive, even corrosive impact of the West. Still, the special problems women incur from his revival focus on a general question: Does modernization not only permit but require an attendant "feudalism" for women?

"Women in China," a Chinese friend told me, "cannot do what women in the West can do. After all, if peasant women started to act like women in the West, the world would turn upside down." My friend's vision of how Western women act was vague at the edges, but at its heart she correctly perceived a striving for autonomy, which is a goal that threatens the premises of both liberal and socialist revolutions. For, despite the promise to women held out by virtually all modernizing strategies, their actual role has been to stabilize the world; to be the still point around which the axis of revolution can rotate more freely.

Given Mao Zedong's passion for contradictions, it is a pity he does not seem to have reflected more on the subject of women. What he did say indicates that his ideas were more complicated than current official Chinese formulations. Liberating women, he argued, was *not* like manufacturing washing machines. By this he seems to have meant two things—that genuine liberation was not simply a matter of the development of the forces of production, and that the production of devices that cut back on women's household labor would not by themselves guarantee that liberation. Moreover, in philosophical moods, Mao was wont to speculate on the ultimate disappearance of the family altogether—in a thousand years, perhaps, as part of the ongoing evolution of human society. The cosmic, permanent, absolutely indeterminate dialectic on which Mao insisted, a universe in which equilibrium was *of necessity* a sometime thing, has been stilled, frozen. Class struggle has been abolished by the fiat of definition. But the social and gender divisions that mark reality in China no less than in the United States cannot be defined out of existence.

Notes

1. See Phyllis Andors, *The Unfinished Liberation of Chinese Women, 1949–1980* (Bloomington, IN: Indiana University Press, 1983).
2. *Women in China*, April 1983, p. 10.
3. Kay Ann Johnson, *Women, the Family and Peasant Revolution in China* (Chicago: University of Chicago Press, 1983).
4. Anita Chan et al., *Chen Village: The Recent History of a Peasant Community in Mao's China* (Berkeley: University of California Press, 1984), p. 190; Johnson, *Women, Family, Peasant Revolution*, pp. 178–79.
5. Johnson, *Women, Family, Peasant Revolution*, p. 182.
6. The late Nora Astorga, quoted in the *New York Times Sunday Magazine*, September 28, 1986.
7. Mao was reflecting on the meaning of revolution: "It isn't simply a question of replacing the Tsar with Khrushchev, one bourgeoisie with another, even if it's called communist. It's the same as with women. Of course it was necessary to give them legal equality to begin with! But from there on, everything still remains to be done. The thought, culture, and customs which brought China to where we found her must disappear, and the thought, culture and customs of proletarian China, which does not yet exist either, must appear. The Chinese woman doesn't exist yet either, among the masses; but she is beginning to want to exist. And then, to liberate women is not to manufacture washing machines." As quoted in André Malraux, *Anti-Memoirs* (New York: Holt, Rinehart and Winston, 1968), pp. 373–74.
8. Tani Barlow and Donald M. Lowe, *Teaching China's Lost Generation: Foreign Experts in the People's Republic of China* (San Francisco: China Books and Periodicals, 1987), p. 95.
9. See Chris Berry, "Sexual Difference and the Viewing Subject in *Li Shuangshuang* and

      The In-laws," in Chris Berry, ed., *Perspectives on Chinese Cinema* (Ithaca, NY: China-Japan Program, Cornell University, 1985).

10. Ibid., p. 42.

11. Andors, *Unfinished Liberation*, p. 99.

12. Ibid., p. 125. For Andors' final summation of the campaign, see p. 149. See also Elisabeth Croll, "The Movement to Criticize Confucius and Lin Piao," *Signs: Journal of Women in Culture and Society* 2, no. 3 (Spring 1977): 721–26.

13. See, for comparison, Leila J. Rupp, *Mobilizing Women for War: German and American Propaganda, 1939–1945* (Princeton, NJ: Princeton University Press, 1978), and Margaret Higonet et al., eds., *Behind the Lines: Gender and the Two World Wars* (New Haven: Yale University Press, 1987).

14. "Diploma," in Zhang Xinxin and Sang Ye, *Chinese Lives: An Oral History of Contemporary China*, ed. W. J. E. Jenner and Delia Davin (New York: Pantheon, 1987), p. 56.

15. Ibid., p. 57.

16. Liu Binyan, *People or Monsters? And Other Stories and Reportage from China After Mao*, ed. Perry Link (Bloomington, IN: Indiana University Press, 1983). One Chinese friend, who otherwise found the model operas of the period stunningly boring, remarked approvingly that none featured "couples." Kay Ann Johnson would probably interpret this as a feature of the traditionalist/Maoist coalition against romantic love, but it *could* also be understood as a focus on female agency.

17. The one-child family policy has had little impact on this discussion. Arguing for an extended leave, one journalist noted that since women "are the ones who bear children, and because they are, on the whole, more diligent, patient and hardworking, they are the natural candidates for taking charge at home, even if that means they have to do more housework. Conversely, it would be no 'liberation' if they have to work and take care of the home at the same time. Three years of leave would alleviate their physical and mental burdens. This is the way to true 'liberation.'" Xing Hua, "A System of Employment by Stages Should be Instituted among Chinese Women," in *Chinese Women (1)*, special issue of *Chinese Sociology and Anthropology* (Stanley Rosen, guest editor) 20, no. 1 (Fall 1987): p. 83. See also Elisabeth Croll et al., *China's One-Child Policy* (London: Macmilian, 1985).

18. Anita Rand, "To Be a Feminist in Beijing," in Gregor Benton, ed., *Wild Lilies: Poisonous Weeds: Dissident Voices from People's China* (London: Pluto Press, 1982), pp. 195ff.

19. Emily Honig and Gail Hershatter, *Personal Voices: Chinese Women in the 1980s* (Stanford, CA: Stanford University Press, 1988), pp. 25–26.

20. Ibid. My quotation was drawn from the original manuscript of *Personal Voices*. See p. 345, n. 38, for full citation on the symposium.

21. I am reminded of the marathon German film answer to *Holocaust*, Reitz' *Heimat*. Here the most evil man in the village, the only member of the S.S., is a suspiciously effeminate individual who is accused, by the village women, of being a "shirker" and avoiding combat. As Erick Rentschler puts it in "The Discourse on Bitburg" (*New German Critique* 36, [Fall 1985]) "Heimat" illustrates the way "forgetfulness can lie in remembering."

22. Honig and Hershatter, *Voices*, pp. 68–69.

23. Ibid., pp. 34, 35.

24. Ibid., pp. 35–36.

25. Zhang Xiping, "Cultivation of New Women," in *Chinese Sociology and Anthropology*, Fall 1987, pp. 48, 49.

Part 4
Women in Industrialized Socialist Regimes

The "Woman Question" in the Contemporary Soviet Union

Mary Buckley

Soviet Ideology on Women

Throughout its seventy-year history the Soviet state has remained officially committed to equality of the sexes. Soviet ideology has consistently held that only socialism can bring about the liberation of women since unlike capitalism it is an economic system that does not exploit women and men in the labor force. Under socialism, moreover, women are no longer financially dependent on men in the home since access to jobs is guaranteed. Thus the double oppression of the capitalist labor force and the bourgeois family that Bebel, Marx, Engels, Lenin, Trotsky, Armand, and Kollontai talked about no longer exists. Their absence makes women's liberation not just possible, but inevitable.

Soviet theoretical writings on the "Woman Question" have always drawn heavily on the classic Marxist texts. The same can be said of Soviet sociological analyses of the position of women in the USSR that began to appear in the 1960s, flourished in the 1970s, and continued into the early 1980s, although slightly diminished in number. This flow of research is likely to increase in the aftermath of the special All-Union Conference of Women that was held in Moscow in January 1987. Soviet books, articles, and Ph.D. dissertations, whether abstract or descriptive, quote extensively from Marx, Engels, and Lenin. The authority of these men on the Woman Question remains undisputed.

The content of ideology at any given point in time is defined "from above" by the leadership of the Communist Party of the Soviet Union (CPSU).[1] Yet in many respects Soviet ideology on women since 1930 has not gone beyond Marx, Engels, and Lenin. A very strong economic component to official ideology on women has been and remains at its core. Soviet writings, in agreement with Marx, praise capitalism for creating the economic preconditions for the clash between labor and capital that would

251

give rise to socialism, and simultaneously condemn it for the exploitation, oppression, and alienation of all nonowning classes in society.

Much that is said about the position of women under socialism is pitched in contrast to their predicament under capitalism. A persistent thread that runs through Soviet ideology is that however capitalism can be faulted, socialism can be praised. In short, the wrongs of capitalism all have the potential to be corrected once a socialist economic base is established. In this sense, economic determinism reigns supreme, while the superstructure of society receives less attention. The ways in which the institutions of socialist society might discriminate against women or how attitudes might subordinate them to men were ideological non-topics for the first sixty years of the Soviet state. Only now in the 1980s, with Mikhail Gorbachev as general secretary of the CPSU, are more probing questions about the lives of women beginning to be asked, extending beyond the debate on female roles that took place under Brezhnev. Similarly, what women's liberation actually means under socialism ceased to be debated after the 1920s and is only now being tentatively taken up under Gorbachev. But self-determination for women is not the main focus of current discussions, which concentrate instead on how women can contribute to the process of reform and on what reforms mean for women.

So the mechanisms of female subordination to men and the various forms these can take have not yet been systematically addressed in Soviet literature. This is mainly because socialism is claimed to guarantee the eventual solution to all serious problems. In this sense, Soviet ideology has for a long time remained locked in the derivative approach to women implicit in Marxism. It is assumed that equality of the sexes under socialism is unavoidable because the economic root of the exploitation of one class by another was torn up with socialist revolution. So long as private property does not exist, neither working women nor working men can be exploited. Equality of the sexes is bound to "happen" once other problems have been sorted out. Thus the common stress is on elaborating what women are free *from* rather than defining what exactly it is that they are free *to* do. This is very different from the arguments of political activists of the 1920s and earlier, such as Inessa Armand and Alexandra Kollontai.[2] While Armand and Kollontai also drew attention to what socialism could avoid for women, they were much more concerned to address what socialism could bring to them and also how the success of socialism depended on changes in women's lives. Armand, for example, argued that energetic woman as a "soldier of the revolution" acting "not in some distant future" but "now" should actively pursue "new ways" since this is necessary for her liberation and for socialism.[3] There was a pressing call from some women in the 1920s for immediate action on women's issues and a recognition of the mutual interplay between the success of socialism and the nature of women's liberation.

Since 1930 the emphasis has been more unidirectional; socialism allows women to be liberated. Discussion of what liberation actually means for women and exploration of how the direction of that liberation might negatively or positively affect socialism itself have generally not been topics for discussion. It was not until the 1987 All-Union Conference of Women that the following question was finally put: "Who suffers most in society from the negative aspects of our life? Women. And because of this we shall indeed be the main real strength in *perestroika*—we have a vital interest in it."[4]

With Gorbachev's priority of *perestroika*—reconstruction of the economy, politics, and society—and his emphasis on *glasnost* (openness or publicity) as one of the means to achieve these broad reforms, more of the difficulties experienced by women under socialism are being broached. However, it is early yet and how far the questioning will go depends to some extent on Gorbachev's political fortunes. If his opponents do not succeed in blocking his policies, then the official treatment of the Woman Question is likely to become more rigorous at the level of theory, and its unisexual bias may be greatly diluted.

For most of its history, the Soviet state has largely ignored the topic of male roles in a socialist society. Lack of male participation in housework, shopping, and childrearing were not much discussed from 1930 until the late 1960s and 1970s. Even once this was mentioned in connection with the recognition that a female "double burden" or "double shift" existed, radical changes in gender roles were not proposed. Male violence against women has also been a taboo topic, as has homosexuality. Similarly, analysis of the mechanisms used by men—both blatant and subtle—to exclude women from professional contacts and informal social gatherings has been lacking.

In this overwhelmingly unisexual historical context, a statement made at the 1987 Conference of Women carried a radical ring. Quoted in Soviet media coverage of the event it announced: "We strive to achieve the situation in which husband and wife carry out household chores equally and together take responsibility for childrearing."[5] So in the late 1980s men's participation in domestic work and child care is beginning to be made an issue. So too is the absence of women from top jobs in political and economic life. Like Khrushchev thirty years before him, Gorbachev is asking why it is that women are absent from many positions of responsibility. Today the Soviet leadership is giving attention to issues that were best characterized in the past as "ideological silences." Soviet women have not always been so reticent about discussing the hardships of their lives among themselves. So official ideology is now broadening to embrace topics of popular concern. The sorts of questions posed publicly by Soviet leaders help to shape the discussion topics pursued by Soviet journalists and also influence the research of policymakers and their academic ad-

visers. The bounds of acceptable debate are set by direction from "above."
What leaders say about female roles influences how broader discourse
about equality of the sexes is pitched and sets the parameters of what it is
permissible to include.

The Political Construction of Ideology

Soviet approaches to the position of women in society have not been
static, however. In different periods of Soviet history, arguments about
women's roles have varied. This is partly because the problems and policy
priorities of successive Soviet leaderships have differed, even if they have
shared broader long-term aims. Although common ideological goals have
always been present, such as working toward communism, supporting
equality of the sexes, drawing women into the workforce and politics,
providing child-care centers and kindergartens to enable women to participate in social production, easing the "crushing drudgery" of housework,
and building more public dining rooms, they have been differently pack-
aged and variously emphasized to coincide with other policy priorities. So
it is appropriate to talk about the political construction of ideology in the
USSR, and the ways in which successive leaderships use it, select from it,
add to it, and ignore it as suits their purposes.

My object here is to illustrate different uses of ideology from 1930 to
1987 and to suggest the underlying reasons for them. My argument in
summary is that from 1930 to 1956 women were portrayed as a "great
army of labor," consistent with Stalin's policies to industrialize a largely
agricultural country, to collectivize agriculture, and to fight the Great
Patriotic War against the Nazis. In these years the Woman Question won
the proud status of "solved." It was alleged that socialist revolution had
freed the working class and since women were part of that class, they too
had been emancipated. Because the Woman Question had been solved,
women's issues were not given a special focus, except in Muslim parts of
the country. Class, not gender, was the key organizing concept.

Under Khrushchev, the question of women's political roles came back
onto the agenda, in keeping with his broader attempt to revitalize political
participation. The *zhensovety*, or women's councils, were encouraged in
order to target women, to meet their particular needs, and to mobilize
them. Women's lives were now seen to have problems, but the Woman
Question was still officially "solved."

Then, in the 1960s and 1970s, greater attention was given by the
Brezhnev leadership to the double burden of women when it became
evident that participation in the workforce topped with domestic chores
and child care affected economic productivity, absenteeism, free time,
retraining, fertility rates, divorce, and political activity. With the revival of

Soviet sociology it became clear that the way in which women lived their lives had tremendous implications for the economy, society, and politics. Similarly, economy, society, and politics influenced what women could and could not do. In a context of falling economic productivity and smaller family size, a lively debate about female roles sprang up. The limits of acceptable discussion widened, helped by the declaration that the Woman Question was now "unsolved." Ideological lines were less rigid than before and looser at the edges.

By the early 1980s when the Brezhnev era was sluggish with geron- tocracy and lacking the hints of hope of its beginning, there was a lull in the debate about female roles. But now, under Gorbachev, the role of women is back on the political agenda and with it has come a limited reappraisal of some male roles. It would be hazardous to try to predict how far this questioning will go in a society that is in many ways quite conservative and that resists change. In addition, firm notions persist in the USSR of what "femininity" and "masculinity" entail, and these affect socialization processes, the content of the media, and career structures. But the issue is a complex one, shaped not just by attitudes, but by cultural diversity across the fifteen Soviet republics and by the way in which cumbersome bureaucratic structures operate.

Thus official Soviet ideology on women is anchored in a changing context of different leadership priorities as well as in a setting of hier- archically organized party-dominated institutions extending over 100 dif- ferent nationalities. Attempts can be made to modify institutions and to encourage changes in values. But in an industrialized socialist regime with intricate and overlapping institutions, which give rise to inertia and resist- ance to new ways, procedures can be altered only with difficulty. Values can be officially restructured, but putting them into practice is a more arduous step. Not all policies are implemented at the local level in a way that some leaders would like.

Before I elaborate further on how ideology on women has been politi- cally constructed in these different periods, let me first give a brief over- view of the position of women in the economy, politics, and society.

Women in Soviet Reality

At first glance Soviet women are active and visible in the public domain: they make up 51 percent of the labor force and have done so since 1970.[6] Women have entered many of the professions, ranging from medicine to university teaching, and can be found among the ranks of qualified engineers, trolley bus drivers, plasterers, and welders. Soviet women also have a high profile in some forms of political activity. They are prominent in the activities of the Komsomol, which is the youth group of the CPSU, and are found in relatively large numbers on the elected soviets. Although their presence on the soviets falls as they move up the hierarchy, it is stronger than the representation of women in most parliaments in the West and is increasing. After the 1985 elections women made up 50.3 percent of the deputies to the local soviets and 36.2 percent of the deputies to the Supreme Soviets of the fifteen republics.[7] Elections held in 1984 to the Supreme Soviet of the USSR, which draws deputies from all of the republics, gave women 32.8 percent of the seats.[8] Great strides have clearly been made since the prerevolutionary years when most women were illiterate, living in rural areas and bound by the 1836 Code of Russian law to give their husbands unlimited obedience.

Yet this glossy picture of transformation from backwardness to liberation obscures more than it reveals. Even though the Soviet economy is heavily reliant on female labor, women find themselves concentrated in relatively low-paid and unskilled work at the bottom of job hierarchies. Workers in light industries such as textiles and food are predominantly female.[9] Here wages are lower than in the male preserves of heavy industry and Soviet writings indicate that women earn two-thirds of the male wage. Even in some fields where women enjoy a high profile, such as medicine, a disproportionate number of top posts are held by men. In fact, the medical profession wishes to redress the overall imbalance between the sexes by admitting men to medical school with lower grades than women. So whereas in 1960 women constituted 76 percent of Soviet doctors, they now comprise 68 percent of a profession that enjoys a lower status than it does in the West.[10] Concern about the "feminization" (feminizatsiia) of both medicine and school teaching has been expressed in Soviet newspapers. Regarding school teaching it is claimed that a predominance of women teachers has a negative effect on the character development of young boys since they lack male role models and may become weak and passive like women. What is missing here, however, is an analogous critique of the "masculinization" of well-paid and powerful jobs in the economy and politics.

In a similar vein, the growing number of female people's deputies does not tell the whole story about politics. Even though women are well represented in soviets, their membership in the more important CPSU is lower and well below their proportion as citizens. Women make up 53 percent of a large population of over 278 million people and 27 percent of party members.[11] Moreover, their presence in the party hierarchy is much lower than their participation as people's deputies. They comprise 4 percent of the members of the Central Committee of the CPSU and before the Gorbachev era only one woman sat on the Politburo—and that was just for three years, from 1957 to 1960.[12] Recent promotions have indeed been made, such as the appointment in 1986 of Alexandra Biriukova at the twenty-seventh Party Congress to the important Secretariat of the Central

Committee, which liaises with the Politburo and party bureaucracy and in September 1988 to the Politburo. Lower down in the system Svetlana Kasumova was named at the thirty-first Congress of the Communist Party of Azerbaidzhan in 1986 to that republic's bureau and secretariat.[13] This is a powerful combination of posts. But while the number of women in top political posts is increasing, and Gorbachev has committed himself to these increases, the general picture is one of a low female political profile.

Moreover, even where women are more visible than men in politics, they tend to enjoy rather different patterns of involvement. For example, examination of the composition of the 1985 Azerbaidzhan Supreme Soviet shows that even though women make up 39.8 percent of the deputies, they pursue very different occupations from male deputies.[14] Whereas 85 percent of female deputies are factory workers or farm workers, only 25 percent of the males fall into these categories.[15] The bulk of male deputies enjoy high status posts in district party committees, the ministries, Central Committee departments, and administration. In keeping with their higher status male people's deputies enjoy a higher presence on the more important Central Committee of Azerbaidzhan. Whereas 45 percent of male deputies to this Supreme Soviet are also members of the Azerbaidzhan Central Committee, only 10 percent of women fall into this category.[16] The political presence of males is further strengthened by their lower turnover rate on the Supreme Soviet. Only 32 women on the 1980 Azerbaidzhan Supreme Soviet, or 17.8 percent of female deputies, reappeared five years later. By contrast, 152 men, or 56 percent of male deputies, were put forward as candidates and reelected in 1985.[17] So over half of the male deputies enjoyed continuity of tenure compared with under 20 percent of the women.

The higher turnover rate of women combined with their lower professional status must mean that they make less impact on the legislative process. Moreover, among the reelected deputies, males enjoy a much greater mobility across districts than women. This gives them broader experience. In 1985, 40 of the 184 reelected deputies changed the district that they represented. Of these 40 only 4 were women.[18] Of course, the soviets do draw working women into political activity and can be seen as more representative of the broader population than Western parliaments. Yet there is a segmentation of representation according to gender.

Thus despite many advances for women since 1917 their position in the economy and politics differs greatly from that of men. Moreover, the female double burden of work in the labor force topped with a second shift at home—which receives little male support—contributes to lower incentives for career advancement. Cultural patterns and traditional attitudes are often slow to change, notwithstanding the exhortations of ideology to do so. Indeed the commitments made to women in socialist ideology regarding the provision of services have always been extensive.

Table 1: *Preschool Institutions in the USSR* (in thousands)

Year:	1940	1960	1970	1975	1980	1985
Total number of preschool institutions	46.0	70.6	102.7	115.2	127.7	140.1
day-care centers	22.0	27.0	19.6	15.8	12.1	9.6
kindergartens	24.0	37.4	35.4	34.1	32.0	29.4
combined day-care centers/ kindergartens	nil	6.2	47.7	65.3	83.6	101.1

Source: *Vestnik Statistiki*, No. 1, 1987, p. 62.

Since before the revolution the Bolsheviks pledged to ease the strains of family life that fell on women's shoulders. Maternity pay, child-care centers, kindergartens, and public dining rooms have always been supported by Soviet leaders. However, in the early years of the Soviet state resources were scarce and a tension existed between the goals of the state and how much it could deliver. This tension persisted in an acute form for a long time. Services were greatly developed in the 1960s, but throughout the 1970s and into the 1980s, the Soviet press has been pointing out that kindergartens fail to meet the demand for places, particularly in rural areas. In addition, mothers are often anxious about sending children to day-care centers due to the illnesses contracted there. Groups are often crowded and the turnover of instructresses is high due to the low status of the job and low pay. The provision of services has nevertheless increased over the years, as Table 1 shows. The total number of kindergartens and day-care centers rose from 46,000 in 1940 to 140,100 in 1985 and the number of children cared for in them went up from 1,953,000 to 16,140,000. Table 2 gives a more detailed breakdown of these statistics. The expansion of child-care facilities shown here and the development of merged day-care centers and kindergartens after 1959 has been met by

Table 2: *Number of Children in Preschool Institutions* (in thousands)

Year:	1940	1960	1970	1975	1980	1985
Total number of children in preschool institutions	1,953	4,428	9,281	11,523	14,337	16,140
in day-care centers	781	1,313	1,181	1,053	873	685
in kindergartens	1,172	2,756	2,791	2,591	2,387	1,980
combined day-care centers/ kindergartens	nil	359	5,309	7,879	11,077	13,475

Source: *Vestnik Statistiki*, No. 1, 1987, p. 62.

increased expenditure from the state.[19] Although the Soviet system of child care is in some respects inadequate, it does nevertheless look after over 16 million children and continues to grow. Moreover, Soviet sociologists and policymakers are aware of its benefits and inadequacies and with each party congress come renewed commitments to improve the provision of services.

It is regularly admitted that the supply of kindergartens fails to meet demand. At the 1987 All-Union Conference of Women, Valentina Tereshkova, the Soviet pilot and cosmonaut and outgoing chair of the Soviet Women's Committee, pointed out that in 1986 as many as 1.5 million parents were disappointed in their request for places for their children in preschool institutions.[20] She characterized this as a grave problem and went on to regret the high incidence of sickness in kindergartens and day-care centers. Another participant complained that although nine years ago a Young Pioneers camp began to be built in her area, construction had been slow and today the camp still lacks its projected sports complex and swimming pool.[21] Inadequate resources and slow implementation of policies are officially identified as problems. These are no longer covered up. With increasing attention being paid to these shortcomings, there is room for further progress.

In recent years it has become clear that a combination of inadequate kindergarten facilities, women's double burden, and lack of male participation in housework have contributed to working women producing smaller families. One-child families are now the norm in Russia, Belorussia, the Ukraine, Lithuania, Latvia, and Estonia. This contrasts with the picture in Muslim republics, such as Azerbaidzhan, Uzbekistan, Tadzhikistan, and Turkmenistan. Table 3 shows the number of births and deaths per 1,000 population in selected republics, followed by the natural increase in population, which is calculated by deducting the latter from the former. From these statistics it is clear that average figures for the USSR obscure

Table 3: Births, Deaths and Natural Increases in Population in the USSR, Russia, Latvia, Uzbekistan and Tadzhikistan (per thousand population)

Year	1940			1970			1984		
	Births	Deaths	N.I.	Births	Deaths	N.I.	Births	Deaths	N.I.
USSR	31.2	18.0	13.2	17.4	8.2	9.2	19.6	10.8	8.8
Russia	33.0	20.6	12.4	14.6	8.7	5.9	16.9	11.6	5.3
Latvia	19.3	15.7	3.6	14.5	11.2	3.3	15.7	12.9	2.8
Uzbekistan	32.8	13.2	20.6	33.6	5.5	28.1	36.2	7.4	20.8
Tadzhikistan	30.6	14.1	16.5	34.8	6.4	28.4	39.8	7.4	32.4

Source: compiled from Tsentral'noe Statisticheskoe Upravlenie SSSR. Narodnoe Khoziaistvo SSSR v 1984g, Moscow, Finansy i Statistika, 1985, pp. 34–35.

very different patterns across republics. Whereas there were 33 births per 1,000 population in the Russian republic in 1940, the figure fell to 16.9 per 1,000 in 1984. Fewer children per 1,000 population were therefore being born. The natural rate of increase fell from 12.4 per 1,000 to 5.3. A similar trend can be traced in Latvia, although starting with a much lower birth rate and rate of increase. A sharp contrast is provided by Uzbekistan and Tadzhikistan. In 1940 there were 33.8 births per 1,000 population in Uzbekistan and a rate of natural increase of 20.6. The number of births here and in Tadzhikistan has remained very high. In 1984 there were 36.2 births per 1,000 population in Uzbekistan with a natural increase of 28.8. Such a large natural increase makes 2.8 in Latvia and 5.3 in Russia pale by comparison.

These statistics should be interpreted very carefully alongside information about age structures and numbers of men and women in the population. However, without exploring them here, it is safe to conclude that very different life styles and cultural values affect reproduction. In 1985 in Latvia, for instance, women comprised 54.7 percent of the workforce, compared with 38.0 percent in Tadzhikistan.[22] Traditional Muslim values, which stress the importance of large families, encourage women to have more than one child. Divorce is rare among Soviet Muslims, but has been growing among Slavs and Baltic peoples.

Declining family size and an increase in divorce can in part be interpreted as evidence of discontent among some Soviet women. They seem unwilling to rear large families in strenuous conditions and are reluctant to tolerate unsatisfactory marriages. Every year 1.4 percent of married couples divorce, leaving more than 700,000 children up to eighteen years of age to live with one parent. Yet the family remains a popular institution and most Soviet citizens do marry. Aggregate statistics on marriages and divorce are presented in Table 4. These reveal that while the incidence of divorce is increasing, the number of marriages is not declining. According to other official Soviet statistics only 2.6 percent of men in 1985 and 3.5 percent of women between the ages of forty-five and forty-nine had never married. It has been calculated that by twenty-five years of age over 80 percent of women and around 70 percent of men are married.[23] Evidence also suggests that within ten years of divorce, 50 percent of Soviet men remarry, but only 25 percent of Soviet women.[24] We should not, however, jump to the conclusion that divorced women are overwhelmingly rejecting the institution of marriage. Divorced men tend to marry younger women, rather than their peers.

Divorce then is increasing in the USSR among non-Muslims, families are becoming smaller, and yet the institution of marriage remains strong. Both ideology and popular culture stress the importance of the family unit and childbirth. They are portrayed as instrinsically valuable to the individual development of women and as stable elements of socialism. This has

Table 4: Number of Registered Divorces and Marriages

Year:	1970	1975	1980	1985	1986
					(estimate)
Number of divorces (thousands)	636	783	930	933	943
Divorces per 1,000 inhabitants	2.6	3.1	3.5	3.4	3.4
Number of marriages (thousands)	2,365	2,723	2,725	2,718	2,727
Marriages per 1,000 population	9.7	10.7	10.3	9.8	9.8

Source: *Vestnik Statistiki*, no. 1, 1987, pp. 67–68.

been a constant theme of official ideology since 1930. So has the argument that participation in the labor force is essential for women's independence and for socialism. However, different emphases in official ideology can be traced over time and are frequently tied to more practical concerns of economics, politics, and demography. Official images of women have ranged from a "great army of labor" and a "colossal strength against fascism" to mothers, mother heroines, political actors, part-time workers, and home workers.

1930–56: Women as a Great Army of Labor

In 1928 the first economic plan was set into motion under the leadership of Joseph Stalin.[25] His overriding goal was to build the industrial economic base that the USSR so badly needed in order to become a viable socialist state. According to Marxist theory, socialism developed out of the advanced economic base of capitalism. Since the new Soviet state had only islands of industry in a vast "agricultural sea," it needed to industrialize quickly.[26] As revolutions had not taken place in Western Europe it was not possible to draw support from a Western economic base. Stalin, therefore, resolved to build socialism in one country. This entailed forced industrialization "from above," the collectivization of agriculture, and a disciplining of the workforce and family life.

Labor power was needed to meet these goals, so women were encouraged to join the labor force. The propaganda themes of building a great socialist society, the threat of war, and the importance of patriotism helped to mobilize women into the workforce. Female participation in the economy was also spurred on by economic necessity and by the socialist notion that those who do not work do not deserve to eat. In 1928 there were 2.8 million Soviet women working in the national economy. This amounted to 24 percent of Soviet workers. By 1940 the number of women at work had increased to 13.1 million or 39 percent of the total.[27] Throughout

these years ideology stressed that participation of women in the workforce
led to the liberation of women and equality of the sexes. However, the
emphasis of ideological lines was tightly tied to the priorities of economic
policy rather than to liberation itself. In addition, the link between the two
was asserted rather than discussed. Collectivization and industrialization
were claimed to be necessary for equality, but what equality of the sexes
entailed was not reflected on at length.

What then was said about female roles and what images of women were
projected? Throughout the 1930s and 1940s women were portrayed as "a
great army of labor," a "colossal reserve of labor power," the "great
strength" of Soviet socialism, and "the pride of the Soviet people." These
images were linked to women's contributions to the construction of the
economy and to the war effort after the Soviet Union was invaded by
Hitler in 1941.

Media treatment of International Women's Day on March 8 every year
often boldly illustrated the regime's overriding concerns. The front page of
Izvestia on March 8, 1930, for example, carried an article entitled "On the
Anti-Soviet Front," which addressed not women's liberation but the struggle for socialism and its relevance to all workers.[28] Alongside, a large
sketch of an enthusiastic woman driving a tractor over pots and pans
constructed the image of mobilization into the workforce and an end to
traditional domestic roles. Woman's role in productive labor was para-
mount.

Woman's role in the economy was described as a vital component of
socialist construction and was cited to illustrate the liquidation of unemployment. It was argued that the economic roles of women coupled with
early Soviet legislation showed the existence of equality. The general
message of the Stalin years was that "one of the outstanding achievements
of the Great October Socialist Revolution is the complete liberation of
women."[29] This liberation was rather narrowly tied to the class struggle.
Since the triumph of socialism meant that the class struggle had been
resolved, it therefore followed that the liberation of women was part of the
package. Equality of the sexes was seen as a result of more fundamental
changes happening elsewhere. So "from the first day of the October
Revolution" Soviet woman "stood shoulder to shoulder with her husband,
father, and brother in the struggle for a new enlightened life."[30] The
argument ran that the class struggle under capitalism leads to class conflict, which is successfully resolved only by socialist revolution. The
working class is then liberated, which means liberation for working women
and men. Alongside men, argued Stalin, and equal to them, women can
be found in every sphere of the economy and in science and the arts.[31]
Female labor and male labor together advance socialism. In this way, the
Woman Question was subsumed under the human question, which was
answered satisfactorily with the advent of socialism.

The position of women in rural areas was particularly hard due to a heavy manual work load and a prevalence of conservative peasant views. In addition, electricity and running hot water were not common. The literature on rural women, however, did not in the 1930s focus on the various dimensions of their subordination to men. Instead it declared that what stood in front of rural women was not the Woman Question, but "all questions of collective farm development."[32] The small amount of literature on women in these years tended to take the following line: "Woman has now understood that only collective farm life opens a wide road of new things for her and leads to full emancipation from the old oppressed life of need."[33]

The Woman Question was defined relative to broader socioeconomic needs as defined by the political leadership. Theorizing was framed around the priorities of the state, which at this time were collectivization, industrialization, and disciplined families. Similarly, during the Great Patriotic War from 1941 to 1945, Soviet women were described as a "great strength" or "great force" in the war against fascism.[34] They were praised above all for their patriotism and courage. Although these official images of women fitted the needs of the state, they were nevertheless active images. Women were not construed just as passive recipients of the benefits of socialism but also as positive contributors to it.

Throughout the upheavals of the 1930s and 1940s stable nuclear families were a priority and Stalin argued that the family grows stronger as socialism progresses. In part, this fitted a more general reaction against the debates of the 1920s about sexuality and emancipation. Many party members disapproved of the liberation of female relatives and friends and coped better with abstract arguments about emancipation, so long as the result did not touch them. The stress on the nuclear family also coincided with an economic and political context of rapid change, in which discipline at work and the terror of the secret police made life for many both difficult and unsettling. The privacy of the family unit not only gave background support and servicing to a hard working life demanded by the regime, but also provided a largely "safe" intimate circle of moral backing (with some exceptions where family members informed on others). The pace of change in the 1930s meant disruptions in family life, too. Rural dwellers moved to towns to work in factories, farmers pooled their land to live in larger units, kulaks or rich peasants were dispossessed of their land and deported miles from home, and purges meant that family members and friends disappeared overnight and ended up in camps. This disruption was one reason among several for official ideology to bolster the family. Others included concern about birth rates, and by the late 1930s the fear of war. In sum, stable nuclear families were highly desirable for the state for reasons of social change, discipline in the workforce, dislocation, reaction to the liberation of the 1920s, birth rates, and fear of war. Consistent with these official concerns, divorce was made difficult to obtain and costly and abortion declared illegal.

Abortion had been legalized in 1920 on the grounds that it was a necessary evil. In 1936 it was prohibited. Ideology confronted this policy reversal in *ex post facto* fashion by arguing that the object of the new law was the protection of working women's health. It was admitted that abortion was illegal in capitalist systems too. The ban, however, took on a different meaning in different systems. Under capitalism, unemployment and the hard lives of workers made abortion a necessity since large families in such circumstances were unhappy families. Yet the bourgeois state denied women the opportunity to abort.

In the Soviet state, ran the argument, the situation was "entirely different."[35] Abortion was to be prohibited only now that socialism had achieved "exceptional improvements in well-being" and the "prosperity of the working population was increasing with every year, with every month."[36] Abortion was no longer necessary because the nature of Soviet society rendered it redundant. The choices of individual women were apparently irrelevant. Yet again official policies—in this case the promotion of stable families and an encouragement to reproduce—affected the content of ideology.

Whereas the 1920s had seen debates about emancipation, the 1930s brought assertions about female roles. Lively and critical discussions did not take place and the Woman Question was effectively closed. Nevertheless, it was admitted that all was not perfect. Alongside the gushing praise of the Soviet state for liberating women came regret that certain problems still existed. These included the persistence of religious ideas about woman's place and weak Komsomol activity among girls and young women. However, these problems and "the disgraceful distortions of Soviet democracy in Kuibyshevskii oblast," which kept women out of the labor force and politics, were not the fault of Soviet power itself but due to the failure of citizens to follow Soviet policy.[37] Thus, where class war continued and where Islam played a reactionary role, as in Soviet Central Asia and the Caucasus, the liberation of women was cast as part of continuing struggles. As *other* issues were resolved, the Woman Question could be solved.[38] The implication here was that the Woman Question lacked a dynamic life of its own and was seen as highly derivative. It was characterized as lacking any independent solutions and as offering no independent input to other questions. Equality of the sexes was seen as a result of more fundamental changes happening elsewhere in society.

1956–65: Democracy and Female Roles

The Woman Question remained officially solved until the second half of the 1960s. However, this did not stop Khrushchev from raising questions about female political roles at the famous Twentieth Party Congress in 1956.[39] Here he scolded those working in party and state institutions for putting women forward for leadership posts "with timidity."[40] He regretted that women were not visible in top jobs.

This rebuke was consistent with Khrushchev's aim to instill democracy into Soviet politics now that Stalin was dead. The terror of the Stalin years and the totalitarian monolith in which it was embedded was under fire. Khrushchev set out to breathe fresh life back into the party and to mobilize the people into greater participation in society—be it in the soviets, the Komsomol, the party, comrades' courts, or housing committees.[41] Given this preoccupation, Khrushchev inevitably posed the question: Who is active in Soviet politics and who is not? At a time when women made up over 55 percent of the Soviet population, they amounted to 3.9 percent of the Central Committee of the Communist Party. In 1956 there were just 10 women on a Central Committee of 254.[42]

So Khrushchev's speeches, party congresses, and Central Committee resolutions began to refer to women. The late 1950s and early 1960s witnessed official efforts to move female roles onto the agenda where relevant to other prominent issues. More space was devoted to women's issues in *Pravda* and *Izvestiia* on March 8, sometimes extending to coverage on March 9. The Woman Question was more prominent than it had been in the two previous decades, but was still not tackled head-on and certainly not declared "unsolved." On the one hand the Soviet press could claim that socialist construction "brought women liberation, freedom and equal rights" but on the same page could report "the Central Committee of the CPSU calls upon Soviet women to participate more actively in politics and society," thereby implying that the rights women had won were not necessarily exercised to the full.[43] Similarly, the message that socialism had brought "genuine emancipation" to women was juxtaposed with references to the difficulties of combining the roles of worker and mother. It was acknowledged that more kindergartens were needed and local soviets were reprimanded in a Central Committee resolution of 1957 for their lack of initiative in improving public dining rooms.[44] Yet women were still described as "equal."

Some writers, such as Vera Bil'shai, argued that the new Soviet state had not only granted women formal equality in law, but "had done everything" for securing equality in production and administration. Indeed, she claimed that along with the resolution of the national question and the peasant question, "one of the great achievements of Soviet socialist construction is solving the woman question."[45] Others, however, stressed the importance of the Soviet road, but did not claim that all had been accomplished. Ekaterina Furtseva, the only woman ever to have sat on the Politburo, remarked: "Only with the origin of the revolutionary movement of the proletariat was the woman question put on course in practice, only the working class and its vanguard, a Marxist-Leninist Party, indicated the sole correct path for the solution of this question."[46] Furtseva did not here go so far as to proclaim the Woman Question "unsolved." The path was right, but how far down it the Soviet state had trodden was not really discussed. The inequalities of capitalism were over, yet the inequalities of socialism had yet to be explored.

Nevertheless, the Khrushchev years opened up the possibility of delving further into inequalities. Evidence indicated that the lives of women were not as ecstatic as socialist realism had frequently proclaimed. Moreover, it was suggested that women had certain distinct needs. In his attempt to mobilize the people into political activity, Khrushchev argued that a "differentiated approach" to different groups should be adopted.[47] Women, he suggested, constituted a distinct category of the population, just as pensioners and young people did. Different groups had different needs and problems and so in order to draw them into politics a variety of approaches would be necessary. He encouraged lectures, conferences, and discussion for women and the development of *zhensovety* or women's councils.[48] These were women-only groups whose activities were geared to promoting the priorities of the party.

The early post-Stalin years then began to raise questions about female roles that had not been taken so seriously in the 1930s and 1940s. At the Twenty-second Party Congress in 1961 it was announced that "remnants of inequality in the position of women in everyday life must be completely eliminated."[49] Longer maternity leave was granted and more household appliances and public dining rooms were called for.

Given the issues raised in the Khrushchev years and given this cue at the Twenty-second Party Congress, readers of *Partiinaia Zhizn'* (Party Life) should not therefore have been surprised when in 1965 the First Secretary of Turkmenistan argued:

> Profound revolutionary changes have come about in the position of women and their psychology. However far from all has been done to allow women to use their rights and knowledge to the full or to display more completely their talent. There are still many unanswered problems. Vestiges of the past and traditional views still hold back women's development and curb their political and economic activity.[50]

Unanswered problems were edging more squarely onto the agenda. But this did not preclude subsequent articles in the same journal from giving prominence to Soviet success rather than devoting a couple of paragraphs to Soviet shortcomings. It was not until the late 1960s that the Woman Question was officially opened. Although the direction of the Soviet Union under Khrushchev can be viewed as building up to this possibility, the Khrushchev years were a time when theoretical developments lagged behind political statements. It was not until the Brezhnev leadership that it was theoretically possible for the Woman Question to be declared unsolved.

1965–81: Declining Birth Rates, Labor Shortages, and Developed Socialism

So far I have argued that immediately after the Russian revolution there was debate about female roles followed by a period of relative silence under Stalin when the Woman Question was officially "solved." Then renewed discussion took place under Khrushchev, consistent with his broader political goals. How was it possible for the Woman Question to be declared unsolved under Leonid Brezhnev?

In one of his frequent optimistic moments Khrushchev had pronounced that the Soviet Union would see communism in the 1980s. As time passed this prediction became increasingly embarrassing to the Soviet leadership since the probability of such an achievement was low indeed. By introducing the concept of "developed socialism" into Soviet ideology Brezhnev managed to get around this claim. Reformulated ideology maintained that while the fundamentals of socialism had already been built, the Soviet Union was now in the long protracted stage of "developed socialism" or "mature socialism," which had to be passed through before communism could be reached and which was characterized by unsolved problems or "nonantagonistic contradictions." Such contradictions were not serious, since they could be solved without revolution and without a radical change in the economic substructure.[51] The Woman Question thus became "unsolved" and was described as possessing nonantagonistic contradictions.

This change in status affected arguments about equality. The Woman Question now needed to be solved and a lively debate was triggered off about how this could best be done. The newly unsolved status of the Woman Question meant that some action had to be taken to tackle it. In practice, this meant that policies affecting women, such as maternity pay and opportunities for part-time labor, were taken more seriously and additional resources were filtered into them. In keeping with this, in 1981, after just over a decade of debate, women with one year's work experience were eligible for partially paid leave to care for children up to the age of one. Mothers were also allowed to take additional leave without pay to look after newborn babies up to the age of eighteen months. After maternity leave women could return to their jobs with an uninterrupted work record. Before these changes women had been allowed fifty-six days off work before and after childbirth with full pay.[52] More investment was also devoted to expanding child-care facilities and to extending the network of public dining rooms. The production of washing machines and other household appliances increased too.

In the past it had been claimed that equality of the sexes had been won. Now it was proclaimed that "formal equality" or "legal equality" had been established immediately after the revolution. However, "factual equality,"

sometimes referred to as "factual social equality," was being worked toward.[53] So the distinction was increasingly drawn between "equal rights"
and "equality." The latter was much broader, embracing political, economic, and everyday life. Formal equality entailed no more than legislation whereas factual equality demanded changes in behavior and attitudes.
These distinctions had really been glossed over in earlier literature and
some writings of the 1930s had stated that factual equality had already
been won.

Alongside more realistic Soviet writings on equality in the Brezhnev era
came pressing concerns about the Soviet economy. Whereas Khrushchev's
priority of reinvigorating the party had shone a spotlight on women's
political roles, concern about falling economic productivity, declining
birth rates, and labor shortages led the Brezhnev leadership to scrutinize
the relationship between women's domestic and economic roles.

A very serious requirement of the economy—labor—was not only in
inadequate supply, but becoming scarcer. The dilemma was that as a vital
51 percent of the Soviet workforce, women were needed both at work and
in maternity wards. How women could increase their productivity at home
and at work was of increasing importance to the Soviet state.

Throughout the 1970s party congresses drew attention to the double
burden suffered by women. Social scientists began to conduct the most
systematic research into the position of women in society that the Soviet
Union had ever seen. This was helped by the development of research
institutes under Brezhnev, the growth of the social sciences, and greater
collaboration between policymakers and academics. At the same time a
huge debate about female roles took place. The Soviet press, journals, and
books all carried contributions from sociologists, economists, demographers, and lawyers on the position of women. Themes such as the
significance of part-time labor for women, the seriousness of declining
birth rates, the relevance of the availability of services, and the advantages
of further mechanization of the economy were all aired with an enlivened
frankness.[54] The leadership of the CPSU wanted these issues to be discussed for reasons of policy, and official ideology was no barrier to this
since the Woman Question was now officially unsolved. In short, political,
economic, and theoretical context gave space to official debate in a way
that the political context of the 1930s had not.

So with greater determination than ever before policymakers set out to
tackle how best to reduce the female double burden. The main solution to
woman's heavy domestic load, however, was thought to be an increase in
state services. Yet while the emphasis was very much on diminishing the
female domestic load, some economists and sociologists, frequently
women, mentioned the need for all family members to contribute to
housework and suggested the desirability of changes in the structure of
family domestic roles.[55] Zoia Iankova and Elena Gruzdeva, in particular,

made this point. But their proposals were rather timid ones. Iankova qualified her thesis very heavily with the caution that a sharing of the domestic shift was just temporary. The long-term goal of socialism was the "liquidation of these functions." In the meantime, she argued, it did not follow that domestic duties should be divided "in equal parts between men and women."[56] This was not viewed as an issue directly connected to attaining factual equality since state measures rather than personal ones were allegedly the key to the solution of domestic work.

Arguing in this way in the 1970s, Iankova and others by-passed questions of the nature of female/male relations and their relevance to equality. Discourse around the theme of the personal is political was precluded. At best, Iankova maintained that domestic duties should not fall entirely on women's shoulders. It was not until the 1980s that bolder statements were forthcoming and it is unlikely that they would have been voiced at all had it not been for Gorbachev's attempts to shake the Soviet Union into what he calls "new ways."

The 1980s: Current Soviet Policy

The political setting changed again in the USSR with the death of Brezhnev in 1982, the brief leaderships of Iuri Andropov and Konstantin Chernenko, and the accession of Mikhail Gorbachev in 1985. Although no fundamental changes in policy toward women have been outlined, women's issues appear to be taken more seriously by Gorbachev, who displays a willingness to tackle them in policy formulation as well as at the level of political rhetoric. The All-Union Conference of Women held in 1987 picked up some of the threads only touched upon in the draft party program of 1985.

When the new draft party program was printed on the front page of Soviet newspapers in October 1985, updating the previous program of 1961, consistencies with the past were the hallmark of policy toward women. This new document was released in the run up to the Twenty-seventh Party Congress of 1986 and described as a "precongress document." Soviet citizens were invited to study it and to comment on its content before it was finally approved in amended form at the congress.

The draft party program made explicit commitments to women as political actors and mothers. Regarding politics, it announced that more politically mature and competent individuals capable of taking initiative would be appointed to leading jobs. Among their numbers would be women. This echoed the message of the Twenty-sixth Party Congress of 1981 at which it was regretted that "the opportunities for the promotion of women into responsible posts have still not been fully realized. Such a situation ought to be rectified."[57]

Concerning motherhood, the draft party program pledged further improvement in the position of women with children and reiterated its promise to create favorable conditions for the successful combination of motherhood with work in social production. In keeping with this, a longer break from employment after childbirth was recommended and more flexibility in employment patterns was supported, in particular part-time labor for women. In addition, commitment was made to a broadening of the network of sanatoria and rest homes for family relaxation.

The draft party program acknowledged what it called "the great significance for the state" of improving care for the family.[58] The nuclear family was portrayed as playing an increasingly important role in the health care and education of the younger generation, in promoting the social and economic progress of society, and in improving demographic processes. The party program stressed that it is in the family that the basic characteristics of individuals are formed and their attitudes toward work and morality developed. The family, therefore, is an institution to be strengthened.

As expected, these themes were echoed in Gorbachev's Political Report of the Central Committee presented to the Twenty-seventh Party Congress. Problems of strengthening the family were raised yet again. In Gorbachev's words: "The formation of a new family is not a simple matter. It is a complicated process."[59] He went on to regret the high divorce rate, despite a slight downturn, and lamented the existence of unhappy families. Such families, he pointed out, negatively affect the education of children and the moral condition of husband and wife and their participation in economic, social and political activity.

Young families in particular, Gorbachev stressed, need protection. In fact, young people need to prepare for family life. However, the precondition for the solution of many family problems is the creation of work conditions and service provisions that enable women successfully to combine motherhood with active participation in the workforce. In keeping with this, the twelfth Five-Year Plan for the years 1986–90 is committed to further growth of part-time labor for women, to a shortening of the working week, and to the development of work for women to perform at home. In addition, mothers can now enjoy a year and a half's paid maternity leave after the birth of a child. Commitment was also given to meeting the demand for kindergartens through further construction.

As far as women's political roles were concerned, Gorbachev could proudly announce that "women are being moved into leadership posts more actively. They have become more numerous in the composition of the organs of the party and the soviets."[60] And he was right. The recent promotions of Alexandra Biriukova and Svetlana Kasumova were cited above. And connected to the general mobilization of women, Gorbachev recommended that the *zhensovety* or women's councils be revived in the workplace and in residential areas and come under the unified structure of the Soviet Women's Committee. The *zhensovety*, he suggested, could exert serious influence on the solution of a wide range of social questions.

So leadership priorities for female roles in Gorbachev's first year were several: first, a successful combination of motherhood in stable families and participation in the labor force; second, expanding opportunities to work part-time; third, greater promotion into top jobs; and fourth, involvement in the reviving women's councils or *zhensovety*. Before his second year in office was out, an All-Union Conference of Women was organized, which Gorbachev attended. It discussed various ways in which the *zhensovety* could be developed, called for male participation in housework and childrearing, and admitted how women suffered from the "negative aspects" of Soviet society.

As argued above, if the boundaries of discourse continue to widen at their current pace, a much more interesting literature on gender roles may soon begin to emerge. However, the current official ideological lines that surround policies largely reiterate the themes of the Brezhnev era that Soviet socialism has freed women from the economic and social oppression of capitalism and has given women and men equal rights in education, work, and social and political life. Formal equality is guaranteed under socialism, but factual equality is harder to attain.

Equality in a contemporary Soviet context does not mean identical work for men and women or identical roles in the home. This is to be avoided because of "psycho-physiological differences" between the sexes.[61] Women are portrayed as kind, gentle, supportive, nurturing, weak, and in need of protection, whereas men are strong, determined, and capable. Motherhood is a natural pursuit for women, which involves both childbirth and childrearing.

In keeping with this, and consistent with the desire to boost the birth rate of Russians, Belorussians, Ukrainians, and Baltic peoples, literature of the 1980s has started to describe women as a "sociodemographic group."[62] Whereas literature of the 1970s referred to women as possessing "psycho-physiological characteristics" that rendered them different from men, they are now described as having special "anatomical-physiological" qualities that give rise to "sociopsychological characteristics" befitting their "sociodemographic group," which are accompanied by specific needs, interests, and relationships.[63]

Woman's biological and social nature, according to current Soviet ideology, coexist "in complex interaction" since motherhood is influenced by social conditions.[64] Thus the nature of motherhood depends on customs, norms of behavior within the family, the position of women in society, class background, and the legal position of the family.

Ideology contends that because women as a "sociodemographic group" have special needs, interests, and relationships, they occupy a special place in the social division of labor, and have to fulfill a definite social function, which is accompanied by certain moral traits and a particular pattern of life, different from that of men. However, the extent of the differences between the sexes is acknowledged to be unclear. Writing in *Pravda* in 1984 the Soviet psychologist Kon regretted that no one in the USSR had systematically studied the differences between men and women.[65] In her recent book *Women in Developed Socialist Society* Novikova concludes that "women always have been and always will be more or less feminine" and men "more or less masculine."[66] These stereotypes help to block discourse along the lines that men might be caring and gentle, too, and quite capable of rearing children. Indeed, it is the concept of parenting that has hitherto been missing from Soviet writings. If these images of women and men persist, they will create a tension with any future policies to involve men more actively in child care. Either an ideological dissonance will exist or images of gender roles will have to be modified. If some of the sentiments expressed in January 1987 regarding male roles in the home are taken seriously by policymakers, then we may soon see attempts to reconstruct the notion of "masculine." This would challenge dominant stereotypes and could in turn make past ideological silences into current issues.

However, the context in which this would take place would be one that includes propaganda to boost the birth rate. So far, fatherhood has been a largely unknown quantity in this. One 1981 publication that was translated into Russian from Czech argued, in a chapter entitled "Soon a Child in the Family": "Pregnancy and birth are necessary for the female organism. It is well known that after childbirth woman blossoms for a second time, and starts to live a full life. Women who have many children usually look younger than their age and younger than those without children."[67] This line is quite consistent with the policy priorities of the Twenty-sixth Party Congress of 1981, at which it was announced that the Central Committee of the CPSU was giving serious attention to drawing up and implementing a demographic policy to tackle the population problem of declining birth rates among Slavic and Baltic peoples.

Such policy priorities have affected the content of writings on the Woman Question. Not only has the notion of women as a sociodemographic group become popular, but in the 1980s it is argued that solving the Woman Question is explicitly tied to solving demographic problems. One sociologist has contended that the Woman Question is of growing importance to the Soviet state and has now taken on a new significance. Its fresh topicality is explicitly tied to "the problems of encouraging a growth in the birth rate and rearing the future generations."[68] Given the difficulties women experience in having a job, producing many children, and suffering a double burden, policymakers may be concluding that the best way to encourage larger families is to call for a male mini "double shift" too. Many women, it seems, are refusing to accept the load on their own.

Interestingly, the boundaries of the Woman Question in the 1980s have, on the one hand, become very narrow. This question is linked to the specific goal of increasing family size. Yet paradoxically at a time when such limited concerns are stressed by some, particularly demographers, those who produce more general books and articles on ideology in the USSR and those who take a more historical approach to the position of women, give the Woman Question immense breadth, as permitted by the concept of developed socialism. These authors emphasize that the complexity of solving the Woman Question is now connected in the abstract to processes of social integration, attaining social homogeneity, achieving equality, developing democracy, and pursuing communist morality.[69] And Gorbachev's rather flexible notion of *perestroika* is providing more space for some redefinition of gender roles. Its companion—*glasnost*—facilitates exposure of the negative aspects of women's lives. With this greater relaxation under Gorbachev more elements of the acknowledged complexity of the Woman Question are being examined. Before long these could include more sophisticated discussions of male roles and of various forms of female subjugation under socialism.

Historical Roots of the Arguments of the 1980s

How then do ideological concerns of the 1980s compare with past Soviet ideology on women? It seems that current ideology draws together various strands of the past. For example, Khrushchev's goal of mobilizing women into politics and of recruiting more women into prominent posts in party and state structures is reiterated today. The differentiated approach to political mobilization is popular in the 1980s, along with the recognition that women constitute a distinct category of labor, with special needs separate from those of men. Therefore, special institutions such as the *zhensovety* are necessary to cater to these needs.

Discussions about the significance of special institutions for women date back to early Bolshevik history. Before the revolution in 1917 there was suspicion in the party of female institutions. They were thought to smack of "bourgeois feminism," to divide the working class, and to divert attention from revolutionary goals. In short, their emphasis was thought to fall in the wrong place. Class, not gender, was the main focus for socialists. A vanguard party was the crucial institution to direct the working class, not distracting feminist offshoots. This mistrust of institutions tailored to women persisted in the 1920s. The *zhenotdel*, or Women's Department of the party, was only reluctantly accepted by some male party members on the grounds that women workers were more backward than males and in need of special encouragement. Much criticized in the 1920s, it was disbanded in 1930.[70]

The revitalization of the *zhensovety* should be viewed against this historical backdrop. At the Twenty-seventh Party Congress in 1986 Gorbachev did recommend that they be revived, but he also suggested that they be organized in a more structured and hierarchical fashion under the umbrella of the Soviet Women's Committee. Although their role was discussed at the special Conference of Women in 1987, as yet it remains unclear precisely what form this restructuring will take. It is possible that party control over the *zhensovety* will tighten, even though Gorbachev is stressing the need to enliven politics by a broader participation of nonparty members. Nevertheless, one should not dismiss the new commitment to the *zhensovety* out of hand. They are special institutions for women. At a time of change, fresh opportunities for women may open up, especially if women become inspired to use these institutions to their advantage. The same can be said of the recent Conference of Women. Such women's conferences have historical precedent in the USSR and in the 1920s convened at the local level several times a year.[71] If they were to become a more regular event throughout the Soviet Union, they could be harnessed not just by the CPSU to get its messages across to women, but also by the women participating in them to define future agendas.

Whereas Khrushchev's drive to mobilize citizens into political activity continues, so Brezhnev's support for part-time labor for women wins increasing backing from the Soviet state. The Twenty-seventh Party Congress applauded the commitment of the Twenty-sixth Congress of 1981 to this, and also extended official backing. The theme that it is one way to render the combination of motherhood and work in productive labor possible is one that was raised in the 1960s, debated in the 1970s, and conclusively agreed to in the 1980s.

The topics that are not addressed in the same way as they were in the past are those of sexuality under socialism and domestic labor. Sexual relations are mentioned in the 1980s, but not in the way in which Kollontai approached them.[72] Where Kollontai had talked about the changing nature of female/male relations, current Soviet ideology stresses the durability of the nuclear family structure and the desirability of early marriage and early childbirth. This has been a recurring theme since 1980. Today it comes across rather loudly in Soviet writings and media. One Soviet television program shown in December 1985 was entitled "Children of the Twenty-first Century." The camera focused on a room packed with Soviet students with their children sitting on their knees. The questions put to them all revolved around the topics of the difficulties and advantages of being students and parents. The replies of the students coincided with the sentiment that it was much better to have children while one is young and that families should not be put off until education is over. The central message was that the joy of parenting is overwhelming, and why put off until later what can be achieved today. Sex manuals are being produced in the 1980s, but as we have already seen, they are geared to the goal of "soon a child in the family" rather than to a general discourse of how female/male relations might change with historical context.

Just as writings on sexuality have moved away from Kollontai's central concerns, so too articles on domestic labor are inspired by different preoccupations from those of Inessa Armand in the 1920s. Armand argued that the success of socialism depended on changes within the family.[73] This argument no longer takes the same form. It was, however, returned to in the period of debate about female roles in the 1970s, as illustrated above, and is receiving even more attention in the 1980s.

Publications are beginning to point out that an unfair distribution of household responsibilities leads to female discontent in marriage. Since the stability of family life is a Soviet goal and seen as a prerequisite of large families, the possible positive correlation between female overwork in the home and the incidence of divorce and the definite link between the double burden and smaller families have forced male roles onto the ideological agenda. If men assumed domestic roles, not only would the female double burden be alleviated, but marriage might be more stable, divorce less likely, and more children a possibility.

Before the 1980s Soviet ideologists were reluctant to develop a firm thesis on male domestic roles. Whereas ideological tracts pushed motherhood for women with little hesitation, the most that was said in connection with male domestic roles was that they were desirable but that an itemized distribution of family chores was unnecessary. In sum, it seemed that male roles edged onto the agenda not because of their relevance to equality per se but because of their significance for easing the female double burden, lowering the divorce rate, and producing larger families. Only with the All-Union Conference of Women in 1987 was there explicit reference to an "equal" division of domestic chores.

Conclusion

The Soviet Union has often been criticized by writers in the West for possessing an ideology that misrepresents reality. The charge is that ideology suggests all in the Soviet garden is rosy, when in fact serious problems in the economy, society, and politics are obvious to any informed observer. Ideology therefore does not fit reality, but distorts it; it fabricates a false picture that is distant from the lives of Soviet citizens; ideology specifies how leaders would like the USSR to appear, rather than how it actually is.

These accusations are somewhat simplistic. Although numerous examples could indeed back them up, the evidence cited would overlook the significance of the changing content of Soviet ideology. The nature of the discrepancy between Soviet ideology and Soviet reality has in fact changed over time, and there are historical, political, economic, cultural, and theoretical reasons for these alterations. I have argued above that not only has the content of Soviet ideology on women carried different emphases in different periods of Soviet history—alongside certain ongoing consistencies—but that these changes can be understood only by locating them within the broader context of policy priorities of a given leadership.

Seventy years have now passed since the Russian revolution. Despite the Soviet regime's consistent theoretical support for equality of the sexes, evidence suggests that in each period of Soviet history the formulation of women's issues has been relative to other policy priorities. It is the CPSU that draws up policy and defines the relevance of women to policy priorities and the significance of policy for women. Rather than being discussed head-on in their own right, women's issues are subordinate to other overriding concerns. In keeping with this, there are no women's organizations outside the party or official trade unions to speak for women's independent interests. These are thought to be unnecessary since the CPSU works for everyone. Separate women's institutions, runs the official line, would therefore be divisive and serve to pander to the mistaken views of bourgeois feminism. The growth of unofficial women's organizations in 1979 and the publication of the first feminist *samizdat* was met with official disapproval and harassment.[74]

The productionist bias of Marxism-Leninism has pervaded policy since the 1930s. Female roles in the paid workforce and in the home have been applauded and women have been encouraged to remain productive in both spheres. The nuclear family remains an officially revered institution and traditional gender stereotypes persist: it is "natural" for women to be feminine and to please men and appropriate for men to be strong and to protect women. Sexuality is rarely discussed critically. A very conservative society with traditional cultural values does not help to promote debate on these topics.

Must we then conclude on a negative note? Perhaps not. There are, after all, a myriad of historical, economic and cultural reasons why the USSR could not have progressed at a faster pace or shaped the Woman Question to fit the predilections of Western feminists. Although Soviet women are largely absent from the key decisionmaking arenas, and despite the fact that a division of labor according to sex persists in the paid workforce and in the home, the Woman Question is at least recognized and addressed in ideology and in policy. Women's issues are indeed in the public arena.

Moreover, within the broadening limits acceptable to the system recent publications are becoming more critical of the status quo and more probing questions are now being put by women writers. Novikova, for example, recently asked why it is that when a woman works well she is described as "clever woman" rather than a "clever worker" and when she makes a mistake it is attributed to a "woman's brain." By contrast, when errors are made by men they are the individual mistakes of Pavel and Ivan and have nothing to do with the sex of the person involved. These "psychological barriers" in attitudes to women, criticizes Novikova, coexist alongside progressive laws for women.[75] More work in this vein may lead to a heightened sensitivity toward the mechanisms and forms of male domination over women. While there is currently little literature in this area, the possibility of its developing should not be ruled out.

Furthermore, so long as the concepts of nonantagonistic contradiction and developed socialism allow for problems to exist under Soviet socialism, difficulties in women's lives will remain on the official agenda. Even though these are generally cast as relative to other policy priorities and not formulated by women in groups independent of the CPSU or trade unions, they are nevertheless aired. Moreover, the acceptable limits to debate are widening under Gorbachev due to the changes demanded by *perestroika* and the criticisms of Soviet society encouraged by *glasnost*. Despite the fact that institutions concerned with women's issues are "official" ones, they do have a potential to influence aspects of policy by making recommendations.

These institutions are various and crop up at different points of the Soviet system. For instance, the Supreme Soviets in the republics and at the All-Union level have standing committees concerned with women's work, motherhood, and daily problems. Similarly, the trade unions employ economists who conduct research into the position of women in the labor force, paying special attention to working conditions. The revived *zhensovety* have a rather undefined potential, but could be harnessed to pursue several issues. One report from Soviet Azerbaidzhan indicates that in this Muslim republic they promote ties with women in other Soviet republics, spread "atheistic education," and call for better clothes for women, improved health care, and more kindergartens. They are currently raising questions too about the high level of chemical fertilizers in the countryside and the effect of these on children's health.[76] Rather different sets of questions about the position of women are explored by academics working in the universities and in the research institutes of the Academy of Sciences. So the "official" indigenous bases of questioning and critique are relatively broad. They also provide access points for Soviet citizens with complaints. Women with grievances can turn to the trade union or to a deputy to the local soviet, who is very likely to be based in their factory or workplace. Newspapers also print letters on a wide range of topics about Soviet life and women frequently air their views here. Similarly, the local soviets and party institutions receive thousands of letters every year on numerous topics.

So it is very likely that the Soviet future will see more lively and wide-ranging critiques of aspects of the Woman Question, albeit constrained by official priorities. But these priorities sometimes coincide with women's needs and can be used by women. Recent statements quoted in the Soviet press from the 1987 Conference of Women testify to this. One participant announced: "I think that in reconstructing society, it is necessary to reconstruct men."[77] And another from Soviet Uzbekistan frankly declared:

> With pain we must say that in our republic there is a high infant mortality rate. This is undoubtedly connected with the poor organization of medical services. On top of this, not everything is right with the production of children's food. It is just not being produced in our factories. We should ask the appropriate ministry to examine this question.[78]

If statements continue in this vein, Soviet literature on women in the next few years will burst out of past ideological straitjackets and address overdue topics with enlivened frankness. The nature of discourse about women could become very eclectic, contradictory, even volatile, but much richer. And there are likely to be disagreements among specialists about how to tackle various problems. Nevertheless, issues such as violence against women and the need for more contraception are likely to be addressed by the policy process as well as the theoreticians.

The Woman Question generates complex issues in the USSR of the 1980s, which in turn overlap with questions of economic productivity, promotion, discrimination, self-determination, nationality, fertility, child care, health, housing, gender roles, personal relationships, political leadership, the nature of institutions, and the use of ideology. Soviet theorists currently acknowledge that there are no simple solutions and admit that as soon as one batch of issues has been tackled, others will emerge. Thus, the Woman Question is seen to be one that changes its form over time. It is dynamic, protracted, and far from clear cut.

Notes

I am grateful to the British Council, the Soviet Ministry of Higher and Special Education, and the Society for Cultural Relations with the USSR for trips to the Soviet Union in 1979, 1980, 1984, and 1985. Without these some of the information used here could not have been gathered.

1. For discussion of the role played by the CPSU in Soviet society see Ronald J. Hill and Peter Frank, *The Soviet Communist Party*, 2nd ed. (London: Allen and Unwin, 1983).
2. Exploration of ideas on women in nineteenth-century Russia and into the early twentieth century can be found in Richard Stites, *The Women's Liberation Movement in Russia* (Princeton: Princeton University Press, 1978), and in Linda H. Edmondson, *Feminism in Russia, 1900–1917* (London: Heinemann, 1984).
3. Inessa F. Armand, *Stat'i, Rechi, Pis'ma* (Moscow: Politizdat, 1975), pp. 67–70.
4. *Bakinskii Rabochii*, January 31, 1987, p. 2.

5. Ibid.
6. "V Pomoshch' Agitatory i Propogandisty: Zhenshchiny v SSSR," *Vestnik Statistiki*, 1 (1986): 53.
7. Narodnoe Khoziaistvo SSSR v 1984g (Moscow: TsSU SSSR, Finansy i Statistika, 1985), p. 11.
8. Ibid.
9. Further details can be found in Gail Warshofsky Lapidus, *Women in Soviet Society: Equality, Development and Social Change* (Berkeley: University of California Press, 1978); Norton T. Dodge, "Women in the Professions," in Dorothy Atkinson, Alexander Dallin, and Gail Warshofsky Lapidus, eds., *Women in Russia* (Sussex: Harvester, 1978), pp. 205–24; Michael Paul Sacks, *Women's Work in Soviet Russia: Continuity in the Midst of Change* (New York: Praeger, 1976); and Martin McAuley, *Women's Work and Wages in the USSR* (London: Allen and Unwin, 1981).
10. *Zhenshchiny v SSSR 1984* (Moscow: TsSU SSSR, Finansy i Statistika, 1984), p. 11.
11. *Narodnoe Khoziaistvo SSSR v 1984g*, p. 6; *Vestnik Statistiki*, no. 11 (1986): 72.
12. This was Ekaterina Furtseva. She was relieved of her post on the Politburo, then called the Presidium, on becoming Minister of Culture. She retained this position until her death in 1974.
13. *Bakinskii Rabochii*, February 2, 1986.
14. Further details can be found in Mary Buckley, "Female Workers by Hand and Male Workers by Brain: The Occupational Composition of the 1985 Azerbaidzhan Supreme Soviet" (Paper presented at the Annual Meeting of the Political Studies Association, Nottingham, April 8–10, 1986).
15. *Bakinskii Rabochii*, February 28, 1985.
16. Ibid.
17. Ibid.; *Bakinskii Rabochii*, February 28, 1980.
18. Ibid.
19. *Vestnik Statistiki*, no. 1 (1987): 58.
20. *Bakinskii Rabochii*, January 31, 1987.
21. Ibid.
22. *Vestnik Statistiki*, no. 1 (1987): 51.
23. *Vestnik Statistiki*, no. 1 (1987): 67–68.
24. Ibid.
25. An accessible introduction to Soviet history can be found in J. P. Nettl, *The Soviet Achievement* (New York: Harcourt, Brace and World, 1970). A more detailed discussion of political change is presented in Mary McAuley, *Politics and the Soviet Union* (Harmondsworth: Penguin, 1977), and Jerry Hough and Merle Fainsod, *How the Soviet Union Is Governed* (Cambridge: Harvard University Press, 1982).
26. More detailed treatments of Soviet industrialization can be found in Maurice Dobb, *Soviet Economic Planning Since 1917* (London: Routledge & Kegan Paul, 1966); and Alec Nove, *An Economic History of the USSR* (Harmondsworth: Penguin, 1982).
27. Lapidus, *Women in Soviet Society*, p. 166.
28. *Izvestiia* is the daily newspaper of the Soviet of People's Deputies of the USSR and *Pravda* is the daily newspaper of the Central Committee of the CPSU.
29. *Izvestiia*, March 8, 1949.
30. *Pravda*, March 8, 1936.
31. *Pravda*, March 8, 1939.
32. *Izvestiia*, March 8, 1933.
33. V. Frolov, *Zhenshchiny v Kolkhozakh—Bol'shaia Sila*, Partizdat, Severnoe Kraevoe Otdelenie, 1934, p. 17.
34. *Pravda*, March 8, 1945; V. C. Murmantseva, *Sovetskie Zhenshchiny v Velikoi Otechestvennoi Voine* (Moscow: Mysl', 1979), p. 178.
35. Z. Tettenborn, "Materinstvo v Sovetskoi Strane," *Vlast Sovetov*, June 11, 1936, p. 7.

36. Ibid.
37. *Izvestiia*, March 8, 1937.
38. Saida Iman Zade, "Osvobozhdenie Azerbaidzhanki—Odno iz Vazhneisikh Zavoevanii Velikoi Oktiabr'skoi Sotsialisticheskoi Revoliutsii (1917–1939)" (Candidate degree diss. abstract, Baku, 1954).
39. It was at this Congress that Khrushchev condemned Stalin for his cult of personality and method of rule. See *Khrushchev Remembers*, trans. and ed. E. Crankshaw (Harmondsworth: Penguin, 1977).
40. *Pravda*, February 15, 1956.
41. George W. Breslauer, "Khrushchev Reconsidered," in Stephen F. Cohen, Alexander Rabinowitch, and Robert Sharlet, eds., *The Soviet Union Since Stalin* (Bloomington: Indiana University Press, 1980), pp. 50–70.
42. Lapidus, *Women in Soviet Society*, p. 219.
43. *Pravda*, March 8, 1957.
44. "Postanovlenie Tsk KPSS o zadachakh partiinoi propagandy v sovremennykh usloviiakh," January 9, 1960, in *KPSSv Rezoliutsiiakh i Resheniiakh S"ezdov, Konferentsii i Plenumov Tsk*, Vol. 8 (Moscow: Izdatel'stvo Politicheskoi Literatury, 1972), p. 49.
45. Vera Bil'shai, *Reshenie Zhenskogo Voprosa v SSSR* (Moscow: Izdatel'stvo Politicheskoi Literatury, 1959), pp. 3–4.
46. *Pravda*, March 8, 1960.
47. "Postanovlenie Tsk KPSS o sostoianii i merakh uluchsheniia massovopoliticheskoi raboty sredi trudiashchikhcia Stalinskoi oblasti," March 11, 1959, in *KPSS v Rezoliutsüakh i Resheniiakh S" ezdov, Konferentsii i Plenumov Tsk*, Vol. 7 (Moscow: Izdatel'stvo Politicheskoi Literatury, 1971), p. 516.
48. For further details see Genia Browning, "Soviet Politics—Where Are the Women?" in Barbara Holland, ed., *Soviet Sisterhood* (London: Fourth Estate Books, 1985), pp. 207–236.
49. *Materialy XXII S"ezda KPSS* (Moscow: Gosudarstvennoe Izdatel'stvo Politicheskoi Literatury, 1961), p. 393.
50. B. Ov-ezov, "Vydvizhenie i Vospitanie Zhenskikh Kadrov," *Partiinaia Zhizn*, January 1969, p. 9.
51. For discussions of "developed socialism" see B. Mochalov, *Requirements of Developed Socialist Society* (Moscow: Progress Publishers 1980), p. 40, and Alfred B. Evans, Jr., "Developed Socialism in Soviet Ideology," *Soviet Studies*, 29, no. 3 (1977): 409–28.
52. L. Rzhanitsina, *Female Labour Under Socialism: The Socio-Economic Aspects* (Moscow: Progress Publishers, 1983), and Vera Tolkunova et al., *Women in the USSR* (Moscow: Progress Publishers, 1985).
53. S. V. Brova, "Sotsial'nye Problemy Zhenskogo Truda v Promyshlennosti" (Candidate degree diss. abstract, Sverdlovsk, 1968), p. 4; and Elena Gruzdeva, "Uchastie Zhenshchin v Obshchestvennom Proizvodstve Kak Forma Realizatsii Ikh Ravnopraviia v Sotsialisticheskom Obshchestve," in E. Klopov, ed., *Vo Imia Cheloveka Truda* (Moscow: Profizdat, 1979), p. 182.
54. For elaborations of the positions put forward see Lapidus, *Women in Soviet Society*, pp. 285–334; and Mary Buckley, ed., *Soviet Social Scientists Talking: An Official Debate About Women* (London: Macmillan, 1986).
55. E. E. Novikova, T. N. Sidorova, and S. Ia. Turchaninova, *Sovetskie Zhenshchiny i Profsoiuzy* (Moscow: Progress Publishers, 1984).
56. Zoia Iankova, "Razvitie Lichnosti Zhenshchiny v Sovetskom Obshchestve," *Sotsiologicheskie Issledovaniia*, no. 4 (1975): 42.
57. *Materialy XXVI S"ezda KPSS* (Moscow, 1981), p. 72.
58. *Bakinskii Rabochii*, October 26, 1985.
59. Ibid., February 26, 1986.

60. Ibid.
61. A. E. Kotliar and S. Ia. Turchaninova, *Zaniatost' Zhenshchin v Proizvodstve* (Moscow: Statistika, 1975), p. 6.
62. E. E. Novikova, *Zhenshchina v Razvitom Sotsialisticheskom Obshchestve* (Moscow: Mysl', 1985), pp. 9–32.
63. Ibid., pp. 9–11.
64. Ibid., p. 10.
65. Cited in ibid., pp. 14–15.
66. Ibid., p. 15.
67. N. M. Khodakov, *Molodym Suprugam* (Moscow: Meditsina, 1981), p. 99.
68. Rzhanitsina, *Female Labour Under Socialism: The Socio-Economic Aspects*, p. 73.
69. Novikova, Sidorova, and Turchaninova, *Sovetskie Zhenshchiny i Profsoiuzy*; R. I. Kosalapov et al., *Developed Socialism: Theory and Practice* (Moscow: Progress Publishers, 1983).
70. For early Bolshevik arguments about women and criticisms of the Zhenotdel turn to Ann Bobroff, "The Bolsheviks and Working Women, 1905–1920," *Soviet Studies* 26 (October 1974): 540–67; and Carol Eubanks Hayden, "The Zhenotdel and the Bolshevik Party," *Russian History*, 3, part 2 (1976): 160–66.
71. P. M. Chirkov, *Reshenie Zhenskogo Voprosa v SSSR (1917–1937)* (Moscow: Mysl', 1978).
71. Alexandra Kollontai, *Selected Writings*, trans. Alix Holt (New York: W. W. Norton, 1977), pp. 237–49.
73. Armand, *Stat'i*.
74. Alix Holt, "The First Soviet Feminists," in Holland, *Soviet Sisterhood*, pp. 237–65; Mary Buckley, "Soviet Religious Feminism as a Form of Dissent," *Topic: 40* (Journal of Washington and Jefferson College) Fall 1986, pp. 5–12.
75. Novikova, *Zhenshchina v Razvitom Sotsialisticheskom Obshchestve*, p. 69.
76. *Bakinskii Rabochii*, February 1, 1987.
77. *Izvestiia*, February 2, 1987, p. 4.
78. Ibid., p. 3. Indeed there is a good reason for concern about relatively high infant mortality rates in the USSR. Since 1970 they have been increasing in rural areas and have not decreased much in towns. An official Soviet source recently released the following statistics:

Number of Child Deaths Up to the Age of One Year (per 1,000 births)

Year	Total	Urban	Rural
1970	24.7	23.4	26.2
1980	27.3	23.5	32.5
1981	26.9	22.8	32.7
1982	25.7	22.2	30.7
1983	25.3	21.7	30.6
1984	25.9	21.9	31.8
1985	26.0	21.7	32.0

Source: Vestnik Statistiki, no. 12, 1986, p. 71

Socialist Emancipation:
The Women's Movement in the German
Democratic Republic

Barbara Einhorn

Socialist Emancipation vs Feminism: The Frame of Reference

The German Democratic Republic (GDR) has had a policy of combating sex discrimination, indeed of positive discrimination toward women, since its foundation in 1949. This means that independence, forthrightness, initiative, career ambition, and confidence in one's rights as an equal member of society are taken for granted by women as well as by men. Contradictions originate in the fact that these gains have been made largely in the field of paid labor. The level of women's qualifications has been raised immeasurably, equal pay for equal work has been implemented since 1946, and women have made substantial inroads into many formerly male-dominated occupations and sectors of the economy. However, the converse is not true: there has been no marked shift of men into traditionally female occupations. Moreover, there is very little awareness in the GDR of gender-defined behavior patterns as they affect social relations, particularly at the level of personal/domestic life. The feminist concept that the personal is political, which has filtered through to many fields of public life in the West, is virtually unknown in the GDR and contravenes the prevailing ideological framework. This explains why what is known about Western feminism tends to be misinterpreted or maligned.

The situation now emerging exemplifies Hilda Scott's observation that emancipation in the countries of "socialism as we know it" has been seen, on the whole, as something given to women without taking anything away from men.[1] To put it another way, men never envisaged that they would have to change themselves as well as the laws in order that women should be enabled to develop their full potential. A possible explanation for this is that the limitations in the concept of emancipation emanate directly from the GDR's espousal of classical Marxist theory on the situation of women as formulated by Marx, Engels, Bebel, Zetkin, and Lenin. This legacy provides stability and gives the legitimacy of historical continuity to the

GDR's endeavors in favor of women, yet simultaneously explains the exclusion from the parameters of official discourse of whole areas of concern to women, such as those of personal autonomy and sexuality (Kollontai, for example, is not regarded as an integral link in the historical chain). The confines of this framework are that emancipation is attained through participation in social production, with child care and domestic labor being largely socialized in order to facilitate this participation. Concentrating on the socialization of domestic labor as an aid to emancipation has had the effect of excluding domestic social relations and the division of domestic labor from official discourse.

What is not on the agenda, therefore, is any discussion or evaluation of the theoretical contribution that Western feminism may have to make, both because of the closures operating in the theoretical framework adopted by the GDR and because of what is seen as the reformist nature of Western feminism. The latter's highlighting of issues surrounding sexuality and self-awareness is seen as a diversion from the main goal of socialist revolution. In focusing on the sensationalist media view of Western feminist concerns to the exclusion of a wider reading of feminist literature, an academic volume on the situation of women in the GDR oversimplifies and misrepresents the Western movement.[2] Even while conceding the heterogeneous composition and diverse demands of the women's movement in the West, the authors simultaneously condemn the "crass" actions of "bra-burning extremists." Kuhrig and Speigner suggest that what they term "neo-feminism" in the West mistakenly substitutes gender warfare for the class struggle and hence concentrates on the need for ideological change rather than on the abolition of capitalist production—and social—relations. The authors conclude from this that the women's liberation movement is not merely tolerated by the imperialist system as not constituting a threat to it, but that, worse, it "ultimately stabilizes the capitalist social system."

Perhaps paradoxically, the flow of information and influence in women's issues operates between the two Germanies in precisely the opposite direction to most assumed influence, namely from East to West. The practice of the GDR has had a far greater influence on women's struggles in West Germany than has the latter's theory on the thinking of GDR women. The only partially successful and subsequently undermined campaigns in West Germany to reform para. 218 of the Penal Code (which restricted and still restricts access to legal abortion) and to extend paid maternity leave on the model of the GDR's so-called baby year are cases in point.[3]

The Democratic Women's Federation of Germany (DFD— Demokratischer Frauenbund Deutschlands): Aims and Achievements

The economic, legal, and social status of women in the GDR as workers, as mothers, and as individuals is undeniably far in advance of that enjoyed by their sisters in West Germany and many other Western capitalist countries and even that in the other countries of "socialism as it actually exists." The credit for this achievement must go in large part to the efforts of the Demokratischer Frauenbund Deutschlands (DFD), the official (and only) women's organization in the GDR.

From its inception in 1947, the DFD saw itself as inheriting and perpetuating the Marxist tradition on the question of women, but with one important distinction. Their comrades in the Soviet Union followed Stalin's mechanistic interpretation of history, whereby the "Woman Question" (the double exploitation of women under capitalism analyzed by Marx, Engels, and Bebel) would automatically be resolved following the overthrow of capitalist property relations. The German Communists and Social Democrats returning from exile in the Soviet Union at the end of World War II differentiated themselves from this view. They felt that social relations and attitudes did not change spontaneously, but required conscious direction and ideological guidance. In this they based themselves on Lenin rather than on Stalin.

As a consequence of this difference in perception, the Demokratischer Frauenbund Deutschlands was founded, whereas several other Eastern European socialist countries considered it unnecessary to have an organization independent of the Communist Party concerned solely with women's issues.[4] As early as October 1945, before the formation in 1946 of the Sozialistische Einheitspartei Deutschlands (SED—the Socialist Unity Party, the ruling party in the GDR), antifascist women's committees were set up to involve women in the laborious task of sorting through and clearing the rubble left by the Nazi-wreaked devastation of Germany. The DFD grew out of these antifascist women's committees and was founded in March 1947.

From the outset, the DFD saw its task as twofold: (1) mobilizing and educating women in a political sense, encouraging them to participate in the democratic reconstruction of Germany, and (2) mobilizing them to break out of their domestic fetters (to which Nazi ideology had confined them) by entering the sphere of social production. The latter aim was never conceived of purely in terms of expediency, motivated by the acute shortage of male labor power following the decimation of the male population during the war. Rather, it was always viewed as the essential precondition for emancipation, not only in terms of the economic independence from men that women would thereby gain, but also in terms of social labor being the crucial ingredient in the development of individual consciousness and the unfolding of personal potential.

The DFD was later responsible for initiating and drafting legislation on behalf of women in the GDR. The Act for the Protection of Mother and Child and the Rights of Women, an all-embracing piece of legislation that laid the basis for all subsequent laws regarding women, was promulgated in

1950, in advance of all relevant United Nations (UN) conventions, with the exception of the Convention of March 1950 prohibiting slavery and prostitution. This act provided for the creation of state child-care facilities, maternity grants, and paid maternity leave, for revisions in marriage and family law, and for measures designed to help women improve their level of qualification and gain access to previously male-dominated occupations. Similarly, the 1946 decree of the Soviet military administration giving women equal rights in all spheres and equal pay for equal work predates the relevant UN Convention (no. 100) by five years.[5]

The DFD is enabled to play such an influential role in legislating on behalf of women and in monitoring the implementation of measures in their favor in part by virtue of its fixed quota of seats in the Volkskammer, the GDR parliament, where it enjoys the same status as a political party. With its 32 seats, it accounts for a large proportion of the 161 seats held by women and 6.4 percent of the total 500 seats in the Volkskammer.[6] In a sense, however, these very figures point to the curiously anachronistic position of the DFD today.

The anachronism arises from the fact that 80 percent of all women of working age in the GDR are currently employed outside the home (as compared with 32 percent of West German women). Yet the DFD has continued to gear its activities toward what now constitute minority groupings: full-time housewives, women temporarily out of the workforce (for example on maternity leave), tradeswomen and craftswomen (or the wives of men in this private sector), and women in the churches.[7]

The DFD's aims have remained constant too, namely encouraging those not already doing so to become involved in social production by conducting political, cultural, and educational activities centered on residential and especially rural areas. For example, the DFD is involved in various projects to give a facelift to old towns or to build or renovate child-care facilities, often providing voluntary labor for such projects. Also at the residential level, it has representatives on school committees.

Two other central concerns of the DFD help to reinforce its somewhat stereotypical gender-defined image: the advice centers it runs to give hints on household maintenance and decor, diet and nutrition, child care and marriage, aimed primarily at young couples contemplating setting up house together; and the organization of waste collection for the recycling of raw materials. Recycling is a major undertaking in the GDR due to the fact that raw materials often have to be imported, costing scarce hard currency, so that the DFD's activity in this area is of central importance. The DFD is also active on the international level, working for world understanding and peace within the International Democratic Women's Federation.

It might be said, therefore, that the activities of the DFD are mainly concentrated in areas traditionally viewed as "women's work" and largely unremunerated. In addition to household maintenance and holding a special brief for peace, they pick up other people's rubbish. This participation in the recycling of raw materials is the DFD's sole direct contribution to the fulfillment of the economic plan, an objective that dominates GDR life. In fairness, however, one must point out that the DFD's efforts to educate women operate not, as is so often still the case in the West, within a framework geared simply to making them better mothers, but in terms of widening women's horizons both politically and culturally, encouraging them to change their lives and assert their concerns in the public arena.

The problematic nature of the DFD's constituency is bound, however, to become an issue over the next few years. With its membership of just 1.5 million out of a total adult female population of over 5 million, it remains the only organization specifically oriented to the needs of women, with the exception of the trade union women's commissions operating at the workplace level in large factories. In addition, only 25 percent of the DFD's membership is under thirty-five as compared with 45 percent of the female population as a whole.[8] Can this organization continue to be seen as representative of all women's interests? Surely the question of how adequately women are represented at their place of work will become more crucial than their education at the residential level? Or will the DFD, by espousing gender issues as yet not addressed in the GDR, be able to ensure that it remains an organization relevant to women's current needs?

The Representation of Women: Politics and the Trade Unions

At the workplace level, there are several structures designed to ensure that equality for women becomes more than a paper right. The function of the women's commissions, set up by the Politburo of the ruling Sozialistische Einheitspartei Deutschlands (SED) in 1952 in agricultural and industrial enterprises employing large numbers of women, is to police legislation affecting women, to delegate women to courses of further education open to them through so-called women's promotion schemes (Frauenförderungspläne), and to support the appointment of women to more senior posts.

In 1965, these women's commissions were subordinated to the enterprise trade union committees. While official GDR sources interpreted this change as giving the women's commissions more clout, one can argue that their role has in fact become subordinate to the trade union in substance as well as in structure. This argument is lent some weight by the following somewhat paternalistic extract from directives on the women's commissions issued by the FDGB, the federation of trade unions in the GDR:

> Enterprise trade union committees shall be fully responsible for their [the women's commissions] activities, for giving guidance to them and instructing

their members. They shall ensure that decisions, laws, and documents important for the responsible work of the women's commissions are explained to them and provide them with the relevant analyses and information.[9]

Aside from the issue of subordination to the trade union, the women's commissions exist only in enterprises employing large numbers of women—hence women working in traditionally male-dominated sectors of the economy, where they still constitute a minority of the workforce, lack this kind of representation and support.

Female membership in the trade unions as a whole accounts for 53 percent of the total (as compared with only 23 percent in West Germany), and 48 percent of shop stewards are women. The latter figure of course includes the members of the women's commissions in large enterprises. At the national level, while women comprise 45 percent of the executive of the FDGB, they make up only 20 percent of its ruling council.[10]

The GDR justifiably vaunts the fact that women participate in public and political life to a far greater extent than do their counterparts in the West. Many hold positions of public responsibility. Twenty-five percent of local mayors are women; 47 percent of residential area arbitration commissions are female; county, district, and borough councils average 40 percent female representation. At the national level, there are 161 women in the Volkskammer (People's Chamber, the GDR parliament) holding 32.2 percent of the total 500 seats. This percentage representation of women compares with only 5 percent in the U.S. House of Representatives and 2 percent in the U.S. Senate. This very impressive figure must nevertheless be viewed within the GDR context where the SED and not the Volkskammer constitutes the most important decision-making body in the country. Yet the 35 percent of SED members who are women have only 13 percent representation on the Central Committee and no full members on the Politburo. As GDR spokespeople will readily admit, women have a diminishing presence in the higher echelons of political structures in the GDR.[11]

Economic Needs and Ideological Commitment: Measures for the Promotion of Women

The GDR's commitment to women's emancipation was couched from the outset not only in terms of involvement in the production process and economic independence from men, but also in terms of the full development of individual potential. It would therefore be inaccurate to see the host of legal and social measures in favor of equality purely in terms of the shortage of labor power in the aftermath of war and of the large-scale exodus of GDR citizens prior to the closing of the border in 1961. One concrete example of this ideological commitment to full equality is that the GDR is the only one of the Eastern European socialist countries to have systematically transformed universal rhetoric on the subject of child-care facilities into an almost totally available reality. In 1986, 81 percent of children under three were cared for in day-care centers; there was kinder-garten provision for 89 percent of three- to six-year-olds, and the trained supervision of 84 percent of six- to ten-year-olds in after-school day-care centers facilitated full-time work for their parents. [12] The 1988 report of the GDR's Central Statistical Office on the fulfillment of the 1987 National Economic Plan states that places in kindergartens and after-school day-care centers were sufficient to meet demand. In fact the proportion of three- to six-year-olds in kindergartens has fallen during the 1980s and is now back to its 1979 level. This reflects not only the increasing number of women taking advantage of extended maternity leave provisions, but also a slight degree of resistance to full-time day care on the part of young mothers who themselves attended such day-care facilities as children.

The reader may wonder how nonsexist the practice of these institutions is, or if they do take care to give all children equal access to dolls and cars, caring and technical skills, and just how effective this is in breaking down the conditioning many of the children still receive at home. While the preamble to the Education Law stipulates equal rights and equal opportu-nity for girls and women in education, to be achieved in part by positive discrimination, this applies mainly to the generation that is already work-ing. For the younger generation, equality of educational opportunity is assumed. Hence the decree on preschool facilities requires that they "shall ensure a harmonious physical, mental, and linguistic training of children and the formation of socialist qualities and modes of behavior and encour-age their independent activity," but there is nowhere any mention of the need to break down gender-based differentiation. There was a passing reference, in the report to the Ninth Party Congress of the Central Committee of the SED in 1976, to the need to overcome "obsolete traditions and habits" in the next generation. That this need exists is exemplified in research into gender-based attitudes among GDR school and preschool children. Results showed that by the time children started school at six years of age, traditionally stereotyped preconceptions about whether boys or girls are cleverer, better behaved, have more fun, and so on, were firmly entrenched in both sexes. [13]

Extremely generous maternity benefits enable women to stay at home on full pay for a year after the birth of child—the "baby year" as it has become known. And monthly child benefit payments were raised in May 1987 by over 100 percent for the first and 500 percent for the second child. A women's job must be held open for her throughout the duration of this year, and if she is a lone parent unable to find a day-care place for her baby after this time, the leave may be extended up to the child's third birthday. [14]

While a cynical view might suggest that both child-care facilities and maternity leave exist only in order to combat the declining birth rate of the 1960s and 1970s, this interpretation could not be justified with reference to the facts. For, unlike several other socialist countries of Eastern Europe, the GDR did not, for example, revoke its abortion law in the face of the falling birth rate.[15] Indeed the wording of the Abortion Act (passed somewhat belatedly in 1972), albeit somewhat patronizing in tone, makes clear its commitment to the principle of women's autonomy on this issue:

> The equality of women in education and vocation, in marriage and family makes it necessary to leave it to the discretion of women themselves to decide whether and when to have a child . . . Women have the right to decide on their own responsibility on the number and timing of children they bear and shall be able to decide upon this through a termination of pregnancy.

Free access to birth control (mainly the pill) for all women over sixteen regardless of marital status (in a society heavily committed to marriage and the nuclear family) and to abortion gives women in the GDR a degree of control over their own fertility that is but a dream to most of their sisters elsewhere in the world.

Hence it must be said that although the GDR is undoubtedly anxious to raise the birth rate, and has succeeded in halting its decline since the introduction of extended maternity leave in 1976 and 1978, it has simultaneously preserved women's right to reproductive self-determination.[16] Expanding child-care facilities and the baby year give women discretion over when to return to work if they have small children, while the availability of birth control and abortion allows them to choose whether and when to have children in the first place.

Underrepresentation at the Top: Some Causes

The main thrust of policies designed to achieve equality has been in the sphere of social production. This emphasis has its legal reflection in Article 20 of the GDR Constitution: "Men and women shall be equal and have the same rights in all spheres of social, political, and personal life. The promotion of women, particularly with regard to vocational qualification, shall be a task of society and the state." The undoubtedly impressive achievements of this policy may be seen in figures showing that the number of women workers classified as semi- or unskilled fell dramatically in the period 1970–85. In 1986, 82 percent of women workers counted as having completed training.[17]

Women have made substantial advances in formerly male-dominated professions, accounting in 1977–79 for 45 percent of judges, 30 percent of lawyers, and in 1983, for 57 percent of dentists and 52 percent of doctors. (According to 1987 statistics, only 4 percent of lawyers and 16 percent of doctors were women in the United Kingdom; 15 percent of judges and 14 percent of lawyers were women in West Germany, as were 23 percent of doctors and 20 percent of dentists; and only 8 percent of lawyers, 6 percent of dentists, and 17 percent of doctors were women in the United States.) Nevertheless, there is a disproportion between the number of women working in certain professions or sectors of the economy and the percentage in posts of responsibility. In education, where women accounted for 77 percent of the GDR workforce in 1985, only 32 percent of head teachers and a very low figure of only 7 percent of college and university lecturers and fewer still professors were women. While 45 percent of the workforce in agricultural production cooperatives (LPGs) are women, as of 1983 only one in six of these cooperatives was headed by a woman.[18]

This disproportion raises many questions, for the women's promotion scheme was specifically introduced to raise the level of women's qualifications with a view to promoting them to responsible posts. Yet the Central Committee Report to the Eleventh SED Party Congress in 1986 makes only vague, perfunctory mention of further efforts to fulfill women's special needs. This would seem to indicate that current policy assumptions regard equality as having been achieved, hence there is no perceived need for further measures involving positive discrimination for women.[19]

The causes of continuing underrepresentation toward the top of professional and political pyramids are complex. They may be attributed to structural factors, which in turn tend to perpetuate outmoded discriminatory attitudes on the part of husbands and colleagues. An example is the greater absenteeism on the part of women: it is still mothers who take time off work tending sick children, as it is working mothers with two or more children who are entitled to paid leave in order to do so. How can such absenteeism be compatible with the demands of a responsible post? The fact that more men than women are employed at high levels at the present time makes these men ostensibly less dispensable than their wives, tending to provide a further structural reason for women to go on being the absentees, which in turn perpetuates the situation. In addition, generous maternity leave provisions mitigate against career enhancement for women in a situation where work is still regarded as synonymous with full-time and continuous paid employment. There are very few innovations in terms of part-time or flexi-time provisions in the GDR. New legislation introduced in 1986 gives husbands or grandmothers the option of staying home during the "baby year." Although utilized by only a tiny minority of men until now, this legislation may provide potential for future change in gender-divided career hierarchies.

It appears that many women themselves decline to take on positions of responsibility, whether at work or in a political capacity. In the absence of substantive change in the division of domestic labor, women feel, like their Western sisters, stressed and overstretched in their dual role as mother and worker, hence may well reject what they see as a potential third role as manager of an enterprise or as public figure within the political structures.[20]

In recent years there has been official recognition of women's underrepresentation in decisionmaking bodies, whether at work or in the administration of the state, and public policy has been committed to improving the situation. The FDGB stressed at its Ninth Congress in 1977 that "the proportion of soundly educated and talented female college and technical school graduates has grown remarkably in all sectors of the national economy. The time has come now to raise the question concerning their systematic appointment to responsible positions. The trade unions should redouble their influence in regard to this matter, primarily in sectors where the overwhelming majority of staff members are women."[21]

It is significant, first, that this imbalance has existed even in sectors of the economy dominated by women; second, that efforts to redress the balance are to be made specifically in those sectors rather than in the economy as a whole; and third, that these sectors continue to be the ones traditionally dominated by women. This trend is exemplified in 1986 statistics for selected occupations. They show a predominance of women in the caring professions (health—84 percent female employment, social welfare—93 percent); education—77 percent; and in the service sector (broken down into commerce and trade—72 percent, secretarial and administrative—77 percent, commercial cleaning—99 percent, hotels and restaurants—92 percent).[22]

Within the industrial sector too, women are more heavily concentrated in those branches that have historically had a predominantly female workforce. In the textile and clothing industry, women comprise 69 percent of the workforce, these figures differing little from those in West Germany and Britain (64 percent and 48 percent, respectively). This tendency is confirmed and even exacerbated by figures for the percentage of women apprentices in selected occupations in the GDR in 1986. Here we see that 95 percent of trainee salespersons and hairdressers are women, as are virtually 100 percent of trainee secretaries, while only 9 percent of those being trained in machine building are women, as are only 8 percent of apprentices in the construction industry. These statistics also imply that the trend is worsening, since current female participation rates in heavy industry are much more favorable than these apprenticeship figures suggest.[23]

While women in the GDR have made significant inroads into formerly male-dominated occupations in industry and agriculture, especially when compared with female participation rates in Western countries, the converse is not true. In their useful short article on women in the GDR, Taylor and Vanovitch claimed, for example, that only one in one hundred nursery teachers was a man.[24] In part this is a question of attitudes, but more concretely it is a matter of money. No man is going to become a nursery or primary school teacher when he could earn far more as a skilled industrial worker. Skilled day-care workers in particular are relatively poorly paid. Hence the care and education of young children, which is given a nominally high status as a socialist task, and the social functions of cooking, cleaning, typing, and serving are still largely "women's work" in the GDR today. There is no government policy to lure men into these fields by means of higher material incentives or even ideological exhortation.

Uncomfortable Partners: Equality and the Dual Role

There is a more general sense in which the complex problems of inequality outlined above are structurally determined. This arises because all the measures for equality and the encouragement of women in the GDR are expounded within a context that explicitly accepts the dual role of women as a natural "given." The program of the SED states, in a formulation similar to that contained in the GDR's Labor Code:

> The GDR will make every effort to create everywhere conditions enabling women to make ever fuller use of their equal status in society and allowing for further improvements in women's working and living conditions. The consolidation of women's status in society and the development of their personality require determined efforts to ensure that women can reconcile the demands of their job still more successfully with their duties towards child and family.

This acceptance of women's dual role reappears in the report of the SED's Central Committee to the Eleventh Party Congress in 1986, though as achievement rather than goal, the report lauding the successful creation of the necessary "preconditions to enable women to better harmonize employment, social commitment, and maternal duties, which generally benefits family life."

It is significant that the phrase regarding measures to enable women to "do full justice to their noble function as mothers" in the 1966 Labor Code was excised in the 1977 version, but all legislation continues to refer to women as workers *and* mothers without any attempt being made to classify men as workers *and* fathers. The reality of the dual role thus enshrined in law is clearly reflected in figures based on market research done in the GDR showing that women are responsible for 80 percent of domestic labor, in effect putting in virtually another forty-hour week on top of their full-time shift outside the home.[25]

The implications of this definition have long been recognized at an official level, as the following extract from the report of the Central Committee to the Eighth SED Congress in 1971 makes clear: "What matters now is the gradual solution of all those problems which determine whether women are really able to make full use of their equal rights. . . . Without underestimating the help given by men in the household, it remains a fact that the main burden is borne by women."

The solution proposed by the Eighth SED Congress and confirmed as the correct approach by the Ninth Congress in 1976 is to develop further the socialization of domestic labor, namely by expanding child-care facilities, workplace canteens and restaurants, and laundry and dry-cleaning facilities (there are no launderettes in the GDR), and making available a wider range of prepared and frozen foods, as well as improving the distributive and service sectors in order to shorten (women's) time spent on shopping, household maintenance, and repairs. The Tenth and Eleventh Party Congresses in 1981 and 1986 make no explicit mention of ongoing problems in the domestic division of labor, nor do they address themselves to measures for the resolution of any such problems, again appearing to confirm the assumption that equality is now taken as given and hence as requiring no further state intervention to guarantee its implementation in everyday life.

Women only are also entitled to a so-called household day off work on full pay once a month. Positive discrimination introduced in 1976 in an attempt to deal with the problems of the dual role was the extension of the forty-hour week—until then restricted to mothers of three or more children and shiftworkers—to mothers of two or more children. The normal working week is still forty-three and three-quarters hours spread over five days. This step introduced from above as an interim measure to alleviate the double burden had the opposite effect from that intended, namely to reinforce the traditional division of labor. A letter in the magazine *Für Dich* (No. 30, 1976) pointed this out, asking why the forty-hour week could not have been made available to either parent, to be agreed by the partners in mutual discussion based on individual circumstances. In fact the shorter working week is explicitly barred to men, as is the household day, unless the man is a single parent (still unusual for men in the GDR) or his "wife is certified ill by a doctor"(!).

Consciousness-raising: The Role of Literature

Limiting the conceptual framework means that many of the more subtle aspects of emancipation, the questioning and reappraisal of social roles by individual women, do not receive a hearing in GDR political debate. The fate of the anthology of short stories entitled *Blitz aus heiterm Himmel* (A Bolt from the Blue) exemplifies the restricted hearing given to, and hence limited dissemination of, some broader feminist issues. [26] In its original conception, the *Blitz* volume was to contain an equal number of stories by male and female writers. Each author was asked to fictionalize the experience of waking up one fine morning to find oneself transformed—not, like Kafka's Gregor Samsa (in *The Metamorphosis*) into a fearsome insect-like creature, but into the opposite sex. Some of the male authors who were approached seem to have regarded this prospect as no less horrific, so that they felt unable to countenance such a possibility, even in fiction. Then there were the publishers. Initially they welcomed the idea, but there were difficulties on presentation of the completed manuscript that delayed publication for several years. The questioning of male-dominated social structures and of gender-based role differentiation implied in many of the stories appears to have been more than the publishers were prepared to take. Only after court proceedings for breach of contract were initiated against them with the backing of the official writers' union of the GDR did the volume eventually appear. Even then it had an edition of only 8,000, which represents a limited edition in the context of the mass readership existing on the GDR literary scene. Subsequently, the publishers have resisted all demands for a second edition.

Issues rarely dealt with in public discourse include violence against women—rape and wife-beating—and the whole area of sexuality and identity, sexuality and autonomy, including homosexuality. While the mass weekly *Für Dich* spent its earlier years encouraging women to be forthright in their relationships with men and to make a life alone if necessary, the extraordinarily high divorce rate in the GDR has led to discussions on how to mend rather than end marriages. [27]

Homosexuality has not since 1967 had the extrasocial stigma of illegality, but it was until very recently regarded as an unfortunate abnormality to be treated with compassion and tolerance but avoidance. A medical comment in the first issue of *Für Dich* for 1986 points out that prejudice against homosexuals is still widespread, resulting in discrimination with regard to employment opportunities. Homosexuality is taken in this column's abstract terminology to apply to either sex, but it remains largely true that in advice columns and other public comment lesbianism is neither explicitly acknowledged nor directly addressed.

Violence against women belongs to a whole area of social reality that the GDR has difficulty in publicly acknowledging. This situation arises from the mechanistic view that with the abolition of private ownership of the means of production, all forms of exploitation would automatically disappear. For this reason rape, mugging, and other forms of violence against the person have no official existence, so that it is almost impossible to gain any idea of the scale of such problems. Interesting questions remain unanswered, such as whether the immeasurably higher status of women in the GDR has meant a decrease in such offenses, or how often they occur compared with the West.

Some of the issues excluded from public debate, as well as the contradictions that are publicly discussed, are finding expression in recent literature in the GDR. It is precisely because of literature's sociological—or in this case one might say consciousness-raising—function in providing often the only forum for topical problems to be aired that the authorities are so sensitive about writers and their views. Western onlookers often fail to grasp the significance of this multiplier function, especially since the impact of literature is so incomparably greater than it is in the West, as a result of the cultural policy followed in the GDR in earlier years. This policy aimed to make literature accessible not just to an intellectual elite, but to the mass of the people. Writers were exhorted to use simple colloquial language. In addition, educational policy and the provision of library facilities were designed to raise the reading level of the population as a whole. The outcome has been a mass readership for all literature, not merely for detective fiction or historical romance. Novels are published in far larger editions than in the West and tend to be sold out almost immediately.

An example is Maxie Wander's *Guten Morgen, Du Schöne* (Good Morning, Beautiful One) a volume of first-person testimony by GDR women of varying age, occupation, and family status.[28] It was the first published work in the GDR in which women spoke for themselves with a previously unheard frank and explicit expression of their frustrations, hopes, and aspirations, including their feelings about their own sexuality. Its impact was sensational, both at the private level and in public, where both theater and television dramatized excerpts from it.

In a reflective essay on Maxie Wander's protocols, the internationally acclaimed GDR author Christa Wolf observes that women in the GDR are in a position, on the basis of the tremendous gains in status and self-confidence they have made through their legally guaranteed economic and social equality, to pose new questions, to widen the horizon of their aspirations, encompassing social relations in their entirety.[29] They are asking, maintains Wolf, not "What do we have?" but "Who are we?" in a search for identity and meaning within the framework of a socialist future. With a newly acquired consciousness based on cooperation rather than on domination, the women speaking in Wander's protocols are questioning the inherited hierarchical structures and "rational" models of behavior that have so crippled and emotionally debilitated men. The vision implied in these women's aspirations as interpreted by Wolf is that of a truly humane society whose norms are based not on expediency, pragmatism, and rationality, but on sympathy, self-respect, trust, and friendliness—a society of fulfilled and liberated individuals.

In the West German edition of Wander's book, a revised version of Wolf's essay is included as an introduction. In the GDR, despite the fact that the book has had many reprintings as a result of its dynamic effect on discussions of the frustrations and aspirations of women, the Wolf essay with its positive speculation on possible future social relations has remained confined to the minority readership of the literary journal in which it first appeared. Wolf herself has furthered her analysis of gender relations in more recent works set in a historical context. In her speech on receiving the Büchner Literary Prize in 1980, she uses the world of nineteenth-century author Georg Büchner's plays. Her revitalization of the Cassandra story (1983) treats this contemporary theme against the backdrop of Greek mythology.

Some of the more subtle, less visible problems involved in the struggle to realize the equality legally guaranteed women have been expressed in short stories by young women writers.

In "Bolero," Helga Königsdorf gives a grotesque twist to her portrayal of one woman's reaction to perceived emotional exploitation by men.[30] After years of "being there" for her married colleague and lover, being "available" at his convenience and "at his service" both sexually and domestically—he likes a good meal with his sex—in a relationship that has long bored her and she would leave were it not for her fear of loneliness, the female narrator takes her revenge. She feels resentful and exploited, robbed of initiative and autonomy in a situation where not only does she feel sexually and emotionally used, but even her intellectual creativity gains him credit at the institute where they both work. One fine day she tips him over the balcony of her twelfth-floor flat, just as he is getting dressed before returning to respectability. No one questions, she remarks, musing whimsically as to why she did it, the fact that such a careful and "proper" person should have committed suicide without his shoes on.

The wry humor of this story is a new ingredient in GDR literature. It is characteristic of several stories by women authors exposing contradictions and the persistence of gender-based social relations with which women have to contend on a daily basis.

One particular target has been the superwoman image much publicized by the media, the woman who "masters" her dual or triple role effortlessly, holding down a position of responsibility at work, being an exemplary wife and mother and active on school parents' or party political committees as well.

Several stories by women suggest through irony that it is possible to achieve such superefficiency only with the help of magic, a means totally incompatible with scientific socialism. One such story is Charlotte Worgitzky's "Karriere Abgesagt" (Farewell to a Career), in which a woman "confesses" as to how she made it to superwoman status.[31] Her secret lies in the help of an angel (probably female, she thinks), who grants her the ability not to need sleep. Hence the six to twelve hours that most people require for sleeping are hers for the fulfillment of her double shift. While awaiting her turn at a televised presentation of medals "in honor of our best people," of whom she is the only woman, she wonders about this: "I had the suspicion that they, like me, had made a midnight pact, but even before I was called onto the stage, the light dawned. The fundamental difference between me and those honored with me was: they were men. The wives sitting in the audience will be the ones who cope, who see to and deal with all the things for which I need my night-time hours."

New Developments: The Women's Peace Movement

The aspirations as well as the dissatisfactions voiced in literature about women's role will reverberate throughout GDR society over the period to come. It must be borne in mind, however, that the difficulties implied in this literature and in the pages of *Für Dich*, while they may appear similar to those faced by women in the West, occur on a fundamentally different level. This results both from the legal and social realization of the preconditions for women's emancipation, and from the greater self-awareness and self-confidence enjoyed by women on the basis of these preconditions. In this respect we are witnessing a transitional period, one in which women have a crucial role to play. These developments will be watched with great interest by socialist feminists everywhere.

The writer Christa Wolf feels that women in the GDR are in the unique situation of having reached a new level of self-expression on the basis of their social situation, while continuing to shoulder multiple responsibilities. But perhaps this in itself avoids their becoming, like so many men, single-track—emotionally imprisoned in and crippled by rigid career hierarchies. The structural impediments preventing most women from reaching the top of the pyramid can be viewed, Wolf suggests, as an advantage, enabling women to retain a broader and more all-embracing vision of a future where social relations would be structured not by dominance and subordination, but by true equality and mutual respect.

But if women have the vision, the question remains as to whether their voices will be heard and taken seriously. In *Cassandra*, Christa Wolf turns to Greek mythology in order to address this question.[32] In parable form she links these questions of socialist feminism to the wider issues of war and peace facing us today, on which our whole future depends, not merely its shape in terms of gender relations.

Cassandra was blessed with the gift of prophecy, but when she spurns the god Apollo's love she is cursed by him. The curse consists in not being heard, not being given credence; indeed worse, for as a messenger she is held responsible and blamed for the message she brings. What she foretells is the destruction of Troy; she warns that this destruction will be self-inflicted—the inevitable outcome of preparations for war, which undermine all the cultural and moral values of Trojan society, even to the extent that an external enemy is "invented" to justify the military buildup. (The parallel in today's arms race, its consequences in terms of anxiety levels and the undermining of the social fabric this brings, as well as in the treatment meted out to voices of warning from the women's peace movement, is striking.) The reaction to Cassandra's prophecy is incredulity, which turns to vindictiveness, even in her beloved father, King Priam. She is proclaimed insane, locked up in isolation in a tower, for years on end, and is finally killed by the "enemy" whose booty she has become, yet whose face, says Christa Wolf, resembles Cassandra's own.

Parallels abound between Wolf's portrayal of the Cassandra story and the present-day cold war situation. In the GDR, as in many Western countries, women increasingly speak out with an independent voice against the dangers of the escalating arms buildup. The women at Greenham Common have experienced a whole spectrum of reactions to their opposition to Cruise missiles, paralleling those Cassandra was subjected to by the Trojan power structures. They have been ignored, locked up and derided, declared mad, and labeled punk lesbian extremists, pronounced dead by media silencing, yet their symbolic strength and worldwide impact persists, based on the fact that political, juridical, and military authorities have been at a loss to know how to handle these women as resisters and voices of warning.

Within the women's movement both in Britain and West Germany there have been debates about the feminist implications of the women's peace movement. Does it represent a step backward, into women's role as mother and nurturer with a special responsibility for the sustenance of life and hence for "keeping the peace"? Or is it the manifestation of a new strength, the expression of a new voice such as that envisaged by Christa Wolf, pointing in the direction of a better future? Whatever the answers, women have raised their voices and have been heard globally. The debate has itself leapt over the cold war divide, like an unquenchable fire jumping a carefully cleared firebreak, igniting discussion among women in the GDR, a discussion fanned by the winds of change.

In the GDR, a loose-knit group of friends and acquaintances formed themselves into the Women for Peace. The group has had an impact far beyond its numerical strength. First involved on behalf of their men, in supporting the families of those men imprisoned as conscientious objectors, the women became active on their own behalf in 1982.[33] This followed the promulgation, in March of that year, of a revised law on conscription, without the prior public discussion stipulated by the GDR Constitution in relation to laws involving matters of fundamental importance. A new clause in this law provided for the conscription of women in times of emergency, with call-up to take effect at any time, in preparation for hypothetical future conflict situations.

Several hundred women wrote letters to Erich Honecker, head of state of the GDR, declaring their opposition to war as a viable means of conflict resolution in the present era, where we stand "on the brink of a nuclear abyss," and hence their unwillingness to serve in the armed forces.

During 1982 and early 1983 it seemed that the women were being treated, like Cassandra, with disbelief—not taken seriously. The Constitution guarantees citizens the right to a reply within thirty days to such petitions. The women never received a reply. Instead, they were summoned, individually, to be questioned at their place of work or in their homes and were asked questions such as which man had "put them up to it." This response angered the women and made them bolder, more determined to be heard. They are opposed to all nuclear weapons (indeed many of them are pacifists, and their insistence on addressing both superpowers stands in conflict with official GDR policy, which while committed to multilateral nuclear disarmament, in effect addresses itself only to the problem of American missiles on the grounds that the United States has been responsible for the escalation of the arms race at every stage). The women's courageous stance subsequently became more openly expressed in small-scale public demonstrations. This did gain them a hearing—with the state security police, who held several of them for questioning on various occasions.

Yet the women did have an effect. Call-up procedures, instigated in the autumn of 1983, shortly before the West German government decision to deploy Cruise and Pershing missiles and the consequent GDR decision to accept the deployment of Soviet SS21s and SS23s on its territory, were curtailed abruptly after effective demonstrations by the GDR Women for Peace. Dressed in black, about thirty of them had congregated on the Alexanderplatz, the central square in East Berlin, in order collectively to post their refusals to report for medicals.

Following this incident, four women were arrested and two of them imprisoned for six weeks on charges of treason. This allegedly involved the gathering of information that, if passed to citizens of another state, could potentially be used to damage the interests of the GDR. What seemed to worry the state security forces most of all about the women's actions, including their wish to maintain contacts with women in the Western peace movement, was their potential as a basis for grass-roots activity, which might be perceived as a political threat and could not therefore be tolerated.

As in the case of the Greenham women in Britain, the single most threatening thing about the Women for Peace seems to have been their ability to organize spontaneously and without an apparent hierarchy of authority or leadership. The inability to identify "ringleaders" or organizational structures, and the realization that women can organize in a non-hierarchical way yet speak with a collective voice, baffled the GDR authorities just as much as it did their British counterparts. Eventually, the charges against the two Women for Peace members were dropped and they were freed (unlike Cassandra), free to continue their courageous opposition to the nuclear threat that clouds our future. Meanwhile, their government—and the DFD and the official Peace Council with it—has continued to oppose only NATO warheads, deeming Soviet missiles necessary to the maintenance of peace and the defense of socialism. [34]

Conclusion

The situation of women in the GDR is both unique and of crucial significance in the struggle to achieve socialist feminist goals. On the one hand, state intervention in the legal, economic, educational, and social spheres has achieved an internationally unprecedented degree of self-determination for women, coupled with the guarantee of rights for which Western women still struggle. Simultaneously, the nature of central control operative in the countries of "socialism as we know it" ensures that women's voices, be they expressed in a literary forum or raised against the nuclear arms race and the militarization of society, will not only be heard, but will also be situated at the precarious leading edge of what it is possible to say and do to change society.

Women's freedom to move and develop in new directions is therefore circumscribed—not least by organizational constraints. There is no easy access to photocopying or other duplicating facilities, nor does everyone have a telephone, so that the "telephone tree" type of rapid communication for organizing actions begun by the Greenham women in Britain is not a viable option for women in the GDR. Neither is it easy to meet and discuss the issues, since all meetings involving more than seven people are required to be reported and officially authorized. Hence the mechanisms for possible future change in the situation of women in the GDR remain unclear. The contradictions expressed in literary form or in the media have no alternative outlet in public debate, other than within the framework of the DFD itself, and it remains an open question as to whether this organization will prove able to adapt itself to the changing needs of GDR women. There is currently no prospect of an alternative, grass-roots women's movement such as that represented by the Western feminist movement, since the emergence of such a grouping could be perceived as an alternative political organization and hence as a threat to the state. It is in this context that the state security forces have attempted to label the Women for Peace as dissidents, a characterization that conflicts with their own self-image.

Despite the constraints, the gains already made by women in the GDR and the strength and potential of their views make their voices ones that all socialist feminists will want to hear. What happens to women in the GDR over the next few years, the directions they take toward full self-expression, and the way the development of their potential affects and shapes GDR society as a whole—these are questions of vital relevance to women's struggles all over the world.

Notes

This is an updated and revised version of an article written for *Women's Studies International Quarterly* 4, no. 4 (1981). A version of it appeared in the journal *East Central Europe* 14–15 (1987–88): 211–48.

1. Hilda Scott, "Eastern European Women in Theory and Practice," *Women's Studies International Quarterly* 1 (1978): 189–99.
2. Herta Kuhrig and Wolfram Speigner, eds., *Zur gesellschaftlichen Stellung der Frau in der DDR* (Leipzig: Verlag für die Frau, 1978).
3. After a long campaign involving many setbacks as a result of opposition from the conservative Christian Democrats and Bavarian Christian Socialists as well as the Catholic church in West Germany, limited reform of para. 218 was achieved in 1976, four years after the GDR promulgated its Abortion Act. The West German law allowed abortion on four grounds only: medical (danger to the woman's life), eugenic (the baby would be abnormal), ethical (the pregnancy is the result of rape), and emergency or need (a vague catchall that embraces financial hardship and gives leeway for, while not specifically allowing, social reasons). In the first two cases, abortion is legal within the first twenty-two weeks, but in the latter two only within the first twelve weeks. This time limit is a seriously limiting factor in a context where the woman can*not* decide on her own responsibility, as is the case in the GDR, but only after consultation with an approved counselor and a doctor other than the one who performs the abortion. The consultations can cause serious delay. Moreover, the Catholic church has conducted a sustained campaign to reverse even this limited reform. In 1984, the CDU government of the Federal Republic launched a Foundation for Mother and Child—to Protect Unborn Life, funded initially with DM50 million per year. This was specifically designed to persuade couples or women contemplating abortion on economic grounds to rethink, offering them grants for baby clothing and equipment, subsidizing accommodation and offering assistance with debt repayment, as well as paying the mother to stay at home while bringing up the child. Not surprisingly, women's organizations were very skeptical of this move, as Alice Schwarzer explains in "Die Klima-Wende um den Abtreibungsparagraphen" (*Der Spiegel* 40, 1.10.84). Pro Familia counseling centers, which support the view that all children should be wanted children, stated their determination not to accept monies from this foundation on the grounds that this would make a mockery of unbiased counseling.

   In many areas of solidly Catholic Bavaria, it is now impossible to obtain a legal abortion. The Bavarian state judiciary prosecuted a gynecologist and 156 of his patients in September 1988 for supposed offences against para. 218, in a court case labeled "the Memmingen witches' persecution" by opposition political parties and protesting women.

   On maternity leave, a new law of July 1979, again several years behind the relevant GDR laws, allowed women in West Germany to take four months' leave at a fixed rate of pay (DM750 per month) in addition to fourteen weeks' maternity leave, making a total of seven and one-half months. During this period, a woman's job was to be held open for her. Despite the fact that these provisions are considerably less generous than those applying in the GDR, they have been severely eroded by the present West German government. The DM600 to be paid for one year after the child's birth by the above-mentioned foundation was intended to improve unemployment statistics, but clothed in rhetoric about women's "ethical duty" to become mothers and provide the emotional stability of the family unit. Although the payment is linked with guaranteed return to one's job, this is not necessarily at the same level of employment. Much preferred by the CDU is its suggestion that women should return to work at age thirty-five and preferably in the voluntary sector, that is, that area of society abandoned by a government committed to monetarist values.

Mechthild Jansen describes how the "family politics" expounded by the CDU government represent the return to traditional roles and women's status as linchpin of the family and unpaid social worker ("Die Frauenpolitik der Bundesregierung" [Cologne: Demokratische Fraueninitiative, 1984]; and "CDU-Frauenpolitik in der Offensive," *Wir Frauen* 3 (1985): 10–12). This trend in West Germany highlights the GDR's ongoing commitment to freedom of choice for women.

4. On the need for ideological work to change gender-based attitudes and behavior, using Lenin as the reference point, see Kuhrig and Speigner, *Zur gesellschaftlichen Stellung*, pp. 30–40. On the differences of opinion among socialist countries as to the need for and relevance of a women's organization, see esp. pp. 33–34.
5. For the provisions of the 1950 act, see Marlies Allendorf, *Women in the GDR* (Dresden: Verlag Zeit im Bild, 1978), p. 77; and Kuhrig and Speigner, *Zur gesellschaftlichen Stellung*, pp. 50–51, 60.
6. See *Statistisches Jahrbuch der DDR 1987* (Berlin: Staatsverlag der DDR, 1987), p. 393.
7. Ibid., pp. 17, 348; *Statistisches Jahrbuch für die BRD 1987* (Stuttgart: Verlag W. Kohlhammer, 1982), p. 98; Ilse Thiele, "Der wirkungsvolle Beitrag des DED zur Vorbereitung des XI. Parteitages der SED," *Neuer Weg* 40, no. 1 (1985): 10.
8. *Statistisches Jahrbuch der DDR 1987*, p. 404.
9. Quoted by Allendorf, *Women in the GDR*, p. 145.
10. Allendorf, *Women in the GDR*, p. 34; Kuhrig and Speigner, *Zur gesellschaftlichen Stellung*, pp. 42–43; Jane Hall, chapter on West Germany in Joni Lovenduski and Jill Hills, eds., *The Politics of the Second Electorate: Women and Public Participation* (London: Routledge & Kegan Paul, 1981), p. 156; *Statistisches Jahrbuch der DDR, 1987*, p. 403; *Statistisches Jahrbuch für die BRD 1987*, p. 600; Gerd Meyer, "Frauen in den Machthierarchien der DDR oder: Der lange Weg zur Parität—Empirische Befunde 1971–1985," *Deutschland Archiv* 19, no. 3 (1986): 309.
11. For comparative figures on the political representation of women in various countries, see Allendorf, *Women in the GDR*, pp. 30, 154; Herta Kuhrig, *Equal Rights for Women in the GDR: A Contribution to International Women's Year 1975* (Berlin: GDR Committee for Human Rights, 1973), pp. 15, 144; Kuhrig and Speigner, *Zur gesellschaftlichen Stellung*, p. 24; Harry G. Shaffer, *Women in the Two Germanies: A Comparative Study of a Socialist and a Non-Socialist Society* (New York, Oxford, Toronto: Pergamon Press, 1981), p. 89; *Statistisches Jahrbuch der DDR 1987*, pp. 393, 396, 398, 400, 403; *Statistical Abstract of the United States 1987* (Washington, D.C: Dept. of Commerce, Bureau of the Census, 1987), Table 408, p. 237. While two women have long been nonvoting candidate members of the Politbüro of the SED—Inge Lange since 1973 and Margarete Müller since 1963—neither was promoted to full membership even at the Eleventh Party Congress in April 1986. This failure to promote women to full membership of the SED's highest ruling body stands somewhat in contradiction to Erich Honecker's speech of February 1985, written as a paper in preparation for the forthcoming Eleventh SED Congress. In it, he exhorted district party secretaries to devote greater efforts to the promotion of women to party leadership positions.
12. For these figures, see Allendorf, *Women in the GDR*, p. 168; *Statistisches Jahrbuch der DDR 1987*, pp. 57, 62, 295. Of all the East European socialist countries, the GDR has by far the highest level of child-care provision: 84 percent of all preschool children attend

educational facilities, as compared with 67 percent in Hungary, 57 percent in Czecho-slovakia, 46 percent in the Soviet Union, and only 30 percent in Poland (see *Statistisches Jahrbuch der DDR 1987*, p. 29*).

13. For stipulations covering the aims and methods of preschool education, see Allendorf, *Women in the GDR*, pp. 135–136; and Kuhrig and Speigner, *Zur gesellschaftlichen Stellung*, pp. 275–87. See Gwyn Edwards, *GDR Society and Social Institutions: Facts and Figures* (London: Macmillan, 1985), pp. 54–56, for a description of nonsexist educational practice at preschool level. For an evaluation of the GDR psychologist Heinz Dannhauer's research into gender-based attitudes among preschool and school children, carried out in the late 1960s, see Jutta Menschik and Evelyn Leopold, *Gretchens rote Schwestern: Frauen in der DDR* (Frankfurt: Fischer Taschenbuchverlag, 1974), pp. 148–52. Edwards, *GDR Society*, p. 39, also refers to a second GDR study.

14. These most recent improvements in the maternity leave provisions, granting women the full baby year as paid leave even after the birth of the first child, together with the increases in child benefit payments, are contained in the Report of the Central Commit-tee to the Eleventh SED Party Congress of April 1986. See also Edwards, *GDR Society*, pp. 46–47.

15. In varying degrees, Czechoslovakia, Hungary, Rumania, and Bulgaria have restricted access to abortion, granting it in the main to women who have already had at least one and in most cases several children. See Scott, "Eastern European Women," p. 193; and Alena Heitlinger, *Women and State Socialism: Sex Inequality in the Soviet Union and Czechoslovakia* (London: Macmillan, 1979), pp. 187, 198.

16. Birth rates in the GDR and FRG are among the lowest in the world. In 1960, the rate of births per thousand inhabitants was 17.7 for West Germany and 17 for the GDR. This had fallen still further by 1970, to a rate of 13.3 and 13.9 respectively. The positive maternity provisions introduced by the GDR have managed to halt though not to reverse this declining birth rate. This is significant, however, when the 1985 GDR figure of 13.7 per thousand of the population is compared with that of 9.6 for West Germany, the latter together with similar rates in Denmark and West Berlin representing an all-time low in population reproduction levels. See *Statistisches Jahrbuch der DDR 1987*, p. 37.

17. See Allendorf, *Women in the GDR*, p. 158; *Statistisches Jahrbuch der DDR 1987*, p. 124; *Vocational Training: Equal Opportunities for All—the Options Open to Young People in the GDR* (Dresden: Verlag Zeit im Bild, 1985), p. 16.

18. Menschik and Leopold, *Gretchens rote Schwestern*, p. 80; Allendorf, *Women in the GDR*, pp. 66, 154, 163–64; Hall, "West Germany," p. 155; *Statistisches Jahrbuch für die BRD 1987*, pp. 336, 400; *Statistical Abstract of the United States 1987*, pp. 91, 167; *Statistisches Jahrbuch der DDR 1987*, pp. 182–83, 320; Shaffer, *Women in the Two Germanies*, p. 76; Meyers, "Frauen in den Machthierarchien," p. 306.

19. Positive discriminatory measures for the promotion of women were always aimed at older women already in the workforce, the assumption being that for women under thirty-five equal opportunity would be guaranteed in the education system. Indeed the effects of the GDR's educational policy have been stunning—girls achieved consistently better aca-demic results than boys throughout the 1970s. This has resulted in a form of positive discrimination in the reverse direction, to enable boys to maintain their considerably less than 50 percent of college and university places. See Martin McCauley, "Social Policy under Honecker," in Ian Wallace, ed., *The GDR under Honecker 1971–1981* (Dundee: GDR Monitor Special Series, 1, 1981), p. 13; and Edwards, *GDR Society*, p. 60.

20. For GDR discussions of the reasons why women reject positions of responsibility at work and in politics, see Inge Lange, "Die Verwirklichung der Beschlüsse des XI. Parteitages der SED zur Förderung der Frau" (lecture held on April 9, 1975), and the dissertation by W. Graupner, "Einige wesentliche Wirkfaktoren bei der Frauenqualifizierung" (Martin Luther Universität, Halle, 1975), both quoted in Michael Dennis, "Women and Work in the GDR," in Wallace, *The GDR under Honecker*, pp. 104, 105.

21. Allendorf, *Women in the GDR*, p. 143.

22. Sources: *Women in the GDR* (Dresden: Verlag Zeit im Bild, 1975), pp. 45–47; *Handbook of the Economy of the GDR* (West Berlin: German Institute for Economic Research, 1977), pp. 168, 283, 284; Shaffer, *Women in the Two Germanies*, pp. 72–73; *Statistisches Jahrbuch der DDR 1987*, pp. 18–20, 320, 344.

23. *Statistisches Jahrbuch der DDR 1987*, pp. 117, 156, 299–300, 39*; *Statistisches Jahrbuch für die BRD 1987*, pp. 106–09; *Women and Men in Britain: A Statistical Profile* (London: Equal Opportunities Commission, 1985), fig. 3.5; *Statistical Abstract of the United States 1987*, p. 404.

24. Sheila Taylor and Kathy Vanovitch, "The German Democratic Republic," in *Women, Oppression and Liberation*, Part 3 (London: Communist Party Education Department, 1980).

25. The figure for the domestic division of labor comes from a survey conducted by the GDR Institute for Market Research in 1970, which is summarized by Menschik and Leopold, *Gretchens rote Schwestern*, p. 145. The results of a 1970 UNESCO study comparing the situation in various West and East European countries are discussed in ibid., p. 145, and in Edwards, *GDR Society*, pp. 37–40. Although there has been change since these studies were conducted, McCauley, "Social Policy Under Honecker," p. 12, and Edwards, *GDR Society*, p. 41, suggest that the imbalance remains, with young women still responsible for the bulk of household work and hence having fewer leisure hours at their disposal than their partners.

26. Edith Anderson, ed., *Blitz aus heiterm Himmel* (Rostock: VEB Hinstorff Verlag, 1975).

27. In 1986, divorce rates in the GDR reached the unprecedented level of 32 per thousand of the population. This figure was slightly higher than that for West Germany, which has no family policy comparable with that in the GDR. See *Statistisches Jahrbuch der DDR 1987*, p. 373; *Statistiches Jahrbuch für die BRD 1987*, p. 606. Herta Kuhrig claims in "Familie und Familienglück," *Einheit* 40, no. 12 (1985): 1099, 1103–05, that any improvement in the West German figures can be put down to high female unemployment rates and other economic factors that militate against women opting out of unsatisfactory relationships. The GDR figures point on the other hand, she asserts, to objective difficulties in the historic process of creating partner and family relationships suited to a developed socialist society in which women have equality. Interestingly, Kuhrig makes no mention whatsoever of marriage guidance counseling in her treatment of the conflicts arising from the attempt to establish relationships based on equality, while at the same time emphasizing the dangers inherent in individuals' attributing such conflicts to their own or their partner's failure. She stresses (p. 1104) the importance of recognizing the objective nature of such conflict, but the only resource she points to as an aid in this process is the many recent publications giving helpful hints on how best to manage conflict resolution within relationships.

28. Maxie Wander, *Guten Morgen, Du Schöne* (Berlin: Buchverlag Der Morgen, 1978).

29. Christa Wolf, "Berührung: Maxie Wanders *Guten Morgen, Du Schöne*," *Neue Deutsche Literatur* 2 (1978): 53–63.

30. Helga Königsdorf, "Bolero," in *Meine ungehörigen Träume* (Berlin: Verlag Neues Leben, 1977).

31. Charlotte Worgitzky, "Karriere abgesagt," in *Vieräugig oder blind* (Berlin: Buchverlag Der Morgen, 1978). A further example of a story citing magic as the only means of coping with the demands of equality, GDR-style, is Irmtraud Morgner's "Das Seil" in Irmtraud Morgner, *Leben und Abenteuer der Trobadora Beatriz nach Zeugnissen ihrer Spielfrau Laura* (Berlin: Aufbau-Verlag, 1975).

32. Christa Wolf, *Kassandra. Vier Vorlesungen. Eine Erzählung* (Berlin: Aufbau-Verlag, 1983); *Kassandra* (Darmstadt und Neuwied: Luchterhand Verlag, 1983); *Voraussetzungen einer Erzählung: Kassandra*—Frankfurter Poetik-Vorlesungen (Darmstadt und Neuwied: Hermann Luchterhand Verlag, 1983). Wolf's postulation of women's new aspirations and demands on the basis of the equality already achieved in the GDR are

echoed in relation to the formation of social policy regarding marriage and the family by Kuhrig, *Equal Rights for Women in the GDR*, pp. 1104–05. Irmtraud Morgner uses the voice of the siren in her novel *Amanda* (Berlin: Aufbau-Verlag, 1983) to signal the need—in view of the nuclear threat—for a voice with a new and unexpected register, one that might by virtue of its very strangeness be heard. There is a sense of urgency in both authors' work, relating specifically to the need to avert a nuclear holocaust. For Morgner's explicit views on this issue, see Doris Berger, "Gespräch mit Irmtraud Morgner," *GDR Monitor* 12 (1984): 29–38.

33. While some people in the GDR opt for conscientious objector status and incur a prison sentence, it must be borne in mind that the GDR remains the only one of the East European socialist countries to offer the option of nonweapon carrying military service in construction units.

34. Since Gorbachev's far-reaching disarmament proposals were made, this situation has undergone some change. Although the GDR supports the abolition of medium-range weapons and the creation of a nuclear-free zone in Central Europe, *glasnost* and *perestroika* have not been applied to internal politics. This means that while supporting a change of foreign policy initiated by the Soviet Union, the GDR government's treatment of the Women for Peace has remained unchanged. In January 1988, several members of the Initiative for Peace and Human Rights, including some former members of the Women for Peace, were arrested and imprisoned. A new element, however, was that some of them were given GDR passports on the understanding that they would be free to return to the GDR after a certain period, rather than simply being expelled and stripped of their citizenship as has been common practice in the past. Two of these people, Bärbel Bohley and Werner Fischer, were indeed allowed to return to the GDR in July 1988, after a six-month period outside the country.

Biographies of Liberation: Testimonials to Labor in Socialist Hungary

Martha Lampland

Introduction

With the advent of Communist Party rule in Hungary after the war, adult women were accorded full legal rights under the law, rights of citizenship giving them equal status with their fellow adult male citizens. Realization of those rights in everyday life was seen, by party and government officials alike, to depend on the active participation of women in the wage labor force. "The joining of women in the social division of labor is the condition of their economic, political, social equality; it has always been considered a desirable social goal in the workers' movement."[1] As formulated in the New Family Law of 1952, "Women's equality within the marriage is therefore primarily ensured by the wife also being a working man,[2] participating in productive labor, economically independent of her husband."[3]

Why should the participation of women in the wage labor force, the so-called social division of labor, have been nearly the sole criterion advanced for attaining equality in socialist society? A group of essays written by women for a contest sponsored jointly by the Women's Committee and the Cultural, Agitprop Department of the National Council of Trade Unions sheds interesting light on that question.[4] Organized in honor of the 1975 International Women's Year, the contest had as its theme "Work is My Calling." The preface states: "The two hundred and forty confessions submitted demonstrate through experience how the life path of working women developed, how their preparation for work, education, and further training progressed, how work became their calling, and how they succeeded in establishing harmony between work and family."[5]

It is my purpose in analyzing these essays to reach an understanding of the socialist state's definition of women in and at work. In other words, I am using these essays to construct a coherent picture of the prevailing ideological assumptions about women's identity as laborers that inform the actions taken by officials in the party and bureaucracy of the state. The essays are particularly illuminating in this regard, for two primary reasons: first, as entries to a state-sponsored contest, the essays, though written voluntarily, nonetheless exemplify rhetoric and themes found in party and bureaucratic materials, thereby underscoring the significance of citizens as participants in the construction of their identity as socialist workers. Witness several titles, which convey the tone of the most ardent party circular: "The Meaning of My Life Has Been Given by the Work of My Two Hands," "Work Is My Life," "The Machine and I Are One," and "Work Will Become a Calling When One Completes It with Spirit." Second, all the essays, without exception, portray a growing love for wage-labor activities in terms of the history of the essayist's career, thus providing a historical and personal depth generally lacking in party or state proclamations on women under socialism.

Biographies of Liberation

Before discussing the essays, let us first examine the social background and labor history of these women. Table 1 shows the age distribution, marital status, and number of children in the families of contest participants. Table 2 provides figures for comparison with the entire female population.[6]
A comparison of the two tables shows two major discrepancies between the essayists and the wider population, namely age composition and marital status. In contrast to the population as a whole, a much higher percentage of contest participants were represented in the thirty-one to forty age group, and a much lower percentage of participants were older than sixty years of age. This discrepancy is no doubt an artifact of the self-selection exercised by participants in the contest. Older women as a group are less apt to share so unreservedly the ideals of socialism espoused in these essays, since unlike younger women, they have not always lived under socialism. One might also speculate whether the disproportionate number of contestants between the ages of thirty and forty can be traced to the well-known advantages that accrue to advancement within the workplace as a result of active political participation, an issue of particular importance to those with budding careers. The differences in numbers concerning marital status most probably derive from the age composition of the group. The number of children in the family appears to be fairly similar.

The areas of education, training and employment, and political participation also suggest that contest participants differ in significant ways from most of their compatriots. Forty-three percent of the contest participants finished high school or technical school, in contrast to 18.5 percent

Table 1: Contest Participants

Age		Marital status		Number of children	
20–30	21%	Unmarried	9%	One child	32%
31–40	35	Married	74	Two children	37
41–60	40	Divorced	11	Three children	11
61–	4	Widowed	5	Four children	3
		Separated	1	Five and more	3
				Childless	14

Source: Compiled from E. Horváth and P. Keszei, eds., *Hivatásom a munka* (Budapest, 1977).

Table 2: Hungarian Women, 1978

Age		Marital status		Number of children	
20–29	21.0%	Unmarried	14.5%	One child	28%
30–39	17.8	Married	64.2	Two children	37.7
40–59	34.5	Divorced	5.2	Three children	12.8
60–	26.6	Widowed	16.1	Four children	4.8
		Separated	—	Five and more	5.2
				Childless	11.5

Source: Central Statistical Office, 1979.

of Hungarian women generally. These statistics, compiled in 1973, also show that an additional 32.5 percent of Hungarian women had not even finished eighth grade. Among the contestants, 26 percent had acquired a college or university degree, which strongly contrasts with the average figure of 4.5 percent in the general female population.[7] Clearly, these women have been more highly educated than their contemporaries. Many of the experiences depicted in the essays focus on their quest for further education, often pursued alongside responsibilities of a job and childrearing. The character of their work also differs from that of most of their fellow women: in 1975 16 percent were employed in industry or agriculture, and 77 percent were employed in intellectual or service positions. In the general population, 62.5 percent of women were employed in industry and agriculture, and the remaining 37.5 percent were employed in intellectual or service occupations.[8]

It is perhaps not surprising to learn, again owing to the voluntary character of the contest, that 60 percent of the contest participants were characterized as holding elected social and political office, as, for example, within the party, the trade union, the Red Cross, the town council, the

Communist Youth League, or the Patriotic People's Front (an umbrella group for numerous social and cultural organizations). Furthermore, nearly every participant recounted the moment when she was honored with a medal or award for her outstanding contribution to the workplace or to socialist society at large: the awards included Excellent Worker, Excellent Worker of the Machine Industry, Excellent Worker of the Food Industry, Second Rank State Prize, Silver Rank of the Honor of Work, and Red Challenge Pennant from the Central Committee of the Student Youth League. As this background information demonstrates, the essayists have pursued many of the advantages women were to enjoy under socialism. The significance of the transition to socialism for their identity as women and for their careers is clear in all the essays, which bear closer examination.

The predominant issue highlighted throughout all the essays is the process whereby a job or means of earning a living became a calling, a satisfying activity, and a moral purpose. This clearly follows from the theme of the contest. The essays, however, also share other similar features. A strong opposition was frequently made between the pre- and postwar periods; more accurately, between the capitalist and socialist periods. Some women spoke of the difficulties they experienced before the war because of social injustice, or of the restrictions on their advancement, to education or a better job or simply to respect. In one essay, a woman writes, "Today my mother would be crowned with the honor and respect accorded an excellent worker, but back then she was given starvation wages, and she didn't dare say anything, because there were thousands who could have taken her place" (p. 16) or another, "In the old days we worked to survive, now we do so to get somewhere" (p. 72). This stark distinction between the capitalist and socialist periods is very common in public forums and everyday speech as well. The two periods are often denoted as "in capitalism" and "in the democracy." The second expression is clearly not used descriptively; it has acquired currency as a popularized catch-phrase because of its frequent use in the media, schools, and other official forums. A careful reading of the essays suggests, however, that significant improvements occurred for these women during the mid- to late 1960s, after collectivization and the brutal socioeconomic pressures of hurried industrialization during the 1950s lessened.

Another common theme was the pleasure of being appreciated for their work. Though never explicitly articulated, the contrast with their home life was evident. As one woman wrote, "By then I was forty years old, and I thought about how much I had worked until then, yet no one had ever praised me. . . . I was only recognized here, in the group" (p. 65). The pleasure of recognition and respect was also strongly associated with the value of group or collective work. Many of the women described how, over time, they had come to enjoy working collectively. "I gladly go to work, and the collective [work group] plays a large role in this" (p. 66). Recent surveys in Hungary have indicated that a prominent reason for women to return to the workplace earlier than is required by maternity leave is to rejoin the community of their fellow workers.[9]

Nonetheless, the weight of women's double burden on the shoulders of the essayists was noticeable. The disproportionate burden of domestic duties borne by women within the family was exacerbated for many of the contestants by the pursuit of further education or training. As one contestant observed: "During the day there was the workplace, the family, domestic work. One could only snip off time for studying from one's sleep" (p. 77). In many cases husbands and children had to be enlisted to assist, or at least coaxed to be tolerant. In the words of one essayist: "The growing pile of unmended socks at home didn't bother anyone any more" (p. 26). With one exception, no one questioned the propriety of women doing the lion's share of domestic chores. It is interesting to note that rarely did contestants speak of the joy of mothering or of the reward of women's domestic responsibilities, as is so often done when officials attempt to explain away the compounded burden of wage labor, domestic work, and childrearing women endure. Indeed, the essayists consistently portrayed the source of their joys to have been found in recognition of their contribution, in a job well done at the workplace, and in service to the broader community.

Yet group or collective work for the essayists represented far more than the pleasure of community or of public service alone. Working at a job outside the home was clearly defined throughout all the essays as *the* truly rewarding and valuable activity. "I can only really be pleased with collective work well done. My own work is worth nothing alone, only in the collective [work group], together with the community" (p. 99), or "For my generation a life is complete only with a calling. The monotonous drudgery of housekeeping cannot satisfy us, nor can the beautiful and responsible task of childrearing" (p. 92), or "Writers and poets have written much and elegantly about this most human, most noble, most amazing activity—about work" (p. 93).

It is significant to note that the term used in the essays to denote work was almost exclusively the word used to refer to work that is pursued outside the home or for wages (*munka*). As I have discussed elsewhere, an alternative term (*dolog*) is generally used to refer to all activities outside the realm of work for wages, such as women's domestic chores, agricultural activities prior to collectivization, or certain agricultural tasks performed in the so-called second economy.[10] The literal absence of reference to a general concept of labor outside the realm of wages, and the concomitant description of domestic responsibilities as less valuable to the community, strongly conveyed the absolute definition of one's calling or social contribution to be found only in wage labor outside the domestic unit.

It bears emphasis that work in the public, nondomestic sphere is not merely significant as a rewarding and valuable contribution to society. It is patently clear that productive labor is symbolically central to the Hungarian socialist economy, understood both by ideologues and the person on the street as the direct production of physical objects, not with reference to Marx's more complex formulation, which defines productive labor in terms of the relationship between the extraction of surplus and use versus exchange value. Yet the emphasis here is not only on the specific character of work per se, but on its location in the public, not the domestic, realm. Only in working here, in the public realm, is it in fact possible to become fully human. Witness the following passages: "Work *(munka)* and man *(ember)*, the first makes the second" (p. 15); " . . . it is truly worthwhile to find the job where we can see joy in our work, and through our work *(munka)* become a complete man *(ember)*" (p. 84); " . . . work *(munka)* is the most important condition for the existence of human society" (p. 100); "Numerous worker women have worked among us whom the *man-making* power of the community raised to an excellent worker" (p. 67; emphasis added). Thus, the pursuit of wage labor is perceived by the contest participants to be a necessary condition for the acquisition of full humanity, of full subjectivity in the socialist community.

Socialist Policies Toward Women

The central value of defining one's ideal self as a wage laborer participating in the collective, public domain is stressed in all the essays. Let us now turn to examine women's participation in the Hungarian wage-labor market since 1945 more closely, and consider the policies propagated by the socialist state regarding women's labor, inside as well as outside the home.

Between 1930 and 1975, the number of active wage earners in Hungary increased by 1.3 million, 93 percent of the increase attributable to women's entrance into the wage labor market.[11] Whereas in 1949, 60 percent of women between the ages of fourteen and fifty-four were housewives, students, or dependents, the figures from 1975 showed only 16.4 percent of this age group could be so characterized.[12] During the period between 1949 and 1974, the percentage of women among active earners increased from 29 percent to 44 percent. The increased participation of women in various fields during the same period may be demonstrated by the following figures: the percentage of women among active wage earners in industry grew from 23 percent to 50 percent, in construction from 4 percent to 17 percent, in transportation and communications from 10 percent to 24 percent, in commerce from 36 percent to 64 percent, and in agriculture, forestry, and water management from 28 percent to 39 percent.[13] According to the 1970 census, 20 percent of the active workers in technical fields were women, 29 percent of workers in the area of state administration and economics were women, 63 percent in health and cultural fields were women (this includes elementary and high school teachers), and 69 percent of office workers and accountants were women.[14]

Proclamations issued in the early years of the Hungarian socialist state consistently emphasized the equality of women, and exhorted them to join in the noble project of building socialism. Nevertheless, state policies in the early 1950s placed an enormous burden on women.[15] The images of women dominating this early period were twofold: the heroic worker and the proud mother. Female tractor drivers and bricklayers joined their Stakhanovite brethren in colossal feats of effort; all the while policies encouraged a dramatic increase in the birthrate. Posters in factories and offices urged *all* women to give birth, dismissing any hesitations on the part of unmarried women. Providing the socialist state with children was a dignified act, worthy of married and unmarried women alike. This period is still referred to as the "infamous Ratkó period," named after the minister of health services during whose tenure very strict policies limiting the availability of birth control and abortions were propagated. Despite these pressures to have babies, women were nonetheless constrained by economic necessity to seek jobs outside the home. One salary was insufficient to maintain a household, as wages were very severely depressed. Families who engaged in private agricultural production, or those who had joined cooperative farms, often had very limited access to money, and so would encourage some family members to find a job outside the home.

After 1956 abortions again became legal, and by the early 1960s women were frequently availing themselves of medical interventions to pace and limit the size of their families. These decisions were predominantly motivated by difficulties with a persistently low income and problems securing adequate housing, despite the improvement of economic fortunes throughout the country. It was also during this period that new regulations were formulated to protect women's health in the workplace more stringently. Reversing policies characteristic of the early 1950s, women were prevented from holding jobs such as tractor driver or other types of strenuous physical labor, jobs that perhaps not so incidentally offered higher wage scales than most women's jobs, and often enjoyed greater prestige. The drudgery of housekeeping tasks was eased slowly, and only by the increasing availability of household appliances, not by any concerted effort on the part of state authorities to assist in the provisioning of services or the general participation of men in the labor of the household. Data from a 1976–77 survey show that men's average daily household tasks totaled 1.4 hours, whereas women worked in the home 3.9 hours on a daily average.[16]

With time, however, more and more state supports were made available to assist families with day care and housing. For example, the proportion of nursery school–aged children provided with day care increased dramatically: 23.5 percent in 1950, 33.7 percent in 1960, 55.7 percent in 1970, 75.5 percent in 1975, and 87.2 percent in 1980. The figures for day care for infants up to three years of age are less impressive: 1.4 percent in 1950, 7.4 percent in 1960, 9.5 percent in 1970, 10.7 percent in 1975, and 15.7 percent in 1980.[17] Housing problems lessened somewhat in the 1960s and early 1970s, as factories began to make apartments available to workers who agreed to have a certain number of children over a prearranged period of time. Credit sources also became increasingly available for purchasing apartments or for building houses. In the countryside, there was a boom in house construction.[18]

The introduction of maternity leave (GYES) in 1967, hailed as the enlightened policy of progressive policymakers, was welcomed in many quarters. Hungary was one of the first countries in Europe to establish maternity leave (Austria did so in 1960); moreover, a mother is allowed to stay home with her child for up to three years after birth. This still remains the most generous provision concerning home-based child care in Europe.[19] Although in 1967 the monthly payment offered for maternity leave represented approximately 42 percent of the average woman's salary (or 32 percent of the overall average salary), by the mid-1970s it was closer to one-fourth to one-third of the average woman's salary.[20] At no time were maternity leave payments truly adequate to cover costs incurred with the birth of children into the family. Nonetheless, as the following numbers indicate, many women chose to take time at home with their young children: in 1968, 92,000; in 1970, 167,000; in 1972, 185,000; in 1974, 229,000; in 1975, 265,000; in 1977, 290,000; in 1978, 277,000; and in 1980, 254,000 women were on maternity leave (the total population of Hungary hovers around ten million).[21] More recent policies have calculated the size of the monthly payment in terms of a certain percentage of the monthly income of the mother on leave.[22] And it is now possible for men to choose to stay home with young children, although rarely is this option chosen because of the general discrepancy in earnings between men and women.

Although reform legislation concerning salaries in the past has apparently attempted to address the discrepancy between men and women's salaries, there are still significant differences. For example, statistics from 1974 demonstrate that among factory workers, female skilled laborers are paid only 71.4 percent of their male counterpart's monthly salaries, female semi-skilled workers 72.6 percent, and female unskilled workers only 76.6 percent. Among factory management and administration, the figures show the following discrepancies: women who are managing directors or presidents of small industrial cooperatives earn 86.7 percent of their male counterparts' salaries, assistant managers 78.7 percent, technical or sales managers 83.8 percent, directors of production or sales 77.5 percent, and higher level technical or sales administrators 76 percent.[23]

Serious differences in the distribution of men and women within the workforce are evident, as are patterns of schooling that diverge between girls and boys.[24] Girls are generally at a disadvantage when seeking training in skills perceived to be traditionally male fields, or in pursuing higher education. The only exception are those fields in which women have been disproportionately represented since the war, such as teaching or training leading to lower-level positions in administration or sales. Accordingly, women are still encouraged to pursue training and seek positions in work traditionally defined as women's work, like weaving or food preparation, or in a myriad of service positions.[25] If we examine the fate of women who have acquired more advanced educational credentials, we find that their ability to attain positions of influence is still limited.

> According to the level of authority, the discrepancy between men and women is especially great. Among men who have advanced degrees, 37% work as upper or middle level managers, while only 12% of women do so. Thirty-five percent of men with middle-level degrees fill middle management positions, or in other words, for a middle-management position men only need a high school diploma, while only 7.5% of women who have a high school degree work in middle-management positions. Therefore, women have managed to join the ranks of professionals with advanced and middle-level training, but they have succeeded in breaking into management jobs in only small measure: 90% of them work in subordinate positions.[26]

The absence of significant participation by women in decisionmaking positions also extends to political office. The percentage of women holding office in town councils and district and county offices varies across the country from 10 percent to 30 percent, but their numbers decrease in higher positions and in those positions closer to central authorities, as in urban areas.[27] At present, there is only one female member in the Politburo, and only fourteen female members in the Central Committee, constituting only 13 percent of its membership.[28]

As can be seen, women have been buffeted back and forth between policies encouraging their participation in the wage-labor workforce, and the roller coaster of pronatalist policies.[29] Though the rapid absorption of female labor into the wage-labor market was stated to be an unequivocal goal of the socialist bureaucracy and party apparatus, policies addressing women's more complex role in society were never clearly formulated. Ferge maintains, in fact, that although work was proclaimed the right and responsibility of all adult citizens, the notion of a woman's right to work never came to be considered a responsibility, that is, an action bearing legal sanctions, either in principle or as understood in public opinion.[30] She traces this ambivalence to a general reluctance to confront the consequences of changing roles of women in Hungarian society, for such consequences would at the least have entailed a partial redistribution of state support away from primary productive industries to support for traditionally defined social services, such as improved health services, day care for school-aged children, facilities to provide for elderly citizens, and for more innovative policies, including substantial reorganization of the educational system and state investments in labor-saving machinery to aid housework. In the final analysis, then, women were treated as a flexible (and cheap) reserve army of labor, whose fortunes in the workplace would vary as the demands for labor in the economy at large changed.[31]

In the early years of industrial expansion, the demand for labor was great:

> Therefore, while social changes demanded rapid mobilization, and set it in motion, mobilization could only truly be realized in the contradictory process whereby the level and structure of the economy presumed and required an uneducated stratum of humble origins, who in great numbers would produce large volumes of industrial products at a low level of technology and for low pay. For this task masses of women from the ranks of the poor were the "most suited," for whom the fact of employment meant social advancement. Putting them to work served the ideologically proclaimed goals of emancipation, while at the same time satisfying the demand for poorly qualified and cheap labor power.[32]

By the mid-1960s, the first phase of extensive industrialization had slowed down, reducing the need for a large mass of unskilled laborers. Moreover, abortion had been legal for over a decade, contributing to a fairly constant negative birthrate. The introduction of maternity leave in 1967, then, should be considered in light both of shifts in the character of the economy and pronatalist concerns. Furthermore, the policy zigzags between enticing women into the wage-labor force, or seducing them back home to motherhood did not end with the 1967 law. The slow deterioration of the value of monthly maternity-leave payments by the mid-1970s, and the introduction of a variety of options such as the possibility of interrupting maternity leave or of caring for a number of children in one's home while on maternity leave were the result of policy debates that focused on the renewed demand for female labor in the public economy in the 1970s.[33]

Yet the consequences of a policy of maternity leave extend far beyond shifting attitudes of policymakers toward the momentary combination of women's roles as producers and reproducers. In effect, this policy has reinforced woman's traditional role within the family: as housewife, child-care provider, dependent.[34] Moreover, the conservative trends bred of the policy directly influence women's careers in the wage economy. Young women are perceived as "imminent mothers" who are bound to be absent from the workplace for years on end. Hence they are not hired for positions of responsibility, or are denied promotions that would be in accordance with their abilities.

The clear articulation of women's contribution to Hungarian society, and creative policies facilitating their possibly new role(s), would have required debates questioning the most central assumptions of women's identity, and the most central assumptions among Marxist-Leninist theorists about productive and worthwhile activities within the economy and society at large. In the absence of such debates, policies grappling with these problems tended to heighten the demands on women in the home and restrict their possibilities in the workplace. As H. Sas has observed, "Despite the fact of employment [for wages, *munka*], the different possibilities that women and men still have today in the areas of training, the character of work, advancement, [and] mobility conserve or only slightly modify traditional life styles, family roles, the character of family life, and related attitudes."[35]

Discussion

What, then, were these central assumptions, held by Marxist-Leninist theorists and policymakers, about women's identity and labor, which remained uncontested? To return to the question posed in the introduction, why should the participation of women in the wage-labor force have been nearly the sole criterion advanced for attaining equality in socialist society, a criterion just as firmly embraced by the contest participants themselves? The answer to this question lies in a closer examination of a series of cultural assumptions underlying the development of political forms in Europe over the last several centuries.

In recent years much attention has been focused on the relationship between the rise of the modern state in Europe and the construction of new forms of subjectivity, largely inspired, of course, by the work of Foucault. As a consequence of these examinations, the genesis of a whole set of oppositions—now so very familiar—between mind and body, self and object, private and public, civil society and the state, are seen to be specifically historic products, forming the foundation of bourgeois thought, of politics, and of subjectivity.[36] The dialectical character of these oppositions presupposes an identity through opposition, each term being implicated in its antithesis. In regard to the division in bourgeois society between self and object, the dialectical process entails the objectification of both terms of the opposition, of self and society. The individual is defined and identified in terms of an objectified universe: In what more classic terms do we see this than in the work of Marx himself? These oppositions remained unquestioned in Marxist-Leninist theory; hence although termed bourgeois, they clearly also form the basis of socialist notions of work. For while the relative symbolic significance of consumption and production for social identity varies between capitalist and socialist societies, theorists and social planners in the Bolshevik tradition did not undertake radical changes in the social relations of production, and so perpetuated or even fostered the commodification of social life. [37]

To return to the essays, then, it becomes evident why the focus is so squarely on wage labor. To acquire full human subjectivity, women understand they must pursue wage labor, must abandon the devalued sphere of domestic activities to engage in the objectification of self in public communities. A woman's (and a man's) subjectivity must be established *against* the collective community of fellow wage workers, for what is the process of objectifying labor if not its very commodification? The commodity as universal equivalent renders all social processes, and social subjects, as objects: time, money, labor, society, and surely self, all come to be objectified. To quote a teacher who entered the contest: "The raw material [of teaching] is man, which is more breakable than glass, speaks up if something hurts, and takes a long time to forget if it has been unfairly treated. With such "material" one can only work in a calm and tempered way" (p. 108). Thus, the drive by socialist politicans to bring women into the wage-labor force signifies far more than a simple emphasis on the centrality of public, nondomestic production: it is the very foundation of civic subjectivity, the basis for equal political participation in socialist society.

Another avenue of exploration into the problem of subjectivity and the rise of the modern state has followed changes in confessional practices. Foucault and Asad's work on Europe, Rafael's work in the Philippines, and Sánchez's work in Peru all emphasize the significance of changing practices of confession and the categorization of acts and ideas that become the focus of attention by religious authorities. These shifts not only radically alter the character of authority and power relationships among its participants, but also fundamentally influence the development of notions of self and subjectivity. It is interesting therefore to return to the passage I quoted from the introduction to the collection of essays, in which the entries were called "confessions." Actually, a more accurate but more awkward translation is "self-avowal" or "self-admission" (*önvallomás*). [38] It would appear significant, then, that the form of the so-called self-admission submitted to the contest was always autobiographical, since emphasis was placed on the history of one individual, on the development of one's self as called to work. I would suggest that although the process of participating in this contest—in writing autobiographies—bears none of the stigma of self-criticism, it appears to share in its result: the empowerment and reification of the socialist state. [39] The representation of self in these writings as truly realized in objectification through commodification surely qualifies as a triumph of bourgeois alienation. The state thus insinuates itself into one's being, making its presence natural and its role necessary.

The contest analyzed here represents just one of myriad opportunities for socialist citizens to address the state as actor, as subject, as reified object. The form may be in reference, as in the common use of the term Uncle State (*állam bácsi*) in phrases like "Uncle State should take care of that," or directly, as in the following passage drawn from one of the essays: "I must take this opportunity to say thanks because I was able to study, because our state has provided this possibility" (p. 92). And yet what has kindly Uncle State—such an appropriate name for patriarchal dominance—done for women lately? Having examined the centrality of commodification for the subjectivity of men and women in the socialist economy, let us now turn to the problem of gender and subjectivity.

The seminal contribution of Foucault to a rethinking of the concept of power and the production of modern subjectivity is undisputed. However, as de Lauretis has recently pointed out,[40] his analysis in *History of Sexuality* does not address the manner in which both men and women are "en-gendered" through practices, epistemologies, and discursive forms he would call sexuality. The tendency to ignore gender, or more accurately to portray one (male) self, would seem to follow precisely from the general logic of bourgeois thought: building on essentialist definitions, social beings are rendered objects of fixed and unchanging character. To step beyond these epistemological constraints, de Lauretis proposes we conceive of a social being as

> a subject constituted in gender, to be sure, though not by sexual difference alone, but rather across languages and cultural representations; a subject engendered in the experiencing of race and class, as well as sexual, relations; a subject, therefore, not unified but rather multiple, and not so much divided as contradicted.[41]

Subjectivity then may be understood as a historical process of multiple and contradictory dimensions. Thus, the engendering of social beings is both a product and a process, at once historically constituted and emergent.

I would propose, then, that the product and process of Hungarian socialist policies has been a subject unified as commodity. The categorical definition of wage labor as the sole means to acquire economic and political equality rests on the denial of multiplicity, on the divestment from human subjects of their complexity. The multiple dimensions of subjectivity are excised from social identity, as the private is excised from the public, the self from nature, the mind from the body. Indeed, the denial of multiplicity appears to be a gloriously bourgeois victory. The complex historical process we identify as the development of bourgeois discursive forms, epistemologies, and practices creates highly circumscribed realms of action and of subjectivity, albeit their unity and integrity presuppose an opposition to other forms and categories. Perhaps the best example of this is the (essentialist) notion of the individual him-self.

Moreover, by denying the manifold character of social subjectivity the modern state reproduces conditions of inequality among its citizens. Sub-jectively impoverished, male and female citizens alike privilege a fixed domain of social action to define their (multiple) selves, thereby realizing an alienation central to the exercise of power by the modern state. The absolute hegemony of singular identity is perhaps no better demonstrated than in the new goal set by feminists in Hungary. Women are now calling for the right to stay at home with their children, to become full-time mothers. Thus, rather than challenge the public/private, workplace/home distinction, or mount a call for men and women to participate across all realms of social experience in varied and multiple ways, Hungarian feminists have kept their goals firmly within the categorical distinctions propagated by the state.

The lessons to be found in this humble contest are sobering. One is painfully reminded of the weight of historical experiences, of the difficulty of breaking out of time-worn habits of thought and action. After all, the categories constraining feminist practice in Hungary today were born in the seventeenth century. But I hasten to add that the tender age of socialism only partially mitigates responsibilities for the difficulties en-countered. The socialist program in Hungary has been poorly realized, even if considered within the narrow boundaries set for the emancipation of women through workforce participation. Women are still paid less than their brothers, sons, and husbands, are limited in their ability to advance within schools and the workplace, and are drastically underrepresented in existing political bodies. Clearly, to effect major changes in both the home and the workplace would require far greater attention to restructuring educational institutions and other influential forms of socialization, to begin the long process of shattering the bonds of currently engendered identities.

Yet the problem extends beyond piecemeal changes in policies con-cerning wage scales or educational organization. The (Bolshevik) Marxist-Leninist program in Hungary has often consciously modeled forms of labor organization, remuneration, incentive, and managerial hierarchies on those of capitalist firms. The introduction of socialism in Hungary was not accompanied by a radical rethinking of the nature of the social form or of politics: hence neither the personal nor the productive would be seen as inherently political. Indeed, the dialectical materialist representation of the socialist economy as a natural fact, in which problems of exploitation and of class are singularly absent, could rival essentialist bourgeois repre-sentations of naturalized markets. I might hazard the suggestion that the contributions of feminist criticism to ideas of subjectivity, focusing on its multiple and contradictory manifestations, could well be inspirational for renewed socialist practice. In Hungary, the growth of the environmental movement, the rise of concern about religious persecution, the problem of conscientious objectors in civil life, disparate forms of artistic expression, and, most importantly, dissatisfaction with oppressive work loads in both the primary and secondary economy could finally break the monolithic hold of factory production ideology on socialist society. Perhaps then diverse aspects of social subjectivity could be realized, born of the toleration of contradiction and the freedom of multiplicity.

Notes

I wish to thank the Center for Russian and East European Studies at the University of Michigan, Ann Arbor, for their generous award of a Mellon Postdoctoral Fellowship, which permitted me the leisure during the 1987–88 academic year to work on this project. I wish to thank John Comaroff, Bette Denich, Michael Herzfeld, Rayna Rapp, Akos Róna-Tas, and Rafael Sánchez for their very helpful comments in the drafting of this article, which was initially prepared for a panel entitled "Gender Contradictions/Gender Transformations: Cases from Eastern Europe," for the 1987 meetings of the American Anthropological Association. This article will appear in very different form in a collection of the papers delivered at the original panel. I would especially like to thank Eva Huseby-Darvas for enlisting me to participate in the panel, and for her constant professional and personal help during its gestation.

All translations of Hungarian texts are my own.

1. Zsuzsa Ferge, *Társadalmi újratermelés és társadalom-politika* (Social Reproduction and Social Policy) (Budapest: Közgazdasági és Jogi Könyvkiadó, 1982).

2. Although nouns carry no gender markers in Hungarian, traditional usage justifies translating the word *ember* as man rather than as the more neutral term of human. As will become evident, translating texts about socialist women in terms of "working men" is not meant to be facetious, but is relevant to the argument.

3. Ferenc Mikos, "Az új családjogi törvény" (The New Family Law Statute), in Sándor Balogh, ed., *Nehéz esztendők kronikája, 1949–1953: Dokumentumok* (The Chronicle of Difficult Years, 1949–1953: Documents) (Budapest: Gondolat Kiadó, 1986), p. 434.

4. Erika Horváth and Pálné Keszei, eds., *Hivatásom a munka* (Work Is My Calling) (Budapest: Szakszervezetek Országos Tanácsának Nőbizottsága, 1977).

5. Ibid., p. 5.

6. As the essays examined here were written in 1975, I have chosen to rely on figures from the mid-1970s throughout to reflect contemporary distributions.

7. Tiborné Erdész, "A dolgozó nők iskolázottsági és szakképzettségi szinvonala, kulturális aktivitása" (The Level of Schooling and Training, and the Cultural Activity of Working Women), in Egon Szabady, ed., *Nők, Gazdaság, Társadalom* (Women, Economy, Society) (Budapest: Kossuth Könyvkiadó, 1976), p. 142.

8. András Klinger, "Társadalmunk gazdasági szerkezete, az ország munkaerőforrásai" (The Economic Structure of Our Society, the Country's Sources of Labor Power), in Szabady, ed., *Nők Gazdaság, Társadalom*, p. 42.

9. Edit Fülöp, personal communication. Increasing concerns have been voiced by analysts examining the rise of what is called "maternity leave neurosis," which they claim primarily afflicts women living in urban housing projects. The studies point to the problems of social isolation from a wider community and the radical change in life style often occasioned by maternity leave (see Horváth Erika Sándorné, *A GYEStöl a GYEDig* [From GYES to GYED] ([Budapest: Kossuth Könyvkiadó, 1986], p. 62). Although it is important to remain skeptical of the psychological labeling of women as feeble neurotics, there is no question but that nervous problems among women have become culturally salient in Hungary. I have been struck by the frequency with which

women will speak of problems with "their nerves." Unfortunately, virtually their sole recourse to calming their nerves is to take medication.

10. Martha Lampland, "Working through History: Ideologies of Work and Agricultural Production in a Hungarian Village, 1918–1983" (Ph.D. diss., University of Chicago, 1987).

11. Judit H. Sas, *Nöies nök és férfias férfiak* (Feminine Women and Masculine Men) (Budapest: Akadémiai Kiadó, 1984), p. 96.

12. The opposition between housewives and wage earners in these statistics, clearly an artifact of assumptions about productive and nonproductive labor, is problematic and we need only emphasize here its cultural and historical specificity. However, these numbers also mask other things as well, specifically agricultural tasks performed around the house and in the fields. As women's active participation in agricultural work at home and at cooperative farms was for a long time organized outside standard forms of wage contracts, e.g., as family contributions or through sharecropping arrangements, it is easily over-looked in statistical compilations. Recent statistics comparing the labor market participation of women in urban and rural communities still demonstrate this disparity (ibid., pp. 96–97).

13. László Molnár, *A munka szerepe a nök életútjában* (The Role of Work in Women's Course of Life) (Budapest: Akadémiai Kiadó, 1981), p. 129.

14. Judit Háber and Júlia Szalai, "A pedagógusnök helyzete, egy pálya elnöiesedése" (The Situation of Women Teachers, the Feminization of a Field), in Szabady, ed., *Nök, Gazdaság, Társadalom*, p. 246.

15. Although the burdens of birthing and childrearing fell disproportionately on women during this time, jokes typically criticized the state's appropriation of male sexual organs, not female wombs.

16. Ferge, *Társadalmi újratermelés*, p. 147.

17. Ibid., p. 145. The figures should also be considered in light of the discrepancies between infrastructural investments in town and countryside. In the early 1950s in particular, day care was often provided at factories and other sites of employment for female workers, services that were thus absent in many villages across the country. Today state-sponsored day care in Hungarian villages is as extensive as in urban areas. Nonetheless, throughout the country difficulties still arise in coordinating the hours when day care is provided and when working mothers and fathers need to be on the job. See György Konrád and Iván Szelényi, "Social Conflicts of Underurbanization: The Hungarian Case," in *Social Consequences of Modernization in Communist Societies* (Baltimore: Johns Hopkins University Press, 1976), pp. 162–78.

18. Shifts in attitudes toward private house construction parallel those held about the second economy (that is, the nonstate sector) in general. The rapid growth of private con-struction in the late 1960s and 1970s was well received: many families were able to build pleasant and spacious homes in the countryside, just as many people increased their income through agricultural and service work in their private, second-economy work. However, in more recent years, the state has severely limited its role in building apartments, coming to rely on rural residents to provide the monetary investments, energy, and labor themselves. Similarly, the varieties of activities called the second economy, once considered the haven of freedom and crucible of creativity, have now come to be seen as a necessary evil, an inescapable means of supplementing a meager wage, all the result of the state's poor economic policy and the oppression spawned by a huge international debt.

19. Sándorné, *A GYEStöl a GYEDig*, pp. 118–21.

20. Ferge, *Társadalmi újratermelés*, p. 152–53.

21. Ibid., p. 151.

22. Debates surrounding pronatalist policies in Hungary have at times bordered on racist hysteria. In recent years many have voiced concern over the size of gypsy families,

fearing that (nongypsy) Hungarians may soon be outnumbered as their families tend to be much smaller. Measures such as the weighing of income in calculations toward monthly subsidies were promoted to encourage wealthier, i.e., nongypsy, Hungarians to take advantage of the supports of the state to bear children.

23. H. Sas, *Nöies nök*, pp. 113–14.

24. Notions about procreation still current suggest that boys are considered to be the product of greater development or higher elaboration than girls from the very moment of insemination on. If one's child is overdue, then it is automatically assumed to be a boy (this is also believed to be true for animals). Following the same logic, it was explained to me that a couple had a baby girl because the very act of copulation had been hurried.

25. H. Sas, *Nöies nök*, pp. 98–99.

26. Molnár, A *munka szerepe*, p. 149.

27. Ibid., p. 153.

28. Central Intelligence Agency Directorate of Intelligence, *Directory of Hungarian Officials, July 1987* (Washington, DC: Central Intelligence Agency, 1987), pp. 5–7.

29. John Cole and Judith Nydon, "Class, Gender and Fertility: Contradictions of Social Life in Contemporary Romania," unpub., 1987, present an insightful discussion of the problems of pronatalist policies and economic pressures on women in Romania.

30. Ferge, *Társadalmi újratermelés*, p. 140.

31. Ibid., p. 155.

32. H. Sas, *Nöies nök*, p. 122.

33. Ferge, *Társadalmi újratermelés*, pp. 151–52.

34. Ibid., p. 141.

35. H. Sas, *Nöies nök*, p. 97.

36. Francis Barker's *The Tremulous Private Body* (London: Methuen, 1984), an analysis of works by Shakespeare, Descartes, Milton, and Samuel Pepys, is one of the most stimulating recent books on problems of modern (bourgeois) subjectivity. I have relied heavily on the analysis for my argument here.

37. Philip Corrigan, Harvie Ramsay, and Derek Sayer's critique of Bolshevism is equally relevant to Hungarian society, for obvious reasons: "The Bolsheviks continued to adhere to that impoverished notion of what production is, and what is entailed in developing it, which we met in the Second International's 'theory of productive forces,' and that this in turn eventuated in the separation of politics from production, and thus an effective fracturing of the spiral of productive and political liberation fundamental to a socialist programme. . . . In short, and unsurprisingly, to foster capitalist forms of productive activity eventuates in the reproduction of various defining relations of the bourgeois Stateform that is their condition and consequence" (*Socialist Construction and Marxist Theory: Bolshevism and Its Critique* [New York: Monthly Review Press, 1978], pp. 39, 46).

38. The word for confession to a Catholic priest is entirely different *(gyonni)*. The fact that these essays were written "to the state" makes the distinction between Catholic confession and legalistic self-avowal all the more trenchant.

39. I am indebted to Rafael Sánchez for this observation, as well as for his substantial contribution to the genesis of the argument as a whole.

40. Teresa de Lauretis, *Technologies of Gender* (Bloomington: Indiana University Press, 1987), pp. 2–3.

41. Ibid., p. 2.

Part 5
Roundtable:
Toward a Feminist Socialism?

Capitalism and Socialism: Some Feminist Questions

Lourdes Benería

Why Socialism Anyway?

In this age of continued Reaganism, deregulation, and privatization, to raise the issue of socialism almost seems to be a futile exercise. And in the age of post-modernism and deconstructionism this exercise almost seems out of fashion, even within progressive circles. Among feminists, there has always been a healthy mistrust of male-defined socialism, which is not to say that feminists have not been interested in progressive social change that might have a lot to do with what we losely tend to call "socialism." Likewise, tired of the effort to deal with the unhappy marriage between Marxism and feminism, some feminists seem to be opting for their separation rather than reconciliation—thereby indirectly raising again the connection between socialism and feminism. [1]

Perhaps the time has come for socialism to be given a different name, or for asking, for the Nth time, what do we mean by the term "socialism": What can we, as feminists, say about it? More specifically, what might feminist socialism mean? Public ownership of the means of production or worker-owned firms? Elimination of hierarchies related to class and gender? Ecologically conscious production and consumption? Full employment? A centrally planned economy or market socialism? Equal share of domestic chores by men and women or collectivization of domestic work? Elimination of racism and homophobia? A moneyless utopia? All of the above? How relevant are these questions and how reconcilable, for example, with feminist utopias like Marge Piercy's *Woman on the Edge of Time?* I do not think that we can give up thinking about these questions if we want feminism to be a source of progressive social change.

More basically still, we may want to ask why we need socialism at all. Capitalism has, after all, proved to be a very dynamic system, producing ever larger amounts of goods and services with progressively less amounts of labor. In the industrialized Western countries, it has resulted in higher standards of living for the majority. The working class can now afford what would have been classified as luxuries in the past. For many, it has facilitated the acquisition of skills, access to knowledge and professional privileges, and a significant increase in individual freedoms. Why then are we talking about socialism? About feminist socialism? Could we not achieve our goals within the existing capitalist structures?

What follows is not an attempt to answer these questions. It is instead a brief reflection on and a reiteration of some of the most basic criticisms of capitalism and, in particular, a discussion of directions for progressive social change with a feminist perspective. It is done with the conviction that, if feminism is to continue to be a source of inspiration for this change, women need to discuss, as much as ever, the overall economic and social aspects of this transformation.

One of the basic features of capitalism is its foundation on private ownership and control of the means of production. This implies that social decisions are made on the basis of private (as opposed to social/public) interest. But private and social needs may be convergent or in conflict. For Adam Smith and subsequent advocates of a laissez-faire economy, the genius of the market mechanism is that the pursuit of individual self-interest results in the maximization of "the wealth of nations." But, as Fritjo Capra has pointed out, the word "private" comes from the Latin verb *privare*, which meant depriving or taking from communal property.[2] This appropriation by private interests of what were in the past (and could be in the future) communal resources and production is at the heart of why capitalism (and not necessarily the market) produces negative as well as positive results.

Some of the most persuasive arguments for socialism come from the negative results of capitalism: great disparities in the distribution of income and wealth, with corresponding inequalities in control over resources and political power; the appearance and reappearance of poverty in the midst of an ever-increasing capacity to produce goods and services (witness the recent growth in the number of the homeless and beggars in the midst of the extreme affluence and lavishness displayed in the centers of world trade and finance); high levels of unemployment or underemployment with human costs that go far beyond economic survival; the all-encompassing hidden and not-so-hidden injuries of class and their connections with race and gender; the increasing disparities between rich and poor countries and the permanence, and even increase, of hunger and malnutrition despite the existence of food surpluses; the destruction of the environment and the disappearance of natural resources and ecological balances through exploitation for private profit.

Underlying these problems there is the fundamental role played by greed in capitalist institutions and its penetration into the realm of social and individual relations in everyday life. This is not to say that the social experiments of the so-called socialist countries have not created their own set of problems. However, this provides no argument against the need to transcend capitalism and move on toward new social experiments that respond more closely to the objectives of a just society in which the gap between our values and real life is minimized.

Women have not played the same role as men in either the positive or negative aspects of capitalist societies. First, they have often been exceptions to the pursuit of individual self-interest by virtue of their *primary* responsibilities in the sphere of the household, where the pressures of the market have penetrated less directly and at a slower pace. Second, given the concentration of resources and power in male hands, men have benefited more than women from the ownership and control of private property and from the benefits derived from capitalism. This is not to say that women have remained outside of the system, but that they have been part of it in different ways.

Similarly, the inequalities generated by capitalism have a specific gender dimension. The feminist literature of the past twenty years has extensively analyzed the specific forms that the subordination of women has taken in capitalist societies. To be sure, gender subordination can also be observed in countries that have moved away from capitalist institutions, despite the many achievements registered, as the essays in this volume point out. As feminists, we want to make note of these achievements while, at the same time, asking critical questions about the reasons behind their limitations.

What Directions for Change?

The second wave of feminism has generated profound social criticisms, many of which have implications for any discussion of social change. In what follows, I briefly summarize what I think are fundamental aspects in a feminist consideration of alternative societies. My suggestions are not meant to be exhaustive, but simply to contribute some general points to this discussion:

1. The interaction between class and gender in determining women's lives should remain central to our understanding of what sort of changes we want. Thus, some feminist objectives of eliminating gender asymmetries can be met within the structures of a capitalist society. In the industrialized capitalist world, for example, we have recently witnessed much progress in women's access to traditionally male strongholds, such as politics and the corporate world. Yet to the extent that women's position in society is determined by class and economic and social structures, some of the inequalities affecting women require basic changes in these structures

and institutions. For example, affirmative action and comparable-worth policies have proved to be important instruments in the pursuit of gender equality in the countries where they have been implemented.[3] Yet the progress made through these policies at some levels is being undermined in the current restructuring of the economy through the creation of new structures of production—such as the low-paid service sector, part-time work, and other practices of work flexibilization—that relegate women again to the lower echelons of the labor hierarchy.[4] This is because these policies cannot address the more basic questions of control, exploitation, and organization of economic life.

Similarly, the permanence of structures and institutions that benefit from gender inequalities also explains the dangers of a backlash and tendencies toward retrogressive policies that wipe out previous gains—as has happened in the United States and other Western countries in recent years. In other words, it might be difficult to implement long-lasting changes toward equality between the sexes without structural changes to build a more egalitarian society.

2. The complexity of the interaction between the material and the ideological aspects of women's condition is a second factor to be underlined. Many of the debates on the transition to socialism as well as platforms of left regimes have been dominated by an economistic approach: their emphasis on economics tends to overlook other basic areas of human development and well-being.[5] To the extent that women's condition is affected by economic factors, the debates are relevant for a discussion of women and socialism. But to the extent that the debates neglect ideological dimensions and their interaction with the material,[6] they cannot easily incorporate what Maxine Molyneux has called "strategic gender interests" or short and long-term feminist demands.[7] Thus, how gender roles are constructed and reproduced within the family and throughout the educational system, or through the media and other institutions, takes on a special meaning for women (as it does for racial and ethnic groups); not only do they effectively define women socially and politically, they also carry economic significance, when translated into, for example, sex-typing of jobs, occupational segregation, lower wages, different promotional ladders, and even job accessibility.

On the other hand, emphasis on the ideological only is likely to be ineffective unless it is accompanied by economic change. Campaigns challenging the traditional division of labor within the household are not likely to be very effective unless women have opportunities for employment in the paid labor market. Similarly, an effort to increase women's labor-force participation will be limited by the extent to which child care is available and by the economy's capacity to generate jobs. In Cuba, for example, the government's effort to increase women's labor-force participation seems to have been limited by an insufficient industrial base and its corresponding lack of growth in industrial and service employment.[8] Similarly, campaigns against male violence are likely to be more effective if accompanied by policies that increase women's economic autonomy and self-esteem.

3. A fundamental obstacle to the elimination of gender inequalities has proved to be in the sexual division of labor at the domestic level. The evidence along these lines is overwhelming and cuts across countries and economic systems. In the United States, the lack of adequate child-care services for all working women and the very limited or nonexistent maternity leaves and maternity benefits continue to be a major handicap to the elimination of women's double day, and to their participation in the labor market and in social life under conditions of equality with men.

In countries attempting to build socialist institutions, the commitment to these policies tends to be much greater, as a number of contributors to this volume argue. However, as most of them go on to point out, the evidence shows that the private sphere of the household is at the root of continuing asymmetries between men and women. In some of these countries, an attempt has been made to influence the household sphere through the introduction of family codes, as in the case of Cuba. What we can learn from the Cuban case is that, despite its intrinsic interest and worthy objectives, and despite the debate that the Family Code was subject to, its "spirit" cannot be imposed solely from the top down. Instead, what is also needed is a vigorous questioning at the bottom, fed by women's concerns and channeled through women's own networks and organizations.

4. Feminism has many implications for the question, "What sort of alternative system," or, "What form of socialism?" For example, given its emphasis on democratic and bottom-up processes of decisionmaking, feminism is less compatible with centralized planning and control of the economy than with more decentralized forms that emphasize individual or community control over resources. Thus, social ownership of the means of production does not necessarily imply government control and public enterprise. Other forms of collective ownership that allow control at the community level are likely to be more compatible with feminist processes of participatory decisionmaking and control. What specific forms these might take will depend on cultural specificity and traditions and might vary across countries.

Similarly, a preference for collective forms of ownership does not automatically have to exclude private ownership of the means of production, particularly when private accumulation is regulated to prevent the creation of inequalities and the concentration of resources in the hands of a small proportion of the population. For example, retail trade and small business in the service sector do not seem to function efficiently under socialized forms of ownership. Given that resources in the small-business sector are not very concentrated, a system that allows them to organize production privately does not pose a serious threat to socialist principles of equality. Since a characteristic of feminism is its lack of dogmatism with respect to "solutions," it can opt for what seems more compatible with feminist objectives without having to adapt to a rigid model of social change.

In this sense, feminists should pay attention to the now fashionable debate on "the global march to free markets," which argues that a new emphasis on the advantages of the invisible hand of the market can be found in both Western and centrally planned economies.[9] In both cases, it is argued, the state bureaucracies linked to public ownership and government regulation of the economy create inefficiency and distortions in the price system that slow down growth. Although such arguments need to be heeded, we should keep two points in mind. One is that even in the United States we hear many voices pointing to the serious problems created by the new emphasis on the market, deregulation, privatization, and cuts in government services and welfare funds. The new polarization of income and wealth is intensifying social inequalities at a point in history when the tolerance for it has been decreasing. Second, it is not clear whether the new trend toward the use of the market in noncapitalist countries such as the Soviet Union and China implies a return to capitalism. At the moment, they represent new experiments, the results of which can not yet be fully evaluated.

As feminists, we want to pay attention to these experiments in order to best evaluate how compatible they are with our own objectives and practice. This might lead to contradictory conclusions. Thus, on the one hand, we want to be aware of the dangers of creating male-controlled bureaucracies and institutions insensitive to gender inequalities.[10] On the other, if these bureaucracies are eliminated through the market, we also want to be aware of possible negative consequences. For example, the reprivatization of land in China has eliminated the system of work points. This, together with a feminization of agriculture corresponding to men's tendency to take jobs in the towns, has meant that women's contribution to the household is no longer accounted for socially. The return to the market therefore has implied the reemergence of old male privileges by eliminating mechanisms that decreased gender inequalities.[11] These contradictions, however, can be properly evaluated only at the level of each country's experience.

5. A fundamental aspect in the discussion of any alternative system is how production is organized and controlled and how its surplus is distributed. While this may appear to be a very economistic statement, here I want to emphasize the connections between what Burawoy has called "the

politics of production" and other aspects of everyday life.[12] Thus, hierarchical productive structures—beginning with the differentiation between those who own capital and those who need a wage to survive but including also the multiple dimensions of job differentiation—determine the distribution of income and wealth, shape class differences as well as social and political structures, and therefore have a bearing on individual and household location in society. Where we live and work, whether our children attend school or not and what kind of school, whether we eat at home or can afford to eat out, what we do with our leisure time, who our friends are and where we meet them, are all affected by where we are located within these productive structures.

Control over production and the sharing of the surplus also affect our lives in other ways. Thus, workers' control over production is likely to have an influence on the nature and direction of technological change and on the distribution of the firm's surplus. If women are involved, they are likely to press for day-care facilities and maternity leaves, and to stress policies affecting gender differentiation in the workplace.

Emphasis on the politics of production is also important in terms of evaluating proposals for social change. Maria Mies, for example, has called for a "consumer liberation movement," to be led by women as primary consumers, that would aim at boycotting certain goods and struggling against business manipulation of consumers, and channel a social awareness about existing commodities in the market.[13] There is of course much ground to argue for actions that would create the true "consumer's sovereignty" assumed by orthodox economic analysis of the market. Yet it seems naive to expect much from those actions alone. A more effective way to control what is being produced, and how, would be through the exercise of some form of collective control over production and surplus appropriation—hence creating the basis for future decisions on investment and growth. The question is how to do so without creating oppressive bureaucracies of centralized planning. If our objective is to move toward "an emancipated society in which people make their own history" rather than having history being made "behind their backs,"[14] feminism is likely to emphasize its preference for a fusion of production politics and state politics that work from below. This requires a subtle combination of the need for collective work on the one hand, and respect for the individual and culturally determined social norms on the other.[15]

By way of a conclusion, production under socialism holds the potential to be organized so that it responds to social *need* rather than *profit* and to collective rather than individual planning. Thus, it opens the possibility of addressing those problems of concern to women whose solution may be in conflict with *private* profit-making production. How exactly a socialist collectivity might operate is not easy to establish by way of general principles and needs to be subject to new social experimentation. It is for this reason that socialism represents more a *direction* for change than a set of definitions.

Notes

I want to thank Phyllis Andors, Günseli Berik, Nulifer Cagatay, Bill Goldsmith, Porus Olpadwala, Christine White, and all participants in the New York Women and Development group for their useful comments and suggestions on the preliminary draft of this paper.

1. See, for example, Michèle Barrett's "Introduction to the 1988 Edition" of her book *Women's Oppression Today* (London: Verso, 1980).
2. Frijto Capra, *Turning Point* (New York: Simon and Schuster, 1982).
3. Brigid O'Farrell and Sharon Harlan, "Job Integration Strategies: Today's Programs and Tomorrow's Needs," in Barbara Reskin, ed., *Sex Segregation in the Workplace* (Washington DC: National Academy Press, 1984); and Heidi Hartmann, ed., *Comparable Worth: New Directions for Research* (Washington, DC: National Academy Press, 1985).
4. Barry Bluestone and Sarah Kuhn, "Economic Restructuring and the Female Labour Market: The Impact of Industrial Change on Women," in L. Benería and C. Stimpson, *Women, Households and the Economy* (New Brunswick, NJ: Rutgers University Press, 1988).
5. There are of course exceptions and interesting efforts to include a wider range of topics. See, for example, Richard Fagen, Carmen Diana Deere, and José Luis Coraggio, eds., *Transition and Development: Problems of Third World Socialism* (New York: Monthly Review Press, 1987).
6. See Barrett, *Women's Oppression Today* and L. Benería and M. Roldán, *The Crossroads of Class and Gender* (Chicago: University of Chicago Press, 1987).
7. Maxine Molyneux, "Mobilization Without Emancipation? Womens Interests, State, and Revolution," in Fagen et al., eds., *Transition and Development*, pp. 280–302.
8. Margaret E. Leahy, *Development Strategies and the Status of Women: A Comparative Study of the United States, Mexico, the Soviet Union, and Cuba* (Boulder: Lynne Riener, 1986).
9. Steve Greenhouse, "The Global March to Free Markets," *New York Times*, July 19, 1987.
10. Christine White, "Socialist Transformation of Agriculture and Gender Relations," in John Taylor and Andrew Turton, eds., *Sociology of Developing Societies—South East Asia* (London and New York: Macmillan and Monthly Review Press, 1988).
11. Phyllis Andors, personal communication.
12. Michael Burawoy, *The Politics of Production* (London: Verso, 1985).
13. Maria Mies, *Patriarchy and Accumulation on a World Scale* (London: Zed Books, 1986).
14. Burawoy, *Politics and Production*, p. 157.
15. Many differences exist, for example, among countries of different cultural norms and traditions. Thus the emphasis on the individual by feminists in Western countries tends to be culturally biased and without meaning in societies where the collective, be it the household or a larger social group, is more prevailing. The search for the right combination between the collective and the individual is therefore likely to be influenced by these factors.

Reflections

Zillah Eisenstein

The articles in this book that discuss the Soviet Union, Nicaragua, China, and other post-revolutionary societies explore the possibilities of feminism—for sexual equality—*within* socialist societies. Although this is a crucial question, particularly for people living in these countries, it is also a troublesome question. It is troublesome because socialism, whatever particular form it takes as one's starting point, one's framework to work *from*, is a framework that assumes a "phallocratic" stance. It is a stance that privileges the economy and the public sphere while using abstract notions of equality that assume the male body as its referent. As such, feminism at best can be used to reform socialism, as it has reformed capitalism; it is clear from this book that socialism(s) can adapt to and incorporate feminist demands. But this is different than arguing that socialism has been transformed by feminism, or that feminism sets the agenda *for* socialism. Feminism, in part, remains derivative because the phallus—the symbolization of man—is the referent.

My point here is not to say that socialism(s) is irrelevant to feminism, or that it does not hold significant promise for women's equality. Rather, my point is that the phallocratic basis of socialism—the oppositional dualisms that privilege the real over the ideal, public over private, economics over sexuality—must be challenged to subvert the epistemological underpinnings of women's subordination. My point is that the way we think and talk about socialism and feminism is as intimately tied up with the promise of "real" equality as are the structural and so-called material relations of society. We must recognize that there is a dialectic between ideas about equality and the structures of equality. Although distinct, they are not completely separate realms. And if this is the case, then we need to rethink the epistemological base of the relations of power. More specifically, we need to rethink the meaning of difference, particularly sex difference(s) and the way it defines the relations of power; in terms of present inequality *and* a promissory radical egalitarianism.

The "unfinished task" of women's liberation within socialist societies is then not only "circumstantial" and "structural" as the editors have stated. It is also epistemological and theoretical. Although several of the contributors—including Wendy Zeva Goldman (the Soviet Union) and Muriel Nazzari (Cuba), argue that the problem—which renders women's liberation unfinished—is one of material poverty, the problem is at least in part a "poverty of philosophy." The way one speaks and thinks about women's lives, their bodies, their equality, their "difference" is as much an issue as the social circumstances, because our language interprets the meaning(s) of these circumstances.

Socialist societies are organized around the differentiation of woman from man, although clearly in a variety of ways. It matters how this division is interpreted and explained. Mostly, the differentiation of woman *from* man is taken as natural. The focus on culture in the nature/culture divide, which on the one hand can be used to liberate women from their so-called nature, instead obfuscates the fact that the body does not fit neatly on one side or the other. Although Marxist theory, as Joan Landes points out, promises to rescue women from the naturalist, patriarchal discussion via its social, historical, and cultural interpretation of "nature," it instead assumes the naturalist stance on the woman's body and its place in the sexual division of procreative sex.

A problem here is that woman's body cannot be fully contextualized or deconstructed: there is a biological thing called the body, whatever it is named, and the process of naming it brings culture with it. The historical aspects of the Marxist method that deny the "reality" of nature per se, and attribute social intervention to all social relations, does not help one to understand the biological components, the particularity and specificity of the female body, especially although not only when pregnant, and silently assumes the male body as standard, as the referent. Hence there is no theorizing of difference(s), meaning the specificities of the female body as part of the continuum of human experience. Difference(s) between females and males rather is treated as woman's "difference" *from* man and, as such, "difference" becomes a problem, an expression of inequality, a lack. Sameness—being like men—becomes the standard, but through a universal and abstract language of equality. Individuals are represented as classes and classes are made up of men and equality means equality between men, like men. But equality cannot mean sameness of treatment between men and women because males and females are both similar *and* particular; they have similar needs *and* specific needs. Equality must recognize more than homogeneity; it must recognize heterogeneity as well. Difference(s) must be theorized and specified as part of the meaning of equality. A notion of equality that encompasses the pregnant body but does not establish it as a new referent can refocus and specify the meaning of sexual equality in socialist theory. Diversity and radical pluralism dislodge sameness (to a male referent) as the criterion for egalitarianism. Equality must take into account individual specificity and not falsely demand a similarity that silences difference(s) or silences the body as natural within an epistemology that supposedly rejects the notion of "nature."

The oppositional stance of Marxist theory, which assumes the clear division between nature/culture, real/ideal, true/false, stunts the promise of socialism and feminism. It is a way of thinking about the relations of power that construct women's lives while limiting the capacity for addressing their inequality. And this is true for liberal democratic societies as well. The problems here are not limited to Marxist theory. The phallocratic discourses that engender the meaning of sex difference(s) operate in liberalism and Marxism. Marxism, as an attack on the economic inequalities of capitalism, and liberalism, as a defense of capitalism as a system of equality of opportunity, both utilize a naturalist doctrine on sexual "difference." They assume a division of labor requisite of the biological "difference" of woman from man; woman is seen as the mother in an institutionalized form instead of as a female who has the potential to bear a child but is not consigned to this potential. And although much of the socialist legal reform tied to reorganizing family responsibilities is done in the name of equality, it is a notion of equality that does not applaud difference(s). A notion of radical pluralism—which recognizes difference(s) as illuminating the meaning of equality—is not part of socialist or liberal theory. Difference(s) is assumed to mean inequality because there is a silent referent: a woman's body is *not* like a man's, she is less than man. In order to be equal she must be the same. Homogeneity becomes the standard and individuality a problem. But socialism cannot be feminist until individuality, difference(s), and the female body transform the meaning of sex equality. It must be specified in more than economic and legal terms.

Radical pluralism is not a part of a socialist theory of sex equality because heterogeneity, particularly individual, and specifically bodily difference(s), are not theorized as a distinct aspect of social relations. The individualist concern with diversity must be incorporated into the socialist vision of equality. But in this instance the concern with individuality must be deconstructed for its engendered representation of maleness. Individuals should not be represented as men; individuals are rather diverse, disparate, particular females *and* males. The point is not to de-sex equality but rather to allow it its sexual diversity without engendering it: without setting up difference(s) in an oppositional, dualist mode that is then further articulated through the economic class inequities of abstract individualism.

What then is the promise of socialism for women's struggle for equality? There is no one answer to this question. The essays in this book depict very different societies, with different histories, different cultures, different possibilities. Just as there is no one feminism there is no one socialism. And there is no one relationship between socialism(s) and feminism(s). There *are* specific societies, particular histories, generalized theories of equality, and the specific struggles for equality that take place. There are also the languages—with their politics and epistemological stance—that interpret and depict these specific struggles.

The similarity among socialist countries arises through the somewhat generalized language of egalitarianism. The promise of egalitarianism is both real *and* ideal, concrete *and* abstract. That is why it is so important to recognize that the distinction between socialist theory and practice is somewhat overdrawn when it is used to privilege practice over theory; the real over the ideal. If socialism is about the changed relationships of the economy toward an equality that specifies the needs of the worker it must also be about the changed way we think and speak about the female body. Establishing the material basis of equality in part requires a language to think about it and this requires a refocusing of the relations of sexuality and reproduction: that the individual always has a body, which is never completely natural or totally cultural. And that conceptions of the body are already engendered through the political discourse(s) that prevails.

It is a false split to argue that issues related to the body and sexuality are different in kind (and import) than issues of food, clothing, and shelter, in that the latter are what first must be met by socialist societies. They are integrally related: food and sex, hunger and equality. We need to think about them as such. Universal humanitarianism needs to be specified, as Marilyn Young points out in her discussion of China, because women cannot be human in a male sense, or an abstract sense for that matter. Socialist theory needs to move beyond the nature/culture split and instead theorize the body in terms of its biological specificity. By deconstructing the "difference" of woman from man equality can come to recognize specificity *and* individuality.

Both liberalism and socialism are constructed in and through phallocratic discourse. Whereas liberalism promises equality of opportunity while mystifying economic and sexual class inequity, socialism demystifies economic exploitation while obfuscating sex inequality. To the extent that socialism is *already* committed to economic equality, and to the degree that economic equality is a significant part of sex equality, socialism holds out a better promise for women than liberalism can or does. But it cannot make good on its promise without deconstructing the political meaning of (sex) "difference." It needs to theorize sex equality while recognizing the specificity of bodily and individual differences. Socialism needs a sexed and individuated theory of equality. Egalitarianism must be specified through the body, male or female, in order that it not require women to be the same as men; or that homogeneity and sameness replace diversity and difference(s). Such a feminist vision can promise socialism a radical egalitarianism that recognizes individuality.

Third World Revolution and First World Feminism: Toward a Dialogue

Delia D. Aguilar

Back in the Philippines for a year's stay after over two decades of residence in the United States, I think back to a New England study group in Marxist-feminism that a handful of us women of color were participants in at the onset of the 1980s. Our identities and commitment defined by and bound to the goal of national liberation of our respective countries—Puerto Rico, Bangladesh, Iran, the Philippines—we soon concluded that, given our differences with the feminist consensus, the mission that devolved upon us was to represent the "third world women's perspective."

True enough, as heterogeneous as our experiences were, our discomfiture with a vocabulary thick with allusions to patriarchy and gender antagonisms but utterly deficient in the language we were more attuned to (capitalism, imperialism, national democracy, revolution, etc.) ineluctably drew us together to puzzle out among ourselves and question what, indeed, was Marxist about this particular group. I distinctly remember thrashing out at the end of the initial session some of the major points under discussion with the white activist who had invited us to join. "But that's not Marxism," I protested. "They're not Marxists," she explained somewhat exasperatedly, distancing herself from the others through the use of the third personal plural. "They're Marxist-feminists!"

In light of our pronounced alienation, only the compulsion to communicate the urgency of our distinct struggles, along with sheer bullheadedness, made it possible for a few of us to remain in the study group. We talked about the status of women, but whether the narration was of women's lives in Puerto Rico, Iran, or the Philippines, the recurrent and pervasive motif was the determining force of U.S. imperialism. Its effect was, as one might well expect, an oversimplified, unidimensional rendition of women's subordination, but one that was necessary in the face of an abysmal ignorance of the "third world perspective" and its corollary, cultural chauvinism. In spite of our cognizance of racism as a hallmark of life in the West, we found ourselves sorely ill-equipped to handle the callous query of one academic who all but obliterated both our presence and the impact of any of our previous statements with one stroke: "Should U.S. Marxist-feminists support national liberation struggles that are patriarchal?"

We were to discover before long that the tensions we felt, while attributable to the confrontation between third world aspirations and racist discourse, were concurrently generated by unresolved issues in the ongoing Marxist-feminist debates. I began to comprehend the more complex, intricate elaborations of the arguments only in the space permitted by individual reading and reflection. Within the study group itself, the attempt to construct a theoretical position—or, as it were, to presuppose a unity among women—meant, in practice, the glossing over of neocolonialism and the assertion of the lived experience of white professional women as universal.[1] In order to challenge this hegemony, we women of color were forced to assume an adversarial posture (that is, to contrapose national sovereignty as the major project and unshifting arena of struggle), a course of action that in turn could effectively retard our conceptualization of gender-specific forms of oppression. Realizing this, we decided to get together for the purpose of exploring the implications of feminism for third world social movements in general and for women in particular. Needless to say, we were alert to the dangers of totalizing these struggles.

In the safety of the smaller group, we voiced our predicament: as progressive third world women situated in the United States, we were pulled in one direction by the primacy of production posited by the classical Marxism of our revolutionary movements, and now pushed in the other by the feminist critique shifting the categories of analysis to sexual politics and reproduction. Our experiences, as women, previously flattened by an exclusive focus on imperialism, now began to be fleshed out and acquire the rich textures of our diverse life histories. In our exchanges—enthusiastic, vigorous, and always impassioned—we accepted the necessity for a philosophical framework that could analyze gender while rejecting the chauvinist impulses with which one model had been prescribed. To be sure, the consciousness that was raised in this process was never limited to the confines of gender asymmetry. In one case, the most conscientious student among us, a Filipina, decided to withdraw rather than confront the growing dissonance presented by the unmasking of racist and sexist tendencies fused in her white leftist husband whose participation in movement activities superseded hers. For him the Philippines served as an area of academic specialization where he could carve himself a little niche. What was it for her except the land of her birth and home of her people?

As entangled as the issues had become for us in the process of our exploration, the questions we sought to answer remained simple. What kind of feminism can we subscribe to? How do we handle male chauvinism in our ranks? This is not to say that we anticipated easy or premature resolutions. For myself, the sessions operated in the manner of a long-delayed, much-needed catharsis, permitting me to recollect in relative tranquillity my bitter frustration, in the mid-1970s, over the refusal of Filipino comrades to constitute gender relations as a legitimate site of struggle. Dispatching letters documenting women's active involvement in the New People's Army (NPA, the military arm of the Communist Party of the Philippines) as proof of their deliverance from sexual oppression, revolutionaries took a view of women's liberation that was class reductionist, mechanical, and instrumentalist. More personally annoying than their denial of sexism as a problem among Filipinos were innuendos about how prolonged stay in the United States, exacerbated by affliction with the individualist character of bourgeois feminism, results in estrangement from one's native culture, an ad hominem fallacy difficult to take kindly to.

Propelled by such a dismissal to seek alternate avenues, I launched into a project investigating Filipino women's position through an examination of the politics of gender at the heart of the family. Held sacrosanct by revolutionaries no less than by the popular mind, the family, perceived as the repository of all that is of value in Philippine life, has been exempted from critical scrutiny and interrogation. I recorded interviews with ten Metro Manila women, all wives and mothers, whose narratives to me revealed unmistakable male dominion over household arrangements, the daily conduct and management of which were the exclusive responsibility of women. I was gratified to have summoned evidence for my contention, indisputable because grounded on testimony from women themselves.

In the meantime the political landscape in the Philippines was being altered with breathtaking rapidity. The airport murder of former senator Benigno Aquino in 1983, inflaming with extraordinary intensity the passions of the Filipino people, found expression in the unprecedented proliferation of "cause-oriented" organizations, cross-class women's groups among them. In 1984 Gabriela, a coalition of women's associations, was formed. A noteworthy facet of this turn of events was the articulation by some insistent women of the hitherto unacceptable, discordant label "feminist," now a linguistic practice to which the party line has had to concede.

It is difficult to predict at this point what influence current campaigns waged by women will have on the long-term project for social liberation in the Philippines. At a conference in Connecticut last fall, a U.S. woman who had just returned from the Philippines conveyed to me her amazement at the extent of Filipino women's organizing. The network of women's associations is truly impressive. Integral to this is research by women activists which, if it proceeds at its present pace, threatens to take over turf formerly occupied by mainstream social scientists funded by U.S. development agencies. But "feminist" or not, the gravitational pull in analysis toward the material sphere of the productive structure indicative of orthodox Marxist dogma remains overpowering. Hence, daily news about skirmishes between government soldiers and the NPA—a recognition, at the very least, of the revolutionary movement's enduring potency in the countryside—sits uneasily with a popular consciousness that is disturbingly retrograde.

Let me illustrate. The other day I was among progressive friends, feminists included, who were describing with great amusement the well-advertised flirtations of a U.S. colleague in energetic pursuit of a Filipino wife. Bothered by their pleasure in the telling of such juvenile antics—to them apparently innocent of the taint of race and gender prejudices—I maneuvered a flashback to my third world women's study group and imagined how we might have dissected the situation. No doubt we would have called up the obvious connection with the phenomenon of the Filipino mail-order bride, her appeal to a clientele of Euro-American males (in many instances social rejects in their own countries) resting on a presupposed disposition toward obsequiousness, service, and loyalty. Even granting how the warm interpersonal bonding governing life in the Philippines can act to obscure this analogy for these friends (the fellow was part of their circle), one wonders how exhortations to combat imperialism, together with that self-critical designation" colonial mentality" can fail to invade the essential realm of the "superstructure."

The incongruity of such naivete, positioned in a transformational movement whose tenacity under the Cory Aquino government continues to trouble Washington, can only be symptomatic of a version of Marxism that, relying on a base/superstructure metaphor, privileges economic factors and obfuscates the interweaving of class, race or nation, and gender. Moreover, mired in the dichotomy that mechanically rank-orders contradictions as either "primary" or "secondary" within a predominantly productivist paradigm, cadres are locked into the perennial subordination of the "Woman Question" to the issue of national self-determination.[2] Yet there is no denying that our sensitivity to suggestions of racism as third world women in the metropole had been sharpened precisely by life in the United States. It is to this that I will now turn, for if I have been unhappy with the blind spots traceable to a doctrinaire Marxism identified with "revolutionaries in a hurry," the deformation of the highly sophisticated theorizing in U.S. Marxist feminism by the buried presumption of a unified female subject tends to sour the most fervent entreaties for international solidarity.

This immediately brings to mind an exchange I had with a columnist in a "Marxist-Humanist" newspaper whose founder took pride in being an exponent of the feminism of Rosa Luxemburg. The writer decried Nicaraguan Minister of Culture Ernesto Cardenal's failure to explain to her satisfaction the Sandinista government's efforts to address the problems confronting women. In point of fact, she had prejudged from a U.S. feminist's perspective the regime's implicit sanction of "butcher abortions" as signaling (to quote her loosely) " a rollback of gains the women's movement in the West had made in the past fifteen years." Only arrogance of immense proportions, the kind sporting a "made in U.S.A." label, can manage the facile equation of the two struggles, and then to admonish one for not learning the cosmic lessons established by the other! When I emphasized how U.S. Marxists engaged in solidarity work need to be attentive to their own location in the United States (the power wreaking havoc on the Nicaraguan people, among others), the columnist ignored my point and instead sent me a news clipping featuring an indigenous campaign for abortion rights in Nicaragua. Had she, by dint of global sisterhood, been transformed into a Nicaraguan? Or had the Nicaraguan woman's identity been subsumed in the U.S. woman's persona?

Impositions pressed on people of color, often released like spasmodic emissions, blemish even carefully formulated treatises that appear sympathetic enough on the surface. A recent conference in Cambridge brought into interesting juxtaposition the concerns of Asian women in the United States and in Southeast Asia, set up panels composed mainly of Asian speakers, and, appropriately enough, drew a largely Asian attendance. In a presentation on Vietnamese women, the only non-Asian panelist roused me from drowsiness induced by a poor night's sleep through her sudden impatient rebuke, fitting only if addressed to a bunch of recalcitrant children or to members of an inferior caste: "Here, read Ann Oakley's book on housework!" As the presenter explained, the valiant struggle of Vietnamese women had been an inspiration for the women's movement in the first world. The time had come for first world women to return the favor.

Now it is hard to say whether a missionary variant of this imperial feminism, which I recount next, is necessarily easier on the stomach. Curious to hear what a policy studies program might have to say about the impact of development strategies on the living conditions of women in the third world (the conference theme was "Dilemmas of Development"), I attended a workshop conducted by a woman of color whose range of professional experience included governmental and non-governmental agencies. Using the life concerns of poor women who comprise the majority in countries of the periphery as the axis of her report, she gave an overview of the prevailing industrial growth-oriented models and cautiously hinted at the need for alternate visions. With that she opened the floor and invited the predominantly white, middle- to upper-middle-class female audience to participate. The response, spontaneous and free-flowing, proceeded without interruption for close to an hour in the direction of how those in the United States can empower (those poor benighted) third world women by convincing them of the value of their housework and by increasing their self-esteem. Bordering on the therapeutic, this demonstration of goodwill is probably not so unusual, emanating as it did from Harvard's John F. Kennedy School. Nor is it puzzling that economic development via production for export subscribed to by the countries in question could be mentioned with no reference whatever to the role of international lending agencies or U.S. government policy.

What is here subject to critique is the denial of a historical context to women with the result that those in the third world are viewed, perhaps charitably, as lagging many light-years behind in developmental terms. This mindset was dramatized in a forum centering on two women prisoners of conscience that was co-sponsored by human rights organizations and a women's studies program. When a poet/prize-winner explains to her listeners that writers in the third world, especially under repressive regimes, are not privileged as are U.S. cultural workers, "to write about themselves as individuals," she presupposes an evolutionary model wherein self-cultivation and self-indulgence represent ascendance to a higher stage. Moreover, she displays a striking lack of appreciation for a worldview in which the self cannot be seen as distinct from sociohistorical process. Thus the editor of a feminist journal, a women in development expert, could offer the following comments on an essay I submitted: "Women need to be at the center of the analysis in a way that they are not now. The piece reads as a discussion of the Philippine situation, with women added rather than an analysis of Philippine women per se." I had begun the article expressly to clarify my position. I tried to distinguish the ahistoricity dominant in Euroamerican feminism from the contextualized perspective that third world women revolutionaries, in particular, insist on. Evidently the four pages of introduction I devoted to explicating this outlook missed the target. I have not submitted this essay to the persual of friends here in the Philippines. Could they conceivably judge it as giving undue stress on feminism?

What are the theoretical cross-currents imbricating this personal odyssey in which two worlds, both guided by a shared visionary politics, are traversed? Clearly, one can easily choose to restrict the meaning of this narrative to the boundaries of a sketch where close encounters with a distinct variety of culturally-formed biases are seen as illustrative of barriers to solidarity-building. There is no denying that this is in large measure the message I would like to get across. These experiences, above all, substantiate the need for a critical examination of the framework in which feminism is inscribed, discarding imagined notions of "international sisterhood" whenever references to empire and race are carelessly omitted or glossed over. Further, as some of the incidents demonstrate, a Marxist-feminist analysis does not in itself prevent the casting of a hegemonic feminism, particularly when the human agent begins to act in a free-floating, neutral capacity; that is, as though unanchored in concrete territory. Here we would have to acknowledge that the undeveloped state of Marxism applies as much to race as to the Woman Question, and that the formulation of theory to account for racial inequality is a project that could prove illuminating for gender oppression.

This brings me to another mode of interpretation that ought not detract from the one just suggested. This one seeks to diagnose the strains and tensions that have been here dramatized by different players on various stages as engendered by contradictions and antinomies embedded in Marxist theory and practice. From this vantage point, the tremendous complexities—not to say absence of uniformity—in the construction of socialism are bared. In particular, two distinct, competing trends rise to the surface: the economic determinism seen in many third world revolutions with its heavy emphasis on the transformation of productive forces at one end and, at the other, the affirmation of consciousness, ideology, and subjectivity represented by Marxist-feminists. Deconstructed thus, the oppositions in Marxism as embodied by the key protagonists in my narrative, Marxism and Marxist-feminism, come alive to engage in creative tension. This engagement is an example of how, through collaborative ventures, exchanges, and dialogues at all levels on all fronts, a more liberating social practice might emerge in the heat of contradictions.

Notes

1. Of enormous help to our understanding of this were essays by women of color, among which were: Floya Anthias and Nira Yuval-Davis, "Contextualizing Feminism—Gender, Ethnic and Class Divisions." *Feminist Review* 14 (Winter 1983): 62–75, and Jenny Bourne, "Towards an Anti-Racist Feminism," *Race and Class* XXV (Summer 1983): 1–22.
2. It is this same mechanism that led to the virtual paralysis of the organized left, barring its affiliate associations from electoral politics and from forging vital alliances against Ferdinand Marcos during the period culminating in the televised "revolution" of February 1986. The result, in the face of Cory Aquino's present popularity is the isolation of the left in Metro Manila and other urban centers.

   For an elucidation of such problems as inherent in the tensions in Marxism, and not solely in its faulty interpretation in the hands of "Third World revolutionaries under pressure," see John S. Saul, "The Role of Ideology in the Transition to Socialism," in *Transition and Development: Problems of Third World Socialism*, Richard R. Fagen, José Luis Coraggio, and Carmen Diana Deere, eds. (New York: Monthly Review Press, 1986), pp. 212–30.

On Promissory Notes

Christine Pelzer White

The title of this book, "Promissory Notes," reflects a consensus among socialist feminists that socialism's promise to bring about equality between men and women has yet to be achieved. In country after country, after decades of "transition to socialism," structured inequalities between men and women persist, in the family, in political life, and in the workplace. This consensus, no matter how qualified, must be accompanied by an equally close examination of gender relations within Western countries and of the ramifications of anticommunist militarism. In Vietnam, for example, we need to consider the implications of the war waged by the United States against the Vietnamese revolution not just for gender relations in Vietnam, but for gender relations in the United States. What are the connections between the struggles for gender equality in Vietnam and in the United States? How were, how are, American women involved in their government's opposition to socialism in Vietnam? What effect will the ongoing reconstruction of women's war and anti-war experiences during the Vietnam period have on the attitude of American women toward future wars yet to be waged against the possibility of the emergence or consolidation of socialism in Central America, the Middle East, Southern Africa, or Southeast Asia? What are the implications for American and third world women of increasing militarization globally? What promissory notes to ourselves as well as to third world people remain unredeemed because of the failure of Western feminists and Western socialists to transform deeply entrenched sexist and militarist institutions in our own societies?

The feminist critical examination of the relationship between socialist transformation and women's liberation needs to be accompanied by an equally careful analysis of the dynamics of international solidarity among women. The concept of "sisterhood," which transcends class, ethnic and national boundaries, constitutes a core assumption distinguishing the Western feminist world view. Studies such as Arlene Eisen-Bergman's

345

pathbreaking *Women of Vietnam*, Margaret Randall's *Spirit of the People*, Arlene Eisen's second book, *Women and Revolution in Vietnam*, and Robin Morgan's *Sisterhood is Global* have introduced Vietnamese women's struggles for national liberation and socialism to Western readers.[1] *Sisterhood is Global*, described as "the International Women's Movement anthology," includes an excerpt from an article by Nguyen Thi Dinh, a Vietnamese woman who played an important role in both political and military leadership during Vietnam's struggles first against French colonialism, then against American neocolonialism. Now president of the Vietnamese Women's Union, during the war she was deputy commander of the armed forces of the National Liberation Front—the so-called Vietcong.

Wartime solidarity with Vietnamese communist women leaders, as well as with ordinary Vietnamese women who were victims of the conflict, was facilitated by a view of the Vietnam war as a man's war, planned by white male policymakers and fought by male soldiers. American feminists' feelings of sisterhood with Vietnamese women were reinforced by the fact that the women's liberation movement was born during the period of the anti-Vietnam war movement. This was probably no coincidence: rather, mobilization against one form of injustice led to mobilization against another. The civil rights, antiwar, and women's movements developed in quick succession. In a similar way, the nineteenth-century women's movement in the United States followed close on the abolitionists' struggle against slavery. The example of the struggle of the Vietnamese people for national liberation contributed to the militancy and radicalism of politics in the late 1960s and early 1970s; oppressed "minority" races and genders in American society—blacks, Hispanics, native Americans, women, and gays thought that if the Vietnamese could fight back against overwhelming odds, they too should be able to resist the forms of oppression they faced.

During the early "consciousness raising" period of the American feminist movement the virulently macho character of the U.S. war machine and its crimes against Vietnamese women threw into bold relief the male chauvinist nature of the American polity. For example, Susan Brownmiller's *Against Our Will*, a pioneering feminist study of rape, includes several accounts of the kidnapping, gang rape, and murder of young Vietnamese peasant girls by American soldiers.[2] The American military did not, in practice, consider rape and murder of Vietnamese civilian women a serious offense, and few offenders were brought to trial. Similarly, in the United States, Brownmiller pointed out, violent crimes against women were often not taken seriously, and assault on women was a favorite sensationalist topic for both tabloids and TV programs.[3] By contrast, Brownmiller noted, it was common knowledge among American reporters in Vietnam that cases of rape by "Vietcong" and North Vietnamese soldiers were extremely rare. The revolutionary Vietnamese armed forces considered rape a capital offense, and executions were publicized as a deterrent for this serious crime.[4]

There was no unanimity between the women's movement and the antiwar movement at this time. Brownmiller concludes the section on Vietnam with an account of her anger at the fact that for some male antiwar leaders the slogan "Stop the Rape of Vietnam" referred only to the defoliation of crops, not the abuse of Vietnamese women,; her offer to speak on the topic of rape and prostitution in Vietnam at antiwar rallies was not accepted.[5] Despite such tensions, the emergence of the women's movement at this time added an important dimension to international solidarity, especially given the apparent demise of proletarian solidarity, which was partially, but only partially, an artifact of the media's headlining of "hard hat" American workers' prowar demonstrations and downplaying of opposition to the war by many sections of organized labor. It was overwhelmingly young working-class males of Euro-American and "minority" ethnic origins who did the actual fighting in the war, not women.[6] The "women warriors" in the consciousness of feminist writers during the antiwar period were on the NLF side.

However, it would be misleading to imply that there was a strong and dominant feeling of international sisterhood between American and Vietnamese women during the war. In the antiwar movement as well as in the wider society, most American women felt a pained and bruised sisterhood with American soldiers along with, or instead of, a sisterhood with Vietnamese women. Furthermore, in real life the abstract category "Vietnamese women" includes political activists with opposing political views ranging from members of the Vietnam Communist Party to militant anticommunists. To be in solidarity with one is to be the enemy of the other. In the postwar period, many American women, including antiwar and socialist women, have opened their hearts to "the boat people," refugees from communism, ongoing war and poverty in Vietnam. Solidarity is a complicated issue, with gender, political, national, and class dimensions. As a result, to date, international women's solidarity, like international proletarian solidarity, is more aspiration than reality.

There has been a shift since the antiwar period in the attitude of the American women's movement toward the military, and the admiration of Vietnam's "women warriors" such as Nguyen Thi Dinh has been superseded by the demand that the contribution of American women to the Vietnam war, particularly as nurses, be recognized. I recently saw a poster with a photo of dogtags and the caption "In the sixties not all women wore love beads" at a conference on "the Vietnam Experience" organized by the local chapter of Vietnam Veterans of America. The political slant of this poster, and the drive for a statue to honor the American women who served in Vietnam which it was advertising, are part of an ongoing effort to recast the Vietnam war in the American political imagination.[7] In the summer of 1988 at the Seneca Falls 10th Annual Convention Days, organized to commemorate the anniversary of the historic First Women's Rights Convention held there on July 19 and 20, 1848, the major topical political issue was recognition of the role of 10,000 American women stationed in Vietnam during the war. Former army nurse Nellie Coakley of the Vietnam Women's Memorial Project addressed the anniversary festival, saying "We suffered, we served, and we died alongside the soldiers. We deserve the recognition." This, she explained, was not just for the sake of women Vietnam veterans but also for women who may become involved in future wars. "If any of the next generation must face the choice of going to war, then, whatever path they take, it is our duty to be there for them when they return."[8] In the next war the slogan "support our boys" may be replaced with: "support our men and women." In the early 1970s a college student would most likely have associated the words "women and Vietnam" with Nguyen Thi Dinh, or Nguyen Thi Binh, the negotiator in Paris for the Provisional Revolutionary Government. Today the association is women veterans, the debated issue of a fourth, female, Vietnam memorial statue, women refugees, or "China Beach," the TV serial about the wartime R and R center near Danang which features a number of American women in Vietnam.

Valiant Women in War and Exile, a recently published collection of interviews by Sally Hayton-Keeva, is exemplary of the new attention to American women's war experiences.[9] Reared on her father's World War II stories, the author had identified with the anti-Vietnam war movement and had a brief marriage to a draft resister in a politically motivated attempt to be involved with the political drama of the time. Her enterprise of collecting women's "war stories" includes a reevaluation of her initial concept of woman as innocent victim and pacifist in favor of an examination of the complexity of women's relationship to war. The book includes a relic of the wartime feminist consciousness of Vietnam: a photograph of General Nguyen Thi Dinh reviewing an all-woman guerrilla unit in the Mekong Delta which appears to be reprinted from Arlene Eisen-Bergman's 1974 book, *Women of Vietnam*. However, there is not a single inteview with a Vietnamese woman in the book. Three interviews with women with such nicknames as Peggy and Kathy are labeled "Vietnam" in the table of contents. They are all Americans: an army nurse, a war correspondent, and a flight attendant on military flights carrying troops to and from Vietnam.

A similar recent book, entitled *Women in War*, also totally ignores Vietnamese women. The women interviewed discuss important aspects of gender relations during the war: both the blatant sexism and the strong sister-brother bond that characterized the relations between the American men and women who served in Vietnam. These American women saw themselves as the emotional sisters of American soldiers in Vietnam, a very different concept of "sister" from that of the Robin Morgan anthology. Nurses suffered deep distress dealing day after day with severely wounded and dying young American men who reminded them of their brothers, and were appalled to realize that as a result "unfeminine" emotions of hatred and desire for revenge often replaced sympathy for Vietnamese men and women as fellow human beings. Some found it difficult to treat POW patients in a professional manner. One nurse remembers feeling hostility toward a woman guerrilla prisoner under her care.[10] These women feel pain and guilt at these lapses in human sentiment and the ethics of their profession. Their bravery in openly discussing the shadows and complexity of their wartime experiences contributes an important corrective to the view of women as innocent of the atrocities and guilt of "men's" wars. This recent recognition, in memoirs and fiction, of women's war experiences does not exclude solidarity between women on opposite sides. For example, the TV serial "China Beach" includes an episode portraying the development of sisterly feelings between an American nurse and a Vietnamese wounded female POW who had been a nurse before the war.

Yet there was a darker side to gender relations in the Vietnam war that is just beginning to come out. While Susan Brownmiller summarized the documentation on the brutal treatment of Vietnamese women by American men at war, the recently published oral histories of American women's war experiences recount case after case of American women murdered or raped by American men in Vietnam.[11] Nurses with an ideal of dedicated service were shocked and hurt to find that many of the American men they encountered there regarded them as camp followers rather than respecting them as brave and dedicated professionals and equals. As a result of their direct experience of the horrors of war, several of these women veterans have become militant antiwar activists in the 1980s. For example, one of the nurses interviewed by Hayton-Keeva has visited Nicaragua with other veterans of the Vietnam war and is active in the campaign against U.S. military intervention in Latin America.[12]

It is crucially important to heal the psychic wounds of the Vietnam war in American society by paying attention to the voices and experiences of both male and female Vietnam veterans. However, a necessary part of this process will be coming to terms with Vietnam itself. At the present time the United States government does not recognize the Socialist Republic of Vietnam diplomatically and has long maintained a trade and aid embargo.[13] In the recent outpouring of scholarly, journalistic, and imaginative works on the Vietnam war the point of view of the Vietnamese "other" is eerily absent. The process of "reconciliation" and "healing the wounds of war" cannot be accomplished without including Vietnam itself in the dialogue. This, it seems to me, is an outstanding "promissory note" of both women and men of the "Vietnam generation" to their own moral, political, and psychic development as well as to the women and men of Vietnam who are still suffering from the aftermath of war.[14]

One of the fruits of the women's movement has been a marked opening of the military to women, and I have even heard young women argue that one of the most important feminist issues for them is equality between men and women in terms of military obligations and combat roles. There appears to be a generational difference in American women's attitudes; it has been argued that women who came to maturity during the Vietnam era are more likely to oppose militarism. For example, Susan Jacoby cites the unhappy reaction of a poor black women who lost a son in Vietnam to her daughter's desire to enlist in the army on graduating from high school.[15] Given the effect of American military involvement overseas on the lives of third world women, the "gains" of the American feminist movement in integrating women in the military are problematic indeed in terms of international sisterhood.

When I was a graduate student at Cornell in the late 1960s there were no women in ROTC. On returning to Cornell as a teacher in the late 1980s one of the most striking changes on campus was the sight of coeds in ROTC uniforms—white and black navy uniforms, brown army uniforms, and military camouflage outfits. One result of the women's movement seems to have been a militarization of acceptable female roles. Women, a high percentage of them from minority groups, now make up about 10 percent of America's armed forces.[16] American feminism thus has an outstanding "promissory note" not only to third world women whose lives are adversely affected by American military involvement in their countries but also to the internal "third world" of ethnic minorities in the United States for whom the military is the best employment option available.

At the present time the Philippines, with the largest American bases outside of American territory, is the site of a rerun of many aspects of the years of the Vietnam war. Clark airforce base and Subic Bay have had social effects similar to those of U.S. bases in Vietnam, much to the concern of Philippine citizens, researchers, and feminist organizations.[17] To give some idea of the magnitude of the problem, in Olongapo City by Subic Bay alone it has been estimated that there are as many as 20,000 prostitutes and that some 30,000 Amerasian children are born each year, of whom only one-fourth are acknowledged by their servicemen fathers.[18] Many of these children are sold, either to childless couples, to brothel keepers, or to recruiters of domestic servants. The rest end up on the street, where some survive as child prostitutes catering primarily to American clients.[19] Sexual experiences overseas can reshape the sexuality and gender attitudes of American men and can affect their relationships with American women after their return home.[20]

The American government, which has taken the unprecedented step of assuming responsibility for the children of American servicemen in Vietnam, and the American press, which has devoted a great deal of attention to the story of Vietnam veterans' reunions with their Amerasian children, have both been silent on the subject of Amerasian children in the Philippines. This issue should be of concern to American women, not just out of international solidarity with Filipino women (although that would of course be laudable) but because it is not in the interest of American women to turn a blind eye to the processes by which young American men are socialized by the military to attitudes of sexism and irresponsibility to the offspring of their sexual activity. [21]

Most Western research in the field of "women and development" has focused on the sexual division of labor and gender differences with regard to access to the means of production; very little has been written on the implications of gender differences in regard to access to the means of violence. One exception is the work of Maria Mies who argued that from prehistoric times male specialization in weapons used against large animals and people has been crucial in structuring the power relations between men and women. [22] In another pathbreaking study, Cynthia Enloe argues that militarization introduces new ideas of what it means to be a man into third world countries and depends on transforming cultural norms of manhood. [23] Men aren't soldiers because they are "naturally" violent, they have to be trained that way.

The sexual terrorizing of young village women by armed men of their own nationality which Enloe graphically depicts in contemporary Central America is just the tip of the iceberg of increasing violence against women in the third world where many military governments, often with United States backing, station armed indigenous soldiers in rural areas, an internal army of occupation. To date socialist-led national liberation movements (e.g., in Vietnam and Central America) and autonomous women's organizations have been the major forces countering the increase in violence toward women.

Women's role in national liberation struggles has been summed up in the Vietnamese proverb: "When the enemy comes to the door, even the women must fight." Since fighting is the male role par excellence, and since women's liberation has so commonly been thought of as women taking on what have been traditionally male roles, there has been a tendency among socialist-feminists in the West and on the left generally to romanticize women's role in national liberation armed struggle and to see it as an index of women's liberation rather than see it either as defense of traditional values or as a sign of desperation. The impact of militarism on gender relations both in the industrialized and third world needs to be added to the research agenda, and the feminist admiration of "women warriors" whether on the imperialist or anti-imperialist side needs to be critically reexamined. It is tragic, not "exciting" or "heroic," when men and women in the third world have no option but to kill other human beings dressed as soldiers in order to defend their lives and their homes. It is doubly tragic because we know that the soldiers of imperial armies, as well as local troops serving foreign or upper-class interests, are primarily men (and in the new integrated American army, women) from economically and socially disadvantaged groups.

Notes

1. Arlene Eisen-Bergman, *Women of Viet Nam* (San Francisco: People's Press, 1974); Margaret Randall, *Spirit of the People* (Vancouver: New Star Books, 1975); Arlene Eisen-Bergman, *Women and Revolution in Viet Nam* (London: Zed Books 1984); and Robin Morgan, *Sisterhood is Powerful* (Garden City, NY: Anchor Books, 1984).

2. Susan Brownmiller, *Against Our Will: Men, Women and Rape* (New York: Simon and Schuster, 1975), pp. 98–111. It is thanks to the political courage of those American servicemen who dared to expose the widespread phenomenon of rape of Vietnamese women that she had information on this topic. Her sources are not Vietnamese accounts but rather Daniel Lang's *Casualties of War* (New York: McGraw-Hill, 1969) which first appeared in *The New Yorker*, October 18, 1969, and the testimony in Vietnam Veterans Against the War, *The Winter Soldier Investigation: An Inquiry into American War Crimes* (Boston: Beacon Press, 1972).

3. E.g. section entitled "Blonde Ex-Showgirl Slain in Hotel Suite" in Brownmiller, *Against Our Will*, pp. 336–41.

4. Ibid., pp. 90–91.

5. Ibid., pp 112–13.

6. Cf. James Fallows, "What Did You Do in the Class War, Daddy?", in A.D. Horne, ed., *The Wounded Generation: America After Vietnam* (Englewood Cliffs, N.J.: Prentice-Hall, 1981).

7. Two excellent summaries of right-wing revisionism (which do not, however, deal with the gender dimension) are Walter LaFeber, "The Last War, the Next War and the New Revisionists," *Democracy*, 1, no. 1 (January 1981): 93–103 and Paul Lyons, "Vietnam: Ambiguous Reconciliation" *Socialist Review* 2(1988): 55–71.

8. Tony Hall, "Seneca Falls Women's Rites," *The Ithaca Times*, July 21–27, 1988, p. 14.

9 Sally Hayton-Keeva, *Valiant Women in War and Exile* (San Francisco: City Lights Books, 1987).

10. One former nurse describes deliberately inflicting pain under the guise of medical care: "I had seen all of these young American boys who had been blown away and now I was being asked to take care of this person who, while probably not directly responsible for what had happened, was a part of what had happened to all the boys I'd just been with. I know that I could probably have gotten the IV in on the first try, but I didn't. His wounds were not such that he needed a urinary catheter, but he got one. That was my way of reacting." Shelly Saywell, *Women in War* (Harmondsworth: Penguin, 1985), p. 254.

11. E.G. in Kathryn Marshall, *In the Combat Zone: An Oral History of American Women in Vietnam* (Boston: Little, Brown and Co., 1987), and in Janice Rogovin, *Let Me Tell You Where I've Been*. I am grateful to Peggy Perri of the Joiner Center at the University of Massachusetts at Boston, who served as a nurse in Vietnam, for information on the importance of this suppressed issue for many women Vietnam veterans.

12. Hayton-Keeva, *Valiant Women*. pp. 70–71.

13. Joel Charny and John Spragens, Jr., *Obstacles to Recovery in Vietnam and Kampuchea: U.S. Embargo of Humanitarian Aid* (Boston: Oxfam America, 1984).

14. Lyons, in "Vietnam: Ambiguous Reconciliation," analyzes the right-wing attempt to mold a new concensus around the concept of "the Vietnam generation" which dismisses the issues raised by the antiwar movement and advocates healing of the Vietnam war wounds in the American body politic with no mention of the Vietnamese and their dead and wounded.
15. Susan Jacoby, "Women and the War," in Horne, ed., *The Wounded Generation*, pp. 203–4.
16. Judy Mann, "No Excuse for the Harassment Women Face in Armed Forces," *The Washington Post*, September 23, 1987.
17. See, for example, Gabriela, *Proceedings, Fourth National Congress*, March 14–15, 1987, Davao City, the Philippines. Gabriela, a feminist organization, can be contacted at P.O. Box 4386, Manila 2800, the Philippines.
18. Pilar Ramos-Jimenez and Ma. Elena Chiong-Javier, *Social Benefits and Costs: People's Perceptions of the US Bases in the Philippines*, mimeo, Research Center, De La Salle University (Manila, 1987), pp. 15–17. The social impact of the bases on gender relations in the Philippines goes far beyond the phenomenon of prostitution; it includes the breaking up of Philippine marriages and the problem of socially unrecognized unions between American servicemen and Philippine women.
19. Ibid., p. 17.
20. The testimony of a professional sex worker, Margo St. James, COYOTE union of prostitutes organizer, who numbered many Indochina war veterans among her clients, is especially valuable given the lack of academic research on this subject:

> I had one trick who was a police officer, sent to Cambodia [? *sic*] in 1963 as an advisor to train their police. He wasn't physically injured but he had changed psychically. He had been kind of a macho guy, but nice. . . . Then he came back and we met again. He had got to where he had no sense of the worth of human life. Women and children were nothing to him. He'd talk about twelve-year-old girls who were 'so lovely.' I thought, 'My God, he was never into pederasty before.' But over there in that war atmosphere and the poverty is great and people would sell their little girls to pimps who would sell them to the officers and their staff. I thought that was truly disgusting. For a long time, I couldn't even bear to talk to him. The worst part was, he didn't even seem to see anything wrong with it. Before the war he'd been kind and considerate; it was a bad thing that happened to this guy (Hayton-Keeva, *Valiant Women*, pp 78–79).

21. Initial steps have been made in this regard. A report published by the Defense Advisory Committee on Women in the Services (DACOWITS), set up to defend the interests of American women in the military, noted that officially overlooked on-base prostitution in the Philippines creates an environment in which "all females are regarded with little or no respect and abusive behavior toward all women is not only passively accepted and condoned, but encouraged." (Jacquelyn Davis, "Summary of Findings of 1987 DACOWITS WestPac' Trip" (August 26, 1987), unpub. mimeo, Washington, Institute for Foreign Policy Analysis.)
22. Maria Mies, *Patriarchy and Accumulation on a World Scale: Women and the International Division of Labour* (London: Zed Press, 1986), pp. 44–73 and 145–74.
23. Cynthia Enloe, "Bananas, Bases and Patriarchy; Feminist Questions about the Militarization of Central America," *Radical America* 19, no. 4 (1985): 7–23. See also Cynthia Enloe, *Does Khaki Become You? The Militarisation of Women's Lives* (London: Pluto Press, 1983) and Gita Sen and Caren Grown, *Development, Crises, and Alternative Visions; Third World Women's Perspectives* (New York: Monthly Review Press, 1987), p. 73.

Of Dogma, Dicta, and Washing Machines: Women in the People's Republic of China

Delia Davin

It is not, I think, generally known in China that Mao ever said, "To liberate women is not to manufacture washing machines."[1] The dictum does not belong to that central canon of Mao's writings with which everyone in China now over thirty was once so familiar, but to the apocrypha, the off-the-cuff remarks made to foreigners and then reported abroad. No matter that Malraux, to whom we owe the report, was not best-known as a faithful recorder of history, the challenge to washing machines spoke to us and our concerns in the West in the 1970s and we have treated it as authentic. When an enthusiastic Marxist-Leninist quoted it to me in 1975, I couldn't help thinking, "Maybe not, but it does help." In Beijing, where I lived at the time with my small daughter, we got hot water for two hours a week and I found laundering hard work, although, unlike most of my Chinese colleagues, we did get hot water twice a week for two hours. My Austrian friend told me I was being ethnocentric, assuming that the Chinese had the same bourgeois needs and aspirations that I had.

Today, I watch the mounting sales of washing machines to those in China who can afford them with a certain satisfaction. Yet, at the same time, I feel a better understanding of Mao when I see the deplorable consistency with which detergents are advertised by a woman standing proudly beside "her" machine.

Washing machines are welcomed because domestic work and child care are very real problems. In the countryside they take time, almost always from women, which could otherwise have been given to income-earning activities. In the cities, one study indicates that Chinese, both men and women, spend more time on domestic chores than the citizens of any other nation for which we have data, but that the load falls far more heavily on women.[2] In some periods the Chinese Communist Party (CCP) has ignored this double burden, in others it has suggested that household work should be collectivized or shared by the men in the family. In the 1980s, modernization has taken the place of collectivization on the agenda.

Women's domestic burden is to be lightened by better housing, fuel, and water supplies, easily prepared food, and labor-saving devices such as washing machines. Men are still urged to share domestic chores, although as Elisabeth Croll has observed, a dual standard operates in media articles on model workers.[3] Husbands of model women are shown as supportive men who take on a share of cooking, laundering, and shopping while male achievers are often portrayed as being entirely serviced by their devoted wives. This message has certainly got through to young men. Surveys of the qualities they are looking for in a wife come up depressingly often with the idea that she must be a good housewife and not too career-minded so that she can offer a man the support he needs to succeed.

Long before washing machines appeared in reality or in discourse in China, the Chinese Communist Party had taken up the orthodox Marxist line that women's exclusion from production lies at the root of their oppression and that their mobilization for production is an essential pre-requisite for their liberation. Hardly surprisingly, Engels' analysis of women's oppression, written in capitalist nineteenth-century Europe, did not entirely fit the circumstances of an Asian peasant society. For example, it failed to explain the oppression of women in those large areas of southern China where they were not traditionally excluded from productive work. And while the mobilization of women for productive work under collec-tivization did improve their position, it certainly did not end their oppres-sion. They remained clearly disadvantaged within the peasant family, a strong preference for sons persisted, and only very small numbers of women attained positions of authority within the commune structure. It has been convincingly argued that what held them back was the structure of the patrilineal family and the custom of virilocal marriage.[4]

Since the abandonment of collective farming the peasant family has once more become the basic unit of production and ownership in the countryside. The household head, generally the oldest working male in the family, usually contracts for land on behalf of all the family members. Most small private enterprises in the countryside are also now family-owned. There are exceptions. Women sometimes run businesses as indi-viduals and may occasionally contract for land themselves. In general, however, the restoration of the family economy seems likely to disadvan-tage women further.[5] Despite the legal position that gives them theoretical equality with men, women's property rights in rural society are still very weak.[6] A woman rarely asserts her right to inherit from her father's household because she leaves it on marriage and its property passes to her brothers. Unless widowed, women have no right, even in law, to inherit in their own right from their parents-in-law. A widow's property rights are likely to be bitterly disputed if she marries out of her deceased husband's family, while a divorced woman rarely succeeds in taking more than personal effects with her when she leaves the marital home.[7] Now that so much of the means of production is in private hands, the failure to implicate women's property rights will reinforce the dependency of peasant women, most of whom have access to the means of production only through their relationship to a man.

Urban women seem to have gained more from the application of Engels' analysis of women's oppression. Participation in productive labor in the cities meant participation in the individual waged economy. Peasant women's earnings went to enlarge the pooled household income, while women in the cities received their wages into their own hands, a fact that would tend to increase their say in the family. Although almost nothing has been done to reduce the concentration of women in the lower paid areas of the economy and the serious underrepresentation of women in positions of authority has met with little more than ritual condemnations of feudal attitudes, there has been consistent official support for the employment of women outside the home (except for a brief period in the mid-1950s).[8]

At one stage recently it looked as though this support might be withdrawn. In the early 1980s there was great concern about increasing levels of cynicism, disaffection, and even hooliganism, especially among the young. A solution was sought in the introduction of a pro-family campaign and a new emphasis on the importance of mothering.[9] This coincided with the encouragement of consumerism on a scale quite new to China. These developments seemed to imply the increased domestication of women, and in fact the idea that women might be encouraged to withdraw from paid employment was raised in the press in 1980–81. As it was by then admitted that there was a serious problem of urban unemployment, the suggestion was made in the press that it could be solved if married women surrendered their jobs to men.

The National Women's Federation, China's official party-led women's organization, which was an important vehicle for the pro-family campaign, opposed the suggestion strongly.[10] Its practical arguments were that the unemployed would not necessarily perform the work currently done by women, and that most families needed the wife's earnings. It relied much more heavily, however, on arguments of principle. It sent letters to the Central Committee and to the press pointing out that the party's policy toward women had always been based on Engels' analysis: "To emancipate woman and to make her the equal of man is and remains an impossibility so long as the woman is shut out from social productive labour and restricted to private domestic labour. The emancipation of women will only be possible when women can take part in production on a large social scale."[11]

In their statements the leaders of the Women's Federation made it clear that any change of policy on women's employment, any attempt to ease women out, would be retreating from all that the federation, as a party-led women's organization, had attempted to achieve in its long history. For the moment at least the federation stand has been successful. Official pronouncements on women still insist on the beneficial effects of their employment outside the home.

In these pages I have tried to give some brief indications of the positive and negative aspects of the Marxist heritage for women in China. Engels' analysis has formed the basis of the theoretical approach to women and this has produced the emphasis on productive labor. Problems such as marriage, the family, domestic labor, and property have all been spotlighted at various times, only to be obscured again when they give rise to too much dissension.

On the one hand, Engels' prescriptions for the emancipation of women have limited the scope of permissible struggles; on the other they have placed women firmly on the agenda of the revolution and their partial implementation has produced some improvements for women. Moreover, the Women's Federation has been able, through an appeal to ideological orthodoxy, to defend gains already made for women in the towns. This was not even attempted in the countryside; the return to family farming was a far more complex matter involving many other issues and was basic to the reformers' strategy for growth. In the debate over the employment of married women, the Women's Federation was strengthened by the very fact that it had a long history as a party-led organization to which its leaders made deliberate reference.

It is difficult to make judgments about women in other countries and cultures. Marilyn Young, in her article in this volume, has rightly reminded us that China's revolution is not our revolution. When I am made uneasy by a China in which women are portrayed as decorative rather than heroic and fashion triumphs over comfort, I recall my Austrian friend's criticism of my ethnocentricity. She used to like two lines from one of Mao's poems, which significantly seem dated now:

> China's daughters have high aspiring minds,
> they love their uniforms, not silks and satins.[12]

Mao himself once said, although again these words come only from his apocrypha: "A thousand years from now, all of us, even Marx, Engels and Lenin will probably appear rather ridiculous."[13]

This is Mao at his undogmatic best. If such an attitude prevailed, theory would always be subject to refinement or improvement. When it does not, inadequate theories may gain a stranglehold and block further progress. In China, this has perhaps occurred in some areas. There is a real need for a strong women's movement to take up women's issues and work out new approaches to them, but it is difficult to see how this could develop in the present circumstances.

Notes

1. Quoted in André Malraux, *Anti-Memoirs* (New York: Holt, Rinehart and Winston, 1968), p. 374.
2. Wang Yalin and Lin Jinrong, "Research on Housework Performed by Urban Employees," *Zhongguo Shehui Kexue*, no. 1 (1982). For comment on this study, and data that give a less sanguine view of men's sharing role, see Martin King Whyte and William L. Parish, *Urban Life in Contemporary China* (Chicago: University of Chicago Press, 1984), pp. 216–21.
3. Elisabeth Croll, *Chinese Women Since Mao*, (London: Zed Press, 1983), p. 64.
4. See Norma Diamond, "Collectivisation, Kinship and the Status of Women in Rural China," *Bulletin of Concerned Asian Scholars* 7, no. 1, January–March 1975, and Judith Stacey, *Patriarchy and Socialist Revolution in China* (Berkeley: University of California Press, 1983).
5. Delia Davin, "Women, Work and Property in the Chinese Peasant Household of the 1980s," in Diane Elson, ed., *Male Bias in the Development Process* (Manchester: Manchester University Press, forthcoming).
6. *Inheritance Law of the People's Republic of China* (Zhonghua Renmin Gongheguo Jichengfa), adopted at the third session of the Sixth National People's Congress, 1985. Text from *Selected Major Laws of the People's Republic of China* (Zhonghua Renmin Gongheguo zhongyao falu xuanbian) (Shanghai: Shanghai People's Publishing House, 1986). See also Delia Davin, "China: The New Inheritance Law and the Peasant Household," *Journal of Communist Studies* (forthcoming).
7. William L. Parish and Martin King Whyte, *Village and Family in Contemporary China* (Chicago: University of Chicago Press, 1978), p. 195.
8. See Delia Davin, *Woman-work, Women and the Party in Revolutionary China* (Oxford: Oxford University Press, 1976), pp. 170–72.
9. This campaign can be monitored through almost every issue of *Zhongguo Funu* (the official women's magazine) for the early 1980s.
10. Letter of August 15 from the secretariat of the National Women's Federation to comrades Wan Li and Peng Chong, in National Women's Federation, ed., *Selected Women's Movement Documents from the Period of the Four Great Modernisations (1981–1983)* (in Chinese) (Beijing: Chinese Women's Press, n.d.). I am also drawing here on an interview with Women's Federation leaders in March 1981.
11. Friedrich Engels, *The Origin of the Family, Private Property and the State* (New York: International, 1972), p. 221.
12. Mao Zedong, Inscription on a photograph of women militia, February 1961.
13. Mao in conversation with Edgar Snow, reported in Edgar Snow, *The Long Revolution* (New York: Vintage Books, 1973).

Some Thoughts on the Left and the "Woman Question" in South Asia

Kumari Jayawardena

The Left in South Asia, where I come from, has been active in mobilizing women workers and peasants (as well as women of the petty-bourgeoisie and bourgeoisie) in many activities. These range from independence struggle, trade union actions, peasant agitations, student movements, and housewives' campaigns against higher prices, to party activity at election time. In India, for example, Communist-led women played a crucial role in all the historic movements of the twentieth century. These include nationalist agitation (both violent and nonviolent), the 1951 Telegana peasant uprising, strikes such as that of the militant Coimbatore mill workers in 1946, famine relief work in Bengal in 1943–44, antifascist campaigns during World War II, and many militant class actions of recent years. In fact the tendency has always been to emphasize women's equal rights of *participation* in nationalist and class struggles. Moreover, political leaders have always been aware of the importance of women's involvement for the success of struggles and, of course, for electoral politics. However, the question of *women's* liberation—as opposed to *national* and *workers'* liberation—has been merely subsumed under "class struggle." This, it has been said, will automatically liberate women when it succeeds. In this subordination of women's specific interests and liberation to those of class liberation, left movements in South Asia parallel all too closely the problematic assumptions and practical weaknesses of many other left movements and regimes discussed in this volume.

Although it frequently tries to forge alliances with other "democratic" organizations, the Left has always had problems with organizations where party members were not in control. Thus autonomous women's groups, although raising issues of importance to socialists, were regarded as hostile, and even attempts by women of the Left to unite across party lines were seldom tolerated for very long. In 1947, Sri Lanka women from the Communist and Trotskyist parties got together with other socialist women to form an autonomous United Women's Front to campaign for women's economic and social rights. Although the organization made significant gains and received a lot of publicity for its programs to mobilize working women, within a year the male leadership of the two parties had forced the dissolution of the organization because of conflict on other issues between the parties. In West Bengal too, although the Communist Party split in 1964, women party members of both communist parties continued to work in a single women's organization until 1971, when increasing problems between the two parties also resulted in a split in the women's organization.

In recent years, when many issues affecting women's rights have arisen in South Asia—including the extreme cases of the Hudood Ordinance (1979) in Pakistan (which includes stoning to death and lashes for adultery), and *sati* (burning women to death on their husband's funeral pyre), or killing women for bringing inadequate dowry in India—the Left has failed to come forward *to give leadership* to these struggles that have been taken up by feminist groups. The relationship today between the Left and feminists in South Asia remains an uneasy one.

A Glance at History

It is interesting to note that when the "Woman Question" came up in India from the ninteenth century onward, it was discussed in terms of social evils to be eradicated by legislation. British bureaucrats along with Indian social reformers, nationalists, and Christian missionaries supported the campaigns against *sati*, child marriage, and the ban on widow remarriage, and promoted the rights of women to education, property, and political participation. It was predominantly a campaign of Indian and Western men whose aim was to liberate, modernize, "civilize," or Christianize women, as the case may be. Nevertheless local women were also involved not only as victims but also as agitators, activists, and reformers, often receiving support from European women feminists, theosophists, and socialists residing in South Asia.

Since the agitation for legal, franchise, property, or education rights for women was part of a package of democratic demands, support for such campaigns came also from the liberal nationalists in India. As the nationalist movement grew, the leaders saw the advantage of drawing the masses of women into the movement and for this purpose they urged women to come out of their homes and into the streets. Thus liberal ideology on women's rights coincided with the need for mass support. It is this that accounts for the enlightened stands Gandhi and Nehru took on the subordination of women.

The nationalist reformers of course had to be careful; they needed to take from the West to combat the West, but in the process, they wanted to also retain their self-identity in terms of national culture. Chatterjee has suggested that there was a separation of social space into the *home (ghar)*, representing "the inner-spiritual self, our true identity" and the *world (bāhir)*, representing the external, the domain of the material. The *world* was where

> the European power had challenged the non-European peoples and, by virtue of its superior material culture, had subjugated them. But it had failed to colonise the inner, essential identity of the East which lay in its distinctive, and superior, spiritual culture. . . . No encroachments of the colonizer must be allowed in that inner sanctum. In the world, initiation and adaptation to Western norms was a necessity; at home, they were tantamount to annihilation of one's very identity. [1]

Hence, the Westernization of the women had to be very selective—in Bengal the new "respectable woman" could acquire "the cultural refinements afforded by modern education without jeopardizing her place at home.[2]

Of course one may add that the home represented not only spiritual but also strong *material* interests and *ideological* domination, providing the men of all classes with unpaid labor and other privileges as well as unlimited power over the lives of women. Thus the home was the primary source of women's oppression and exploitation, which few males were (or are) willing to change.

In India, the opponents of social reform for women were a mix of orthodox Hindu and Muslim conservatives who, ironically, included some of the most militant opponents of British colonialism. One such example was B. G. Tilak, the leader of the "extreme" group in the Indian National Congress. When, in 1908, he was tried for sedition and deported, there was a major wave of strikes in the mills of Bombay, in which many women workers participated. But Tilak, although politically militant, was socially conservative. He regarded legislation on social issues affecting women as an unwarranted and objectionable interference by the colonial state in local tradition and custom. He even joined the social reactionaries in the campaign against the Age of Consent Bill of 1891, which raised the legal age for female sexual intercourse from ten to twelve years.

Sri Lanka, ahead of India in terms of female education and quality of life in the nineteenth century, produced no liberal demands for women's rights from reformist males. The "Westernizing" men of the bourgeoisie were concerned with moderate constitutional reforms, limited male franchise, and equal opportunity with Europeans in the professions and government service. The women of the class were given a limited education with the emphasis on "accomplishments" and keeping up with the latest Western fashions. Opposition to these trends came from the Buddhist and Hindu revivalists who urged women to be chaste and docile, discarding Western influences. For example, Anagarika Dharmapala (1869–1933), the most militant spokesman for Sinhala Buddhist consciousness, urged industrialization and scientific advance but criticized the adoption of Western customs and fashions by Sinhala women. "The glory of woman is in her chastity, in the performance of household duties and obedience to her husband," he insisted. [3]

In South Asia, the Left is frequently accused of being too internationalist and secular and of being insensitive to the strength of feelings based on national identity and tradition. Without entering that debate, I would only point out that this is not true of the Woman Question, where one finds a continuity of traditional values, permeating all strands of current political thinking, including frequently, that of the Left. Moreover, many leftists who were prepared to support the national liberation of all peoples and to struggle for the democratic rights of workers and peasants at home and abroad were not only unwilling, but also reacted with great emotional fervor against attempts to raise the question of women's liberation. The strongest reasons given for such opposition have always been linked to arguments for resistance to foreign domination and ideological control.

However, in colonial times there were also some radical male reformers who spoke out against women's subordination, but who tended to be from the more maverick elements of the political spectrum. They were able to make the connection between caste oppression and women's oppression that existed in a hierarchically organized caste and class society. For example, in Maharastra, Jotirao Phule (1827–90), of low-caste origin, led a struggle against Brahmin hegemony. He opposed child marriage and polygamy, set up schools for girls and "untouchables," and, in opposing *sati*, speculated on whether a man would become a *sata* on his wife's funeral pyre; he was an early opponent of sexism in language criticizing expressions such as "all *men* are equal," and in his own writing, changing this phrase to "each and every woman and man."[4] Another outstanding example is that of E. V. Ramaswami Naiker (born in 1879 and known popularly as "Periyar," the Great One), the founder in the 1920s of the Dravidian movement against North Indian and Brahmin domination of the south. Being a great iconoclast, challenging Hindu orthodoxy and excoriating priests, he condemned the worship of gods and religious ritual and went even further to denounce Tamil social customs and the enslavement of women. He hit out at the revered classic texts on women, attacked the sacred laws that enforced chastity, and advocated "self-respect marriages" without clergy or religious ritual, with rights of divorce and remarriage. His boldest suggestions included the plea for sexual freedom, a new moral code for both men and women, intercaste marriages, and a woman's strike against reproduction; he also called for an autonomous, strong movement run only by women, because in his view, male presence would be like having Brahmins in the anti-Brahmin Dravidian movement. [5]

However, while Periyar is venerated as a founding father of what became a powerful political movement that still dominates Tamil politics, little is heard today of his revolutionary views on women. These are regarded as an aberration and are seldom referred to.

The Legacy of Dogmatism

In South Asia, the left parties have tended to be "dogmatic" rather than innovative, and have essentially been parties "of the book"—quoting from Marx, Engels, and Lenin in all cases, to establish their revolutionary *bona fides*, and from Stalin, Trotsky, and Mao to differentiate their Marxism from that of their rivals. Being essentially loyal to the founding fathers, the Left, when in doubt on any issue, and especially in cases where they had not debated the question, often referred to the classic texts. Thus in response to the wave of feminism of the 1970s the Left brought out the old quotations on the Woman Question, while dismissing feminism as a dangerous Western import.

Nevertheless, the resort to the texts was a positive move. In all the countries of the region translations in the local languages were available of the key Marxist texts on women, including those of Engels, Bebel, Lenin, and Mao. From these the standard view—that the advent of socialism would automatically "solve" the Woman Question—was verbally affirmed, but without serious discussion. However, the new women's groups, which were both socialist and feminist, began also to comb the texts, finding good quotes by Lenin on housework and Engels on the proletarian family. They discovered not only Rosa Luxemburg, Alexandra Kollontai, and Emma Goldman (none of them recommended reading by the traditional left parties), but also the little-known communist and anarchist women revolutionaries of early twentieth-century Asia.

Populism and the Bogey of Western Feminism

In the colonial period, before the advent of mass electoral politics, the Left took a firm, principled stand on minority rights, secularism, caste, and social reform; its role was educative and iconoclastic, attacking feudal interests, capitalist exploitation, social inequality, religious bigotry, and chauvinism. The Left thus formed the ideological vanguard, giving leadership in bringing democratic and socialist ideas to the people. It was a period of popular advance, which in the postindependence years was reflected in very significant gains at the general elections. By 1947, a Trotskyist was the leader of the opposition in Sri Lanka, and by the 1950s, the Communist Party in India was not only the leading opposition party in national politics, but had also won an election victory and formed the government in Kerala state.

However, more recently the Left has had a tendency to succumb to populist, fundamentalist pressures. Because it has chosen the option of participating in parliamentary politics and the democratic process based on adult franchise, the Left has on many occasions adapted and tailored its policies to reflect what was seen as "popular opinion." Thus one cannot begin to understand the phenomenon of radical left politics combined with social conservatism without looking at the strong influence of petty-bourgeois ideology on the Left in South Asia. The term "petty-bourgeois" is used to cover an amorphous group including urban and rural small-holders, traders, white-collar workers, students, clergy, and sections of the intelligentsia, from whom the left parties draw their most articulate supporters. In South Asia, this class has contradictory aspirations. It has a strong radical current, favoring modernization, secularism, and political change, while also defending tradition and revivalism. Its nationalism and socialism have been expressed in anti-imperialism and in opposition to class privilege and vested interests. But the nationalism has frequently descended into chauvinism, racism, and xenophobia. A persistent feature of the class has also been the combination of populist radicalism with social reaction—the latter being expressed in terms of women's subordination.[6]

It is important to distinguish between *anti-imperialism* and an *anti-Western* campaign of agitation. There was always a strand in the Left that was internationalist and anti-imperialist, that did not fall into the trap of Europhobia, even during the period of colonial rule. But since opposition to imperialism frequently entailed the assertion of a national self-identity and even feelings of cultural superiority, claims were often made in Asia (as in Africa) that women in those cultures were free in the precolonial period. Some in the left movements identified with such views, the Marxist vision of "primitive communism," perhaps reinforcing them. The future too was the millennium of the classless society, where exploitation and oppression would cease to exist and where women would be free. The good times for women were clearly in the past and in the future; it was the present that was problematic.

Today, countries of the third world are faced with distorted capitalist development causing severe economic crisis, social dislocation, a breaking down of hierarchies, and the explosive phenomenon of unemployed educated youth. This climate of crisis has led to the growth of populist, fundamentalist movements. These use revolutionary slogans against imperialism and capitalism to put forward ideas imbued with chauvinism, religious bigotry, and sexism. The xenophobia about the West has taken many forms, including the denunciation of Marxism, Christianity, secularism, and women's liberation. Such views which are prevalent among right-wing fundamentalists as well as among those calling themselves revolutionaries, have served to cloud and confuse the issues; in Iran, for example the Left and the religious Right for a time seemed to be speaking a similar language and revolutionary intellectuals in that country produced books and articles with such titles as "Marxism and Other Western Fallacies," "Occidentosis; a Plague from the West," and "Westoxication." Writing of this anti-Western agitation, Moghadam points out that "they advanced a critique of Europe and the United States from a radical, populist, Islamic and Third Worldist perspective—not a socialist one," adding that third worldism is "a mirror image of Eurocentrism, an equally misguided and wrong-headed point of departure."[7]

It is not difficult to see the line of descent between the social conservatives and cultural nationalists of an earlier era and their contemporaries today who view feminism as a foreign conspiracy that is trying to undermine society. Like many male-dominated cultures, Asian societies too have their vision of the evil woman temptress, goddess of destruction, witch or sorceress bringing disorder and chaos. Just as the West has its myths of the "noble savage" woman," the East has developed the myth of the "female foreign devil." It is of course accepted practice that the enemy's woman is a target of abuse. In colonial times diatribes against the British often took the form of the vilification of foreign women, and this tradition persists, the current targets being "Western feminists."

The great historical failure of the Left in South Asia has been its inability to give leadership to the movement for women's liberation. Far from recognizing women's subordination as a question of central concern to any movement advocating democracy and socialism, the Left has either ignored the question or made some token gestures. Left parties have mouthed the rhetoric of women's emancipation, quoting the Marxist texts, but in practice have not treated the issue as one demanding any degree of priority. In fact, the Left has raised the bogey of Western feminism and has attacked feminism as a suspect foreign ideology aimed at destabilizing and splitting the family, the working class, and the party. The absence of the Woman Question in the programs of the Left and the Left's lack of support for feminist organizations are matters for concern, especially since the "democratic struggle" has always been an essential part of left theory and practice. One can only hope that this short-sighted policy will soon be changed—especially as there are signs that the Left in South Asia is poised for large gains in the 1990s. There are already some indications of change. As a member of the Women's Power organization in Hyderabad, India, has recently written:

> We have been looked upon critically by the Left and labeled either anti-Marxist or bourgeois feminists. Attempts to co-opt us have alternated with

attempts to denounce us. But our strength has been that we have retained our identity and coherence as a group. After initial attempts to bring us into the "correct path," the Left has reassessed our role. Our relationship with the Left—originally so difficult for both us and them—is now far more balanced and marked with a certain respect for our identity.[8]

Notes

1. Partha Chatterjee, "The Nationalist Resolution of the Woman Question," Occasional Paper of the Centre for Research in the Social Sciences, Calcutta, 1986, pp. 8–9.
2. Ibid., p. 16.
3. Kumari Jayawardena, *Feminism and Nationalism in the Third World* (London: Zed Books, 1986), p. 126.
4. Gail Omvedt, "Caste, Class and Women's Liberation in India," *Bulletin of Concerned Asian Scholars* 7, no. 1 (1975): 46.
5. Gabrièle Dietrich, "Conceptualising Women's Role and 'Power' in the Process of Political Participation of Women," unpublished paper, n.d.
6. In the absence of research on this topic, one can only speculate about why the petty-bourgeoisie in South Asia is inclined to social conservatism. One reason may be that since it is a class with aspirations of upward mobility, it is therefore more subject to "status anxiety" and asserts its status in terms of female chastity and "respectability."
7. Val Moghadam, "Socialism or Anti-Imperialism? The Left and Revolution in Iran," *New Left Review* 166 (1987): 15.
8. Vasantha Kannabiran, "Report from SSS, A Women's Group in Hyderabad, Andhra Pradesh, India," *Feminist Studies* 12, no. 3 (Fall 1986): 611.

List of Contributors

Delia Aguilar is director of the Center for Educational Innovation at the University of Connecticut at Storrs. She is very active in the women's movement in the Philippines, where she spent the year 1987–88.

Lourdes Benería teaches in the Department of City and Regional Planning and Women's Studies at Cornell University and is the Director of Cornell's Program on International Development and Women.

Amrita Basu teaches in the departments of Political Science and Women's and Gender Studies at Amherst College. Her forthcoming book comparing women's radicalism in two Indian states will be published by the University of California Press.

Mary Buckley is a Lecturer in Politics at the University of Edinburgh and has been a frequent visitor to the Soviet Union since 1978.

Delia Davin is Lecturer in Chinese Studies at the University of Leeds. Her interest in women's issues developed during two years spent in China in the 1960s. She is the author of *Womanwork: Women and the Party in Revolutionary China* and co-editor of *Chinese Lives: an Oral History of Contemporary China*.

Barbara Einhorn lectures in German at Brighton Polytechnic, England. Her research interests concern women's literature and the situation of women in the GDR. She is active in the European peace movement and in establishing links between women in the East and West.

Zillah Eisenstein is professor and chairperson of the Department of Politics, Ithaca College. She edited *Capitalist Patriarchy and the Case for Socialist Feminism* and is the author of *The Radical Future of Liberal Feminism* and *Feminism and Sexual Equality*. Her most recent and forthcoming book is *The Female Body and the Law*.

Christina Gilmartin is Assistant Professor of History at the University of Houston. She is currently a visiting scholar at the Fairbank Center for East

368 Contributors

Asian Research at Harvard, where she is completing a book on women and the Chinese Communist Party during its formative years.

Wendy Zeva Goldman is Assistant Professor of History at Carnegie Mellon University in Pittsburgh. She is currently working on a book entitled *Revolution in the Family: Soviet Law and Social Change, 1917–1936*.

Kumari Jayawardena of Sri Lanka received her B.Sc. and Ph.D. degrees from the London School of Economics and was Associate Professor in Political Science at the University of Colombo, Sri Lanka until 1985. She has been an activist in workers' education, civil rights and the women's movement in Sri Lanka. Her interests are reflected in her books: *The Rise of the Labour Movement in Ceylon, Feminism and Nationalism in the Third World*, and *Ethnic and Class Conflicts in Sri Lanka*.

Sonia Kruks is Associate Professor of Political Science at the New School for Social Research. She is author of *The Political Philosophy of Merleau-Ponty, Situation: Existential Perspectives on Subjectivity, Society, and History* (forthcoming) and numerous articles on Mozambique.

Martha Lampland is an anthropologist who specializes in Hungarian political economy and history. She is Assistant Professor of Sociology at the University of California, San Diego.

Joan B. Landes is Professor of Politics and Women's Studies at Hampshire College. She has published numerous articles on gender issues on political and critical theory. She is the author of *Women and the Public Sphere in the Age of the French Revolution*.

Maxine D. Molyneux is Lecturer in Sociology at Essex University, England. She is the author of numerous articles on women and socialism, of *State Policies and the Position of Women Workers in the People's Democratic Republic of Yemen*, and is co-author of *The Ethiopian Revolution*.

Muriel Nazzari teaches Latin American history at Indiana University. She is currently working on a book provisionally called *The Disappearance of the Dowry: The Case of Sao Paulo, Brazil*.

Rayna Rapp is Associate Professor of Anthropology at the New School for Social Research. Her current work focuses on reproductive technology. She is the author of numerous articles on gender and feminism and the editor of *Towards an Anthropology of Women*.

Elizabeth Waters teaches Russian and Soviet history at the Australian National University. She is the author of numerous articles on Soviet social history of the post-revolutionary period and on women and the family in the contemporary USSR as well as *Women in a Bolshevik World: Work, Family and Society in Soviet Russia, 1917–1928* (forthcoming).

Christine Pelzer White, formerly at the Subordination of Women Cluster at the Institute for Development Studies, Sussex, England, is Visiting Associate Professor in the Southeast Asian Studies Program at Cornell University. She is co-editor of *Revolutionary Socialist Development in the Third World* and *Postwar Vietnam: Dilemmas in Socialist Development.*

Ben Wisner is Luce Professor of Food, Resources and International Policy at Hampshire College. He is the author of numerous articles on rural development and the book *Power and Need.*

Marilyn B. Young teaches Chinese history and women's studies at New York University. She is the author of *Rhetoric of Empire: American China Policy, 1895–1901,* co-author of *Transforming Russia and China: Revolutionary Struggles in the Twentieth Century* and editor of *Women in China: Essays on Feminism and Social Change.*

Bibliography

Anderson, Norman. *Law Reform in the Muslim World*. London: Athlone Press, 1976.

Andors, Phyllis. *The Unfinished Liberation of Chinese Women, 1949–1980*. Bloomington: Indiana University Press, 1983.

Angel, Adriana, and Fiona Mackintosh, eds. *The Tiger's Milk*. London: Virago, 1987.

Anthias, Floya, and Nira Yuval-Davis. "Contextualizing Feminism—Gender, Ethnic and Class Divisions." *Feminist Review* 14 (Winter 1983).

Barker, Francis. *The Tremulous Private Body: Essays on Subjection*. London: Methuen, 1984.

Baum, E. "The Women's Question at the IV World Congress." *International Press Correspondence*, no. 2 (1927).

Bebel, August. *Women Under Socialism*. Trans. Daniel De Leon. Intro. Lewis Coser. New York: Schocken Books, 1971.

Beck, L., and Keddie, Nikki. *Women in the Muslim World*. Chicago: University of Chicago Press, 1979.

Benenson, Harold. "Victorian Sexual Ideology and Marx's Theory of the Working-Class." *International Labor and Working Class History*, Spring 1984, pp. 1–23.

Bengelsdorf, Carollee. "On the Problem of Studying Women in Cuba." *Race and Class* 27 (Autumn 1985).

Bengelsdorf, Carollee, and Hageman, Alice. "Emerging from Underdevelopment." In Zillah Eisenstein, ed., *Capitalist Patriarchy and the Case for Socialist Feminism*. New York: Monthly Review Press, 1979.

Benton, Gregor. "The Yenan Literary Opposition." *New Left Review*, no. 92 (July–August 1975).

Beresford, Melanie, *Vietnam: Politics, Economics and Society* London. Pinter, 1988.

Bobroff, Ann. "The Bolsheviks and Working Women, 1905–1920." *Soviet Studies* 26 (October 1974).

Boorstein, Edward. *The Economic Transformation of Cuba*. New York: Monthly Review Press, 1968.

Bourne, Jenny. "Towards an Anti-Racist Feminism." *Race and Class* 25 (Summer 1983).

Brabin, Loretta. "Polygyny: An Indicator of Nutritional Stress in African Agricultural Societies?" *Africa* 54, no. 1 (1984): 31–44.

Brown, Beverly. "Natural and Social Division of Labour—Engels and the Domestic Labour Debate." *m/f* 1 (1978).

Browning, Genia, "Soviet Politics—Where Are the Women?" In Barbara Holland, ed., *Soviet Sisterhood*. London: Fourth Estate Books, 1985.

———. *Women and Politics in the USSR: Consciousness Raising and Soviet Women's Groups*. Sussex: Wheatsheaf Books, 1987; and New York: St. Martin's Press, 1987.

Brundenius, Claes. *Revolutionary Cuba: The Challenge of Economic Growth with Equity*. Boulder, Co: Westview Press, 1984.

Buckley, Mary. "Soviet Religious Feminism as a Form of Dissent." *Topic*: 40, Fall 1986.

———. ed. *Soviet Social Scientists Talking: An Official Debate About Women*. London: Macmillan, 1986.

Buhle, Mari Jo. *Women and American Socialism, 1840–1920*. Urbana, Chicago and London: University of Illinois Press, 1981.

Bujra, A. *The Politics of Stratification: A Study of Political Change in a South Arabian Town*. Oxford: Oxford University Press, 1971.

Butler, W., *Soviet Law*. London: Butterworth, 1983.

Carr, E. H. *Socialism in One Country 1924–1926*. Harmondsworth: Penguin, 1972.

Casal, Lourdes. "Revolution and Conciencia: Women in Cuba." In Carol Berkin and Clara M. Lovett, eds., *Women, War and Revolution*. New York: Holmes & Meier, 1980.

Chalatov, A." Participation of Women Workers in the Activities of Public Feeding." *International Press Correspondence*, no. 87 (1925).

Chanda, Nayan. *Brother Enemy: The War After the War*. San Diego: Harcourt Brace, 1986.

Chandler, David. "Post Mortem on the Wars in Indo-China: A Review Article." *Journal of Asian Studies* 40, no. 1 (November 1980).

Charny, Joel and John Spragens, Jr. *Obstacles to Recovery in Vietnam and Kampuchea: U.S. Embargo of Humanitarian Aid*. Boston: Oxfam, 1984.

Chatterjee, Partha. "The Nationalist Resolution of the Woman Question." Occasional Paper of the Center for Research in the Social Sciences. Calcutta, 1986.

Clements, Barbara Evans. "Working-Class and Peasant Women in the Russian Revolution, 1917–1923." *Signs* 8, Part 2 (Winter 1982).

Cliff, Julie, N. Kanji, and M. Muller. "Mozambique Health Holding the Line." *Review of African Political Economy* 36 (September 1986).

Corrigan, Philip, and Sayer, Derek. *Socialist Construction and Marxist Theory: Bolshevism and Its Critique*. New York: Monthly Review Press, 1978.

Coulson, Noel. *Conflicts and Tensions in the Islamic Jurisprudence*. Chicago: University of Chicago Press, 1969.

Coward, Rosalind. *Patriarchal Precedents: Sexuality and Social Relations*. London: Routledge & Kegan Paul, 1983.

Croll, Elizabeth. *Chinese Women Since Mao*. London: Zed Books, 1983.

———. "Women in Rural Production and Reproduction in the Soviet Union, China, Cuba and Tanzania: Socialist Development Experiences." *Signs: Journal of Women in Culture and Society* 7, no. 2 (Winter 1981).

———. *Feminism and Socialism in China*. New York: Schocken Books, 1978.

————. "The Movement to Criticize Confucius and Lin Piao," *Signs: Journal of Women in Culture and Society* 2, no. 3 (Spring 1977): 721–26.

————, Delia Davin, and Penny Kane, eds. *China's One-Child Policy.* London: Macmillan, 1985.

Dahlstrom, Edmund. *The Changing Roles of Men and Women.* Boston: Beacon Press, 1971.

Davin, Delia. "China: The New Inheritance Law and the Peasant Household." *Journal of Communist Studies.* forthcoming.

————. "Women, Work and Property in the Chinese Peasant Households of the 1980's" In Diane Elson, ed., *Male Bias in the Development Process.* Manchester: Manchester University Press, forthcoming.

————. *Woman-work, Women and the Party in Revolutionary China.* Oxford: Oxford University Press, 1976.

de Lauretis, Teresa, ed. *Feminist Studies, Critical Studies.* Bloomington: Indiana University Press, 1986.

————. *Technologies of Gender.* Bloomington: Indiana University Press, 1987.

Deere, Carmen Diana. "Co-operative Development and Women's Participation in the Agrarian Reform." *American Journal of Agrarian Economics,* December 1983.

Deighton, Jane, Rossana Horsley, Sarah Stewart, and Cathy Cain, *Sweet Ramparts.* London: War on Want and the Nicaraguan Solidarity Campaign, 1983.

Diamond, Norma. "Collectivization, Kinship and the Status of Women in Rural China" *Bulletin of Concerned Asian Scholars* 7, no. 1 (January–March 1976).

Dodge, Norton T. "Women in the Professions." In Dorothy Atkinson, Alexander Dallin, and Gail W. Lapidus, eds., *Women in Russia.* Sussex: Harvester, 1978.

Edmondson, Linda H. *Feminism in Russia.* London: Heinemann, 1984.

Egerö, Bertil. *Mozambique: A Dream Undone.* Uppsala: Nordiska afrikainstitutet, 1987.

————. and Jens-Erik Torp. "What Kind of Socialist Transition in Capitalist Recession?" In J. Carlsson, ed. *Recession in Africa.* Uppsala: Nordiska afrikainstitutet, 1987.

Einhorn, Barbara. "Socialist Emancipation: The Women's Movement in the German Democratic Republic." *Women's Studies International Quarterly* 4 (1981).

Eisen-Bergman, Arlene. *Women of Vietnam.* London: Zed Books, 1984.

Eisenstein, Zillah. "Developing a Theory of Capitalist Patriarchy and Socialist Feminism." In *Capitalist Patriarchy and the Case for Socialist Feminism.* New York: Monthly Review Press, 1979.

El-Saadawi, Nawal. *The Hidden Face of Eve: Women in the Arab World.* London: Zed Books, 1979.

Engels, Friedrich. *The Condition of the Working Class in England.* Trans. and ed. by W. O. Henderson and W. H. Chaloner. Stanford, Ca: Stanford University Press, 1958.

————. *The Origin of Family, Private Property and the State.* New York: International, 1972.

Erhlich, Carol. "The Unhappy Marriage of Marxism and Feminism: Can It Be Saved?" In Lydia Sargent, ed. *Women and Revolution.* Boston: South End Press, 1981.

Evans, Grant and Kelvin Rowley. *Red Brotherhood at War: Indochina Since the Fall of Saigon*. London: Verso, 1984.

————. "The Unhappy Marriage of Marxism and Feminism: Towards a More Progressive Union." In Lydia Sargent, ed., *Women and Revolution*. Boston: South End Press, 1981.

Evans, Richard. *Comrades and Sisters: Feminism, Socialism and Pacifism*. Sussex: Wheatsheaf Books, 1987.

Farnsworth, Beatrice. "Communist Feminism: Its Synthesis and Demise." In Carol R. Berkin and Clara M. Lovett, eds. *Women, War and Revolution*. New York: Holmes & Meier, 1980.

Ferge, Zsuzsa. *A Society in the Making: Hungarian Social and Societal Policy, 1945–1975*. Penguin, 1979.

First, Ruth. *Black Gold: The Mozambican Miner, Proletarian and Peasant*. Sussex: Harvester, 1983.

Foucault, Michel. *The History of Sexuality*. Vol. 1. Trans. Robert Hurley. New York: Pantheon, 1980.

————. "The Subject and Power." *Critical Inquiry* 8, no. 4 (1982).

Gitlow, K., "Women's Work in the United States." *International Press Correspondence*, no. 2 (1923).

Glendon, Mary Ann. *State, Law and Family*. New York, Amsterdam: Elsevier, 1977.

Glickman, Rose L. *Russian Factory Women: Workplace and Society, 1880–1914*. Berkeley: University of California Press, 1984.

Gomori, Edit. "Special Protective Legislation and Equality of Employment Opportunity for Women in Hungary." *International Labor Review* 119, no. 1 (1980).

Gronewald, Sue. "Recent Scholarship on Chinese Women." *Trends in History*, 1986.

Grossmann, Atina. "Abortion and Economic Crisis: The 1931 Campaign Against Paragraph 218 in Germany" *New German Critique*, no. 14 (1978). Reprinted in Renate Bridenthal, Atina Grossman and Marion Kaplan, eds., *When Biology Became Destiny*. New York: Monthly Review Press, 1984.

Halliday, Fred *Arabia Without Sultans*. Harmondsworth: Penguin, 1974.

————"The P.D.R.Y.: The 'Cuban Path' in Arabia." In Robin Murray, Christine White, and Gordon White, eds. *Revolutionary Socialist Development in the Third World*. Sussex: Wheatsheaf Books, 1983.

———— "Yemen's Unfinished Revolution: Socialism in the South." *Merip Report* 8, no. 81 (October 1979).

Hanlon, Joseph. *Beggar Your Neighbor*. Bloomington: University of Indiana Press, 1986.

————. *Revolution Under Fire*. London: Zed Books, 1984.

Harrell-Bond, Barbara. *Imposing Aid: Emergency Assistance to Refugees*. Oxford: Oxford University Press, 1986.

Harris, Hermione. "Women in Struggle: Nicaragua." *Third World Quarterly* 5, no. 4 (1983).

Harris, Lawrence "Agricultural Cooperatives and Development Policy in Mozambique." *Journal of Peasant Studies* 7, no. 3 (1980).

Hartmann, Heidi. "Capitalism, Patriarchy, and Job Segregation." *Signs* 1, no. 3, part 2 (Spring 1976 Supplement).

Hayden, Carol E. "The Zhenotdel and the Bolshevik Party." *Russian History* 3, part 2 (1976).

Heitlinger, Alena. "Marxism, Feminism and Sexual Equality." In Tova Yedlin, ed. *Women in Eastern Europe and the Soviet Union*. New York: Praeger 1980.

————. *Women and State Socialism: Sex Inequality in the Soviet Union and Czechoslovakia*. London: Macmillan, 1979; Montreal: McGill University Press, 1985.

Heldt, Barbara. *Terrible Perfection: Women and Russian Literature*. Bloomington and Indianapolis: Indiana University Press, 1987.

Hellman, Judith A. *Journeys Among Women: Feminism in Five Italian Cities*. New York: Oxford University Press, 1987.

Hill, Ronald J. and Peter Frank. *The Soviet Communist Party*, 2nd ed. London: Allen & Unwin, 1983.

Hindess, Barry and Paul Hirst. *Mode of Production and Social Formation*. London: Macmillan, 1977.

Hirst, Paul. "Law, Socialism and Rights." In P. Carlen and M. Collison, eds. *Radical Issues in Criminology*. Oxford: Martin Robertson, 1977.

Holt, Alix. "The First Soviet Feminists." In Barbara Holland, ed., *Soviet Sisterhood*. London: Fourth Estate Books, 1985.

Honig, Emily and Gail Hershatter. *Personal Voices: Chinese Women in the 1980s*. Stanford: Stanford University Press, 1988.

Hubsey-Darvas, Eva V. "Elderly Women in a Hungarian Village: Childlessness, Generativity, and Social Control." *Journal of Cross-Cultural Geronotology* 2 (1987).

Humphries, Jane. "Class Struggle and the Persistence of the Working Class Family," *Cambridge Journal of Economics* 1 (1977): 241–58.

Hunt, David. "Village Culture and the Vietnamese Revolution." *Past and Present* 94 (1982).

Isaacman, Allen. "Historical Introduction." In Lina Megaia, *Dumba Nengue: Run for Your Life: Peasant Tales of Tragedy in Mozambique*. Trenton: Africa World Press, 1988.

Isaacman, Barbara and June Stephen. *Mozambique Women, the Law and Agrarian Reform*. Addis Ababa: United Nations, Economic Commission for Africa, 1980.

Jaggar, Alison M. *Feminist Politics and Human Nature*. Totowa, NJ: Rowman & Allenheld, 1983.

Jayawardena, Kumari. *Feminism and Nationalism in the Third World*. London: Zed Books, 1986.

Johnson, Kay A. *Women, the Family and Peasant Revolution in China*. Chicago: University of Chicago Press, 1983.

Joshi, Barbara, ed. *Untouchable! Voices of the Dalit Liberation Movement*. London: Zed Books, 1986.

Kannabiran, Vasantha. "Report from SSS, a Women's Group in Hyderabad, Andhra Pradesh, India." *Feminist Studies* 12, no. 3 (Fall 1986).

Keesing, Roger M. "Kwaio Women Speak: The Micropolitics of Autobiography in a Solomon Island Society." *American Anthropology* 87, no. 1 (1985).

Kenner, Martin, and James Petras, eds. *Fidel Castro Speaks*. New York: Grove Press, 1971.

Kibreab, G. *African Refugees*. Trenton: Africa World Press, 1985.

King, Marjorie. "Cuba's Attack on Women's Second Shift, 1974–1976." In Eleanor Leacock, et al., eds. *Women in Latin America: An Anthology from Latin American Perspectives*. Riverside, CA: Latin American Perspectives, 1979.

Kishwar, Madhu. "Gandhi on Women." *Race and Class* 27, no. 1 (1986).

———, and Ruth Vanita, eds. *In Search of Answers: Indian Women's Voices from Manushi*. London: Zed Books, 1984.

Kligman, Gail. "The Rites of Women: Oral Poetry, Ideology, and the Socialization of Peasant Women in Contemporary Romania." In Sharon Wolchik and Alfred Meyer, eds. *Women, State and Party in Eastern Europe*. Durham: Duke University Press, 1985.

Kollontai, Alexandra. *Selected Writings*. Trans. Alix Holt. London: Allison and Busby, 1977; New York: W. W. Norton, 1977.

Konrád, György, and Iván Szelényi. "Social Conflicts of Underurbanization: The Hungarian Case." In *Social Consequences of Modernization in Communist Societies*. Baltimore: John Hopkins University Press, 1976.

Kulcsar, Rozsa. "The Socioeconomic Conditions of Women in Hungary." In Sharon Wolchik and Alfred Meyer, eds. *Women, State and Party in Eastern Europe*. Durham: Duke University Press, 1985.

Landes, Joan B. "Hegel's Conception of the Family." *Polity* 14, no. 1 (Fall 1981).

Lapidus, Gail W. *Women in Soviet Society: Equality Development and Social Change*. Berkeley: University of California Press, 1978.

Larguía, Isabel, and John Dumoulin. "Aspects of the Condition of Women's Labour." *NACLA's Latin America Empire Report* 9, no. 6 (September 1975).

———. "Women's Equality and the Cuban Revolution." June Nash and Helen Safa, eds. *Women and Change in Latin America*. South Hadley, MA: Bergin & Garvey, 1986.

Lazitch, Branko and Milorad Drachkovich. *Biographical Dictionary of the Comintern*. Stanford: Hoover Institution, 1973.

Leith, Suzette. "Chinese Women in the Early Communist Movement." In Marilyn Young, ed. *Women in China: Studies in Social Change and Feminism*. Ann Arbor: University of Michigan Press, 1973.

Liegle, Ludwig. *The Family's Role in Soviet Education*. New York: Springer, 1975.

Liu Binyan. *People or Monsters? And Other Stories and Reportage from China After Mao*. Ed. Perry Link. Bloomington: Indiana University Press, 1983.

MacKinnon, Catharine, "Feminism, Marxism, Method and the State: Toward Feminist Jurisprudence." *Signs* 8, no. 4 (1983).

Mackintosh M. and Marc Wuyts. "Accumulation, Social Services and Socialist Transition in the Third World: Reflections on Decentralized Planning Based on Mozambican Experience." The Open University, *Development Policy and Practice*. Working Paper 9, November 1987.

Machel, Samora. "Defining Woman's Enemy." Speech to the OMM in 1976. In B. Munslow, ed. *Samora Machel: An African Revolutionary*. London: Zed Books, 1985.

Mai Thi Tu and Le Thi Nham Tuyet. *Women in Vietnam*. Hanoi: Foreign Languages Publishing House, 1978.

Marr, David G. *Vietnamese Tradition on Trial, 1920–1945*. Berkeley: University of California Press, 1981.

Marr, David G. and Christine P. White. *Postwar Vietnam: Dilemmas in Socialist Development*. Ithaca, NY: Southeast Asia Publications, 1988.

Marx, Karl. *Critique of Hegel's Philosophy of Right*. Ed. Joseph O'Malley. Cambridge: Cambridge University Press, 1970.

———. "On a Proposed Divorce Law." In Lloyd D. Easton and Kurt H. Guddat, eds. *Writings of the Young Marx on Philosophy and Society*. Garden City, NY: Doubleday, 1967.

Marx, Karl, and Friedrich Engels. *The German Ideology, Part One*. Ed. C. J. Arthur. New York: International, 1970.

Massell, Gregory. *The Surrogate Proletariat*. Princeton: Princeton University Press, 1974.

McAuley, Martin. *Women's Work and Wages in the USSR*. London: Allen & Unwin, 1981.

McAuley, Mary. *Politics and the Soviet Union*. Harmondsworth: Penguin, 1977.

McIntyre, Robert J. "Demographic Policy and Sexual Equality: Value Conflicts and Policy Appraisal in Hungary and Romania." In Sharon L. Wolchik and Alfred G. Meyer, eds., *Women, State and Party in Eastern Europe*. Durham: Duke University Press, 1985.

Mernissi, Fatima. *Beyond the Veil*. New York: John Wiley, 1978.

Meulenbelt, Anja et al., eds. *A Creative Tension: Key Issues of Socialist Feminism*. Boston: South End Press, 1984.

Meyer, Alfred G. "Feminism, Socialism, and Nationalism in Eastern Europe." In Sharon L. Wolchik and Alfred G. Meyer, eds., *Women, State and Party in Eastern Europe*. Durham: Duke University Press, 1985.

———. "Marxism and the Women's Movement." In Dorothy Atkinson, Alexander Dallin, and Gail Lapidus, eds., *Women in Russia*. Stanford: Stanford University Press, 1977.

Miller, Nancy. "Changing the Subject: Authorship, Writing, and the Reader." In Teresa de Lauretis, ed., *Feminist Studies, Critical Studies*. Bloomington: Indiana University Press, 1986.

Moghadam, Val. "Socialism or Anti-Imperialism? The Left and Revolution in Iran." In *New Left Review*, no. 166 (1987).

Molyneux, Maxine. "Mobilization Without Emancipation? Women's Interests, the State and Revolution in Nicaragua." *Feminist Studies*, 11, no. 2 (1985). Reprinted (revised) in Richard Fagen, Carmen Diana Deere, and José Luis Coraggio, eds. *Transition and Development*. New York: Monthly Review Press, 1986.

———. "The Politics of Abortion in Nicaragua." *Feminist Review*, no. 29 (May 1988).

———. *State Policies and the Position of Women Workers in the P.D.R.Y. 1967–1977*. Geneva: ILO, 1982.

———. "Women in Socialist Societies: Problems of Theory and Practice." In Kate Young et al., eds., *Of Marriage and the Market*. London: LSE Books, 1981.

———. "Women's Emancipation Under Socialism: A Model for the Third World?" *World Development* 9, no. 9/10 (1981).

Mondlane, Eduardo. *The Struggle for Mozambique*. London: Penguin, 1969.

Moses, Claire Goldberg. *French Feminism in the Nineteenth Century.* Albany: State University of New York Press, 1984.

Moskoff, William. "Sex Discrimination, Commuting, and the Role of Women in Romanian Development." *Slavic Review* 37, no. 3.

Mumtaz, Khawar, and Fareeda Shaheed. *Women of Pakistan: Two Steps Forward, One Step Back?* London: Zed Books, 1987.

Munslow, Barry. *Mozambique: The Revolution and Its Origins.* London: Longman, 1983.

Mysliwiec, Eva. *Punishing the Poor: The International Isolation of Kampuchea.* Oxford: Oxfam, 1988.

Nafe, G. "The Strike and the Wife." *The Toiler,* December 4, 1920.

Nazzari, Muriel. "The 'Woman Question' in Cuba: An Analysis of Material Constraints on Its Solution." *Signs* 9, no. 2 (1983).

Nettl, J. P. *The Soviet Achievement.* New York: Harcourt Brace and World, 1970.

Nove, Alec. *An Economic History of the USSR.* Harmondsworth: Penguin, 1982.

Omvedt. Gail. "Caste, Class and Women's Liberation in India." *Bulletin of Concerned Asian Scholars* 7, no. 1 (1975).

————. *We Will Smash This Prison! Indian Women in Struggle.* London: Zed Books, 1980.

Ong, Aihwa, *Spirits of Resistance and Capitalist Discipline: Factory Women in Malaysia.* Albany: State University of New York Press, 1987.

————. "Industrialization and Prostitution in Southeast Asia." *Southeast Asia Chronicle* 96 (January 1985).

Ortner, Sherry and Harriet Whitehead, eds. *Sexual Meanings: The Cultural Construction of Gender and Sexuality.* Cambridge: Cambridge University Press, 1981.

Outshoorn, Joyce. "The Dual Heritage." In Anja Meulenbelt et al. eds., *A Creative Tension: Key Issues in Socialist-Feminism.* Boston: South End Press, 1984.

Palmer, R. and S. Parsons, eds. *The Roots of Rural Poverty in Central and Southern Africa.* London: Longman, 1977.

Pankhurst, Sylvia. "The Home and the Housewife." *Workers Dreadnought* 13 (October 1917).

Parish, William L., and Martin K. Whyte. *Village and Family in Contemporary China.* Chicago: University of Chicago Press, 1978.

Peristiany, J. G., ed. *Honour and Shame: The Values of Mediterranean Society,* London: Weidenfeld and Nicholson, 1965.

Pike, Douglas and Benjamin Ward, "Losing and Winning: Korea and Vietnam as Success Stories." *The Washington Quarterly* 10, no. 3 (Summer 1987).

Quataert, Jean. *Reluctant Feminists in German Social Democracy 1885–1917.* Princeton: Princeton University Press, 1979.

Rafael, Vicente L. "Confession, Conversion, and Reciprocity in Early Tagalog Colonial Society." *Comparative Studies in Society and History* 29, no. 2 (1987).

Raikes, Phillip. "Food Policy and Production in Mozambique Since Independence." *Review of African Political Economy* 29 (July 1984).

Ramírez-Horton, Susan. "The Role of Women in the Revolution." In Thomas, Walker, ed., *Nicaragua in Revolution.* New York: Praeger, 1982.

Randall, Margaret. *Sandino's Daughters.* London: Zed Books, 1981.

————. *Afterword*. Toronto: Women's Press, 1974.

Rankin, Mary. "The Emergence of Women at the End of the Ch'ing: The Case of Ch'iu Chin." In Margery Wolf and Roxanne Witke, eds., *Women in Chinese Society*. Stanford: Stanford University Press, 1975.

Reiter, Rayna, ed. *Toward an Anthropology of Women*. New York: Monthly Review Press, 1975.

Reynolds, Sian, ed. *Women, State and Revolution: Essays on Power and Gender in Europe Since 1789*. Amherst: University of Massachusetts Press, 1987.

Ritter, Archibald R. M. *The Economic Development of Revolutionary Cuba*. New York: Praeger, 1974.

Robert, Y. "The Life of the Working Women in the Textile Industry in France." *International Press Correspondence*, no. 73 (1928).

Rodriguez, Anabella, "Mozambican Women After the Revolution. In Miranda Davies, ed. *Third World, Second Sex: Women's Struggles and National Liberation*. London: Zed Books, 1983.

Roesch, Otto. Peasants and Collective Agriculture in Mozambique." In Jonathan Barker, ed. *The Politics of Agriculture in Tropical Africa*. Beverly Hills: Sage, 1984.

Rogers, Barbara. *The Domestication of Women*. New York: St. Martin's Press, 1980.

Ropp, Paul. "The Seeds of Change: Reflections on the Condition of Women in the Early and Mid Ch'ing." *Signs* 2, no. 1 (1976).

Rotenstreich, Nathan. *Basic Problems of Marx's Philosophy*. Indianapolis: Bobbs-Merrill, 1965.

Rowbotham, Sheila. *New World for Women—Stella Browne—Socialist Feminist*. London: Pluto, 1977.

————, Lynne Segal, and Hilary Wainwright. *Beyond the Fragments: Feminism and the Making of Socialism*. London: Methuen, 1979.

Rzhanitsina, L., *Female Labour Under Socialism: The Socio-economic Aspects*. Moscow: Progress Publishers, 1983.

Sacks, Michael P. *Women's Work in Soviet Russia: Continuity in the Midst of Change*. New York: Praeger, 1976.

Sati—A Symposium on Widow Immolation and Its Social Context. *Seminar*. no. 342 (New Delhi, 1988).

Saul, John S. "The Role of Ideology in the Transition to Socialism." In Richard Fagen, Carmen D. Deere, and José Luis Coraggio, eds., *Transition and Development: Problems of Third World Socialism*. New York: Monthly Review Press, 1986.

Schlesinger, R. *The Family in the USSR: Documents and Readings*. London: Routledge & Kegan Paul, 1949.

Scott, Hilda. *Does Socialism Liberate Women?* Boston: Beacon Press, 1974.

Scott, Joan W. "Gender: A Useful Category of Historical Analysis." *The American Historical Review* 91, no. 5 (1986).

Shamiry, N. A. "The Judicial System in Democratic Yemen." In B. Pridham, ed. *Contemporary Yemen: Politics and Historical Background*. London and Centre for Arab-Gulf Studies, University of Exeter: Croom Helm, 1984.

Smedley, Agnes. *Battle Hymn of China*. New York: Knopf, 1943.

Sowerine, Charles. *Sisters or Citizens?: Women and Socialism in France Since 1876*. Cambridge: Cambridge University Press, 1982.

Stacey, Judith. *Patriarchy and Socialist Revolution in China*. Berkeley: University of California Press, 1983.

Stites, Richard. *The Women's Liberation Movement in Russia*. Princeton: Princeton University Press, 1978.

Stookey, R. *South Yemen: A Marxist Republic in Arabia*. London: Croom Helm, 1982.

Strum, Hertha. "On the International May Conference Among Women." *International Press Correspondence*, no. 44 (1926).

Stubbs, Jean. "Gender Issues in Contemporary Cuban Tobacco Farming." *World Development* 15 (January 1987).

Ta Van Tai. "The Status of Women in Traditional Vietnam." *Journal of Asian History* 15, no. 2 (1981).

Taylor, Barbara. *Eve and the New Jerusalem: Socialism and Feminism in the Nineteenth Century*. New York: Pantheon, 1983.

———. "Socialist Feminism: Utopian or Scientific?" In Samuel Raphael, ed., *People's History and Socialist Theory*. London: Routledge & Kegan Paul, 1981.

Terzani, Tiziano. *Gai Phong: The Fall and Liberation of Saigon*. New York: St. Martin's Press, 1976.

Thönnessen, W. *The Emancipation of Women: The Rise and Decline of the Women's Movement in German Social Democracy 1863–1933*. London: Pluto, 1976.

Tobler-Christingen, M. "The Swiss Working Women's Movement." *International Press Correspondence*, no. 11 (1929).

Tolkunova, Vera, et al. *Women in the USSR*. Moscow: Progress Publishers, 1985.

Urdang, Stephanie. *And Still They Dance*. New York: Monthly Review Press, 1987.

———. "The Last Transition? Women and Development." In John Saul, ed. *A Difficult Road: The Transition to Socialism in Mozambique*. New York: Monthly Review Press, 1985.

Vogel, Lise. *Marxism and the Oppression of Women*. New Brunswick, NJ: Rutgers University Press, 1983.

Volgyes, Ivan. "Blue-Collar Working Women and Poverty in Hungary." In Sharon L. Wolchik and Alfred G. Meyer, ed. *Women, State and Party in Eastern Europe*. Durham: Duke University Press, 1985.

Walt, Gillian. "Commitment to Primary Health Care in Mozambique: A Preliminary Review." *Rural Africana* 8–9 (Fall 1980– Winter 1981).

Weinbaum, Batya. *The Curious Courtship of Women's Liberation and Socialism*. Boston: South End Press, 1978.

White, Christine Pelzer. "Socialist Transformation of Agriculture and Gender Relations: The Vietnamese Case." *IDS Bulletin* 13, no. 4 (September 1982).

———. "Collectives and the Status of Women: The Vietnamese Experiences." *Ceres* 16, no. 4 (July–August 1983).

Whitmore, John. "Social Organization and Confucian Thought in Vietnam." *Journal of Southeast Asian Studies* 15, no. 2 (September 1984).

Whyte, Martin K., and William L. Parish. *Urban Life in Contemporary China*. Chicago: University of Chicago Press, 1984.

Wiegersma, Nancy, *Vietnam: Peasant Land, Peasant Revolution; Patriarchy and Collectivity in the Rural Economy*. New York: St. Martin's Press, 1988.

Wield, David "Mozambique: Late Colonialism and Early Problems of Transition."

In Robin Murray, Christine White, and Gordon White, eds. *Socialist Transformation and Development in the Third World*. Sussex: Wheatsheaf Books. 1983.

Williams, Raymond. *Marxism and Literature*. Oxford: Oxford University Press, 1977.

Wisner, Ben. "Social Impact, Socialism and the Case of Mozambique." In W. Derman and S. Whiteford, eds. *Social Impact Analysis and Development Planning in the Third World*. Boulder CO: Westview Press, 1985.

Wolf, Margery. *Revolution Postponed: Women in Contemporary China*. Stanford: Stanford University Press, 1985.

The Woman Question: Selections from the Writings of Karl Marx, Fredreich Engels, V. I. Lenin, Joseph Stalin. New York: International, 1951.

Woodward, Susan. "The Rights of Women: Ideology, Policy, and Social Change in Yugoslavia." In Sharon L. Wolchik and Alfred G. Meyer, eds., *Women, State and Party in Eastern Europe*. Durham: Duke University Press, 1985.

"The Work Among Women and the Task of the Communist Parties. Resolution Adopted by the Conference of the Chiefs of Women's Departments of European Communist Parties." *International Press Correspondence*, no. 49 (1930).

World Bank. *Development Report 1980*. Oxford: Oxford University Press, 1980.

———. "The P.D.R.Y.: A Review of Economic and Social Development." Washington, D.C.: World Bank 1979.

Young, Sheryl. "Fertility and Famine: Women's Agricultural History in Southern Mozambique." In R. Palmer and S. Parsons, eds., *The Roots of Rural Poverty in Central and Southern Africa*. London: Longman, 1977.

Index